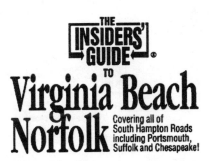

THE INSIDERS' GUIDE TO

Virginia Beach Norfolk

Covering all of
South Hampton Roads
including Portsmouth,
Suffolk and Chesapeake!

by
Suzy Adams Dixon
and
Sally Kirby Hartman

THE INSIDERS' GUIDE

The Insiders' Guides, Inc.

Co-published and marketed by:
Richmond Newspapers, Inc.
333 East Grace Street
Richmond, VA 23219
(804) 649-6000

Co-published and distributed by:
The Insiders' Guides, Inc.
P.O. Box 2057 · Highway 64
Manteo, NC 27954
(919) 473-6100

•

FOURTH EDITION
1st printing

•

Copyright ©1993
by Richmond Newspapers, Inc.

•

Printed in the United States
of America

ISBN 0-912367-29-6

Richmond Newspapers, Inc.

Director, Marketing Development
Bob Bowerman

Manager
Ernie Chenault

Account Executives
Heidi Crandall
Adair Frayser

Project Coordination
Bonnie Widener

Ronnie Johnson, Susan Doyle, Nerina
Lakenda North, Jay Kasberger and
Chris Novelli, artists

The Insiders' Guides, Inc.

Publisher/Managing Editor
Beth P. Storie

President/General Manager
Michael McOwen

Manager/Creative Services
David Haynes

Manager/Distribution
Giles Bissonnette

Editorial Assistant
Georgia Beach

Fulfillment Coordination
Gina Twiford

Controller
Claudette Forney

37748 Ingram 8/93

Preface

Whether you're spending a few days or a lifetime here, we hope this book helps you enjoy your stay in Hampton Roads. Since its many cities are divided by water, bridges and tunnels, this can be a tricky region to explore at first. But it's worth getting out the map and wandering to the different cities since each is unique. In this new edition of *The Insiders' Guide* we've tried to make it easy for you to find your way around.

Rather than segmenting the book by city, we've arranged it by topic. Since we're talking about a unified region, this approach seemed to make the most sense when it came to categories such as History or the Military. However, within sections like Restaurants, Attractions and Recreation you'll find a handy city-by-city breakdown of where to go and what to do.

Although we've included a special section called Kid Stuff, throughout the book you'll find suggestions for entertaining children.

Our goal was to create a book that will become a well-thumbed companion as you explore this area. Even people comfortably settled into the region will find numerous suggestions for activities they've never tried before. We hope *The Insiders' Guide* will be the first place you turn when you show off our region to company.

Although we know this area well, when we sat down to write about it, we were amazed at its diversity. We hope you have as much fun as we've had exploring Hampton Roads.

If we've left out your favorite place, please let us know so we can check it out before the next edition of *The Insiders' Guide* is published.

About The Authors

A lifelong resident of southside Hampton Roads, Suzy Adams Dixon is the owner of an advertising and public relations firm specializing in real estate. As a freelance writer, she has been a frequent contributor to area lifestyle magazines, including *Metro Magazine, Hampton Roads Magazine* and *Port Folio*. She is also the editor of a bi-weekly real estate magazine, *Home Search*, published by the *Virginian-Pilot and Ledger-Star*.

Her best work to date is son Scott, a graduate of both University of Virginia and the Colgate Darden School of Business, now sharpening his own Insiders' skills in Washington, D.C.

Suzy and her husband Rick live the enviable empty nester lifestyle in Norfolk's West Side where both have perfected the advanced art of casual exploration of the Insiders' favorite haunts.

Sally Kirby Hartman first discovered Hampton Roads when she moved to Norfolk in 1985. She is public relations director for The Norfolk Foundation and a freelance writer who specializes in magazine and public relations work. She formerly was associate editor of *Virginia Business* magazine and editor of *Tidewater Virginian* magazine. She has won writing and editing awards from the National Federation of Press Women, Virginia Press Women, Arkansas Press Women and the Council on Foundations. Before becoming a diehard Virginian, Sally spent most of her life in Arkansas. She graduated from the University of Arkansas with a journalism degree and for several years was features editor of the *Arkansas Gazette*. She and her husband, Ron, have one son, Luke.

Acknowledgements

There are far too many people involved in this project to thank individually. However, you all have our gratitude for the information and tips you so eagerly shared. And, we appreciate the encouragement from everyone who asked how the book was going during these past few hectic months.

Sally thanks Gayle Donovan for the photo on the back cover. She also appreciates the help she received from Mallory Copeland at Forward Hampton Roads, Amy Jonak at the Norfolk Convention and Visitors Bureau, Hubert Young of Young Properties, Peggy Haile at the Kirn Memorial Library, Patricia Rawls at the Business Consortium for Arts Support, Jim Raper of Zuni, H.L. and Linda Wilson of the Bibliopath Bookshop & Bindery, Jim and Lisa Bacon of Richmond, Lee Starkey at Earle Palmer Brown, Mike Kensler of the Chesapeake Bay Foundation, Mare Carmody of "Eagle 97," Mindy Hughes of the City of Chesapeake, and Coni Chandler of Virginia's Eastern Shore Tourism Commission. Sally especially thanks her husband, Ron, and son, Luke, for their patience, understanding and willingness to explore new places here at home.

In addition, Suzy thanks Cynthia Carter West, Norfolk Scope; Kristine Sturkie and Priscilla Trinder, GSH Real Estate; and Beth Baker, Public Affairs Office, Commander Naval Base Norfolk.

Suzy especially thanks husband, Rick, for his unselfish contributions of research, astute observations and dish-washing during the writing of this guide, son, Scott, for sharing his enormous wealth of night life knowledge, and mother, Eleanor, for her spunky words of encouragement and brisket dinners.

The Supplementary Publications Department of Richmond Newspapers would also like to thank Coni Chandler, Virginia's Eastern Shore Tourism Commission, Irene Walker, Bed and Breakfast Association of the Eastern Shore, Breda Vaughan, Isle of Wight Tourism, The Norfolk Convention and Visitors Bureau, The Virginia Division of Tourism, and The Virginia Department of Economic Development.

Table of Contents

Directory of Maps

Sand sculpture is a unique form of art on the shores of Virginia Beach.

SOUTH HAMPTON ROADS

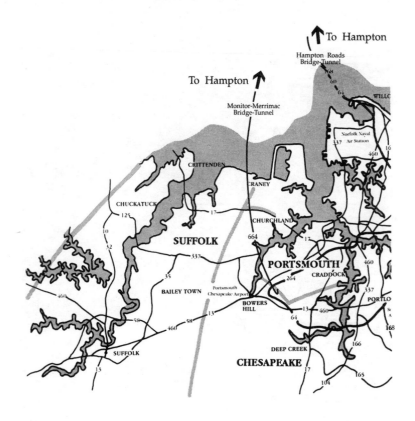

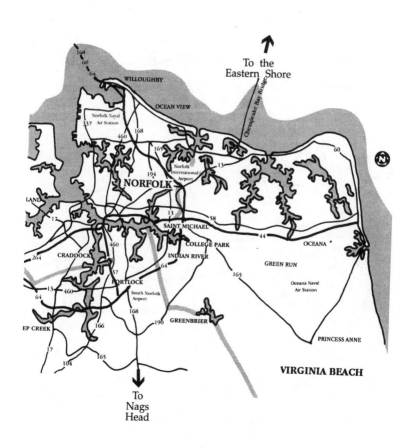

DOWNTOWN NORFOLK

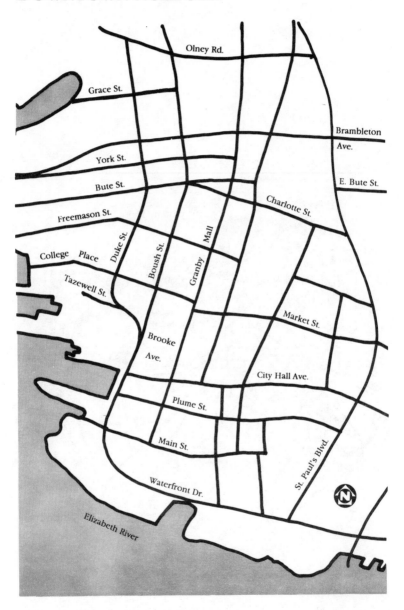

VIRGINIA BEACH

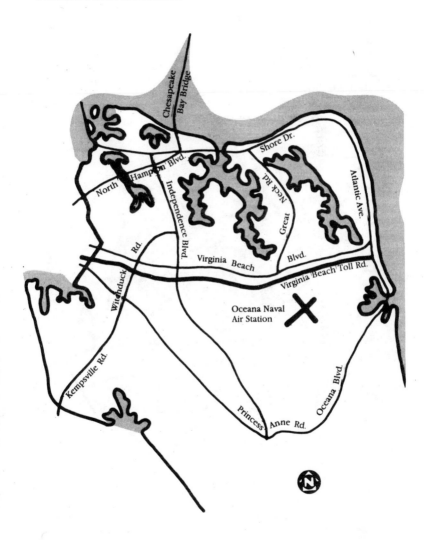

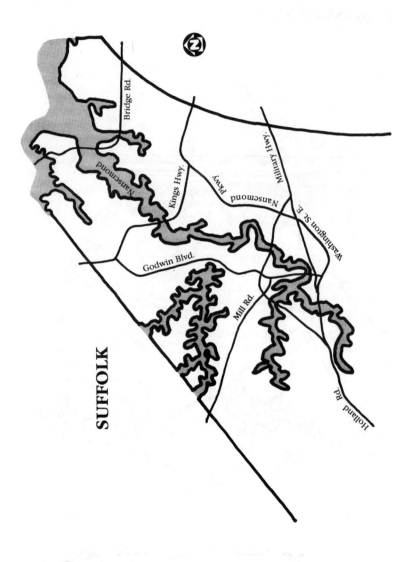

PORTSMOUTH

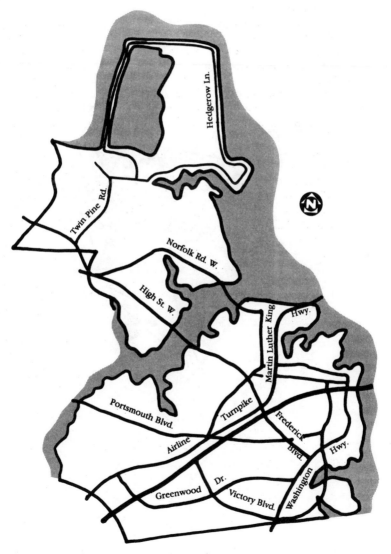

CHESAPEAKE

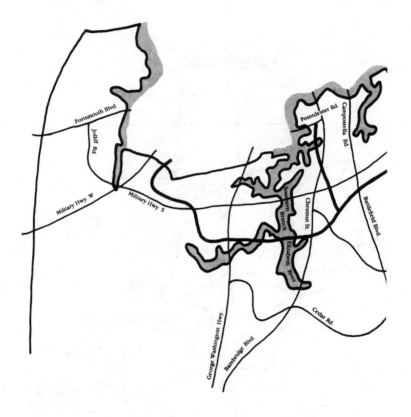

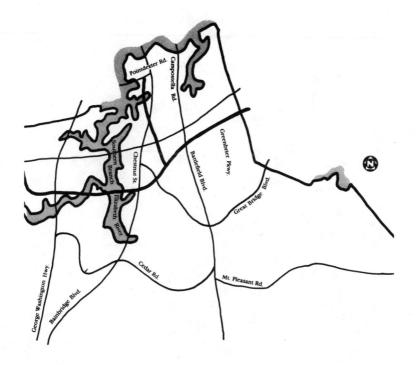

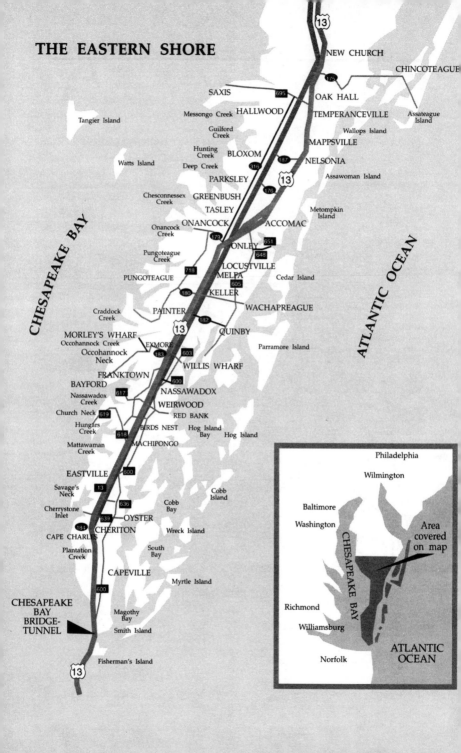

THE EASTERN SHORE

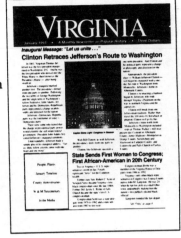

A view of the shipyards across the Elizabeth River.

Inside
Area Overview

As a visitor or newcomer to Hampton Roads your mind will be boggled by all the terms you hear: Southeastern Virginia, Hampton Roads, Tidewater, Southside, South Hampton Roads and Virginia Peninsula. To add to the confusion, residents often use specific names of the nine cities and three counties that make up this vast region of Virginia located where the Chesapeake Bay spills into the Atlantic ocean.

Ask residents where they're from and you'll get a boatload of answers depending on the circumstances. If they're in Illinois or New York, they're likely to say "Southeastern Virginia." If they're visiting Roanoke, Richmond or some other part of Virginia, they might say "Hampton Roads." If the question is asked at the opera, a corporate meeting or elsewhere in the region, the answer is likely to be "Portsmouth," "Virginia Beach" or another specific locality.

All the terminology is accurate. But in today's politically correct times there are some names for this 1,833-square-mile region that are "more correct" than others.

Geographically, this is Southeastern Virginia. Officially, it is the Norfolk-Virginia Beach-Newport News Metropolitan Statistical Area. With nearly 1.4 million residents, this is the 28th most populous MSA in the country. It is bigger than Columbus, Ohio, but smaller than

The region is blessed with a mild climate that can make a beach stroll a pleasant post-dinner activity on Thanksgiving and Christmas. There are four distinct seasons but rarely drastic extremes in temperature. The average January temperature is 40 degrees. The August average is 78 degrees. Remember that the wind blowing off the ocean or bay can make winter temperatures feel much colder. In summer, high humidity can make you swelter. With an average rainfall of about 56 inches, be sure to pack an umbrella, especially during the winter and spring.

Insiders' Tips

the Portland-Vancouver area. Until 1983 the region was broken into two MSAs – South Hampton Roads and the Virginia Peninsula. The two areas are physically divided by the James River and the body of water known as Hampton Roads. To some extent, residents still feel loyalty to one side or the other.

The politically correct term for this region is Hampton Roads. In the 17th century this name was given to the body of water where the James, Elizabeth and Nansemond rivers flow into the Chesapeake Bay to form the world's finest deep-water harbor. The name "Hampton" honors Henry Wriothesley, the Earl of Southampton, who supported the colonization of Virginia in the early 17th Century.

In past decades, the term "Tidewater" was frequently used for this coastal plain as well as adjacent regions that stretch along the York and James rivers. But since "Tidewater" conjures up negative images of mud flats and brackish water, its use has been discouraged in recent years.

In the 1980s, economic developers started touting "Hampton Roads" as the name for the entire region, which includes Norfolk, Portsmouth, Chesapeake, Suffolk and Virginia Beach on the south side of the Hampton Roads Bridge-Tunnel. To the north are Hampton, Newport News, Poquoson, Williamsburg and the counties of James City, Gloucester and York. Since 1990 all the region's mail has been postmarked with "Hampton Roads" rather than the names of individual cities and counties.

For at least a decade, Hampton Roads has ranked second to Northern Virginia as the state's fastest growing region. It has six of the state's 10 largest cities, and Virginia Beach is No. 1 in population.

The region, which is crisscrossed by a half dozen major rivers, feels more unified today than it did 10 years ago. New tunnel crossings link cities separated by rivers, and long-time tolls have been eliminated on them. Today it's common for residents to commute to work through a tunnel from Suffolk to Newport News or Hampton to Virginia Beach. Frequently when they're driving along Interstate 64 or other major arteries, residents aren't sure what city they're in.

To simplify matters for this Insiders' Guide, which concentrates on the five Southside cities, we'll use the names of specific cities if possible. When talking about the region, we'll call it Hampton Roads.

A Vast Region

Semantics aside, Hampton Roads is a fascinating, multi-faceted area that prides itself on its remarkable history. The earliest recorded mention of the region was in 1607 when the first permanent colonists in the New World landed at Cape Henry in what is now Virginia Beach. Hampton Roads survived occupation during the Revolutionary War and the War Between the States. It stepped into modern times with quick build-ups during World War I and World War II when thousands of military personnel and defense workers came here to work. Many of them liked the area enough to become permanent residents.

If there's one thing Hampton Roads is noted for, it is military might. The region's strategic East Coast location has helped it accumulate the world's largest concentration of naval operations. It also has bases representing every branch of the U.S. armed forces as well as the Armed Forces Staff College and the headquarters for the North Atlantic Treaty Organization (NATO). Nearly a third of the region's workers earn a paycheck from the Department of Defense or a private defense contractor.

Mainstays of the economy include shipbuilding and repair, service jobs, tourism and the port. Traditional industries, such as growing peanuts and tonging for oysters, remain the livelihood for some residents. Coal exports are as important to the busy Port of Hampton Roads as they were in the 1890s. These days the area is also a major port for container cargo as well as products such as grain and rubber.

In recent years new industry has come into the region. There are high-tech Japanese companies in Chesapeake producing computer disks and copy machine parts. In the past five years Hampton Roads has become a hub for the service-oriented "fulfillment industry." Various companies use thousands of workers to process credit card transactions, take orders for merchandise and handle insurance claims.

Tourism is one of the most important segments of the economy. Each year more than 2.5 million visitors flock here to enjoy miles of shoreline extending along the Chesapeake Bay and the Atlantic Ocean. Besides soaking up the sun, visitors can tour a variety of museums and historic homes. They can fish for flounder or sea bass, relax on harbor cruises or exert themselves by windsurfing, parasailing or hiking.

Excellent health care is a plus for Hampton Roads. The addition of Eastern Virginia Medical School in the early 1970s attracted experts in most medical fields, including heart transplants. The medical school has a well-respected in vitro fertilization program that produced the United States' first test-tube baby in 1981. The school's researchers are on the trail of a cure for diabetes. Area physicians, many of whom are on EVMS' faculty, attract patients from around the world for corrective urological surgery, sex-

---

In the Commonwealth of Virginia, cities are not located in counties. If you're new, don't feel embarrassed that you haven't figured out the name of your county. If you live in a city, you don't have one.

Insiders' Tips

change operations and cosmetic surgery.

Diverse People

If you're a newcomer, you'll find plenty of company in Hampton Roads. Most residents have moved here from somewhere else. The region ranks second to Orlando, Fla., in the mobility of its residents. Some of these "come-heres" are retirees enjoying the good life along the area's waterways. Others are drawn by work at military bases, defense contracting firms or other private employers. During the 1980s the region added nearly 200,000 new jobs, and many of those workers are still here.

Interspersed among the newcomers are natives who are proud of their region and the strides it has made in the past decades to improve itself. Because they're accustomed to the ebb and flow of military personnel, most old-timers are very accepting of newcomers.

If you've just moved here, you may be surprised at how readily the Hampton Roads community will welcome your time and talents. The region is filled with tireless volunteers working for everything from the Virginia Opera to Habitat for Humanity. Even before you unpack your moving boxes, you may find yourself recruited to help plan a festival or raise funds for the children's hospital. Getting involved in committee work will speed up the process of feeling at home.

Although Hampton Roads doesn't have the ethnic enclaves of Boston or Baltimore, its citizens hail from many places. Its many military residents have lived all over the world. There are thriving Filipino and Hispanic communities as well as a growing number of residents from India. During the last decade, the region had one of the country's fastest-growing Jewish populations. Although the 1990 census showed that 68 percent of the region's residents are Caucasian, in the last decade the region's black population grew slightly faster.

City Rundown

Hampton Roads cities pride themselves on their individuality. Some were created centuries ago; others were formed as recently as the 1970s. They run the gamut from urban to suburban and downright rural. Sum up the strengths of the five southside cities, and you a have a vibrant region with something to offer everyone.

Norfolk: The region's oldest city dates back more than 300 years. During the past decade the city has seen decaying waterfront warehouses replaced by The Waterside festival marketplace as well as hotels, parks and new office buildings. Downtown Norfolk recently gained a new 22-story Marriott hotel and adjacent convention center. Under construction downtown are a new stadium for the Triple-A Norfolk Tides and the National Maritime Center (NAUTICUS). In another part of the city, United Services Automobile Association, a large financial services company, recently completed its East Coast headquarters.

Norfolk, with a population of 261,229, is Virginia's second largest city. Its downtown is the region's financial hub. Within a two-block radius are regional headquarters for all the major banks in the state. One of the gleaming downtown high-rises is headquarters for Norfolk Southern Corp., whose rail lines run through 20 states and Canada. Old Dominion University (ODU), Virginia Wesleyan College, Eastern Virginia Medical School (EVMS) and Norfolk State University (NSU) have their campuses here. Norfolk International Terminals is the state's largest marine terminal.

The city is home to Norfolk Naval Base, the world's largest Navy base. Norfolk is also the region's cultural core and is home base for the Virginia Symphony, Virginia Stage Company, Virginia Opera and numerous smaller arts groups. On the weekends, Norfolk is one of the most fun places to be. Each year Town Point Park, adjacent to the Waterside, is the site of more than 45 festivals and 100 concerts and other outdoor events.

Virginia Beach: With 393,069 residents, Virginia Beach is Virginia's most-populous city. This often surprises visitors focused on the city's resort strip and its 28 miles of beaches. Although tourism is the city's No. 1 industry, there's much more to Virginia Beach than waffle houses, T-shirt shops and sunbathers.

Virginia Beach has more office buildings than any other city in the region and Lynnhaven Mall, the region's largest. Since this is a city with no traditional downtown, offices and stores have cropped up in suburban office parks. The city has numerous manufacturers and

Insiders like to brag that:
- Norfolk has the world's largest Navy base.
- Portsmouth has the world's largest ship repair yard.
- Suffolk is the Peanut Capital of the World.
- The Port of Hampton Roads exports more coal and imports more rubber than any other U.S. port.
- The United States' first in vitro baby was born in Norfolk in 1981 with the help of Eastern Virginia Medical School.
- Norfolk is mile zero for the 1,095-mile Intracoastal Waterway, which takes boaters to Miami.
- With nine underwater tunnels, the region ranks second only to Japan as the world leader in tunnels.

Insiders' Tips

distributors. Stihl chain saws are made here, and Lillian Vernon Corp. ships outs millions of catalog orders from its distribution center.

Virginia Beach also maintains a strong agricultural base. Ride the roads out to Pungo and Sandbridge, and you'll be amazed to learn you're still within the city limits. Stretching for miles are horse farms and fields. This agricultural heritage dates back centuries before the current city of Virginia Beach was formed in 1963 from the merger of vast Princess Anne County and the tiny resort community of Virginia Beach.

The city also is home to The Christian Broadcasting Network. Rev. M.G. "Pat" Robertson lives on the elegant grounds of CBN, where the "700 Club" show is produced. This is home for the fast-growing Family Channel and Regent University. Other educational institutions in the city include Tidewater Community College and Virginia Wesleyan College.

Portsmouth: This is one of the region's most charming cities. Its Olde Towne Historic District adjacent to downtown has the largest collection of historic homes between Alexandria, Va., and Charleston. Portsmouth has more houses on the National Register of Historic Places than any other Virginia city.

Adjacent to the restored 18th-century neighborhood are several museums, including a delightful one for children. On the banks of downtown's Elizabeth River is Portside, an outdoor festival marketplace. A double-decker ferry regularly churns the waters between Portside and Waterside, across the river.

The federal government is the main employer in Portsmouth. The Norfolk Naval Shipyard, the world's largest ship repair yard, is here. Also in the city is the Portsmouth Naval Hospital, the Navy's first hospital. Already the largest Navy hospital on the East Coast, the hospital is in the midst of a multi-year expansion. Portsmouth also has a major Coast Guard installation and a branch of Tidewater Community College.

In addition to government operations, Portsmouth has the Portsmouth Marine Terminal and a strong manufacturing base. Among the products made in the city are Hoechst Celanese fibers and London Fog raincoats.

Suffolk: With 430 square miles, Suffolk is Virginia's largest city in land mass. The city is renowned for its peanuts, which flourish in its rich soil, and calls itself The Peanut Capital of the World. The peanut is the backbone of the city's long-standing agribusiness sector, which includes four shelling companies and six major processors. Planters Peanuts started in the city – as did its mascot Mr. Peanut. Planters, a major employer, roasts peanuts in its plant and gives Suffolk a pleasant aroma.

Besides peanuts, Suffolk manufacturing plants produce Lipton tea and Hills Bros. coffee. The city has a mammoth distribution center that ships merchandise for QVC, the country's largest TV home shopping channel. Suffolk also has a branch of Paul D. Camp Community College.

Suffolk, which has 52,141 residents, maintains a traditional downtown. It also is gearing up for development in outlying areas near the Monitor-Merrimac Memorial Bridge-Tunnel, which opened in early 1992. The tunnel links Suffolk with Newport News, and eager developers have staked their claims on thousands of prime acreage near the tunnel.

Chesapeake: Once the site of the East Coast's largest plant nursery, Chesapeake has been Hampton Roads' boomtown during the past eight years. Although Chesapeake maintains a strong agricultural base, in recent years it has sprouted subdivisions, shopping malls, office parks and manufacturing plants.

Like Virginia Beach, the city of 151,976 has no traditional downtown. Its business hubs are clustered around exits off Interstate 64. Two manufacturers have their North American headquarters in the city. Sumitomo Machinery Corp. of America, makes industrial drives while Volvo Penta North America produces marine engines. Sumitomo is one of several Japanese manufacturers with plants in Chesapeake. The city also has numerous distributors and service companies. Among the largest is Household Finance Corp., which built its East Coast processing center in Chesapeake.

Chesapeake has two of the region's newest shopping malls – Greenbrier and Chesapeake Square. It has recently gained numerous restaurants and retail shops. The city has a branch campus of Tidewater Community College. Popular recreational areas include the Great Dismal Swamp National Wildlife Refuge and Northwest River Park.

Photo: Virginia Division of Tourism

The old and new lighthouses at Cape Henry.

Inside
History

Water and war. These two factors are intertwined in the history of Virginia Beach, Norfolk and the neighboring cities of Portsmouth, Chesapeake and Suffolk. Since the 17th century, the region's location on the Chesapeake Bay and the Atlantic Ocean have made it a prime trading partner with the world. Having one of the finest deep-water harbors has made Hampton Roads a key player in every war from the Revolutionary War to the Persian Gulf conflict of 1990.

Until April 26, 1607 this wooded coastal plain, commonly known as Hampton Roads, was home to about 18,000 Indians. The Algonquins, the Nansemonds and the Chesapeakes thrived on oysters and fish harvested from the ocean, the bay and their many tributaries as well as on crops grown on rich soil. On that spring day in 1607 when the Indians' world changed, three small ships carrying 104 Englishmen led by Adm. Christopher Newport sailed to what is now Cape Henry in Virginia Beach. Twenty-eight explorers ventured ashore, fell to their knees and thanked God for carrying them safely to land. That night they were attacked by the Chesapeake Indians.

The next day the newcomers hiked for eight miles, frightening Indians tending a smoldering fire. The explorers raked aside the coals and sampled their first delicacy in this new land – roasted Lynnhaven oysters. The third day the group continued on about 50 miles to Jamestown Island where they established the first permanent English settlement in America. They later returned to hammer a wooden cross at their landing spot at Cape Henry, where the Chesapeake Bay flows into the Atlantic Ocean.

Capt. George Percy, a member of the expedition, wrote of his first encounter with Virginia, "There we landed and discovered fair meadows and goodly tall trees with such fresh water running through the woods so I was almost ravished at the first sight thereof."

To the British, Virginia's land was so abundant that they eagerly granted colonists 100 acres to establish plantations. By 1634 Virginia was divided into eight counties and several settlements had sprung up along the region's riverbanks. Within four years smaller counties were created. Suffolk fell into Upper Norfolk County, which became Nansemond County a few years later. The rest of South Hampton Roads ended up in Lower Norfolk

County, which later yielded Princess Anne County, Norfolk County and several cities. By 1703 Virginia had a population of 60,606 living in 25 counties. Norfolk County had 2,279 residents; neighboring Princess Anne County was home to 2,017 people.

Norfolk, chartered as a town in 1682 and a borough in 1736, is the region's oldest city. Suffolk became an incorporated town along the Nansemond River in 1742. Portsmouth, across the Elizabeth River from Norfolk, officially became a town in 1752 when 65 acres was set aside for a community named after the famous English seaport. Virginia Beach, Chesapeake and Suffolk are the region's newest cities. Virginia Beach and Chesapeake were created in 1963 by merging large counties with smaller towns. The current city of Suffolk was formed in 1974 by merging a smaller Suffolk with vast Nansemond County.

In the 17th and early 18th centuries, tobacco was the mainstay of the local economy. Farmers grew the cash crop along the region's numerous rivers, cured it and shipped it overseas from their private wharves. By 1736, foreign trade had helped make Norfolk the largest town in Virginia with 1,000 residents. Thirty-three years later its population had swelled to 6,000.

During this time the region was plagued by pirates who plundered ships coming into the port. The most famous was Blackbeard, who built his headquarters in what is now Virginia Beach.

In 1763 George Washington surveyed land in what is now Chesapeake and Suffolk for the Dismal Swamp Land Co. He dug the first spade of dirt to create a canal through the Great Dismal Swamp, a 200,000-acre wilderness area.

As the region's prominence as a world port grew, local docks were filled with turpentine, cheese, corn, lumber and other products awaiting export. Besides Europe, the region had a thriving trade with the West Indies. In 1767 Andrew Sprowle, a merchant and shipbuilder, started Gosport Shipyard near Portsmouth. By the late 1700s three-fourths of Portsmouth's land owners worked in the maritime trade as merchants, shipwrights or other craftsmen.

Revolutionary War

The region's harbor and its proximity to Williamsburg, meeting site of the First Continental Congress in 1774, made it an important player during the Revolutionary War. Since Virginia had the strongest navy of the 13 original colonies, this area's harbor was vital to winning freedom for the colonies.

That fact wasn't lost on the British. In November 1775 Lord Dunmore, the last royal governor of Virginia, captured Portsmouth and boasted that Norfolk was defenseless. Less than a month later, the British were defeated at the Battle of Great Bridge, near the current site of Chesapeake's city hall. Lord Dunmore's only victory had already come during a battle at Kempsville in 1775, in what is now one of Virginia Beach's most populous neighborhoods.

New Year's Day 1776 was the most fateful day in Norfolk's history. In the afternoon British soldier opened fire on the city and continued their assault for 11 hours. With the wind whipping flames, two-thirds of the city was destroyed. By the end of February, colonists had torched the rest of Norfolk. The government of Virginia ordered the second burning to prevent sheltering Lord Dunmore and his soldiers. Of more than 1,300 Norfolk buildings only the brick walls of St. Paul's Church remained. Even they were marred by a cannon ball wedged in one side. Norfolk held the dubious distinction of being the most devastated community in the colonies during the Revolutionary War.

To try and protect the harbor, in early 1776 the Commonwealth of Virginia ordered the con-

The Witchcraft Trials

By the early 17th century, Virginians were swept up in the frenzy of witchcraft trials that gripped Salem, Mass.

In 1655, Lower Norfolk Court, which contained what is now Virginia Beach, Norfolk, Portsmouth and Chesapeake, enacted a law stating that anyone making a charge of witchcraft was liable for a fine or court censure if the charge couldn't be proven. As a result there were several suits and counter-suits involving witchcraft charges.

The most famous case concerned Grace Sherwood, a resident of the Pungo area of what is now Virginia Beach. Grace, a carpenter's wife and mother of three sons, was charged with witchcraft in 1697. When she sued her accuser for defamation the case was settled without trial. In 1687 Grace and her husband James sued another couple for slander for accusing Grace of bewitching the couple's cotton.

Grace was named in two other suits, including one that accused her of riding and whipping the plaintiff and sneaking out a key hole like a black cat. In 1706 after several searches, the county court ordered Grace to "be tried in ye water by Ducking." The dunking took place in July 1706 in the Lynnhaven River.

Grace was tied with ropes with her right thumb touching her left big toe and her left thumb tied to her right big toe. Trussed like a turkey, Grace was tossed in the river in front of hundreds of curious onlookers. Because she did not sink, Grace failed the trial by water and was immediately jailed. She later was released and sent home to live without further recorded incident.

Although Grace Sherwood died in 1740, her legacy lives on in Witchduck Road, a major thoroughfare in Virginia Beach. The site of Grace's dunking is known as Witchduck Point.

struction of Fort Norfolk. Across the Elizabeth River from it, the commonwealth established Fort Nelson in Portsmouth.

During the war the Gosport Shipyard in Portsmouth was one of the busiest places in the colonies. The British burned the yard in 1776 but the colonists quickly built new wharves and scaffolding so they could produce new ships. Although the British were routed from Hampton Roads by the burning of Norfolk in 1776, they returned in 1779 and took over Portsmouth. They promptly proceeded to ransack homes and burn ships anchored in the harbor. Suffolk also was burned in 1779 during a raid that originated in Portsmouth. The traitor Benedict Arnold set up headquarters in Portsmouth in 1781 before moving 50 miles away to Yorktown with Lord Cornwallis, who surrendered there a few months later.

After the war, the region started the arduous task of rebuilding. Former residents were aided by European immigrants, many of them merchants, who saw opportunity in America. Within a few years Norfolk regained its role as a major world port. Suffolk also saw its port come alive when it was designated as a port of delivery in the Customs District of Norfolk and Portsmouth.

During this time of reconstruction several major projects were built. The Cape Henry Lighthouse, which had been started before the Revolutionary War, was completed in 1791 under orders from President George Washington. Today the Virginia Beach landmark is the oldest public works project in the coun-

try. In 1794 the federal government took over Gosport Shipyard, although it didn't actually buy it until 1801. The yard later was named the Norfolk Naval Shipyard even though it was located in Portsmouth.

In Norfolk, Congress authorized Washington to build a new fort to protect the harbor. In 1795 the government paid 200 pounds of sterling for the dilapidated Fort Norfolk. Permanent brick buildings were constructed about 1810 in anticipation of another war with the British. The region had rebounded from the Revolutionary War when trade restrictions imposed because of the War of 1812 torpedoed foreign trade.

In 1825 there was great fanfare in the region when the Marquis de Lafayette, the French general who had aided the country during the Revolutionary War, visited here as part of his farewell tour of 24 states.

By 1851 the Norfolk and Western Railway had laid track in the region and managed to put a roadbed through the Dismal Swamp.

Prosperity had returned by 1855 when the area was devastated by yellow fever. In June mosquitoes breeding in the hold of a steamer from St. Thomas escaped and wreaked havoc, particularly upon Portsmouth and Norfolk. Within two months all business in Norfolk stopped. Hotels, homes and warehouses were turned into hospitals as up to 100 residents a day died. Only one ship was allowed into the harbor, and its sole cargo was coffins. When those ran out residents were buried in boxes or blankets sometimes in mass graves. By the end of the plague four months later, 2,000 were dead in Norfolk and more than 1,000 in Portsmouth.

At War Again

The region again flexed its military muscle during the War Between the States. On April 12, 1861 it didn't take long for news to arrive that the Confederates had fired on Charleston's Fort Sumter. That day the Confederate flag was raised at the blockhouse on Craney Island near Portsmouth. On April 17, Virginia became the eighth state to secede from the union. Three days later Union soldiers fled the Navy yard in Portsmouth, burning buildings and 11 warships as they escaped.

One of the first battles was the little-known Battle of Sewell's Point in May, 1861. There were no fatalities as local Confederates skirmished with federal troops stationed across the water at Fort Monroe in what is now Hampton.

By November, 1861, more than 20,000 Confederate soldiers were stationed in Portsmouth at the Navy yard, which was at work on eight Confederate vessels. The most famous was the USS *Virginia*, which was forged from the partially burned hull of the ironclad USS *Merrimac.* The *Merrimac's* historic battle of the ironclads with the USS *Monitor* took place March 9, 1862 in the waters between Norfolk and Hampton. Four hours later the *Monitor* retreated to Fort Monroe, the last Union stronghold in Hampton

Roads. Later that year the *Merrimac* ran aground at Craney Island and was blown up by its crew. Fourteen years later its hull was salvaged and hacked up with a few pieces remaining as relics.

In May, 1862, the Confederates ordered residents of Portsmouth, Suffolk and Norfolk to evacuate. They burned the Portsmouth Navy Yard to save it from federal troops landing at Ocean View, a Chesapeake Bay community that is now part of Norfolk.

At the start of the war, Suffolk was a training ground for Confederate soldiers from Georgia and South Carolina. But soon the town was occupied by Union soldiers, just like nearby Norfolk and Portsmouth. This was a humiliating time for these three cities. Federal troops ransacked homes and forced ferry passengers to tromp on the Confederate flag.

After Confederate Gen. Robert E. Lee surrendered in Appomatox, Va. in 1865, the Hampton Roads area began the arduous task of reconstruction. There was no money in Portsmouth's treasury, and the city's Navy yard was in shambles. Norfolk buildings were dilapidated, and the city's foreign trade was nonexistent. There were only 300 residents left in Suffolk, which had boasted a population of 1,395 in 1860.

In the two decades after the end of the war, the region did an about face. Brick three-story buildings soon lined the streets of downtown Norfolk as carts full of oysters, chickens and other provisions rolled toward the city's many hotels and popular farmer's market. Steamships regularly called on the port and a new rail line linked the city with other parts of the country.

Although cotton was the main export commodity after the war, that changed in 1883 when the Norfolk and Great Western Railway sent its first load of coal from western Virginia to Norfolk. To keep pace with demand, the railroad built a new coal pier at Lambert's Point in Norfolk. In 1886 the railroad brought in 504,153 tons of coal. By 1889 trains were hauling more than 1 million tons into Norfolk. At Lambert's Point workers loaded coal on ships bound for overseas or other parts of the United States.

Two other railroads – the Chesapeake & Ohio and the Virginian – also brought coal into Norfolk and Newport News making Hampton Roads the world's largest coal port. A constant line of coal trains became a common sight for local residents.

During this period, Virginia Beach also saw major changes. In 1880 a wooden clubhouse was built at 17th Street and the Oceanfront to entice beach goers. Three years later a railroad line from Norfolk to Virginia Beach provided an easy way for city dwellers to get to the new Virginia Beach Hotel, which held 75 guests. Soon steamers were transporting vacationers down the Chesapeake Bay from as far away as Washington, D.C. and Baltimore.

In 1887 the hotel was enlarged to hold 400 and renamed the Princess Anne Hotel. The luxury resort featured electric lights, elevators, salt-water baths and the top bands of the day. Guests included Presidents Benjamin Harrison and Grover Cleveland as well as inventor Alexander Graham Bell and actor Lionel Barrymore. The hotel burned in 1907 and was replaced in 1922.

By 1888 leading Norfolk area citizens had begun building large cottages with sweeping verandas along a new boardwalk on the beach. In 1906 Virginia Beach incorporated as a city and continued growing as a resort with the opening of Seaside Park Casino. The resort was renowned for its Peacock Ballroom, which bragged it had the largest dance floor on the East Coast. During the 1920s and '30s the lively resort brought in such well-known band leaders as Tommy Dorsey, Duke Ellington and Cab Callaway. Their bands drew crowds for the ballroom's popular 10-cent dances (or three for a quarter). Sadly, the hotel burned in 1955, ending a grand era.

Jamestown Exposition

One of the biggest regional events of the early 20th century was the Jamestown Exposition, held near Norfolk to commemorate the 300th anniversary of the settlement of Jamestown. The Exposition site was 340 acres at Sewells Point, 10 miles from downtown Norfolk. Local organizers, who had raised $1 million in stock to help fund the Exposition, spent several years erecting a mini-city on marshland and pastures. To celebrate the event, other states built replicas of famous buildings such as Independence Hall in Pennsylvania and the Old State House in Massachusetts. Entire halls were devoted to such fields as manufacturing, transportation and art.

The Exposition opened April 26, 1907 with a 100-gun salute as President Theodore Roosevelt arrived on the *Mayflower*, the presidential yacht. During a parade 14,000 soldiers saluted Roosevelt, who called the event the greatest military pageant witnessed in the country since the War Between the States.

Foreign dignitaries from around the world converged on the exposition during its seven-month

The Norfolk Mace

The most prized possession in Norfolk is its sterling silver mace. The ceremonial symbol of power was presented to the Borough of Norfolk in 1754 by Virginia's Lt. Gov. Robert Dinwiddie. South Carolina is the only other American owner of a British-made mace from the 18th century.

Norfolk's mace is 41 inches long and weighs 6 1/2 pounds. Inscribed on it are the initials of Fuller White of London, the mace's silversmith. It also bears an etching of a lion, showing it is pure silver, as well as emblems of England, Scotland, France and Ireland. During the burning of Norfolk in 1776, the mace was hidden in what is now the Kempsville area of Virginia Beach.

The mace was used in 1836 to celebrate the 100th anniversary of Norfolk's charter as a borough. It made an appearance in 1857 during the 350th anniversary of the landing at Jamestown. In 1862 Norfolk's mayor hid the mace under his hearth to protect it from Union soldiers occupying the city during the War Between the States.

No one paid much attention to the mace after the war. In 1894 Norfolk's police chief found it lying in disrepair in a back room of the police station. Norfolk National Bank (now NationsBank) arranged to repair the mace and store it. In 1925 a group of Norfolk third-graders raised money for a bag to protect the mace.

Several years ago the mace moved from the bank to a second-floor gallery in The Chrysler Museum, which is open Tuesday through Sunday. During city parades and other official occasions, police officers lead processions by solemnly carrying a replica of the mace.

run. A decade later, just months after the start of World War I, the Exposition site was included in 474 acres purchased by the federal government for $1.2 million. Its destiny was to become Norfolk Naval Base – the world's largest Navy base. Its development started with $1.6 million allocated in 1917 to build piers and buildings.

World War I

In 1914, as the world stood on the brink of war, the Army took over 343 acres of Cape Henry to build Fort Story in what is now Virginia Beach. Fortified with 16-inch howitzers, during World War I Fort Story was known as the "American Gibraltar." It was considered the Atlantic coast's most strategic heavy artillery fortification. As the Army expanded onto surrounding land, the fort's prominence continued to grow.

The impending world war first touched Portsmouth in 1915 when two German ships were interned in the city. After war was declared in 1917 the Navy yard saw unprecedented growth as three drydocks, four destroyers and a battleship were built. To keep pace, thousands of workers from throughout the country flooded the city. The city's naval hospital, established in 1827 as the Navy's first hospital, quickly expanded into the largest naval hospital on the Atlantic coast. In 1915 Portsmouth had a population of 38,000. By 1918, it was home to about 57,000 residents. At Norfolk Naval Shipyard employment surged

from 2,700 before the war to 11,234 in 1919.

Norfolk also experienced dramatic growth during the war. Within a month in 1917 a training camp for 7,500 soldiers had been completed at the old Jamestown Exposition site. After hastily putting up barracks, warehouses and mess halls, the Navy built a bulkhead, dredged channels and filled in enough areas to add 300 acres to the Navy base. After a year's work the base had added a submarine base, landing fields for airplanes and dirigibles and hundreds of buildings.

Like Portsmouth, Norfolk also had an influx of workers from throughout the country. Besides the military, Norfolk also gained numerous private manufacturing plants. In 1910 the city's population was 67,452. By 1920 it had swelled to 115,777.

World War I gave a great boost to the region's port. With northern ports in New York and other large cities unable to handle increased demand, Norfolk and nearby Newport News filled the gap. Their proximity to the Atlantic and eight area rail lines attracted an endless parade of ships from throughout the world. They came primarily for coal that arrived day and night from West Virginia. Other export commodities included tobacco, cotton and seafood. Norfolk's port also was used heavily by the Naval Overseas Transportation Service, which sent 288,000 soldiers and their provisions to France.

The post-war years were a jolt for the region as it recovered from the days of heady prosperity. To keep solid economic footing in 1922 Norfolk residents approved a $5 million bond issue that created a grain elevator and terminal. The city built a modern downtown farmer's market that cost $500,000. It annexed 27 square miles of adjacent land, including the Navy base and Ocean View resort area.

During the Great Depression, which started in 1929, the region weathered the economic slowdown with help from the Navy. Naval operations gave Norfolk's economy a $20 million a year boost. The port also held its own. When coal exports dropped, sugar exports picked up the slack. In Portsmouth a drop in employment at the Navy yard after World War I was offset by jobs modernizing 15 Navy ships. The 2,538 workers the yard had on the payroll in 1923 had grown to 7,625 by 1939.

Virginia Beach continued to court the resort trade with the completion in 1927 of The Cavalier, a luxury resort near the oceanfront. Agriculture was the mainstay of what is now Chesapeake, while peanuts and lumber remained the backbone of the economy in Suffolk.

World War II

Once again thousands of workers descended on the region during World War II. The Norfolk Naval Shipyard payroll jumped by more than 36,000 workers from 1939 to 1943 as nearly 1,000 workers a month joined the war effort. Employment reached a record high in 1943 with nearly 43,000 workers. To make room for the construction of the 101 ships and landing craft the yard turned out during the war, it expanded from 352 acres to 746 acres in Portsmouth. During the war, the Navy yard did nearly $1 billion in business – half of it going for workers' wages.

In Virginia Beach and Princess Anne County, three military bases were added and a fourth was consolidated from smaller operations. The Army leased a Virginia National Guard rifle range to start Camp Pendleton. The Navy built the Oceana air base and the Dam Neck base, which handles data systems and missile operations. In 1945 the Navy merged four smaller bases into the Little Creek Amphibious Training Command. Off the coast of Virginia Beach, German U-boats patrolled the coast and occasionally sunk Allied ships.

During the war the region benefited greatly from the $12 million the Navy earmarked for construction at the Navy base and the Navy yard. Wooden buildings slapped up during World War I were replaced with solidly built brick and stone structures.

By 1941 apartments and houses were going up faster that they had in the past 20 years. The federal government, the Navy, the Norfolk and Portsmouth housing authorities, and private developers were all busy building new homes. Although Norfolk had two new high schools, they quickly became overcrowded with military dependents. Some schools had to operate in shifts. City buses, restaurants and hospitals filled to capacity, and Norfolk had to quickly expand its water supply. To the rest of the nation, Norfolk was a prime example of wartime overcrowding.

From 1940 to 1944 Norfolk's population swelled by 44,000. As defense workers searched far and wide for housing, adjacent Norfolk County added more than 40,000 new residents. Portsmouth gained 13,000 residents; Princess Anne County grew by 5,000.

Although ship building and ship repair were the area's claim to fame during the war, the region's fertilizer plants, furniture manufacturers and other industries also were expanding. During the war the threat of German U-boats off the coast torpedoed much of the area's commercial foreign trade. But the port made up for that by shipping tanks, bombs and other military supplies to Europe and North Africa.

Post-war Years

After World War II – the fifth major war to have an impact on the region – thousands of war-time workers stayed in Hampton Roads. To keep from falling into a post-war slump, city leaders started aggressively modernizing the region. Norfolk initiated a campaign to annex neighboring counties – a move frequently met with opposition by people living near the land-hungry city.

Inter-city transportation was a key issue during post-war years. Ferries still connected many parts of the region. To speed car travel, the Elizabeth River Tunnel opened in 1952 between Norfolk and Portsmouth. The success of the region's first underground roadway led to another tunnel between the two cities in 1962. In 1957 Norfolk became linked to Hampton by the Hampton Roads Bridge-Tunnel. At the time its 6,860-foot tunnel was the longest of its type in the world.

As marvelous as those accomplishments were, they paled in comparison to the Chesapeake Bay Bridge-Tunnel. Construction on the 17.6-mile roadway started in 1961. It took 3 1/2 years before Virginia Beach was linked with the isolated Eastern Shore of Virginia. For drivers the bridge-tunnel cut 1 1/2 hours off the drive from Virginia Beach to New York. The feat cost $200 million and required two mile-long tunnels, three bridges, four man-made islands and a causeway. The tunnel is considered one of the seven modern wonders of the world.

Mergers were major news in the early 1960s as large counties and small cities struggled to combat Norfolk's annexation mania. As a result, in 1963 the resort city of Virginia Beach annexed rural Princess Anne County and instantly became a city of 125,000. The same year South Norfolk merged with agricultural Norfolk County to form Chesapeake. In 1974 Suffolk merged with Nansemond County to create the new city of Suffolk. The mergers left south Hampton Roads with five cities and no counties and signaled a new era of growth and prosperity.

In recent years the region's

history has been shaped by the rejuvenation of Norfolk and Portsmouth and the coming of age of Virginia Beach, Chesapeake and Suffolk. In the 1960s civic leaders banded together to create Eastern Virginia Medical School. The state's third medical college opened in 1973 in Norfolk and is in the heart of a burgeoning medical complex that includes two hospitals and several research institutes affiliated with the medical school.

During the 1970s and early 1980s dilapidated buildings along Norfolk's downtown waterfront were razed to make way for The Waterside festival marketplace, Town Point Park, elegant condominiums and Dominion Tower. Today the National Maritime Center and a new stadium for the region's Triple-A baseball team are going up on the river banks. A mile away blocks of substandard housing were torn down to create the upscale Ghent Square area. Nearby turn-of-the-century homes in Ghent attracted new residents eager to restore their splendor. Today the city is committed to the revitalization of Ocean View, a hodge-podge of homes, motels and business stretching along the Chesapeake Bay.

Through the years Portsmouth, which has one of Virginia's largest collection of historic homes, has worked to ensure the preservation of Olde Towne. To complement this historic district, the city has gone through major improvements since the 1970s. Recently it has enhanced its downtown business district with wide brick sidewalks, historic lighting and landscaped road dividers. Its seawall is home to Portside, an outdoor collection of restaurants and shops.

In the late 1980s Virginia Beach joined the revitalization movement with a $94 million face lift in its resort area. The effort added mini-parks, attractive lighting, benches and landscaping along Atlantic Avenue and the 2.9-mile oceanfront boardwalk.

In Chesapeake, Virginia Beach and Suffolk, which are blessed with many miles of farmland, the emphasis has been on new

For decades, drivers stopped at the intersection of Hampton Boulevard and Princess Anne Road in Norfolk wondered about the vacant patch of land on the corner. The lot in residential West Ghent was a mass burial ground in 1855 when as many as 100 Norfolk residents a day died during a yellow fever epidemic. With the help of a $10,000 fund-raising effort by a local Brownie troop, Yellow Fever Memorial Park was dedicated in the spring of 1993 -- complete with year round plantings of yellow flowers.

Insiders' Tips

development during the past few decades. Agriculture remains important to the cities, whose major commodities include peanuts, soybeans, strawberries and hogs. However, the temptation to sell the family farm has turned many former fields into subdivisions and office parks in the past decade.

The entire region was an economic hotspot during the early 1980s when federal spending was on the upswing. With military rapidly expanding, eager defense contractors moved in to do business and thousands of workers left tougher economies for the greener pastures of Hampton Roads. As a result neighborhoods, shopping centers and office parks sprung up across the land as the region added 200,000 new jobs during the 1980s.

Development moves at a less manic pace today as the region works to balance its economic prosperity with preservation of its environment. Water still plays a vital role in shaping Hampton Roads history, as does war. During the Persian Gulf war in 1990 and 1991 more than 40,000 military personnel left the region for the Middle East. In addition, thousands of civil service workers and employees of area defense contractors also headed to the Persian Gulf. Half the warships in the Gulf were homeported here. When the war ended, the region celebrated with enthusiastic homecomings that harked back to World War II as bands, banners and tearful relatives welcomed home their heroes.

Today Hampton Roads' heritage is still visible despite the area's high-rise office towers, interstate highways and suburban homes. Its economy, although greatly diversified in recent years, remains rooted in the military and the port. Tourism, started along the Virginia Beach oceanfront in the late 19th century, is a cornerstone of the region's economy. And peanuts remain important to Suffolk.

Like Hampton Roads' early explorers, many newcomers land here because of the area's proximity to the Atlantic Ocean and Chesapeake Bay. They like what they see and decide to make it their home.

Photo: Richmond Nwspapers

Virginia Beach has its own horseback mounted patrols.

Inside
Getting Around

On The Road Again

Welcome to Hampton Roads, where getting from place to place requires going under, over, around, across or, in case of a thunderstorm, through water.

While our bridges, tunnels, major arteries and interstates have undergone extensive renovation and expansion in recent years, it is still wise to know the best times to venture out, especially if you're heading for major shopping centers or beaches. Because this is home to the largest military installation in the country, it is common wisdom to leave the driving to those headed to the bases in the morning, from 6 AM-8 AM, and away from bases in the afternoon, from 3 PM-5 PM. This translates to morning journeys north on Expressway-44/Interstate 64, and afternoon jaunts south on those same routes. The congestion periods hold for all tunnels connecting Norfolk to Portsmouth and Hampton. Helpful automated signage along the interstate system will alert you to pending back-ups, which can delay you an hour or more. If lights are flashing, you might consider following the alternate routes indicated by checker-board directories on interstate signage. While normally longer in mileage than your original route, they will guide you around traffic gridlock to your escape route.

Most local radio stations are diligent in reporting back-up alerts during rush periods; AM 530, the state operated station, broadcasts updates all day although the signal doesn't carry too far beyond the interstate. For information anytime, day or night, you can also call 1-800-792-2800.

For newcomers with a fear of merging, traveling on Hampton Roads' interstate system can be quite a thrill. Because of the diabolically designed entries and exits, use extreme caution when entering or exiting the interstate. Once safely in the flow, it may be helpful to note that you are actually going south when on Interstate-64 East and north on Interstate-64 West.

Enamored with the number "64," the Virginia Department of Transportation has named all the major connectors with that suffix. If I-64 is the wheel that circles the area, these are the "spokes." 464 is a quick, usually desolate shot between Norfolk and Chesapeake; 664 is a new connector between 64 and the new Monitor-Merrimac Tunnel to the Peninsula; 564 zips you from I-64 to the Naval Base and 264 takes you from the heartbeat of downtown Norfolk to 64 where it magically changes to 44, the toll expressway to the Virginia Beach oceanfront.

Speaking of tolls, the only places you will have to fish around for change is on Expressway 44. If you're traveling the full length, the charge at the usually congested Toll Plaza is a quarter; all other exits demand a dime before you can enter or exit.

The rules of the road in Hampton Roads are simple and straightforward. Seat belts are required for all vehicle occupants, and children under age 4 or under 40 pounds must be secured in a child restraint or booster seat. As throughout Virginia, right turn on red after stopping is permitted unless otherwise indicated.

How To HOV

Spanning the distance from Virginia Beach to Norfolk and Chesapeake to the Naval Base is Hampton Roads' answer to rush hour frustrations – the HOV-2 system. The median on I-64 between the Rt. 44/I-64/264 Interchange and I-564 has been designated for vehicles with two or more persons headed westbound to the Naval Base in the morning, eastbound in the afternoon. Readerboards along the interstate system alert you to the traffic direction of the reversible lanes. Entry and exiting is limited, so unless you are really headed to or

from the Base, sticking to the regular interstate with the masses might be your best option. All the details of HOV-2 are available from the Virginia Department of Transportation at 925-2584.

Let Someone Else Do The Driving

To avoid traffic trauma, you might want to consider putting someone else behind the wheel. Although buses are not the transportation vehicle of choice for the majority of Hampton Roaders, Tidewater Regional Transit, our local bus service, can scoot you along major highways for a base fare of $1.10 plus 50 cents for each additional zone. For some interstate-weary business and military folks, there is some interest in TRT's new Express Bus Service with twenty-two spanking new buses that will zip you to Downtown Norfolk or the Naval Base from two convenient Park & Ride locations: Pembroke Mall and Timberlake Shopping Center. A call to 627-RIDE can get you the complete schedule and pick-up points.

If you're headed to someplace a little off the normal beaten track, a taxi is the answer. Unless you're at the airport, don't expect one to be just waiting for your fare. It's best to call one of the many companies listed in the phone book, and plan on adding enough time for them to arrive. Initial charges average $1.25 plus $1.20 to $1.25 for each mile.

From Memorial Day through Labor Day, if charm, not speed, is your fancy, you've got a ticket to ride on one of TRT's darling trolleys. While limited in travel, you can hop aboard for a trip along five Virginia Beach routes (50 cents-$1.25) or take a tour through historic Norfolk or Portsmouth ($2.50). Full information and trolley tokens are available at TRT booths at Waterside in Norfolk, Portside in Portsmouth or 27th at the Boardwalk in Virginia Beach.

The Resort Strip

Amazing what $94 million dollars can do to facelift what was once referred to as the "Redneck Riviera." The Atlantic Avenue resort strip is now undergoing a streetscape program that is turning what was once a dismal counterpart to a beautiful beachfront into a glamorous place to stroll, shop and snack. To this end, you may encounter some bumpy, torn up streets if you're headed to "the Beach," but well-marked detour signs will guide you through the rehab spots.

Take note, this is a tourist alert! A new Code has been entered into Virginia Beach law making "cruising" illegal. Cruising is the debatable pleasure of traveling up and down Atlantic Avenue to show off a hot vehicle or pick a date out of the pedestrian crowd. Now it's a no-no, and friendly Virginia Beach officers, staked out at control spots from the Rudee Inlet Loop through 31st Street, will be delighted to autograph a ticket if you're spotted traveling past a traffic control point two times in the same direction within any three hour period. The Cruising Law is in effect from 2 PM until 2 AM, April 15 through September 30, and was initiated to alleviate gridlock during the busy vacation period. Signs are clearly posted along the violation area, lest you forget.

Airports

NORFOLK INTERNATIONAL AIRPORT

When headed for "ORF" – airline lingo for the Norfolk/Virginia Beach area – you'll most likely set down in an airport situated in the midst of acres of our gorgeous Norfolk Botanical Gardens, quite a beautiful entry to our fair region. Norfolk International, home of the only permanent customs facility between Washington, D.C. and Atlanta, Georgia, is just six miles from downtown Norfolk, and 15 miles from the Virginia Beach oceanfront, so getting from the airport to your destination is a quick and relatively painless trip.

More than 200 daily arrivals and departures are logged at Norfolk International, served by most major carriers and transporting over three million travelers on an annual basis. Non-stop flights zip you to Atlanta, Baltimore, Boston, Charlotte, Chicago, Cincinnati, Dallas-Fort Worth, Detroit, Manteo, N.C., Nashville, New York, Philadelphia, Raleigh-Durham, Richmond, St. Louis and Washington, D.C.

Major carriers (as of this writing) include:

American	800-433-7300
Continental	800-525-0280

Delta   627-2145
Northwest   800-225-2525
TWA   800-221-2000
United   800-241-6522
USAir   622-4350

Commuter service is provided
by American Eagle, Business Express,
Northwest Airlink, TW Express,
United Express and USAir
Express. Air charter service is provided
by Piedmont Aviation Services, Inc.

The airport has recently completed
an expansion that refurbished
the main passenger terminal,
added 10 new gates and built a
new control tower. During the refurbishing,
the Armed Services
YMCA opened a Military Welcome
Center in the airport. This is a
lounge with a television and free
coffee and soft drinks. Outside in
the main lobby is a military information
booth that has a staff person
on duty who will also answer questions
from civilians.

If you must park at the airport,
there are two multi-level, covered
parking garages and one open
lot for long term parking, and short
term open lots at both arrival and
departure sides of the terminal.
Overall, there are 4,000 spaces, so
the parking nightmare typical of
many other large airports just isn't a
factor here. Expect to pay $1 an
hour for short term, 75 cents an
hour up to a maximum of $4.50 per
day for long term. If you're lucky
enough to find a curbside parking
place, meters ask for 25 cents for 10
minutes. Cars with handicapped license
plates park free.

If you're without personal
transportation, taxis circle like vultures
at the arrival side of the terminal,
so you shouldn't have any
trouble hailing one. The cost is
about $18 to downtown Norfolk and
about $25 to the oceanfront in Virginia
Beach. Taking the Norfolk
Airport Shuttle costs about $11.50
to downtown Norfolk and $15.50 to
the oceanfront. To find a shuttle
from the airport, check at the
glassed-in booth in the median outside
the baggage claim area. Some
hotels also offer courtesy transportation
to and from the airport; you
might check on this when you make
reservations. If you do need to make
specific arrangements, here are a
few numbers:

Norfolk Airport Shuttle
857-1231
Beach Taxi   486-4304
Yellow Cab   460-0605,
622-3232 or 399-3077
Black & White   489-7777
B&W Cabs of Chesapeake
543-2727

And, for the truly decadent
traveler:
Celebrity Limousine Service
853-5466
Executive Car Service
622-7441
Atlantic Beach Limousine
471-0068

CHESAPEAKE MUNICIPAL AIRPORT

Owned and operated by the
City of Chesapeake since 1979, this
small airport is located just south of
Great Bridge at 177 West Road and
is capable of handling small jets on
its 4,200-foot runway. The facility is
open to the public every day from 8
AM to sundown, and has 100-oc-

tane, low-lead jet fuel. Pilots arriving after hours can call 804-421-9000 24-hours a day to make suitable arrangements.

Mid Eastern Airways (FBO) is responsible for the operation of the facility, which offers charter, flight school and major maintenance. Hanger space and rentals are also available, with a small pilot's lounge with all the basic layover amenities.

Pilots, take note. The identifier is W36 and there is no landing fee.

HAMPTON ROADS AIRPORT

With two asphalt runways and four reciprocals, Hampton Roads Airport offers runways from 3,500 to 4,000 feet. Mercury Flight Center is FBO at this general aviation airport in Chesapeake just past Bowers Hill off South Military Highway. Flight school, maintenance, hanger facilities and tie-downs are available. The airport is open from 8 AM to 5 PM daily and until 8 PM in the summer. It has 100-octane, low-lead fuel.

The Identifier is PVG, with 24-hour number 804-488-1687. No landing fee is required.

SUFFOLK MUNICIPAL AIRPORT

This city-owned airport, which started in 1943, is at 200 Airport Road on the outskirts of Suffolk. It has four runways ranging in size from 2,500 to 7,000 feet. Two runways are in the midst of a renovation that will be completed in July of '93. Hours of operation are 8 AM to 8 PM from April through October and from 8 AM to 5 PM the rest of the year.

There are hangars, tie downs and a maintenance facility as well as 100-octane low-lead fuel. There is also a full-service restaurant. The airport's identifier is SFQ. Its 24-hour number is 804-539-8295. There is no landing fee.

Train Service

AMTRAK

The nearest station for Amtrak train service is at 9304 Warwick Boulevard in Newport News. Service to Washington, D.C. includes departures Monday through Saturday (8:15 AM) and Sundays (7:45 AM and 3:05 PM). Arrivals from Washington are at 8:25 PM daily. For information, call 800-872-7245.

Travel By Water

THE ATLANTIC INTRACOASTAL WATERWAY

There's more to Hampton Roads travel than gridlocked interstates and backed-uped tunnels. You can escape it all when you travel on water. It may not be as quick as land or air travel, but it certainly is one of the greatest pleasures of living in this region of river, ocean and Bay.

Connecting the area to destinations north and south are the Dismal Swamp Canal and the Albemarle & Chesapeake Canal which form alternate routes along the Atlantic Intracoastal Waterway between the Chesapeake Bay and Albemarle Sound. The Atlantic Intracoastal Waterway provides pleasure boaters and commercial shippers with a protected inland channel between Norfolk and Miami, Florida.

The Dismal Swamp Canal, the oldest operating artificial waterway in the United States, is on the National Register of Historic Places as a Historic Landmark, as well as being noted as a National Historic Civil Engineering Landmark. It is the primary course for recreational craft making a lazy journey from Deep Creek in Chesapeake down to the Pasquotank River in Elizabeth City, North Carolina, which in turn, spills out to the Albemarle Sound. If you travel this route (along with the Yankee rich and famous steering their boats to warmer climates in fall and the reverse come springtime), be sure to stop in at the Mariner's Wharf city docks for a visit with the famous Rose Buddies, Elizabeth City's self-appointed welcoming committee for visiting cruisers.

The second headwater canal is the Albemarle & Chesapeake, primarily used by commercial vessels. It weaves through the locks at Great Bridge out to the less protected waters of Currituck Sound, and on through the locks at Coinjock, North Carolina to the Albemarle Sound.

Both canals and the rest of the waterway are maintained by the United States Army Corps of Engineers. When navigating these waters, you should have both bow and stern lines ready when going though any locks, and reduce speed to eliminate wakes when approaching, motoring through or leaving the locks and bridge structures. You should also stay on the lookout for natural hazards, such as submerged stumps, rocks or logs.

For more information, including charts and available anchorages, contact the U. S. Army Corps of Engineers in Norfolk at 441-7606.

THE CHESAPEAKE BAY BRIDGE-TUNNEL

No discussion of the waterways of Hampton Roads would be complete without a mention of the Chesapeake Bay Bridge-Tunnel, acclaimed one of the Seven Wonders of the Modern World. Considered the world's largest bridge-tunnel complex, it consists of more than 12 miles of trestled roadways, two mile-long tunnels, two bridges, almost two miles of causeway, four manmade islands and 5 1/2 miles of approach roads, totalling an absolutely amazing 23 miles.

The bridge-tunnel connects Southside Hampton Roads to Virginia's Eastern Shore, and those headed north to New York can save 95 miles and 1 1/2 hours by taking a ride across the mighty surge of the Atlantic Ocean and the waters of the Chesapeake Bay. If it is your first trip across the span, you might just want to add those hours back into your itinerary and stop off at the first island for a snack at the Sea Gull Restaurant, a walk down the busy fishing pier, or to snap up a t-shirt at the goodies-packed souvenir and gift shop.

Emergency road service is available, and there are call boxes every one-half mile. One-way crossing toll is $10.

Inside
A Pronunciation Guide

*T*here's a quick way to tell newcomers from Hampton Roads natives. Just ask them to pronounce the name of area cities. OK, Virginia Beach and Chesapeake are pretty easy to fake. But Norfolk, Portsmouth and Suffolk can trip you up if you're not careful.

The region's British heritage remains emblazoned on many of its city and street names. The following guide will have you speaking like a native in no time.

Botetourt: <u>bot</u>-a-tot. Lord Botetourt was the Virginia Colony's governor from 1768 to 1770. In Norfolk there are at least two streets and an apartment complex named for him.

Boush: bush. This major downtown Norfolk artery has been called Boush Street since 1762. It was named for Samuel Boush, who was elected as the first Norfolk mayor but died in 1736 before he took office.

Greenwich Road: <u>grin</u>-ich.

The name of this Virginia Beach road fouls up many a new broadcaster trying to talk intelligently about traffic tie-ups.

Monticello: Thomas Jefferson may have called his estate outside Charlottesville mont-a-<u>chel</u>-lo, but Monticello Avenue in Norfolk is pronounced mont-a-<u>cell</u>-o.

Norfolk: <u>naw</u>-fik. If you go calling this city Nor-folk, that's a dead giveaway that you're not from here. The name is borrowed from the British, who have a Norfolk County. Say the name rapidly, and you'll sound fine.

Portsmouth: <u>ports</u>-muth. Portsmouth, England was the namesake for this city. If you hear someone calling it <u>porch</u>-muth, you will have found a bona fide native who's lived here a lifetime.

Suffolk: <u>suff</u>-ik. This city also has a namesake in England. Like Norfolk, this is a city whose name should be said quickly.

Photo: Richmond Newspapers

Fresh oysters on the half shell.

Dining
in
Ghent

Award Winning
Louisiana & American Cuisine
Live Jazz Fri. & Sat. Night
723 West 21st St.
(804) 625-5427

magnolia
Down South West Cafe
Colley Ave. &
Princess Anne Rd.
(804) 625-0400

FELLINI'S
Gourmet Pizza Cafe

1421 Colley Avenue
(804) 625-0259

123 West 21st St.
(804) 625-3000

1316 Colley Avenue
(804) 622-0033

Inside
Restaurants

*L*et's face it. Hampton Roads is not the best place on earth to go on a diet. You've got your seafood, your corn-fed beef, your antipasto, your Peking duck and your burrito combo platter. You've got so much temptation whipped up by so many prime time chefs that you could eat out three meals a day, seven days a week and never duplicate the menu.

Yes, when it comes to the practiced art of satiating hunger, the cart of many colors – and flavors – is ready to wheel in your direction. Whether you're in town for a night, a week's vacation or to snag a permanent address, you'll soon discover that only your taste buds know for sure where you'll wind up with a napkin in your lap. While delicacies from the deep take top banana in many of our most favorite places, you can broaden your appetite horizons by sampling some of the best ethnic, Mexican, Chinese and good old Southern cooking this side of the burn-off-those-calories-video line.

With so many restaurants to sample, we'll keep this intro brief, but we must mention the grand finale of every meal...the check. Most places accept plastic as payment, although American Express is not welcome at quite a few establishments who hope you leave home without it. Personal checks are likewise not a just dessert for many tabs. Be advised to check out each restaurant's specific payment policies when making reservations.

A word about reservations is in order, too. If it's Memorial Day weekend at Virginia Beach, don't expect to waltz in unannounced to a waiting table. Ditto any holiday or, for that matter, any night during peak summer season. Most better restaurants require, or at least recommend, that you make reservations for your dining party, and that (believe us!) has no bearing whatsoever on the time you may actually be seated. This is no way implies that your restaurant of choice does not want to pamper your every culinary desire, it's just that the party of 12 just ahead of you may be savoring the umpteenth mini-cup of cappuccino. So, wherever your destination for the evening's repast, be prepared to linger at the inevitable well-stocked bar for an aperitif before your name is announced for din-din.

We have chosen to take you through the wonderful world of caloric intake by category rather than city by city. That's because, if you're like us, if you have a taste for mu shu pork, you don't want to have to flip through 47 pages of Cajun spiced American nouvelle to locate the best Chinese places in the area. We'll try to give you the decorative flavor of each establishment, along with the most popular menu items, and throw in a few totally subjective opinions along the way.

Next to each restaurant's name, you'll notice a nifty little dollar sign signal, the Insiders' secret code for what you might expect to pay for a divine dinner plus reasonable cocktail intake or sensible bottle of wine. These all apply to an evening's meal, and you can work the math to subtract about one-third for a lunchtime visit:

Under $20	$
$21-$35	$$
$36-$50	$$$
$51 and up	$$$$

One last note before we're seated. The tour we're about to take is current as of this meal, but we do have chefs that have wings under their white smocks. What's pasta today may be pai fan tomorrow. But menu u-turns and restaurant name-changes are all a part of the thrill of the food chase.

American

Virginia Beach

ARTY'S DELI
Loehmann's Plaza
$ 340-2789

Arty's Deli opened in 1987 with a traditional Kosher menu that includes corned beef and brisket cooked on site. Arty's pastrami sandwiches, chicken soup and chicken salad have big followings. Arty's serves breakfast, lunch and dinner every day but Sunday.

BAJA RESTAURANT
3701 Sandpiper Rd.
$$ 426-7748

Despite its Mexican name, this restaurant specializes in homemade pizza and seafood. The Baja has been a casual Sandbridge beach eatery since 1974. It overlooks Back Bay and has a screened dining area. Fresh fish usually includes flounder, tuna and catfish. The Baja is known for crab cakes. During the summer it serves lunch and dinner daily. In the off-season it shuts down on Sundays. Dinner is served six days with lunch only on Friday and Saturday.

THE JEWISH MOTHER
3108 Pacific Ave.
$$ 422-5430

The Jewish Mother is a Virginia Beach landmark that's been around since 1975. It's a fun, New York-deli type place with a big line-up of sandwiches. Lox and cream cheese, latkes, blintzes and home-made soups are on the menu. The Jewish Mother serves a variety of salads and breakfast items, too. With more than 20 desserts in a showcase up front, it's hard to pass up the sweets. Children eat their sandwiches off of Frisbees they can take home. Live entertainment at night brings in some national bands. Breakfast, lunch and dinner are served daily. People who've dined

Kids and Eating Out

If you're dining with children, you'll find your family welcome almost anywhere. Although there are many familiar fast-food restaurants here, branch out and try some local spots. Even if your children detest seafood, they'll usually find chicken fingers or hamburgers on the menu. The only restaurants where you might hesitate to take the young ones are to some of the romantic Continental or French restaurants and the trendy Nouvelle American or New Southern bistros.

Once the lack of a babysitter forced us to take our 3-year-old son on our anniversary dinner to a candlelit restaurant by the bay. We went early and were treated graciously by the staff. However, if you aren't sure whether a restaurant welcomes children, call ahead and ask.

At most restaurants you'll find children's menus, booster seats and a staff quick to supply a basket of crackers while you wait for food. At places where there is no children's menu (like most Chinese restaurants), we find an appetizer that will work or just share our dinners if portions are large enough. No one seems to mind.

There are numerous restaurants that hand out crayons and menus to amuse children. The following are some that go the extra mile to make young customers feel welcome.

*Elliot's Restaurant, 1421 Colley Ave. in Norfolk, lets children eat free on Monday nights. The children's menu, which they get to color and keep, has a good variety and includes a peanut butter snack plate.

*The Jewish Mother, 3108 Pacific Ave. in Virginia Beach, serves children's sandwiches on a Frisbee they can take home. They usually leave with balloons, too.

*Fuddrucker's Restaurant, 4625 Virginia Beach Blvd. in Virginia Beach, lets children eat free Monday through Thursday in the evenings. Be sure to ask for one of the paper Fuddrucker's hats like the ones the workers wear.

*Hooters, 1776 Laskin Rd. in Virginia Beach and 1160 N. Military Hwy. in Norfolk, is probably the last place you'd think to take your kids. However, children under 12 always eat free, and Hooters is tame enough that we've taken the grandparents there for lunch. The cheerleader-looking waitresses are friendly with children and eagerly haul out hula hoops and bowling sets for them. The hamburgers and big-screen TV get a thumbs-up from the young crowd.

*ShowBiz Pizza, Lynnhaven Parkway and Lishelle Place in Virginia Beach is the ultimate kids' place. Pizza is the mainstay of this restaurant near Lynnhaven Mall. There's an animated musical show and lots of games and rides that require you to buy tokens. ShowBiz also has a big area filled with colored balls for kids to jump and roll around in. This is a popular place for birthday parties and reaches the pandemonium level on weekends and rainy days.

here in the past will be amazed at the new decor. Gone are the graffiti-covered walls. In their place are a pastel and turquoise color scheme.

MARY'S

616 Virginia Beach Blvd.

$ 428-1355

Since 1958 Mary's has been dishing out big breakfasts and good home cooking. It still has the same owners who specialize in barbecue, meatloaf and luscious desserts such as German chocolate cake and banana cake. Early bird specials are real bargains.

PJ BAGGAN

4001 Virginia Beach Blvd.

$ 498-4748

Gourmet sandwiches are the bread-and-butter of PJ Baggan, which opened in 1991. PJ Baggan's sandwiches team up turkey with cream cheese, lettuce, tomato and sprouts, and roast beef with cream cheese, horseradish, lettuce, tomato and onion. The restaurant also makes an excellent pasta artichoke salad. Homemade desserts include turtle brownies. There is a bargain-priced cappuccino happy hour in the afternoons. The restaurant has a large selection of Virginia, California and French wines for sale. It serves lunch and dinner every day but Saturday.

POLLARD'S CHICKEN

100 London Bridge Blvd.,	
Virginia Beach	340-2565
3033 Ballentine Blvd., Norfolk	855-7864
326 E. Bayview Blvd., Norfolk	587-8185
717 Battlefield Blvd., Chesapeake	482-3200

$

There is much more than fried chicken on the menu at this local chain of family restaurants that's been around since 1967. North Carolina-style barbecue, chicken and dumplings and Brunswick stew are as popular as the chicken. Daily specials feature country-style comfort food such as livers and gizzards. Homemade desserts include five-layer coconut cake

and bread pudding. Lunch and dinner are served daily. No credit cards.

PUNGO GRILL
1785 Princess Anne Rd.
$$ 426-6655

This restaurant prides itself on its eclectic menu. On a typical day diners can choose from crab cakes, pasta, lasagna, catfish, Thai and Jamaican chicken and 12 different vegetables. The grill, which opened in 1988, is in a restored 1919 house in the heart of Pungo in rural Virginia Beach. It works local produce into the menu when it's available. Homemade desserts include chocolate mousse, hummingbird cake and lemon meringue pie. Lunch and dinner are served everyday but Monday. Reservations are encouraged.

THE RAVEN
1200 Atlantic Ave.
$ 425-9556

Since 1968, The Raven has been a beachfront mainstay. Its offerings include French dip sandwiches and the Raven champignon – a burger dressed up with bacon and sauteed mushrooms. During off-season Wednesday nights, all-you-can-eat crablegs and shrimp pack in the crowds. Lunch and dinner are served daily.

TOM'S TIKI TAI
3472 Holland Rd.
$$ 468-5940

Naval fans feel at home at Tom's Tiki Tai, which bills itself as the "region's largest private Naval museum." The restaurant is filled with Navy signal flags, diving equipment and historic photos. Among its intriguing memorabilia are a Revolutionary War cannonball and a pressure gauge plate from the *Maine,* which sunk in 1898. Ambiance aside, Tom's has a solid seafood and steak menu and often brings in live entertainment featuring music from the 1940s.

Norfolk

CHARLIE'S CAFE
1800-A Granby St.
$ 625-0824

Hearty breakfasts and comfort food are the hallmarks of this small Ghent eatery that attracts a diversified clientele from police officers to young professionals. Omelettes, waffles, pancakes and fluffy biscuits are on the breakfast menu, which is served all day. At noon burgers, meat loaf and sandwiches share the spotlight with daily specials such as chicken and dumplings and pot roast. Charlie's is open daily for breakfast and lunch. No credit cards.

COLLEY BAY CAFE
5215 Colley Ave.
$$ 451-1641

Opened in 1992 on the Lafayette River, Colley Bay is near Old Dominion University and the Larchmont neighborhood. It is the third restaurant in this former marine supply store and appears to be the one that will survive. This is a casual place with a trendy billiards room in back. The menu features seafood, steaks, pastas, salads and sandwiches. It is open for lunch and dinner on weekdays and only for dinner on weekends. Reservations are accepted.

CRANK'S FAMILY RESTAURANT
1105 N. Military Highway
$ 461-5106

Crank's has been a meat-and-potatoes kind of place since it started in the 1950s as Burrough's. Owner Artis Crank worked for the original restaurant before buying the operation in the 1980s. We know several executives who can't start the day without a Crank's country breakfast. Steaks, fish and chicken are the lunch and dinner staples. Homemade puddings and pies, including chocolate cream and lemon meringue, are irresistible. There's nothing fancy about this place, but it offers all-American food for a reasonable price.

THE DINING CAR
742 W. 21st St.
$ 622-0159

After nearly five years in a more obscure location the Dining Car moved to the heart of Ghent in late 1992. Brother and sister duo Janet and Chris Nagy feature all-American cooking as well as some Southwestern specialties such as chicken and sour cream burritos. Their vegetarian entrees are popular, including sauteed vegetables and pasta. Other items that keep customers coming back are fried potato skins and crab cakes. The Dining Car is open for lunch and dinner daily. Children's dinners include an ice cream sundae. The restaurant also serves Sunday breakfast. Reservations are accepted. The Dining Car is a *Port Folio* magazine

People's Choice award winner.

DO-NUT DINETTE
1917 Colley Ave.
$ 625-0061

If you're a fan of vintage diners, this is the place to go. The dinette opened in the 1940s. Its current owner, Sheila Schneider Mullins, is the daughter of the dinette's long-time owners. When she took over in 1987 she kept the same ambiance. There are only 16 stools, most of them occupied by regular customers. Breakfast and lunch are served daily. The morning meal features eggs, sausage, hash browns and donuts just pulled from the hot oil and dripping with glaze. There's always a lunch special such as fried chicken or fresh seafood. The dinette has some of the best prices in town.

DOUMAR'S
20th and Monticello Ave.
$ 627-4163

Doumar's is a Norfolk landmark that shouldn't be missed. It's been at the same location since 1934 and still has car hops. When they hang a tray on your car window loaded with burgers, fries and milkshakes served in real glasses, you'll think the calendar slipped back a few decades. The food is good and cheap. Doumar's opens for breakfast and keeps serving until late night every day but Sunday. Its standouts include pork barbecue and the best limeades in town. Be sure to end your meal with ice cream in a homemade cone – after all Abe Doumar, the restaurant's founder, invented the ice cream cone in 1904. (See related article.)

(See related article.)

ELLIOT'S
1421 Colley Ave.
$$ 625-0259

This is the granddaddy of the trendy Ghent restaurants. Elliot's has been going strong since 1978 with an unbeatable menu of burgers, pastas, seafood, chicken and beef.

Popular items include mile-high nachos and "the works" brownie loaded with ice cream and fudge sauce. Besides the food, Elliot's is known for its eclectic interior that has a giant silver moon, fun-house mirror, old Norfolk photos and lots of flea-market memorabilia. Elliot's has expanded several times, most recently with a glassed-in side room

Crab Talk

Watermen and restaurateurs have their own lingo when it comes to the region's favorite mollusk – the blue crab. Here are some terms you may hear:

Backfin – Also called the paddle fin, this appendage is where the tastiest crab meat lies. The flat backfin serves as a swimming aid and, when it's time for the crab to molt, it develops the white, pink or red lines crabbers rely on to help them spot peelers.

Busters – A crab who is getting rid of, or busting out of, its old shell.

Doublers – Male and female crabs riding tandem during the mating process. This may last for days while the female molts, is impregnated and develops a new protective shell.

Jimmies – A very hard male crab with a slender apron. (Crabs reveal their sex and state of maturity in several ways, including the shape of their abdominal apron.)

Papershell – A crab who molted about 12 hours ago, but whose shell is already toughening.

Peeler – Often used as bait, these are crabs on the verge of molting with a soft shell ready and waiting under the hard one.

She-crab – A young female crab with a V-shaped apron. These crabs are favorite ingredients in local soups that often include cream and sherry.

Softshell – Just molted, this tired, vulnerable crab is sought by fish and fishermen alike. Softshell crabs are a real delicacy that shows up on menus in late spring and summer where they are battered, cooked and eaten whole, legs and all.

Sooks – Mature female hard crabs who have molted for the last time, characterized by a dark bell-shaped apron.

Sponge crab – A female crab carrying her egg mass on her abdomen.

and patio seats along the sidewalk – a great place for people-watching in warm weather. Lunch and dinner are served daily with brunch offered on Sunday. Children eat free on Monday nights. Elliot's is a winner of *Port Folio's* People's Choice dining award.

FIRST COLONY COFFEE HOUSE
2000-1 Colonial Avenue
$ 622-0149

Java lovers take note: California chic finally landed in Norfolk when this coffee paradise opened in late 1992. Its owners are the Brockenbrough brothers who run First Colony Coffee Co., which has blended beans around the corner since 1902. With First Colony's gourmet coffees taking the country by storm, the Brockenbroughs figured it was time to test the waters with their own coffee house. Gleaming antique coffee dispensers and a copper-top bar create the mood for this classy but casual place. White bean chili, and olive and cream cheese sandwiches will tempt you at lunch and dinner. Desserts are divine and imported from New York. Biscotti is just right for dunking. Linger over the house blend or check out the wilder coffee and tea flavors of the day. On your way out, grab a bag of beans for the road.

FREEMASON ABBEY
Freemason and Boush streets
$$ 622-3966

This aptly-named restaurant is in a former Presbyterian church built in 1873. Before becoming a restaurant in 1988, the building was an Odd Fellows meeting hall. Although the Abbey retains its original exterior, inside it has been remodeled into a modern two-level restaurant. The menu includes seafood, pasta, quiche, sandwiches, chicken and steaks. Perenalli's greens is a notable salad and makes an ideal lunch when accompanied by crab soup or gumbo. Each Wednesday is lobster night with a New England lobster dinner served for a reasonable price. Lunch and dinner are served daily with brunch offered on Sunday. Reservations are accepted.

KELLY'S TAVERN
1408 Colley Ave.   623-3216
1936 Laskin Rd., Virginia Beach   491-8737
$

Kelly's is the only place we go that always makes us toss health care to the wind and chow down on a hamburger with fries. Both are great as is the grilled chicken sandwich. Kelly's has been in its Norfolk location in Ghent since the late 1970s and in Virginia Beach since 1991. Both restaurants serve sandwiches, salads and appetizers. The larger Beach restaurant also has some full dinners. The restaurants serve lunch and dinner daily with the Beach location featuring a Sunday brunch. The Beach establishment also takes reservations.

LOAVES AND FISHES BY DAIL
339 W. 21st St.
$ 627-8794

After years of running Dail's seafood, the Dail family opened a restaurant in the Palace Shops in late 1992. Lunch is served every day but Saturday and features more than the seafood you'd expect. Chicken salad, roasted turkey, pasta and home-cooked specials such as meat loaf and chicken and dumplings are on the menu as well as sandwiches, soups and salads. The daily special runs the gamut from linguine and red clam sauce to meatloaf. Homemade pies are tempting. You can still buy fresh seafood here as well as some produce and baked goods. Loaves and Fishes is open for lunch every day but Saturday. The seafood shop is open longer hours. No credit cards.

No Frill Grille
7452 Tidewater Dr.
$ 587-0949

The name of this restaurant says it all. It opened in 1988 to serve good, basic food at a reasonable price: barbecue ribs, hamburgers, milkshakes and big salads. The place has a '50s feel and is open for lunch and dinner every day but Sunday. No credit cards.

Oh! Brian's
7512 Granby St.
$$ 480-7267

This Ward's Corner restaurant has drawn a loyal following since its opening in 1990. Its hallmarks are fresh fish and pasta. Popular entrees include an Italian fish stew and crab cakes. Homemade bread and desserts – including apple and cherry crisps – round out the offerings. Early bird specials are a bargain. Lunch and dinner are served every day but Sunday. Oh! Brian's is a recent People's Choice winner in *Port Folio* magazine's Golden Fork awards.

Philly Style Steaks & Subs
7456 Tidewater Dr.
$ 588-0602

One Philadelphia expatriate we know swears this eatery turns out the most authentic cheese steaks and subs he's had since he left the City of Brotherly Love. Owners Joe

and Debbie Hatch opened in 1983 and still import their sandwich rolls from up north. They serve lunch and dinner every day but Sunday. No credit cards.

REGGIE'S BRITISH PUB
The Waterside
$ 627-3575

This British pub has a great view of the Elizabeth River from the second floor of The Waterside, and on nice days, Reggie's balcony is a pleasant spot to dine. The menu is a blend of British and American. It offers Cornish pasty's, fish and chips and shepherd's pie as well as sandwiches, steaks, chicken and salad. Desserts include Norfolk County apple dumpling and chocolate mousse pie. Lunch and dinner are served daily. Live music is featured on weekends.

REISNER'S DELICATESSEN
144 Janaf Shopping Center
$ 461-8548

Founded in 1943 by Austrian immigrant Allen Reisner, this deli is still run by Reisner's daughter, son-in-law and grandchildren, who carry on the family tradition of serving some of the best deli food in town. The hot pastrami and Swiss sandwich ranks with the Reuben as

Reisner's best sellers. However, health-conscious diners will also find a grilled chicken breast sandwich. Side dishes include onion rings, corn fritters and potato pancakes. All desserts are homemade, including Kahlua milk chocolate cheesecake. Reisner's is in Janaf shopping center on Military Highway and sells a good variety of bottled wine. It closes on Sunday.

Chesapeake

CARA'S
123 N. Battlefield Blvd.
$$ 548-0006

Opened in 1992 along the Atlantic Intracoastal Waterway, this restaurant has expanded Chesapeake dining options. Its menu includes chicken, seafood, beef and specialty salads such as chicken with macadamia nuts. Cara's is in the Island Wharf shops and has a deck overlooking the waterway. Everything is homemade, including breads and desserts such as Mississippi fudge pie and peanut butter pie. There is a Friday night seafood buffet as well as Sunday brunch and dinner buffets. Lunch and dinner are served every day but Monday.

CHEER'S

1405 Greenbrier Parkway

$ 424-4665

Modeled on its Boston namesake, this casual restaurant opened in 1990 on the outskirts of Greenbrier Mall. Its menu is varied and includes sandwiches, salads, beef, chicken and seafood. Popular entrees include barbecued ribs and a Boston chicken and shrimp combo served over fettucini in cream sauce. There is a fresh fish daily special as well as a cheesecake of the day. An inexpensive express lunch is available for the working crowd. Lunch and dinner are served daily with brunch available on Sunday.

Doumar's

With its car hops and antique ice cream cone machine, Doumar's revels in its history. Founder Abe Doumar was lured to Norfolk in 1907 by the Jamestown Exposition, which promised to attract thousands of new customers to eat his ice cream cones.

Doumar, who came here via St. Louis and Coney Island, invented the ice cream cone during the 1904 St. Louis Exposition. He started out in Norfolk's Ocean View area and by 1913 had opened a second location on the Virginia Beach boardwalk with his brothers. Since 1934 the only Doumar's has been in Norfolk at Monticello Ave. and 20th Street. The current building went up in 1949, and time has stood still since then.

As soon as drivers pull up, a car hop trots out with a menu and tells them to turn on the headlights when ready to order. Within a few minutes the carhop hauls out limeades, cherry Cokes and milk shakes in real glasses. Hamburgers are swaddled in wax paper spiked with a toothpick. Everything comes on a tray that hangs on the car window. Switch on the lights again, and the attendant whisks the tray away.

Doumar's nephew Albert runs the drive-in with his son Thad. Each day at either 3 PM or 7 PM one of them fires up Abe Doumar's original machine and creates hand-made cones. Two car hops have each been on duty for 40 years. Some cooks have been there just as long making Doumar's famous pork barbecue and other sandwiches.

Prices are unbeatable, and the atmosphere is great. There's room to dine inside where walls are lined with blown-up photos of Doumar's early days. There are several photo albums to peruse, and Albert will be happy to show off his cone-making technique if it's time to make a batch. Customers can also buy a big jar of homemade cones to take home.

Doumar's is open from 8 AM-11 PM Monday-Thursday. It stays open until 12:30 AM on Friday and Saturday nights and closes on Sunday. The drive-in is a gathering spot for antique car owners who feel right at home here.

VILLAGE GRILL
2001 S. Military Highway
$ 543-1702

Owner Marilyn Fried opened the grill in late 1992 after leaving The Intermission in Norfolk, which has since folded. Many of her popular items such as spicy steamed shrimp and the hunk of steak have reappeared here. Large salads, 20 different deli sandwiches and daily specials also are on the varied menu. The grill serves lunch and dinner daily. Decadent desserts include a Snickers volcano and a triple layer chocolate cake. The restaurant is in the K Mart shopping center.

Portsmouth

THE MAX
435 Water St.
$$ 397-1866

After a late 1992 move down the street to a new location, The Max has enlarged its menu. It still specializes in what its owner calls "semi-gourmet meals" such as seafood Miranda and chicken piccata, but now there are nachos, fried clams and pizzas on the menu as well. Desserts are homemade. The restaurant overlooks the Elizabeth River. The Max serves lunch and dinner daily with a buffet brunch on Sunday.

MOM'S BEST DELI
3210 High St.
$ 399-1199

One of our favorite stops for a quick sandwich, this small deli also turns out some good home cooking. Daily specials include chicken and dumplings, and corned beef and cabbage. Homemade salads and desserts also are notable. The deli has gained local fame for its chocolate chip cookies and meringue pies. It serves lunch on weekdays and takes no credit cards.

NEW YORK DELICATESSEN
509 Court St.
$ 399-3354

The deli has been in downtown Portsmouth since the 1930s and in its current quarters for about 20 years. Kosher foods include reuben and pastrami sandwiches, lox and bagels and chicken soup. Desserts include homemade cream puffs. It serves breakfast, lunch and early dinners, closes on Sunday, and takes no credit cards.

Suffolk

BUNNY'S RESTAURANT
1901 Wilroy Rd.
$ 538-2325

Bunny's is Suffolk's home-cooking standout. It's been serving up fried chicken, crab cakes and chicken pot pie since 1971 from its location near Wilroy Industrial Park. This is a no-frills restaurant with a big lineup of vegetables such as stewed tomatoes, candied yams and butter beans. Meals are served with homemade hushpuppies. Bunny's is open daily for breakfast, lunch and dinner. Breakfasts feature Belgian waffles, eggs and pancakes. No credit cards.

FRONT STREET RESTAURANT
434 N. Main St.
$$ *539-5393*

Housed in a historic home near downtown Suffolk, Front Street changed hands in 1992. It is open for lunch on weekdays and dinner on Wednesday through Saturday. Dinner entrees range from steaks and scallops to trout and chicken. Specialty dishes include scalloped oysters and chicken cordon bleu stuffed with brie and ham. The lunch menu features mainly salads and sandwiches.

THE PEANUT RESTAURANT
6001 Holland Rd.
$ *657-9846*

Located on Route 58 beside a cotton patch, this restaurant prides itself on its home-cooked daily specials such as pork chops, ham and chicken and dumplings. Vegetables include butter beans, homemade onion rings and collards. Peanut pie and banana pudding are on the dessert menu. On Friday and Saturday nights there are all-you-can-eat

shrimp specials. The restaurant, which also sells country crafts, serves lunch daily and dinner on Wednesday through Saturday.

Bakeries

Virginia Beach

BONJOUR BAKERY AND DELI
336 Constitution Dr.
$ *473-9107*

This European bakery opened in 1986 and is run by a Lebanese baker whose specialties are baklava, eclairs, chocolate mousse cigars and other French pastries. You may have to search to find this spot. Although it is in a shopping center across from Pembroke Mall, it is dwarfed by a neighboring K Mart. Bonjour Bakery is open Monday through Saturday and serves lunch and early dinners. Featured items are sandwiches on homemade bread.

Although you'll find crab on almost every restaurant menu, you may want to buy a bushel for your own pick-and-eat feast. Be aware that crab prices fluctuate wildly depending on how prolific the catch. Before planning your menu call ahead and find out if crabs are on hand and if you can afford them. They're usually most abundant in spring and summer.

Among the places to buy a bushel or half bushel of crabs are: Channel Crab, 714 Stapleton St. in Norfolk (622-3724); Chesapeake Bay Crab House, 2592 Campostella Rd. in Norfolk (454-0653); Loaves and Fishes by Dail, 339 W. 21st St. in Norfolk (627-8794); Wickers Crab & Seafood, 3138 Victory Blvd. in Portsmouth (487-4201), and Leggetts Seafood, 340 N. Main St. in Suffolk (539-5331).

Insiders' Tips

PASTA & PANI BAKERY
1065 Laskin Road
$ 422-8536

This Italian bakery is well known for its breads, particularly the crusty sourdough. It also has semolina and white bread and rolls. Other products include fresh pasta, ravioli, Italian sauces, cheeses and cold cuts. The bakery also makes a wonderful biscotti. It opened in 1990 as part of Pasta & Pani restaurant. In 1992 it moved five doors down to its present location. The bakery is open Tuesday through Saturday. No credit cards.

SUGAR PLUM BAKERY
1353 Laskin Rd.
$ 422-3913

This nonprofit bakery has a tremendous following in Virginia Beach. It started in 1987 to provide training and jobs for young adults with mental retardation. It serves that mission well while turning out what one person we know calls "the best cookies I ever ate." There are more than 200 items in the bakery, making it one of the region's largest. Among the best sellers are chocolate mousse cake, six-grain bread and buttery wedding cookies.

The bakery has a cafe that is a great place to savor a sweet roll and coffee. Sugar Plum also serves lunch, which features a variety of salads and sandwiches and a soup of the day. The menu changes seasonally. The bakery is open Tuesday through Sunday. No credit cards.

Norfolk

BON APETIT
2708 Granby St.
$ 625-4777

This tiny Mediterranean bakery turns out an amazing amount of bread, baklava and specialty pastries. Its products show up in local stores and restaurants, but individuals also can stop by for a coconut macaroon or a bag of croissants. The bakery is part of a small Mediterranean grocery whose wares include filo dough, grape leaves and feta cheese. It is closed on Sunday. No credit cards.

Steinhilber's Thalia Acres Inn

The year is 1922. It's the Lynnhaven Golf and Country Club, and you have traveled hours for a gentlemanly round, far away from the big city of Norfolk, in the rural Town of Lynnhaven in Princess Anne County, long miles from the sleepy outskirts along the Atlantic Ocean known as young upstart Virginia Beach. Life is lazy, slow and genteel. And then comes the Depression.

During the early '30s, Depression takes it's toll. The Country Club flounders, and in comes a young man from the city to buy the property. The young man is Robert Steinhilber, who, along with brothers Walter and Herman, has successfully run a popular eatery on Main Street in Norfolk. While they negotiate, the Club burns to the ground, save the thick concrete foundation and, in 1935, Robert and Herman buy the 140-plus acres out in the country and turn it into a country resort. They build stables to board horses, patch up a driving range, erect log cabins for overnight guests, create riding trails and set up picnic tables for those city folk who need to escape from the hustle and bustle of city living. Robert takes his bride, an avid horsewoman from Berkley, and they build a restaurant so people who visit will have a fine place to eat. It is now Thalia Acres Inn...and then it is World War II.

The trees around the Inn are thick with the war. Just around the bend is a prisoner of war camp, set up as a processing station for German POWs. Steinhilber is a German name, and not to be trusted by those who had never met the gentle man. The military claims the building and the grounds and it becomes an Officer's Club along with drill and tank testing fields, while the young Steinhilbers watch powerless, biding time.

In the early '40s, much worse for wear, Thalia Acres Inn is returned to the rightful owners. The war has ended, and life resumes. The area now has merged into the City of Virginia Beach, the restaurant is enlarged and suddenly there is the new-fangled passion for family flight to suburbia. The country club to driving range to tank testing site becomes...homes...built on land sold by Herman to crystal-balled investors, hungry for the heavily wooded property. Once a long driveway of oyster shells and grass, Thalia Road becomes a yellow-brick pathway, entry into the prestigious neighborhood tucked away on the Lynnhaven River.

Steinhilber's Thalia Acres Inn flourishes, and expands. Tourists flock to Virginia Beach and hear wonderful things about the fine dining in this tucked away restaurant along the Lynnhaven. They come. But, they themselves are not all so wonderful. They're too rude, too pushy and too boisterous for Pop Steinhilber's liking. He is defiant, closing the restaurant during the summer season to avoid the pressure to serve patrons who show no respect. He becomes a legend.

Today, Steinhilber's is still part yesterday, part today, where kind respect for those serving and those served is a way of life. Now operated year round by Robert Steinhilber's children, Steve and sister Jeanne, you can hear the echoes of the past when you sit on the lower level where the locker rooms and rathskeller once roared with country club members and World War II officers. If you choose to drive down what was once an oyster shell driveway to the gracious hospitality and old world charm that awaits at roads end, you might ask your server for a favorite story or two. Many have been there for over 35 years. And oh, the tales they can tell.

FRENCH BAKERY & DELICATESSEN
4108 Granby St

$ 625-4936

This bakery has been run by the Habib family since 1913 and has been in this location since 1942. The Habibs pride themselves on using the same recipes as when the bakery was founded. They produce all types of French pastries, including eclairs and French cigars. One popular seller is the orange donuts. The bakery is open Monday through Saturday. For lunch it serves submarine sandwiches on homemade bread. No credit cards.

LA BANNETTE BAKERY AT CAFE 21
742 G W. 21st St

$ 625-4218

Located in Cafe 21, one of Norfolk's most popular restaurants, this bakery opened in late 1992 and immediately gained a following in west Norfolk. La Bannette sells all types of bread, including crusty French baguettes and loaves of sourdough and raisin walnut. Other popular items include croissants, brioche, chocolate chip cookies, rugulah and brownies. The bakery is open daily.

NAAS BAKERY
3527 Tidewater Dr.

$ 623-3858

Naas has been around for at least 50 years. Its current owners have run the business since the early 1970s and gained a loyal clientele. Even the bakery's relocation in 1992 didn't deter Naas' regular customers. The bakery is known for its danishes, coffee cakes and butter cookies. There are tables for din-

ing. Naas closes on Sunday.

NEW YORK BAGEL SHOPS
161 Granby St

$ 627-2345

This shop has one of the largest selections of bagels we've seen, ranging from banana nut to oat bran and spinach wheat. There are traditional varieties as well as doughnuts. The shop sells several diabetic desserts, including rugulah. Lunch includes deli sandwiches and salads. The shop closes on Sundays. No credit cards.

THE VILLAGE BAKERY
1511 Colley Ave.

$ 625-7422

This Ghent mainstay is the primary bakery for the west side of Norfolk. It has been in business since the 1930s when it was known as Urquahart's. Specialties include almond pound cake, cookies, danishes, bread and eclairs. There are a few tables in the bakery, which is open Tuesday through Saturday. No credit cards.

Suffolk

YE OLDE PASTRY SHOP
353 W. Washington St

$ 539-7181

Don't be put off by the yellowed wedding cake in the pastry shop window. Inside you'll find apple, chocolate and sweet potato pies just pulled from the oven. Donuts, cinnamon buns, cookies and buttery rolls are also sold. The bakery has been in a former downtown dress shop for about 10 years and has done little to alter the decor. Its prices are extremely reasonable, and on Saturday nights its owner sells baked goods from a booth at the Village Auction Barn on the outskirts of Suffolk. The bakery closes on Sunday. No credit cards.

Barbecue

Virginia Beach

THE BAR B QUE GRILL
1601 Hilltop W. Shopping Center
$ 428-7758

This immaculate cafe gives a down-home touch to the tony Hilltop area. The grill's owners hail from Florida but their barbecue style has a Texas twang. Pork, beef and chicken barbecue anchor the menu. Dinner plates come with two side orders and two corn fritters. There are 14 side dishes available, including Brunswick stew, baked beans and stewed apples and yams.

Fried fritters are laced with whole corn kernels and lots of black pepper. Each day there are homemade soup and dessert specials. In true Southern style, the iced tea comes presweetened unless you specify otherwise. The restaurant is open for lunch and dinner every day but Sunday. No credit cards.

THE BEACH BULLY
39th St & Baltic Ave.
$ 422-4222

This casual tavern-style restaurant provides a change of pace for beach goers ready for a switch from the resort city's predominant seafood. The Beach Bully opened in 1985 four blocks from the oceanfront. Barbecued beef, pork and chicken are all on the menu. Platters come with two side orders of homemade specialties, including hand-cut french fries. One popular offering is the baby back rib dinners. The restaurant is open daily for lunch and dinner. No credit cards.

Norfolk

PIERCE'S PITT BAR-B-QUE
The Waterside
$ 622-0738

This is a spin-off of Pierce's outside Williamsburg, probably the best-known barbecue restaurant in Virginia. The Norfolk location is in the food court of The Waterside. It specializes in minced pork barbecue and traditional side dishes like baked beans and cole slaw. Pierce's is open daily for lunch and dinner. It is a winner of *Port Folio* magazine's People's Choice award for favorite barbecue restaurant. No credit cards.

Chesapeake

MR. PIG'S BAR-B-Q
445 N. Battlefield Blvd.   547-5171
1915 Victory Blvd., Portsmouth   485-2048
$

Mr. Pig's has been Chesapeake's main barbecue restaurant since the late 1980s. Vinegar-sauced North Carolina barbecue is the house specialty, however, the restaurant also does a brisk business with its fried chicken. Brunswick stew, boiled potatoes and chicken salad are among the other menu offerings. In late 1992 Mr. Pig's added a second location in Portsmouth in the Triangle Shopping Center. The restaurants serve lunch and dinner but close on Sunday. No credit cards.

Portsmouth

RODMAN'S BONES & BUDDY #2
3562 Western Branch Blvd.   397-3900
RODMAN'S BONES & BUDDY #3
5917 Churchland Blvd.   483-2000
$

Although these restaurants only opened in the 1980s they have a rich history. One of the owners was the founder of The Circle, a Portsmouth dining landmark. His partner is renowned for making Rodman's barbecue. "Buddy & Bones" pays tribute to two deceased Portsmouth restaurant owners who bore those nicknames and served the "square dog" now a staple of Rodman's menu. (Just so you won't be confused, the original Rodman's is in Suffolk and is strictly a catering operation.)

Rodman's has loyal customers who lap up the barbecued pork and chicken. Side dishes include Brunswick stew and navy bean soup. Its hushpuppies are some of the best around. Featured menu items include sliced Smithfield ham sandwiches and, of course, the square dog. This is a sliced grilled hot dog served with lettuce, tomato and a lump of Smithfield ham just as Bones and Buddy would have offered it. The restaurants serve both lunch and dinner every day except Sunday. No credit cards.

Suffolk

HERB'S BAR-B-Q
868 Carolina Rd.
$ 539-9785

This is your classic barbecue joint – the kind you have to be told about to find. Herb Brinkley has run the business since 1951 and maintains a menu that has changed little since then. Barbecue pork comes either sliced or minced on a sandwich or a platter. The combination plate is served with barbecue, cole slaw, corn bread and Brunswick stew. Herb gives cornbread a different twist by serving it as delicious fried nuggets. Herb's maintains a rustic look, and it still has curb service under the metal canopy out front. It closes on Sunday. No credit cards.

Chinese

Norfolk

BAMBOO HUT
1355 Debree Avenue
$ 640-1649

Always good, always fast, always reasonable – that's Bamboo Hut, and, while they may slide somewhat in the category of international "fast food," it's hard to beat their Beef and Broccoli or their Mu Shu Pork. With both Mandarin and Szechuan menu offerings, they've spread out to multiple locations throughout the region, which more or less is a clue to their popularity among Insiders. You'll find them here in the heart of Ghent and in:

Virginia Beach: 2832 Virginia
Beach Boulevard
Lynnhaven Mall
Larkspur Square
2407 Pacific Avenue
1801 Pleasure House Road
College Park Shopping
Center
Norfolk: 6400 East Virginia
Beach Boulevard
7450 Tidewater Drive
Chesapeake: 455
North Battlefield Boulevard

CHINA GARDEN
854 N. Military Highway
$$ 461-3818

The combination lunches and dinners here are tough to top, but, if you insist, you can order from the page after page of their extensive menu. Peking duck by Chef Lu is a house specialty, and you'll really enjoy the Chinese brunch tradition of dim sum served here on weekends. You can find other China Gardens at Pembroke Mall at the beach and 303 High Street in Portsmouth.

SHINE SHINE PALACE
The Waterside
$$ 623-0778

Choose from Hunan, Cantonese or Szechuan fare from the menu, and dine in a most opulent setting for chopsticks with spectacular views of the Elizabeth River from the top floor of The Waterside Festival Marketplace. The smells that greet you as you enter are enough to snap those tastebuds to attention, and we can almost guarantee you'll be satisfied not only with the splendid food, but with the

service as well.

SZECHUAN GARDEN
121 West Charlotte Street
$ 627-6130

Some like it hot, and none serve it spicier than Szechuan Garden, a local favorite for both lunch and dinner. Our most favorite dish on the menu is the gan bien string beans, spicy and tender. (One Insider we know picked up several orders to add to their dinner party menu!) Their sesame pancakes are hard to top, too, and they offer a full selection from secret Hunan, Cantonese and Mandarin recipes. Their Beach counterpart is at 2720 North Mall Drive.

SZECHUAN IN GHENT
1517 Colley Avenue
$$ 625-1551

Ghent has many restaurant choices, but this is a favorite. The interior decor is surprisingly elegant for a Chinese eatery, but the extensive menu and cordial service match the best of them. Peking duck for two is a house specialty, but we're partial to the triple seafood delight. A special vegetarian menu is available, too.

Virginia Beach

FOON'S
4365 Shore Drive
$$ 460-1985

One great benefit of the authentic Hunan and Szechuan dishes here at Foon's is that they are all prepared without MSG. Outstanding on the menu are Szechuan shredded beef, Peking duck and soft-shell crab with ginger and scallions.

FORBIDDEN CITY
3544 Virginia Beach Blvd.
$$$ 486-8823
This is one of the priciest
Chinese restaurants in town, but
once you slide into that private
booth and close the privacy cur-
tains, you can pretend you're not
really in Virginia Beach after all.
Having just completed an extensive
renovation, the exceptional impe-
rial Peking dining with rich, spicy
sauces is rolling again.

MR. YEE'S
2914 Pacific Avenue
$$ 428-3661
Long known as the Golden
Dragon, a Beach landmark, this is
now home to Mr. Yee's. The fare is
standard Chinese variety, and we
haven't had a chance to see if any
remodeling to the dining room has
taken place. It's location is key, however, if you're in the midst of a
Beach vacation and have a hankering for egg roll, won ton and shrimp
with lobster sauce.

Continental/
French

Norfolk

ANTIQUITIES
Norfolk Airport Hilton
$$$ 466-8000
White linen, gracious
maitre'd and attentive wait staff all
add to the luscious menu featuring

continental euro-American favorites
(including wild game) in this el-
egant, candlelit, beautifully ap-
pointed restaurant lurking behind
the stark exterior of the Norfolk
Airport Hilton. This is a place to
truly act out the word "dining," as
lingering at the table is not only
welcome, but encouraged.

LE CHARLIEU
112 College Place
$$$ 622-7202
Elegant, old-style dining still
exists, and it's here at Le Charlieu,
the epitome of traditional French
cuisine. Housed in a former residence, Richard Tranchand and
chef, Mathieu, pour their attention
on haute cuisine and their guests.
Try not to spill any wine from the
massive list on the white damask
tablecloths.

Virginia Beach

LA CARAVELLE
1040 Laskin Road
$$$ 428-2477
Rich French-Vietnamese of-
ferings in an elegant candlelit set-
ting await you at this much touted
restaurant decorated in the country
French manner inside the Seashire
Inn on Laskin Road. Duckling in
Grand Marnier sauce, salmon in
champagne sauce and tornadoes
Caravelle are among our favorite
entrees.

LE CHAMBORD
324 North Great Neck Road
$$$ 498-1234
A wonderful feast for the eyes
as well as the stomach, Le Chambord

is one of the most charming restaurants in the area. It's crisp decor and comfortable seating urges patrons to linger over divine entrees like quail stuffed with crab or chateaubriand bearnaise with red onion confit. Lunches offer a lighter bill of fare, with some marvelous salads, perfect with a glass of wine for a noontime break. Owners Frank and Luisa Spapen have just been awarded the American Automobile Association's Four Diamond Award, one of only two such honorees in the region. (Ship's Cabin in Ocean View is the other.)

THREE SHIPS INN
3800 Shore Drive
$$$ 460-0055

This is one of the most romantic restaurants in the region as far as we're concerned. On a winter's evening, reserve early for a table beside the enormous fireplace, where you will be pampered by knowledgeable servers tempting you by describing the preparation of their duck with black cherry sauce or the brace of quail. A place not just for dinner, but for a most enjoyable evening.

Ethnic

Virginia Beach

ANATOLIA
2158 N. Great Neck Rd.
$$ 496-9777

Anatolia is a stylish restaurant that excels in gourmet Turkish cuisine and has the region's broadest selection of Middle Eastern food. Its owner is a former Greenwich Village restaurateur who decided to head south and opened the restaurant in 1990. The extensive menu includes lamb and beef kebabs; chicken, shrimp or lamb sautes; shrimp dishes and vegetarian specialties. A wood-burning brick oven turns out some of the best pita bread you'll ever eat. Early bird dinners are a bargain. Anatolia is in the Great Neck Square Shopping Center and is open for lunch and dinner daily with hearty breakfasts served on weekends. If you go on Friday or Saturday nights you'll definitely need a reservation since that's when belly dancers entertain during dinner. Anatolia's is a *Port Folio* Golden Fork People's Choice winner.

THE STREET COOK
Lynnhaven Parkway and Princess Anne Road
$$ 471-7810

This Mediterranean restaurant has a cuisine its owner describes as "a little Greek, a little Italian and a little Virginia Beach." It turns out great seafood crepes, veal Erica and poulet florentine among other entrees. Homemade desserts include a chocolate torte and baklava. The Street Cook is open for lunch Tuesday through Friday and for dinner Tuesday through Sunday. Reservations are accepted. No credit cards.

Norfolk

BAVARIAN INN
5541 Iowa Ave.
$$ 858-2758

Unless you've been here before, call for directions. This small German cafe is just off Military Highway but is easy to miss. The inn opened in 1990 and serves some of the best German food in the area. Owner/chef Lothar Nass is from the Black Forest region of Germany. His broad menu has 15 entrees, traditional appetizers and desserts as well as hamburgers and sandwiches. Sauerbraten and grilled pork steak with peppers and onions are the best sellers. The winerschnitzel also comes highly recommended made with either veal or pork steak.

Nass' side dishes are excellent, from the spatzle to the hot German potato salad. Desserts include apple strudel and Black Forest cake. With its blue gingham table cloths and German music, the inn provides a charming touch of Bavaria. Lunch and dinner are served every day except Monday. Reservations are accepted. Since its opening, the inn has been a consistent winner of *Port Folio* magazine's Golden Fork awards.

GERMAN PANTRY
5329 Virginia Beach Blvd.
$ *461-5100*

This tiny, authentic German cafe has been in business since the late 1970s. Its owners are three friends who grew up in Germany and are excellent cooks. Their menu includes a variety of wieners and wursts as well as pork chops with sauerkraut. Daily specials feature such hearty fare as spatzle with goulash served with an excellent green salad and hard roll. Breads are imported from Canada but most everything else is made on premises,

including Black Forest cake.

The Pantry has a small German store selling greeting cards, magazines and cooking supplies. Lunch is served Monday through Saturday with dinner available on Thursday and Friday. No credit cards.

THE MONASTERY
443 Granby Mall
$$ *625-8193*

This is one of the city's most venerable ethnic restaurants. Adolf and Anna Jerabek opened it in 1983 after moving from Czechoslovakia via New York. House specialties include roast duck and an excellent goose in the winter. Schnitzel and goulash are also featured on the 38-item menu. Daily specials range from salmon to roast lamb. Guests are welcomed with a plate of cheese, apples and bread. They will be tempted to end their meal with the Jerabeks' homemade Black Forest cake, strudel or chocolate fondue. The Monastery is open for lunch Tuesday through Friday. Dinner is served Tuesday through Sunday by waiters dressed as monks. Reservations are suggested, particularly if the symphony, opera or other arts group is performing in downtown Norfolk. The Monastery has won so many Golden Fork awards from *Port Folio* that it has made it into the magazine's hall of fame.

NAWAB
888 N. Military Highway
$$ *455-8080*

It was a happy day for Norfolk gourmands when this Indian restaurant opened in 1992 on the outskirts of Military Circle Mall – typically a haven for all-American chain restaurants. Nawab is the only regional restaurant specializing in Indian cuisine. Its vast menu ranges from tandoori dishes cooked in a clay oven to curried chicken or squid. The menu is extensive and includes mulligatawny soup and a good mix of seafood, lamb, beef, vegetarian and chicken dishes. Nawab's bread is the traditional papadam wafer made from lentil flour. The restaurant is open daily for lunch and dinner. Nawab's lunch buffet is reasonably priced and is a good way to sample Indian cuisine.

ORAPAX INN
1300 Redgate Ave.
$ *627-8041*
This is one of our mainstays. When we can't decide where to go for dinner we usually end up here. The inn opened in 1970 in residential West Ghent. This casual restaurant is renowned for its Greek specialties, including pastitsio, spanakopita, Greek salads and a gyro platter. It has some of the best fried calamari around.

Meals come with an irresistible homemade bread and melted butter for dipping. Salads are served with a bottle of the tangy house dressing for you to pour. Popular entrees include the spinach pizza and mousaka. There are daily specials. The Orapax is open for lunch and dinner and has delivery to nearby neighborhoods. It closes on Sunday. In September the owners shut down for most of the month and make their annual pilgrimage to Greece. The Orapax is a recent

People's Choice winner in *Port Folio* magazine's Golden Fork Awards. No credit cards.

TAKIS GYROS
The Waterside
$ *627-5087*
This Greek eatery is one of our favorites for lunch. It is in the food court of Waterside and serves great gyros, Greek salads and spanakopita. Other traditional foods on the menu include souvlaki and baklava. Takis is open for lunch and dinner daily. It has limited delivery in downtown Norfolk. No credit cards.

Italian

Norfolk

LA GALLERIA RISTORANTE
120 College Place
$$$ *623-3939*
Valet parking outside, mahogany, veined marble and hammered copper inside...a tiny hint of the spectacular evening you'll have dining at La Galleria in downtown Norfolk. This place can only be classified as an "event," and has to its credit mucho awards for its wonderful food as well as its decor. Just recognized as one of the 10 most beautiful restaurants in the country by two national trade magazines, fine northern Italian specialities are prepared superbly, and served with panache. Get your taste buds activated with a white pizza from the wood-burning oven, then move on to polla alla Sorentina (chicken

stuffed with spinach, zucchini and mozzarella in wine sauce) or vittello La Galleria (veal with fresh tomato sauce). The bar that floats off-center in the restaurant is gorgeous, and a popular spot for gathering after work or after dinner.

FELLINI'S
123 West 21st Street
$$ 625-3000

Credit owner Mike Cavish with introducing "new pizza" to the palates of Hampton Roads residents and visitors. Cancel Pizza Hut and order one of his Thai Chicken, BLT (the "L" is spinach!) or Cajun pizzas, prepared to order in the open kitchen you can see from any table in the intimate house. A favorite hangout for locals who know every server and bartender by name, plan to push your way through the crowds to the bar on a weekend night. There's more than pizza, though. Their pasta dishes are phenomenal, and they prepare one of the best and biggest Caesar salads in town. You can get the same Fellini's taste at the Beach, too, via their speedy home-delivery service. Place your order by calling 422-3500.

MAMA'S ITALIAN KITCHEN
182 West Ocean View Avenue
$ 587-4262

You had better be hungry! The servings are mammoth and can only be described as comfort food, Italian style. An Ocean View landmark for generations, you may have to wait a bit in the unrushable atmosphere, but all your Italian basics like spaghetti with sausage and lasagna, along with some exotics like

Pasta Putanesca (pasta with anchovies, pine nuts and herbs), are well worth the "weight."

IL PORTO
333 Waterside Drive (The Waterside)
$$ 627-4400

If expansion is a sign of success, Il Porto in The Waterside is on a garlic roll. Since their opening in 1983, they've expanded two separate times to accommodate diners who adore their Northern Italian cuisine. Savor the homemade pasta, veal and seafood while you watch ships slide down the Elizabeth River, and two spacious patios are available for dining when weather permits. Rivaling the food and view for popularity is Charlie Wiseman, a super song-man, who takes his place at the 12-foot concert grand piano bar to entertain the after-work crowd.

REGINO'S
114 East Little Creek Road, Ward's Corner
$ 588-8012

The pizza comes in one size...humongous. And it's amazing how you can eat the whole thing, it's so delish. Antipasto and lasagna to die for are also here in this long and narrow eatery tucked away in Wards Corner. You may have to wait outside the door on a busy evening, but the aroma of garlic that hits you when you step inside makes any wait well worth the time. We've heard a rumor that there may soon be a Regino's, the sequel, in the Hilltop area of Virginia Beach. Updates to follow.

SPAGHETTI WAREHOUSE
1900 Monticello Avenue
$ 622-0151

We're talking volume at Spaghetti Warehouse, a relative newcomer to Norfolk in a totally rehabed old warehouse located on the outskirts of Ghent. Volume number one: the food literally hangs off the platter no matter what you order. The other volume: the number of patrons lined up to take their turn at the vast menu, especially on weekend nights. It's a bit noisy for a romantic bottle of Chianti, but a super place if you have teenagers that never seem to be filled up.

Virginia Beach

IL GIARDINO RISTORANTE
910 Atlantic Avenue
$$$ 422-6464

While it isn't really necessary to dress up to eat here, you'll want to look your best to impress all the beautiful people you'll bump into. There's no doubt you'll be tempted by the dazzling array of appetizers, but do share one. You'll want to save room for the entree...a little veal, perhaps? A supper here may be the very best meal you have at Virginia Beach, both for divinely prepared dishes and superb service. Afterwards, there's a happening piano bar, and the lounge stays open until 2 AM to maintain its social cachet.

ALDO'S RISTORANTE
1860 Laskin Road
$$ 491-1111

Not only will you eat well here,

you'll look good doing it. This is a charming place, with a never-ending turnover of equally charming patrons, all waiting for their personalized platter of homemade pasta graced by light and tasty sauces, one better than the next. Their fantastic pizzas, baked in a wood-burning pizza oven, are likewise delish. Popular for lunch and dinner, it's a fun place when you're in the mood for a taste of Italy.

BELLA PASTA
1423 North Great Neck Road
$$ 496-3333

Take your pick here from northern and southern Italian dishes, with a few creative American specialties tossed in for universal appeal. A bustling place, working magic in the kitchen is sous chef Tracy Kessler, one of the area's youngest female chefs.

CIOLA'S
1889 Virginia Beach Blvd.
$$ 428-9601

What masquerades as a good-old roadside diner is the laboratory for the Italian chemists who can whip up some of the most tummy-pleasing dishes this side of Italy. From pasta to lasagna, the portions are generous and consistently excellent, all cooked to your order. A long-time Virginia Beach landmark, neither the interior decor nor the quality of the food has changed in many of year, a fact for which many of Ciola's fans are quite grateful.

ISLE OF CAPRI
313 Laskin Road
$$ 428-3831

Another Virginia Beach landmark for guaranteed delicious Italian cuisine, the Isle of Capri just has the look of your basic great restaurant. From the constantly packed house, to the aroma of garlic, to the extensive menu, it's a grand place to pig out on pasta. New here is the Back Room Bistro, which features live entertainment on weekends.

PASTA E PANI
1065 Laskin Road
$$ 428-2299

The running battle here is which is more delicious – the homemade pasta or pani (bread). Simplicity is the key, whether it's a pizza from the wood-burning stove or delicately flavored pasta entrees. There's also a separate deli where you can bag some of their specialties along with cheeses, meats and other Italian groceries.

LA BROCCA
608 Birdneck Road
$$$ 428-0655

"Dancing shrimp with cognac" should give you a clue to the fine dining experience that's tradition at La Brocca. Since La Brocca means wine carafe, you can expect an exceptional wine list and, if you're in doubt about your selection, owner Micael Scaramellino and his son are at the ready with the proper suggestion. The medieval decor with its Portuguese tapestries and lattice work gives the restaurant a dark, intimate ambiance, perfect for a romantic dinner for two.

Portsmouth

CAFE EUROPA
319 High Street
$$$ 399-6652

If you ever have a yen for veal cooked to absolute perfection, a trip to Portsmouth's Cafe Europa is almost the only sensible choice. A charming little cafe, all lace curtains and candlelight and long known for it's Italian and French cuisine, it is a multi-time Golden Fork winner for the quality of food, atmosphere and service.

Japanese

Virginia Beach

AJI-ICHLBAN
309 Aragona Blvd.
$$ 490-0499

It's natural, pretty and fresh, with no fat or sugar. It's sushi, and it's the new rage in Hampton Roads. Serving some of the best is Aji-Ichban in Virginia Beach, under the watchful eye of Eunju Kim. After you're done in the sushi bar, settle in to enjoy tempura, teriaki, yakitori, tonkasu and hot pots, washed down with either a Japanese beer or sake.

KYUSHU
400 Newtown Road
$$ 499-6292

Fresh, beautifully presented sushi and sashimi platters are the standard at this award-winning sushi bar. Watching chef Ebigasko deftly layer a touch of wasabi (horseradish root) and a slender slice of yellowtail on an oval of rice is true culinary theatre. Of note here is the "kiss roll" of seaweed and rice filled with garlic, a very different taste for the bored palate.

MATSURI
4768 Shore Drive
$$ 460-5222

Another popular sushi bar serving traditional Japanese seafood dishes, Matsuri has been around since 1986, and owner Chong Kim sees to it that his restaurant offers not only some of the tastiest sushi in town, but the most elegantly presented. Tuna, salmon and yellowtail are the favorite ingredients here, but vegetable sushi is offered to those who can't, or won't, eat raw fish.

SHOGUN
313 Hilltop Shopping Center
$$ 422-5150

You just know you're in for something extraordinary when you first spot those chefs wearing tall, brilliant red chef's hats and neck scarves and bearing mega-sized knives sharp enough to split a human hair. You have entered the Shogun zone, and you are going to have the most entertaining meal of the year – a full seven courses prepared with the speed of lightning right before your very eyes. The food, especially the tempura, is excellent, and watching the skilled preparation is an event. Don't miss it.

Mexican

Norfolk

COLLEY CANTINA
1316 Colley Avenue
$ 622-0033

We can't quite figure out whether it's the food or the fun that keeps this place in Ghent jammed every night. As Mexican food goes, this is all your favorite basics...lots of it for a reasonable price. But toss in a phenomenal margarita and perhaps you've unlocked the secret to this popular place's success. It's especially nice in spring through fall, with outdoor seating where you and your taco can watch the Colley Avenue cruising.

FAJITA FLATS
Hampton Boulevard
$ 423-9126

Just opened across from Old Dominion University, you can slide into a booth for a combo platter, play a little billiards in the back parlor, or cuddle up to the bar that stretches the length of the place. Popular with students and young parents who don't mind if their kids roam aimlessly around, it's got a real neighborhood kind of feeling, along with some spunky spirit-lifting decor. It's great for a quick and cheap meal.

Virginia Beach

LISTA'S
Bonney Road at Lynnshores
$$ 463-8226

Slide into a high-backed booth and unbuckle your belt. This family-owned restaurant offers a break from the typical Mexican taste, but not the overload. Sauces here are so much more delicate than any of the other Mexican restaurants in town, and that makes for very special dishes like chipolte pepper tuna and the ever-popular steak relleno, a NY strip that's butterflied, pounded and stuffed with vegetables.

AMIGOS MARGARITA GRILLE
2272 Great Neck Road
$$ 481-3133

Under the watchful eye of manager Rick Maggard, here's a Mexican restaurant that's on the border...southwest that is. Along with the popular Cantina for a custom margarita, the restaurant offers more than just the standard Mexican fare, tossing in some real tasty items like fish grilled with citrus. Upbeat and spunky, it's a terrific place to go when only a fajita will soothe your nerves.

SAN ANTONIO SAM'S
604 Norfolk Avenue
$ 491-0263

It's Tex-Mex and more in this jumping place packed with Lone Star memorabilia and roadhouse-style tunes on tape. A hint to the creative touches is their wonderful way with enchiladas. Try the crab and avocado or enchiladas del mar,

stuffed with crab, scallops and shrimp. At this writing, a second location in Ghent is being readied at 1503 Colley Ave. in Norfolk. We all plan to make a beeline to the border when it opens.

MI CASITA
Rosemont & Bonney roads
$ 463-3819

New on the Mexican scene in town, this place is so packed with pinatas dangling from the ceiling and draped on shelves that you have to blink to make sure you haven't been whisked to a sidestreet in Tijuana. All your favorites are here, as well as some superb homemade guacamole and chips to wash down with a bottle of Tecate, but we'd advise staying clear of the cactus that's stir-fried with tomatoes and onions. They make a mean margarita, and the huevos rancheros they serve only at lunchtime are muy bueno.

New Southern

Virginia Beach

PUNGO PLACE LIGHTHOUSE RESTAURANT
1824 Princess Anne Rd.
$$ 426-2670

Cajun food is the specialty of this restaurant founded in 1987. Since Pungo Place is in the heart of Pungo – one of Virginia Beach's rural areas – its menu often features seasonal produce grown right down the road. Seafood, steaks, pork and chicken are restaurant staples with a blackened fish of the day and a blackened prime rib always on the menu. Wednesday is Cajun night with creole, jambalaya and other Louisiana favorites. Alligator is a popular appetizer as is a puff pastry stuffed with andouille sausage, shrimp and crab. Homemade fruit cobblers and cheesecakes are available. Ice cream comes from two local sources – Bergey's Dairy Farm and Uncle Harry's Cones and Cream. Pungo Place closes on Tuesdays, and also Mondays during summer. It accepts reservations.

Norfolk

BIENVILLE GRILL
723 W. 21st St.
$$ 625-5427
You'll find Louisiana style cuisine with a kick, with Cajun and Creole dishes that can't be matched in Hampton Roads at this great spot. Chef Mike Hall was instrumental in introducing Cajun to our area, bless his little andouille sausage. A Louisiana native, he's brought a bit of the French Quarter to Ghent, along with some pretty mean live jazz on weekends and, as Mike says, "killer catfish." The restaurant has won so many *Port Folio* Golden Fork awards that it is enshrined in its Hall of Fame.

CAJUN CAFE
The Waterside
$ 626-3711
Bienville Grill's Mike Hall opened this Waterside eatery in 1992 to put some hearty Cajun cooking in the downtown food court. For a reasonable price, diners get a jumbo plate of red or black beans and rice or shrimp creole. All are served with a hunk of homemade French bread. Beef brisket and grilled chicken sandwiches also are served. Open daily. No credit cards.

THE DUMBWAITER
117 Tazewell St.
$$ 623-3663
It is absolutely impossible to describe Dumbwaiter owner Sydney Meers and keep a straight face. The man is a trip, and so is his popular restaurant that boasts perhaps the smallest bar in town.

The place is a whimsical madhouse, crammed with happy people munching on regional dishes with a down-home Southern flair. You've never had real grits, sweet potatoes or meatloaf until you've tasted Sydney's. If you're close to downtown Norfolk, you'd be missing something special if you don't stop in. At lunchtime, a must-order is the grilled chicken breast on black-eyed peas with blue cheese dressing. And, try not to laugh when you see "Dumbketchup" and Dumbmustard" on the table.

The Dumbwaiter was scheduled to move to Tazewell Street in April 1993 from its original location a block away. Meers gets more elbow room in the kitchen, but the dining room remains cozy.

Nouvelle American

Norfolk

BISTRO 210

210 York Street

$$ 622-3210

There have been almost as many rave reviews of this brand new eatery in downtown Norfolk as there have been patrons. That said, we, too, would follow owner/chef Todd Jurich anywhere he chooses to hang his ladle. An upstart and innovator when it comes to combining tastes and textures, Jurich has whipped up some unusual – and unusually delightful -- surprises. Try the carpaccio of pastramied lamb or the salmon glazed with molasses, cayenne and cinnamon. It may sound a bit off the deep end of the griddle, but those, and so many other weird menu concoctions that change with seasonal availability are fantastic.

CAFE 21

742G West 21st Street

$$ 625-4218

A real neighborhood bistro orchestrated under the watchful eye of owner Larry Epplein, Cafe 21 features ethnic and American cuisine. Enjoy their risottos, curries and couscous, along with a mean pasta Alfredo. The fresh-baked desserts are tempting and delicious, and an order from the Espresso Bar makes a savory after-dinner finale.

CRACKERS

821 West 21st Street

$$ 640-0200

If you drive by too fast, you'll miss it. Cracker's may be small in stature, but a giant in the eyes of those who know a great meal when they're served one. Everything is prepared from scratch daily, and nightly specials are the whim of the chef who excels in neoclassical cuisine. It's a popular place to crowd into for Sunday brunch.

MAGNOLIA

Princess Anne & Colley

$$ 625-0400

Billed as a down Southwest cafe, Magnolia is a palate pleaser, although service isn't always the speediest. Owners Tracey and David Holmes must stay up very late at night to concoct new and innovative menu offerings. Try a tuna taco or pizzadilla, the southwestern version of the Italian staple, or stick to the standard favorites like Santa Fe chicken or rib-eye Magnolia. Salad lovers will want to give their Texas Caesar salad a go. It's a regular Caesar enhanced with some Southwestern pizazz, like golden corn kernels. Connected to the main dining area is a handsome bar and lounge that stays hopping with locals until the wee hours.

SIMPLY DIVINE

4019 Granby Street

$$$ 625-0554

It's almost as difficult to describe the talent of owner/chef Bobby Gordon as it is to describe this jewel of a restaurant. The lavish and consistently wonderful menu (angel hair pasta with shrimp and scallops, Norwegian salmon tickled with dill sauce) is served with aplomb in a setting that can only be described as Victorian goes zonkers. From the "living room" where you can comfortably await your table, to the table itself with fine silver service, you feel as though you've been whisked through the century to the dining hall of a manor home of a prince who just happens to have a magic touch in the kitchen. It's well worth making reservations.

PALETTES CAFE AT THE CHRYSLER MUSEUM

245 West Olney Road
$ *622-1211*

Not even many Insiders are aware of this delightful restaurant located on the first floor of The Chrysler Museum. With its dark walls and crisp tablecloths, it is an elegant little bistro offering a seasonal variety of salads, like Thai chicken and fresh tuna Nicoise, as well as sandwiches served on dark Bavarian bread and in pita. Tempting soups and a few selected entrees are available, too, and it's a wonderfully peaceful oasis for a quiet and intimate lunch.

Virginia Beach

THE BIG TOMATO

2nd & Atlantic
$$ *437-0155*

Cioppino with lobster tail, cornflake-fried crab cakes and silk tomatoes dangling from the ceiling...got your interest? The Big Tomato is the newest brainchild of chef Chuck Sass who carries on his

American regional theme with a twist, and a sense of humor. Open only for dinner Tuesday through Sunday nights, the totally renovated location on Atlantic Avenue sports great ocean views along with some tasty eats. Try it.

BOGIE'S

620 19th Street
$$ *428-1865*

Bogie's is funky and fun, what with exposed colored pipes and great antique French posters on the walls. But the real treasures are the men behind the open kitchen, Greg Rhoad and Parker Lee, both culinary veterans. Just try the fresh tortellini with smoked salmon or Mediterranean-style pan-seared shrimp and scallops with wild rice. Yummy! An excellent wine list is available, too, along with acclaimed onion rings served "Texas style" with B-B-Q sauce.

COASTAL GRILL

1427 N. Great Neck Road
$$ *496-3348*

From the minute you land a table at this intimate bistro, you start right off into the wonderful world of food. A waiting basket of Sourdough bread with crocks of unsalted butter may tempt you, but save that appetite for the superb entrees including beautifully prepared and presented lamb, duck, rabbit and fresh seafood. If you think you'll have room, order the spinach salad, topped with a surprising garnish of chicken livers.

FIVE 01 CITY GRILL
501 Birdneck Road
$$ 425-7195

Be advised that this is the hottest meal ticket in town of the moment. It's just smokin' with its cool clientele, big, casual bar and devastatingly delicious menu. Host Mike Atkinson and chef Corey Beisel have got a winner by serving some of the tastiest treats in town. Veal chop grilled with goat cheese is perfect to follow a starter of charred tuna sashimi with spicy kim chee or the house's signature Michelob shrimp. To top it off, sample the sweet bread pudding drowning in Jack Daniels. What a way to go...and you should.

LUCKY STAR
1608 Pleasure House Road
$$$ 363-8410

When chef supreme Amy Brandt puts the pedal to the kettle, wonderful things happen. Here in the sparkling white interior, sprinkled with the works of local artists, Amy and partner Butch Butt lay out one magnificent spread after another. Combinations are innovative and seasonal, influenced by the Pacific rim. Crawfish spring rolls, spicy corn cakes and Thai chicken salad are among our favorites, but when it's apple season, there's no telling what wonderful aromatic delights will greet you at the Lucky Star.

MENUS
Laskin & Holly roads
$$ 422-1511

Long-time local chef Willie Moats has injected a new spirit into this old favorite with his regional and new American food. Have you ever tasted cinnamon roasted chicken breast or pecan crusted salmon? If not, this might just be your selection for an evening of creative cuisine.

PIRANHA: AN EATING FRENZY
8180 Shore Drive
$$ 588-0100

Wherever master chef Monroe Duncan goes, flocks of gourmands are sure to follow. Piranha is no different than any other fine eatery where magician Monroe has hung his culinary shingle. Piranha: An Eating Frenzy is just that. Be prepared for an overwhelming menu with hidden delights like curried conch fritters for starters and Trinidadian shrimp curry with papaya chutney for the main course, then fight over the last morsel of fluffy blueberry cheesecake or sweet potato pecan pie. It simply amazes us how Monroe dreams up some of his offerings (roasted banana halves with zucchini?), but judging from the repeat patronage at this wonderful eatery, where you can watch sailboats bobbing outside the window, he's dreamed up a whimsical winner.

TANDOM'S PINE TREE INN
2932 Virginia Beach Blvd.
$$ 340-3661

Since 1927, an evening at Tandom's Pine Tree Inn has been a treat for the entire family. Starting with the award-winning 60 item salad, hors d'oeuvres and raw bar, you can settle in a comfy chair and watch the parade of Black Angus beef, pasta, seafood and Cajun dishes go by. We're prejudiced to their superbly prepared veal and chicken entrees, presented by some of the most knowledgeable and personable servers in town.

SWAN TERRACE
Founders' Inn
$$$ 366-5777

Putting a spin on Colonial cookery, the Swan Terrace literally sparkles from the beautifully appointed dining room as well as the individual tables set to Miss Manner's smug satisfaction. Seasonal entrees vary, but not the policies that prohibit smoking or consumption of alcoholic beverages.

Seafood

Virginia Beach

ALEXANDER'S ON THE BAY
4536 Oceanview Ave.
$$$ 464-4999

Alexander's terrific view and fine dining make it a favorite special-occasion place. On warm nights, diners can eat on an open deck overlooking the Chesapeake Bay. Since Alexander's opened in 1985 one of its signature appetizers has been Oysters Alexander – sauted herb-coated oysters served with a white wine and shallot sauce. Entrees range from seafood to steak and veal. Popular entrees are sea-

For some wonderfully rich ice cream thats made locally there are two places to go: Uncle Harry's Cones & Cream and Bergey's Dairy Stores. Uncle Harry's has four locations in Virginia Beach and Chesapeake. Each features a dozen flavors of the day, such as chocolate amaretto and raspberry truffle. Owner Harry Tully opened his first ice cream shop in the late 1980s and has been going strong ever since. His stores are at 1412 Greenbrier Pkwy. in Chesapeake and at 606 Hilltop West Shopping Center, Loehmann's Plaza (4000 Virginia Beach Blvd.) and 3623 Pacific Ave. in Virginia Beach. Uncle Harry's is open daily. Bergey's Dairy Farm has three locations that feature its ice cream as well as sandwiches served on homemade bread. Bergey's makes 27 flavors from its own fresh milk, ranging from apple cinnamon to mint chocolate chip. The first Bergey's store opened on the family farm in rural Chesapeake in 1978. It is at 2221 Mt. Pleasant Rd., and while there you can visit the Holsteins to thank them for their milk. Call 482-4711 for directions. Other stores are at 1128 N. Battlefield Blvd. in Chesapeake and 1989 Landstown Rd. at the Virginia Beach Farmer's Market. The stores close on Sunday. The farmer's market shop also closes on Monday.
Bergey's ice cream also is sold at Gray's Pharmacy in Norfolk at 4712 Hampton Blvd. Grays is open daily and is across from Old Dominion University.

Insiders' Tips

food Madagascar – shrimp, scallops and lobsters cooked in a creamy peppercorn sauce – and a mariner's platter loaded with five types of seafood. Favorite desserts are homemade cheesecakes. Dinner is served daily, and reservations are recommended.

ANCHOR INN

2143 Vista Circle   481-1286
135 Kempsville Rd., Norfolk   455-8180
$$

Tucked away on the Lynnhaven River just off Shore Drive, the original Vista Circle restaurant is a locals-only place highly recommended by seafood lovers. The fish is fresh and the view of the river unbeatable. There is a deck and raw bar. Menu offerings include a three-fish platter and crab cakes. Appetizers include fried calamari and crab-stuffed mushrooms. Homemade desserts include chocolate mousse pie and key lime pie. The Virginia Beach inn has been in business since 1983 and is open for dinner daily. Its Norfolk spin-off opened recently near the Koger Center and serves lunch on weekdays. It is open for dinner every day but Monday.

ANGELO'S

37th & Oceanfront
$$ 425-0347

Right next to Howard Johnson's sits a jewel of a restaurant, a Beach favorite for over 20 years. While Angelo and brother George will be pleased to put a 16 oz. Black Angus NY Strip in front of you, we have to suggest the wonderful seafood pastas, like shrimp over

a steaming bed of linguini or our favorite pasta dish with lobster, scallops, mussels and shrimp. If you can't decide between the two, order the famous Land and Sea Platter with a fork tender fillet and delightfully seasoned New England lobster tail. Don't let the homemade desserts overwhelm you, especially the chocolate Chambord cake.

BLUE PETE'S

1400 N. Muddy Creek Rd.
$$ 426-2005

This is the ultimate off-the-beaten-path restaurant. But once diners get to Blue Pete's, they're glad they made the trek. This rustic restaurant is known for its variety of fresh seafood. The house specialty is sweet potato biscuits, and the restaurant cheerfully hands out the recipe for this treat. Blue Pete's typically closes during the winter, but from spring through fall it is open for dinner Monday through Saturday. Call for directions and reservations. Driving to Blue Pete's will take you on a jaunt through rural Virginia Beach. The restaurant was a recent People's Choice winner in *Port Folio* magazine's Golden Fork awards.

CAPT. GEORGE'S

1956 Laskin Rd.   428-3494
2272 Pungo Ferry Rd.   721-3463
$$$

These restaurants originated the gorge-till-you-burst concept in the region. They offer an amazing variety of seafood, salads, side dishes, soups and desserts for one price. For landlubbers, there is a good selection of other foods. The

Growing, processing and selling peanuts has long been a traditional regional industry.

steamed crab legs and shrimp are irresistible to most diners, especially since they can fill their plates as often as they like. The restaurants do a big volume of business so fresh batches of food are continually being hauled from the kitchen. Capt. George's opens daily for dinner.

CAPTAIN JOHN'S SEAFOOD COMPANY
4616 Virginia Beach Blvd.
$$$ 499-7755

If you're really starved, head for this all-you-can-chow-down seafood buffet. It seems to stretch for a mile with a gargantuan array of crabs, clams, fish and shrimp prepared in endless ways. You'll also enjoy all kinds of other entrees, salads, side dishes and scrumptious desserts. You'll find Captain John's anchored next to Pembroke Mall and serving lunch and dinner daily.

CHARLIE'S SEAFOOD RESTAURANT
3139 Shore Dr.
$$ 481-9863

Charlie's is a homey seafood place near the Chesapeake Bay with a 1950s aura. It was started in 1946 and six years later moved across the street to this location. Little has changed since then in this utilitarian restaurant. It remains in the Rehpelz family with the founder's grandsons at the helm. The menu of flounder, fried oysters, steamed clams and seafood platters is still intact. Homecooked side dishes include squash, collards and black-eyed peas. One standout is the she-crab soup. Desserts usually feature key lime, lemon meringue and chocolate banana pies. On most nights there is an all-you-can-eat

steamed shrimp special. Snow crab legs are discounted on Monday and Wednesdays nights. Charlie's is open for dinner daily and serves lunch every day but Monday. Reservations are accepted.

CHICK'S MARINA AND OYSTER BAR
2143 Vista Circle
$$ 481-5757

This casual restaurant on the Lynnhaven River is a local hangout. Fresh fish is the backbone of the menu that features the best of what is currently available. Chick's is one of the few restaurants that serves deviled crab. Steamed mussels and shrimp also are big sellers. You can dine inside or eat outside on the deck and watch the boats. Chick's recently was a People's Choice winner as part of *Port Folio* magazine's Golden Fork Awards.

DICK'S CLAM & COW
1069 Laskin Rd.
$$ 491-9000

The owners of Harpoon Larry's branched out in early 1993 with this casual, fun restaurant. Dick's quickly gained a reputation for its fresh fish tacos and spicy pizzas as well as its lively activities. Diners can take a spin on a human-sized gyroscope or shoot a few hoops on the indoor basketball court. In warmer weather they can compete in tournaments on the outdoor volleyball court. The place appeals to families during the day and early evening and the bar crowd at night. Dick's menu has a lot of fresh seafood as well as salad entrees, burgers and homemade pies. Reservations are accepted.

DUCK-IN & GAZEBO

3324 Shore Dr.

$$ 481-0201

The Duck-In has an ideal location right on the Chesapeake Bay with a beach and gazebo in its back yard. Diners can eat inside or on a deck under a striped canopy overlooking the bay. The restaurant is renowned for its crab cakes, hushpuppies and fisherman's chowder. It's been in business since 1952.

Although its regular menu of seafood platters, crab and shrimp is good, the Duck-in has gained a following for its buffets. The all-you-can-eat buffet is offered nightly during the summer and on Friday and Saturday during off-season. It usually is loaded with snow crab legs, shrimp creole and other seafood dishes. Popular desserts include bread pudding with pecan glaze and the volcano – a brownie and ice cream with all the fixings. The Duck-In serves lunch and dinner daily and has breakfast on weekends. Reservations are accepted.

GUS' MARINER RESTAURANT

57th St. and Atlantic Avenue

$$$ 425-5699

With its ocean view and excellent cooking, Gus' has earned a permanent spot in *Port Folio's* Golden Fork Hall of Fame. It has been in the Ramada Oceanside Tower since 1981. There are usually at least five types of fresh fish on the menu. Hushpuppies are hard to resist. Specialty desserts include Belgium whisky pudding made with pound cake and raspberry sauce. Gus' serves breakfast, lunch and dinner daily with a brunch on Sundays.

HARPOON LARRY'S OYSTER BAR

216 24th St.

$$ 422-6000

Fresh seafood served in a casual atmosphere is the draw at Harpoon Larry's. The restaurant opened in 1990 as a spin-off of a Hampton restaurant. The menu is heavy on shrimp, crab legs and seafood platters. There are lots of appetizers, including chicken wings. Harpoon Larry's has a raw bar. It is open for dinner daily. Lunch is served daily during spring and summer and on weekends the rest of the year.

HENRY'S AT LYNNHAVEN INLET

3319 Shore Dr.

$$ 481-7300

Located on the Lynnhaven River near the Chesapeake Bay, Henry's is a big, busy restaurant founded in 1938. It changed hands in 1986 and underwent a major renovation and expansion. Menu standouts include jumbo fried shrimp, pure crab cakes made with no filler and Turtle Creek salmon - - broiled fish topped with shrimp, mushrooms, crab and Dijon mustard. Henry's also is known for she-crab soup and its blackened scallops. The restaurant is open Monday through Saturday for dinner and for a Sunday brunch buffet. During weekends there is usually entertainment on the deck overlooking the river. Reservations are needed during the summer, especially on weekends.

HOT TUNA BAR & GRILL

2817 Shore Dr.

$$ 481-2888

As Hot Tuna's name suggests,

you'll find tuna prepared many ways – Oriental style, blackened and in fajitas. The menu is much broader than that, however. Hot Tuna also serves barbecue ribs, crab cakes, steaks and pasta. Although the restaurant leans toward heart-healthy cooking, it also prides itself on its fried calamari. Hot Tuna is open for lunch and dinner daily. There are daily early bird dinner specials. Reservations are accepted.

JOE'S SEA GRILL
981 Laskin Rd.
$$ 422-5637

Opened in 1989, this Art Deco-styled restaurant was an immediate hit. Many of its dishes are created over a hardwood grill. The menu is changed at least twice a year but always includes flounder, tuna and salmon entrees. Popular items include barbecued salmon and grilled tuna with artichokes, tomatoes and mushrooms served on spinach. A recent menu switch added more sandwiches and appetizers for patrons of the movie theater next door. Lunch is served weekdays with dinner offered daily. Reservations are available. Joe's has won so many *Port Folio* Golden Fork awards that it has made it into the magazine's Hall of Fame.

KING OF THE SEA
27th and Atlantic
$$ 428-7983

This venerable seafood restaurant has been at the same location since 1965 and was remodeled in 1993. Its draws crowds with its nightly all-you-can-eat crab leg and shrimp specials. The restaurant is known for broiled seafood platters and blackened fish as well as steaks. King of the Sea is open for lunch and dinner daily. Reservations are accepted.

LAVERNE'S SEAFOOD RESTAURANT AND CHIX CAFE
7th & Oceanfront
$$ 428-6836

There are lots of early bird specials to tempt diners at Laverne's and sister restaurant, Chix Cafe. Both are in the Hilton Inn in Virginia Beach. The restaurants have been cooking fresh seafood since 1981 and have identical menus. Specialties include build-your-own-seafood platters as well as a prime rib and seafood combination. The restaurants are open daily for breakfast, lunch and dinner.

THE LIGHTHOUSE
1st Street and Atlantic Ave.
$$$ 428-7974

Located on the Atlantic Ocean at Rudee Inlet, this airy restaurant has a terrific view. To make it even better, outdoor seating is available in summer. The Lighthouse is a special-occasion restaurant that has been in business since 1963.

House specialties are she-crab soup, steamed shrimp and crabs and a variety of broiled fish. Lobster tails are flown in from New England while shellfish come from the Eastern Shore. Steaks brought from the Midwest and trimmed on site also are popular menu items. Dinner is served daily with lunch offered on Saturdays and brunch on Sunday. There usually are early-bird specials for dinner. Reservations are accepted.

LYNNHAVEN FISH HOUSE
2350 Starfish Road
$$$ 481-0003

This popular restaurant is on the Lynnhaven Fishing Pier right on the Chesapeake Bay and just off Shore Drive. Since 1979 it has prided itself on having an atmosphere similar to San Francisco's Fisherman's Wharf. Noted menu items include she-crab soup, Mediterranean salad and at least five types of fresh fish. Crab cakes, oysters on the half shell and surf-and-turf-platters are menu staples. Dessert features Belgium whiskey pudding and a variety of cakes. The fish house is open for lunch and dinner daily. Reservations are accepted. This is a People's Choice winner in *PortFolio's* Golden Fork Awards.

NICK'S HOSPITALITY RESTAURANT
508 Laskin Rd.
$$ 428-7891

Founded in 1952, this is a locals-only restaurant, mostly because Nick's location next to a laundry doesn't seem too exciting. Inside, the menu is another story. Nick's serves fresh seafood in a comfortable atmosphere that's changed little since the '50s. The menu features whatever is in season with bargain-priced daily specials such as lobster tails and all-you-can-eat flounder. This is one of the few places where you can get crack-'em-and-eat-'em steamed crabs. They're usually in season May through October. The menu sometimes has surprises like blackened alligator and other Cajun dishes. Nick's serves breakfast, lunch and dinner daily. One best-seller at breakfast is the crab omelette.

Photo: Virginia Dept. of Economic Development

The Virginia Beach oceanfront stretches for 28 miles.

OYSTER BAY CAFE
3152 Shore Dr.
$$ 496-2755

Oyster Bay opened in 1992 in the former Hog Heaven barbecue restaurant to instant acclaim. The owners are the same, and Hog Heaven fans will still find barbecue on the menu. However, Oyster Bay's emphasis is seafood prepared with Italian zest. Besides grouper Francaise and barbecued or blackened tuna there are many seafood pastas. Froglegs sauteed in butter, wine and lemon also are a popular offering as is the house dressing, an unusual Gorgonzola cheese. Daily specials often include comfort food such as meatloaf and spaghetti. Breakfast, lunch and dinner are served daily during the summer. In winter Oyster Bay closes on Mondays.

ROCKAFELLER'S
308 Mediterranean Ave.
$$ 422-5654

This restaurant and raw bar opened in 1990 on the scenic Rudee Inlet. Its specialties include Oysters Rockefeller and Clams Casino. While seafood is a big part of the menu, Rockafeller's entrees also include pasta, chicken and seafood. Lunch and dinner are served daily with brunch offered on Sunday.

RUDEE'S ON THE INLET
227 Mediterranean Ave.
$$ 425-1777

This Rudee Inlet restaurant is known for its raw bar and steamed-shrimp specials. Steaks, crab, scallop and lobster round out the menu, which also includes sandwiches.

There is a wide variety of seafood appetizers. Desserts range from key lime pie to carrot cake. Rudee's, which was founded in 1983, serves dinner daily and is open for lunch Monday-Saturday with brunch served on Sunday. Reservations are accepted.

SANDBRIDGE RESTAURANT & RAW BAR
205 Sandbridge Rd.
$$ 426-2193

Open only from March through December, the Sandbridge Restaurant has been around since the early '60s and is one of the few restaurants in the Sandbridge beach area. Fresh seafood and prime rib are the house specialties. Baby-back ribs also are big sellers. Dinner is served nightly with lunch on Saturday and brunch on Sunday.

SEA CREST RESTAURANT
1776 Princess Anne Rd.
$$ 426-7804

Located in Pungo, the Sea Crest prides itself on its she-crab soup, broiled seafood platter and prime rib. Its noted dessert is rice pudding. The Sea Crest is open Tuesday through Sunday for dinner but closes during the winter. No credit cards.

STEINHILBER'S THALIA ACRES INN
653 Thalia Rd.
$$$ 340-1156

Steinhilber's is one of Virginia Beach's oldest restaurants, and you can count on it for good food served in an elegant environment Specialties include fried shrimp and steak. Fresh seafood grilled over a mesquite fire is a real delicacy. Steinhilber's is open Tuesday through Saturday for dinner. Reservations are accepted. (See related article.)

SURF RIDER

605 Virginia Beach Blvd.	422-3568
4501 Haygood Rd.	464-5992
723 Newtown Rd., Norfolk	
$$	461-6488

Started in 1979, the Surf Rider on Virginia Beach Boulevard has spawned two popular offshoots. The casual Surf Riders have a loyal following who like their crab cakes and other fresh seafood. Everything is homemade, including cream of broccoli soup with crab, clam chowder and a variety of pies. The Virginia Beach Boulevard location is open daily for lunch and dinner. The other two restaurants close on Sunday.

TRACY'S CLAM AND OYSTER BAR

2917 Shore Dr.
$$ 481-3642

This no-frills cafe is part of the Shoreline Seafood Market. It is run by a former police officer who knows how to boil shrimp with a Cajun flair. Tracy's has a raw bar. Besides serving steamed and broiled seafood it also offers sandwiches and homemade soup. It serves lunch on weekdays with dinner served nightly.

WORRELL'S STEAMED SHRIMP

501 Laskin Rd.
$$ 491-9191

If you're hungry for steamed shrimp, then Worrell's should be high on your list since that's about all that's served. Shrimp is spiced to order – from fiery hot to mildly zesty. Shrimp is served either in the shell, peeled or with cheese melted on top. Orders come with French bread and wild rice. The only other menu offering is shrimp salad. Worrell's opened in 1989 and has done so well that it is branching out in 1993. By late spring it was to have operations in Virginia Beach at Laskin Road and Baltic Avenue, Lynnhaven Parkway and Rosemont Road and Independence Boulevard and Pleasure House Road as well as in Norfolk on Little Creek Road.

Worrell's offers take-out and delivery from its locations and uses one central phone number for orders. Only the Laskin Road and Independence Boulevard restaurants have seating.

Norfolk

BLUE CRAB BAR & GRILLE

4521 Pretty Lake Ave.
$$ 362-5620

With its location overlooking the waters of Little Creek, this is a scenic spot to dine – complete with boats tied up at a neighboring marina. Blue Crab opened in 1989 with a menu that features a lot of seafood prepared in Caribbean and Cajun styles. Salmon, tuna, catfish and crabs are menu staples with seasonal fish offered when available. Blue Crab closes on Monday but serves lunch and dinner the other days. Brunch is offered on Sunday. Reservations are recommended on the weekend.

LEWIS' SEAFOOD RESTAURANT
41st & Colley Ave.
$$ 489-9420

This is one of Norfolk's oldest seafood restaurants, and many of its customers have been dining here for decades. Lewis' was founded in the 1940s and has been at this location since 1966. Its current owners have run it since 1983.

Meals start with crackers served with a good garlic butter and blue cheese spread. The menu features a variety of shrimp, crab and other seafood dishes as well as chicken and beef. Its five-item seafood platter is one popular choice. Sandwiches, soups, salads and homecooking, such as liver and onions, round out the offerings. There is a big selection of vegetables for side dishes. The restaurant is open daily for lunch and dinner. Late at night the restaurant switches identities to become one of the hottest night spots in town.

O'SULLIVAN'S WHARF
4300 Colley Ave.
$$ 423-3753

This is a popular spot near Old Dominion University for dining or relaxing with a beer. It sits on scenic Knitting Mill Creek with boats anchored outside. In warm weather O'Sullivan's deck is a popular gathering spot. Menu offerings include crab cakes and seafood combinations. There also is a variety of sandwiches, soups and salads. The restaurant is open for lunch and dinner daily. Reservations are accepted.

PHILLIPS' WATERSIDE
333 Waterside Dr.
$$ 627-6600

This is one of the anchors for The Waterside festival marketplace. Its view of the Elizabeth River is unbeatable, and on warm days you can dine on an open-air patio. Phillips' is a spin-off of Phillips' Crab House, which opened in Ocean City, Md. in 1956. Menu offerings include a wide variety of seafood, including crab cooked any way you can imagine. There also are some steaks on the menu as well as a raw bar. The restaurant is open daily for lunch and dinner. You may want to call for reservations, particularly on weekend evenings.

SHIPS CABIN
4110 E. Ocean View Ave.
$$$ 362-4659

A Norfolk dining landmark since 1967, the Ships Cabin has been in the Hoggard family for two generations. Owner Joe Hoggard is one of the region's best-known restaurateurs. His lovely restaurant has one of the best views of the Chesapeake Bay and a fine seafood menu to go with it.

Menus frequently change but there are some staples that local diners have come to expect. Servers continually make the rounds with a variety of great bread, including blueberry, raisin, honey wheat and Bavarian wheat. Oysters Bingo (named after a local attorney) are oysters sauteed with shallots, butter and wine. Crab soup and crab cakes are other menu staples. Other offerings include a variety of shrimp, crab and fresh fish as well as steaks.

Regulars know to save room for the whiskey pudding after dinner.

The restaurant is open for dinner daily and takes reservations. The Ships Cabin has a AAA Four Diamond rating. It is a consistent winner of *Port Folio* magazine's Golden Fork awards.

Chesapeake

THE LOCK'S POINTE
136 Battlefield Blvd.
$$ **547-9618**

Overlooking the Atlantic Intracoastal Waterway, Lock's Pointe lets diners watch boats plying the waters. The restaurant opened in 1984 and has never wavered from its emphasis on seafood. Specialties include baked salmon stuffed with prosciutto and Gouda and topped with a crab sauce. A veal, crab and artichoke pasta also is a crowd pleaser. Meals often start with oysters Rockefeller or she-crab soup. There are at least six homemade desserts on the menu. Lunch is served on weekdays and dinner everyday but Saturday. There is a Sunday brunch. Reservations are accepted.

THE OYSTERETTE
3916 Portsmouth Blvd.
$$ **465-3336**

The Oysterette opened in 1992 to give some dining diversity to the Western Branch area of Chesapeake. This small, casual raw bar is in Stonebridge Center at the foot of the Hodges Ferry Bridge. Its menu includes crab cakes, stuffed flounder and a variety of other fresh seafood. There is a large assortment of appetizers and each weekday night a different entree is highlighted with a bargain price. The Oysterette serves dinner daily and also lunch on weekends. It stays open late for night owls.

Portsmouth

AMORY'S SEAFOOD
5909 High St.
$$ **483-1518**

If anyone knows fresh seafood it's George Amory, owner of Amory's Seafood. His family has been in the seafood business for more than 100 years and at one time was the East Coast's largest seafood distributor. Amory opened his restaurant in 1976 in the Churchland area of Portsmouth. The menu offers many shrimp, scallop, crab and fish dinners. Some are made from old family recipes, including crab Maryland and flounder supreme. Popular items include she-crab soup, a New England clambake and homemade marinara sauce for pasta. There is a raw bar, and Amory's oysters come from the family's oyster beds. On every night but weekends there are bargain-priced specials on the menu. Lunch and dinner are served daily. Reservations are accepted.

AMORY'S WHARF
10 Crawford Parkway
$$ **399-0991**

An Amory's Seafood spin-off, this waterfront restaurant opened in late 1992. Its owner is David Amory, a Culinary Institute of America graduate whose father runs the other Amory's. Both restaurants share many of the same seafood dishes. However, the Wharf puts its own spin on the menu with some upscale, trendy dishes such as a mozzarella appetizer wrapped in romaine and prosciutto, grilled with garlic and served with a fresh tomato vinaigrette. Besides seafood, there are pastas, steaks, sandwiches and salads on the menu. The Wharf is in downtown Portsmouth at the end of a marina. It is a small restaurant overlooking the Elizabeth River and downtown Norfolk across the water. It has a small parking lot inside the marina fence, and in the summer it offers valet parking to a nearby parking deck.

THE CIRCLE
3010 High St.
$$ 397-8196

Since its opening in 1947, The Circle has been a Portsmouth dining landmark. It retains the same round, diner look it had back in the days when it had car hops and was a Chicken in the Rough franchise. On one wall are caricatures of Hollywood celebrities whose heyday has long passed. Ambiance aside, The Circle is known for its seafood and steaks. Menu standouts include crab cakes, lobster tails and seafood platters. There also is a raw bar and a solid list of reasonably priced entrees such as ribs, ham steak and a broiled chicken breast. Side dishes include cabbage, yams, black-eyed peas and collards. The Circle is open for three meals a day, including a big breakfast buffet. On Sunday there is a popular buffet, that includes all-you-can-eat crab and prime rib at night. Reservations are ac-

cepted and definitely needed on weekends. Children who clean their plates are rewarded with free ice cream.

LOBSCOUSER
337 High St.
$$ 397-2728

This downtown restaurant bears the nickname for the chef on a ship. Its menu leans toward fresh seafood with some beef and chicken included for balance. There are usually four soups on the menu, and homemade desserts often include bread pudding and strawberry shortcake made with sweet biscuits. Lobscouser is open for lunch and dinner daily. Reservations are accepted. Lobscouser is a People's Choice winner in *Port Folio's* Golden Fork awards.

SCALE O' DE WHALE
3515 Shipwright St.
$$$ 483-2772

Since the opening of the Western Freeway in 1992, this seafood restaurant on the Western Branch of the Elizabeth River has become much more accessible. It is located in a marina and has a varied menu that features seafood, beef and chicken. Noted entrees are the Neptune feast – a dinner for two that includes lobsters, filet mignon and stuffed shrimp – and kebabs laced with shrimp, scallops and fillet mignon. The she-crab soup is excellent. Homemade desserts include apple cobbler and bread pudding with lemon custard. Dinner is served daily with lunch offered on weekdays. Reservations are accepted, and you may want to call for directions to the restaurant.

Brunch

One of our most favorite, and caloric, Sunday pastimes is the long-standing tradition of brunch, prepared, naturally, by someone else. Along with the obligatory eggs and trimmings, many local restaurants go out on a limb to create the most savory offerings you've ever tasted. You must start with a mimosa, then barrel ahead to such delectables as the steak benedict at Tandom's Pine Tree Inn, seafood benedict at Ellliot's in Ghent, huevos rancheros at Magnolia's, also in Ghent and make-and-top-your-own donuts at Tradewinds in the Virginia Beach Resort and Conference Center.

Here's a quick rundown of some of our favorite places to head with the Sunday paper and your partner to waste away a lazy afternoon with a brimming plate of delicious cuisine and attentive service:

Norfolk

Blue Crab Bar & Grill, 4521 Pretty Lake Avenue, Ocean View

Chesapeake Cafe, Howard Johnson Hotel-Norfolk

Elliot's, 1421 Colley Avenue, Ghent

Freemason Abbey, 209 West Freemason, Downtown Norfolk

Harbor Grill, The Waterside

Magnolia, Ghent

Omni Hotel Riverwalk, Downtown waterfront

The Promenade, Norfolk Airport Hilton

Pirahna: An Eating Frenzy, 8180 Shore Drive

Virginia Beach

Bogie's, 620 19th Street

Tandom's Pine Tree Inn, 2932 Virginia Beach Boulevard

Rockafeller's, 308 Mediterranean Avenue

Blue Pete's Seafood Restaurant. 1400 N. Muddy Creek Road

Cafe Zoe, 40th Street & Atlantic Avenue

Henry's Seafood Restaurant, 3319 Shore Drive

Tradewinds, Virginia Beach Resort and Conference Center

Chesapeake

Cara's, 123 N. Battlefield Boulevard

Cheers Cafe and Tavern, 1405 Greenbrier Parkway

Lock's Pointe, 136 N. Battlefield Boulevard

Ruby Tuesday, Crossways Shopping Center and Chesapeake Square Mall

Portsmouth

The Max, 435 Water Street

Vic Zodda's Harborside, Holiday Inn, Portsmouth Waterfront

The interior of the stately Cavalier Hotel in Virginia Beach.

Inside
Accommodations

*P*ull right up...your room's waiting! If you're travelling for pleasure, it's a pretty sure bet that you're headed for one of our ocean- or bayfront hotels. Travelers with business on their minds are drawn to the hotels circling our major business districts, like Downtown Norfolk or the Newtown Road corridor in Virginia Beach. And, if you're in town to visit family or friends lacking in a guest room, you're likely to unpack in a comfortable, moderately priced suburban motel right around the corner.

If you're pillow-counting, there are nearly 20,000 hotel and motel rooms to lay a weary head in Hampton Roads. Virginia Beach alone boasts 10,000-plus and counting! The range of accommodations is nearly as great, from econo-boxes to luxury high-rises, mega conference centers to a charming bed & breakfast. Only your particular destination in our area will dictate which of the many brand-name or independent alternatives you're able to target.

Pick your destination, pick your price. Because of the area's ownership of miles of beautiful beaches along the Chesapeake Bay and Atlantic Ocean, demand for beachfront accommodations is heaviest during the summer season, with rates adjusted upward accordingly. On average, however, rates throughout the area take the big swing from a low of about $30 per room per night all the way to $300 for a drop-dead luxury suite. Your pocketbook, and your need to be pampered, will be your deciding factor, especially if you're planning an extended holiday.

As in any other part of the country, if you are planning a peak resort-time or holiday visit, advance reservations with deposit are definitely a must. On summer weekends and holidays, many hotels require a two or three day minimum stay for confirmed reservations, so plan accordingly. Payment with plastic is the general rule, since it is a rare establishment that will accept a personal check (including restaurants), so pack heavy with credit cards, cash or traveler's checks.

If your plans should change, make certain that you are aware of your chosen hotel's cancellation policy. Some require at least a 72-hour notice for a change in reservation dates, and up to seven day's notice for complete cancellation. Ask about specific rules and refund policies when making your initial reservations.

While it's impossible to list every accommodation alternative in the area, we'll highlight those hotels and motels that are not only local favorites for out-of-town visitors, but generally applauded by the business community for both amenities and consistency of guest service.

Accommodations will be listed in various categories by city, along with from one to five dollar signs ($) based on the typical daily rates for a standard room with two double beds. Keep in mind that, come resort or holiday time, these rates may take a considerable hike, so be sure to confirm prior to making any firm reservation commitments.

Also note the weekly rental possibilities in cities where beach properties are available for extended family vacations. These are often privately-owned, fully furnished and appointed homes, ready to move in for a week or two of beachy relaxation.

Under $30	$
$31 – $50	$$
$50 – $75	$$$
$76 – $90	$$$$
$91 and up	$$$$$

For assistance in selecting the hotel/motel property that best suits your visiting needs, you can call the following for advice, availability and specific rate information: Virginia Beach 1-800-VA-BEACH Norfolk 1-800-843-8030

Norfolk

Norfolk definitely has a split-personality when it comes to accommodations. Downtown is home to our convention hotels, all within walking distance of The Waterside festival marketplace with its restaurants and shopping. Ocean View offers rooms for sandy feet overlooking the Chesapeake Bay, where bathers, anglers and sun-worshippers happily commingle. Undergoing a dramatic rejuvenation, the Ocean View area is regaining its popularity among vacationers, lost during it's decline of the '60s and '70s. Today, with new bayfront parks and well life-guarded beaches, it is once again becoming a favorite for families with small children because of calm, warm waters. Folks headed to the vicinity of Old Dominion University, the airport/Military Circle hub or elsewhere in the city, will find a suburban motel perfect for their overnight needs.

Downtown

BED & BREAKFAST AT THE PAGE HOUSE INN
323 Fairfax Avenue
$$$ 625-5033

You'll enjoy this award-winning bed & breakfast in the heart of Downtown Norfolk's lovely historic neighborhood. Elegant accommodations are available in this Georgian revival (c. 1899) inn, meticulously restored in 1991 by owners Stephanie and Ezio DiBelardino to the tune of $600,000. Six absolutely charming rooms are here, and the

daily tariff includes a homemade, deliciousl gourmet breakfast spread. All rooms are furnished with period antiques and canopied beds, and three of the rooms have fireplaces. There are even two suites that incorporate a touch of today – whirlpool baths. No major credit cards are accepted, except to make advance reservations, so be prepared with either cash or check.

NORFOLK WATERSIDE MARRIOTT HOTEL

235 East Main Street
$$$$ 627-4200/800-228-9290

A jewel in the crown of Downtown Norfolk, this glamorous new facility welcomes you with the most elegant lobby in the area, just a taste of the good life that awaits you during your stay. A favorite of conventioneers, the hotel offers 405 guest rooms, including eight suites and three concierge levels. From health club and roof-top indoor pool to The Dining Room, The Piano Lounge, Stormy's Pub and Sidewalk Cafe, The Marriott is like a plush mini-city you might never want to leave. There's more than 15,000 square feet of flexible conference space, with a ballroom that can accommodate a banquet for 750. Most of the standard guest rooms are small, however, but you can make up for the size by requesting a room with a view of the Elizabeth River.

OMNI INTERNATIONAL HOTEL/NORFOLK

777 Waterside Drive
$$$$ 622-6664

Just having undergone a massive multimillion-dollar renovation to match the elegance of it's Marriott neighbor, The Omni can pamper you in 442 deluxe rooms and 23 executive suites with spectacular views from balconies overlooking the Elizabeth River. Adjacent to The Waterside festival marketplace, you can take advantage of the hotel's fine dining facilities: The Riverwalk Cafe with outdoor veranda seating on the river and The Lobby Bar, a favorite and comfortable place for an aperitif. The International Ballroom can accommodate 1,200, along with 14 banquet rooms. Extra perks are the indoor/outdoor pool and access to the superb health club located next door in Dominion Tower.

HOWARD JOHNSON NORFOLK

700 Monticello Avenue
$$$ 627-5555

Adjacent to Scope Convention Center and Chrysler Hall, this 344- room hotel began life in the '60s as the Golden Triangle, the largest and most elegant hotel of its time. It has gone through many renovations, and names, since those early, popular days, and seems at last to have found a renewed life under the Howard Johnson's banner. The facility includes Harvey's Lounge and the Chesapeake Room restaurant, an Olympic-size outdoor pool and lobby shops. This is a reasonably priced alternative for the Downtown visitor.

RAMADA NORFOLK HOTEL

Granby & Freemason Streets
$$ 622-6682/800-522-0976

A landmark hotel in the heart of the original Downtown shopping

Photo: Virginia Division of Tourism

Tourists can find a multitude of oceanfront hotels at Virginia Beach.

district, The Ramada features 1-, 2- and 3-room suites along with two restaurants, an attractive lounge and complimentary health club and racquetball facilities at the Downtown Athletic Club across the street. There are five meeting rooms with over 5,000 square feet, and banquet facilities can serve 200 guests. Some of Downtown's most popular restaurants are within one block's walking area, and The Waterside is about five blocks to the south, although we do not suggest you attempt the short hike if you're all alone.

COMFORT INN TOWN POINT
Virginia Beach Blvd. at Tidewater Drive
$$ 623-5700

This is a comfortable place to stay if you want a more relaxed atmosphere that's a stone's throw from the downtown financial district. The newly remodeled, 167-room motel has an on-premise health club,

sauna and whirlpool, plus an outdoor pool surrounded by a charming, well-tended courtyard. Continental breakfast is included in your tab, and a courtesy van is available for airport transportation.

Suburban

QUALITY INN LAKE WRIGHT
6280 Northampton Boulevard
$$ 461-6251/800-228-5157

A quick zip to the Interstate and airport, this 304-room resort and conference center has an easygoing attitude. For specifics, there are eight suites, and meeting rooms covering over 12,000 square feet of flexible space, plus a fine restaurant and cocktail lounge. It also boasts a great neighbor: the very popular 18-hole golf course and driving range. Swimming pool and tennis courts are also on the premises.

Convention Facilities

Both Norfolk and Virginia Beach have city-owned convention facilities. Norfolk has Scope and the Waterside Convention Center. Scope has 85,000 square feet of space and is five blocks from the downtown waterfront. It is where the Ringling Bros. Barnum & Bailey Circus performs, the Hampton Roads Admirals play ice hockey and college basketball teams have their games (441-2764).

The Waterside Convention Center opened downtown in 1991. It is connected to a new Marriott Hotel and is across the street from The Waterside festival marketplace. It has more than 36,000 square feet of meeting space (441-1852).

Virginia Beach's Pavilion Convention Center is six blocks from the ocean and has 57,000 square feet of space. Two blocks from the ocean is The Dome, a 10,000-square-foot civic facility (428-8000 – same number for both).

Throughout the region there also are numerous hotels with conference space.

Photo: Richmond Newspapers

Tourists going to Virginia Beach just need to follow the snow geese.

RAMADA INN AIRPORT
AT NEWTOWN
6360 Newtown Road
$$ *461-1081/800-2-RAMADA*

Near Koger Executive Park, the 138-room Ramada offers four suites and five meeting rooms with almost 2,500 square feet and banquet facilities for up to 120. Just off the Norfolk-Virginia Beach Expressway, there's a courtyard pool, fitness center and the very popular Adams's night club. Especially nice touches for guests are the in-room coffee-makers and free washer-dryer, with microwave and refrigerators available.

SHERATON-MILITARY CIRCLE
Military Highway & Virginia Beach Blvd.
$$ *461-9192*

If you were born-to-shop, stash your traveling bags here. An "anchor" of Military Circle Center Mall, you can spill right out of your room into over 150 great stores, shops, restaurants and movie theaters. The 208 recently renovated rooms are quite comfortable, and there's Ginger's Restaurant and a lively lounge with live entertainment.

HAMPTON INN
1450 Military Highway
$$ *466-7474/800-489-1000*

Just a skip from the airport to the north and Military Circle to the south, this is a life-saver for the budget-conscious traveler who wants a lot for the overnight dollar. While there's no restaurant on the premises, there is an outdoor pool and complimentary continental breakfast served each morning. Offered are 130 comfortably-sized rooms, with free local phone and the obligatory cable/HBO.

HILTON HOTEL-AIRPORT
1500 Military Highway
$$$ *466-8000*

A real architectural mystery to many Insiders, this deluxe 250-room hotel is as close to the airport as you want to be, and also close to the new USAA regional headquar-

ters complex. A decorator's vision of contemporary with Oriental overtones, the lobby is impressive with its piano bar accented by polished brass accessories and teak and marble floor. Dining both casual and elegant is here, too, along with a super popular nightclub that rocks to the wee hours. (If you're intent on getting a sound night's sleep, request a room in the back!) A high-tech fitness center with Jacuzzi and sauna, plus a swimming pool and tennis courts round out the amenities. For getting down to business, there are nine salons, parlors and conference rooms, along with the grand ballroom with foyer and a garden. A nice feature of the guest rooms is the mini-bars.

OLD DOMINION INN
4111 Hampton Boulevard
$$ 440-5100
This inn is a relatively new facility and a welcome one for visitors to both Old Dominion and the

major medical complex a short hop down Hampton Boulevard. Sixty guest rooms are surprisingly spacious and well-appointed, and restaurants and shops that serve the University are right across the street.

HAMPTON INN-NAVAL BASE
8501 Hampton Boulevard
$ 489-1000
Minutes from the main gate at Naval Station Norfolk, the Hampton Inn offer 119 rooms with free continental breakfast and local phone calls. There's an indoor pool plus whirlpool, and the rooms have kitchenettes plus modem jacks for those who must stay in touch even when they're on vacation.

COMFORT INN-NAVAL BASE
8051 Hampton Boulevard
$ 451-0000
A few blocks from The Hampton Inn, this 120-room motel also welcomes guests to Naval Station Norfolk. Indoor swimming pool and

on-site laundromat, plus refrigerators in every room and free local phone calls make this a popular place to stay.

Ocean View

ECONO LODGE
9601 4th View Street
$$$ summer, $$ winter   480-9611

While not directly on the Bay, this 70-room, 22-efficiency motel offers clean, comfortable accommodations, worth the easy walk across the street to access the beach. Also close to the popular Harrison's Boat House and Fishing Pier, you'll find a hot tub and sauna along with a guest laundry room and cable-TV.

HOLIDAY INN
1010 West Ocean View Avenue
$$$ summer, $$ winter   587-8761

Find traditional Holiday Inn hospitality in this 120-room ocean-front hotel. It's a comfortable place to hang the family's wet bathing suits in summer, and a nice place for business travelers to watch ships and fishing boats any time of year. You have access to swimming and kiddie pools, cocktail lounge and restaurant, and banquet facilities, too.

QUALITY INN-OCEAN VIEW
719 East Ocean View Avenue
$$$ all seasons   583-5211

Always with a diverse guest list of business people, vacationing families and military guests, this 101-room inn sits directly across from a popular family beach, with next-door tennis courts and the Ocean View Golf Course just a few blocks away. On-site is a swimming pool, restaurant and popular night spot.

Portsmouth

It's not that visitors don't want to stay in Portsmouth, it's just that the competition from neighboring city beaches and business centers preclude many overnight options in this city. Here's where Insiders would stay if they were to overnight in Portsmouth.

HOLIDAY INN-PORTSMOUTH WATERFRONT
9 Crawford Parkway
$$ 393-2573

This is *the* place to stay. Two hundred and seventy rooms and suites on the waterfront in Olde Towne are just the beginning, because you're not only just across the river from Norfolk's Waterside, but also adjacent to Tidewater Yacht Agency marina, one of the area's busiest, as well as Portside. Vic Zodda's Harborside Restaurant overlooking the Elizabeth River has been a local favorite for years, and Madeline's Peppermint Lounge stays busy with its '50s and '60s themed atmosphere. Rooms are comfortable and spacious, but be sure to request one that has a view of the River to catch the harbor activity and spectacular sunsets.

ECONO LODGE-OLDE TOWNE
1031 London Boulevard
$ 399-4414

The overnight choice for those with business at the Portsmouth Naval Hospital or Portsmouth General Hospital, you're only five minutes by ferry to Waterside in Downtown Norfolk. Sixty-one rooms are offered, with fast food restaurants within walking distance in the local neighborhood.

Chesapeake

One city that should be suffering from growing pains, there's always a new hub of activity that seems to spring up out of nowhere in the blink of an eye. For most visitors to Chesapeake, however, the Greenbrier corridor seems to be the most logical overnight destination choice since it puts you smack dab in the hustle-bustle for primo shopping and good food, as well as a quick hop to the Interstate.

HOLIDAY INN CHESAPEAKE
725 Woodlake Drive at Greenbrier Parkway
$$ 523-1500

Here's a real beauty, packed with frills to thrill the overnight guest. There are 190 rooms and suites in seven stories of Holiday Inn at its finest. Our favorite room is the King Executive, with a king-size bed in spread-out comfort, plus a queen-sized pull out sofa and nifty wet bar. There's also an indoor swim-

ming pool, whirlpool, sauna and fully-equipped exercise room. The Key West Restaurant and Lounge is an especially popular spot with its nightly entertainment, and generous banquet facilities can accommodate up to 700 people with ease. Complimentary airport transportation is available on request, and you're just 15 minutes from the airport, Downtown Norfolk and the Virginia Beach oceanfront.

COMFORT SUITES OF GREENBRIER
1550 Crossways Boulevard
$$ 420-1600

One hundred twenty-three all-suite rooms complete with refrigerators, microwaves, cable TV/HBO and VCRs are the offering at this Comfort Suites. An outdoor swimming pool, fitness center with steam room and sauna, and a wide variety of restaurants, shopping and entertainment just around the corner at Greenbrier Mall make it a convenient choice.

DAYS INN
701A Woodlake Drive
$ 420-1550

Just off I-64 and a short distance to restaurants and shopping, the Days Inn offers 119 rooms with free cable/HBO and complimentary continental breakfast. The outdoor swimming pool is open in season.

RED ROOF INN
724 Woodlake Drive
$ 523-0123

Sitting practically on top of the Holiday Inn is the alternative to budget-watching travelers who just

want a clean and pleasant place to stay, hold the frills. To eat or shop, you'll have to drive just a few miles down the road, but there is complimentary coffee and a newspaper waiting for you in the lobby each morning.

ECONO LODGE-CHESAPEAKE
3244 Western Branch Boulevard
$ 484-6143

This is our pick for an overnight other than in the Greenbrier area. This small and down-home friendly, 48-room motel can offer you a clean, comfortable room and morning coffee in the lobby, but no amenities like a restaurant or swimming pool. Its big advantage is its location in the Western Branch section of the city, an older, established neighborhood with nearby shopping and fast food.

WELLESLEY INN
1750 Sara Drive at Woodlake
$$ 366-0100/800-444-8880

Like a corporate bed and breakfast, The Wellesley Inn is a favorite of both businesspeople on the road and visiting families. With 106 rooms, plus outdoor heated pool, you can hop just one-half mile down the street to full health club facilities. The king and queen suites here are especially plush, with coffee-maker, refrigerator, microwave and wet bar. A laundry facility is available to all guests, along with free continental breakfast served daily.

BOARDWALK INN

2604 Atlantic Ave. 106 units. A/C. Rest/Lounge. Coffee Shop. CC/TV. Pool. Balconies.

425-5971/800-777-6070

COLONIAL INN

29th & Oceanfront. 159 oceanfront and economical west side rooms. Restaurant. Gift Shops. Indoor/outdoor pool. Jacuzzis and kitchens available.

Resort Resv. **800-344-3342**

DAYS INN OCEANFRONT

32nd St. 121 units. A/C. Rms & effs. CC/TV. Indr pool. Jacuzzis. Rest/Lounge. Game Rm. Balconies.

428-7233/800-292-3297

DUNES MOTOR INN

10th & Oceanfront. 107 Rms & effs. Balconies. Ocnft pool/Sundecks/Whirlpools. Restaurant. Gift Shop. Laundry. Parking. CC/TV.

428-7731/800-634-0709

NEWCASTLE MOTEL

12th & Oceanfront. 83 units. Doubles available. Kings w/ whirlpool tubs. Efficiencies.

428-3981/800-346-3176

OCEANFRONT INN

29th & Oceanfront. 146 units. A/C. Ocnft balconies. Rest/Lounge. CC/TV. Indr pool. All fire sprinkled.

422-0445/800-548-3879

PRINCESS ANNE INN

25th & Oceanfront. 60 units. A/C. Lounge. Coffee Shop. In/outdr pool. Jacuzzi. CC/TV. Bed/brkfst. Enclosed balconies.

428-5611/800-468-1111

WINDJAMMER MOTEL

19th & Oceanfront. 72 dbls. Kings & effs. A/C. Pool. CC/TV.

428-0060/800-695-0035

Virginia Beach

Now you're talking hotel rooms. From the ocean to the bay, central business district to the suburbs, Virginia Beach uses more hotel-issue bed linens than any city in Hampton Roads. To help you decipher between the 122 choices, we'll divide the city into hotel-heavy areas, like oceanfront, Chesapeake Bay and out there in the Suburbs.

All of these properties offer free, in-room cable TV, refrigerators and microwaves, but you should confirm availability early, especially in peak resort or holiday season. Every on-premise restaurant features a pendulum swing of choices, all constantly changing. Most of the properties along the Boardwalk area are within a short stroll of gourmet, casual and convenience dining, with fresh seafood the predominant bill of fare year round. When you're shellfished-out, you'll find excellent alternatives for beef, Italian, Carib-

bean, Mexican and good old Southern food just another step away.

Ocean Area

(While not noted, count on a $$$$$ rating during the resort season.)

RAMADA OCEANSIDE TOWER RESORT & CONFERENCE CENTER
57th Street & Oceanfront
$$$ 428-7025/800-365-3032

We'll start just off the Board-walk path with this fine facility that's nestled on North Virginia Beach's "Gold Coast" and puts you in the midst of the prime residential ocean-front community. The 215 rooms, including three suites, have recently undergone extensive renovation, resulting in the honor of being named the best Ramada Inn in the Country in 1991. Conference facilities include 12 meeting rooms and banquet facilities for 400. You'll love the swim-up bar in the heated indoor/outdoor swimming pool, and

there's also an exercise room and excellent restaurant on premises.

HOLIDAY INN ON THE OCEAN
39th & Oceanfront
$$$ *428-1711/800-94BEACH*
Everyone is renovating, and this 266-room Holiday Inn is no exception. There's new life to the expanded outdoor pool, a new indoor pool complex with two whirlpools, improvements to the banquet facilities that can serve up to 400, and over 9,000 square feet of meeting space on the top floor overlooking the ocean. It's right on the Boardwalk, so that means if you decide to pass on their excellent restaurant, you've got oodles of dining choices just a short walk away.

THE CAVALIER HOTELS
42nd & Oceanfront and 42nd On The Hill
$$$ *425-8555/800-446-8199*
For sheer Southern hospitality in a seaside manner, nothing comes close to the Cavalier on the Hill, a landmark in the Beach community, and it's newer, slicker sister along the oceanfront. This 18-acre seaside resort offers over 400 guest rooms and eight suites overlooking the 600-foot private beach along the Atlantic Ocean. Boasting the largest hotel ballroom in the Commonwealth of Virginia, you can throw an intimate dinner for 1,400 with no problem. With its AAA four-diamond rating, there are also three restaurants, two lounges, tennis courts, indoor and outdoor swimming pools and a new health club. Other amenities include jogging tracks and facilities for racquetball.

SHERATON INN
36th & Oceanfront
$$$ *425-9000/800-325-3535*
Rising above the Boardwalk, this 203-room hotel also has eight luxury suites, along with nine meeting rooms that cover 12,000 square feet, two ballrooms and banquet facilities for 600. Along with glorious ocean views, the Sheraton offers a heated, outdoor swimming

pool, exercise room, dining room and lounge.

PARK INN INTERNATIONAL RESORT HOTEL
424 Atlantic Avenue
$$$ *425-2200/800-955-9300*
This is a great place for a longer visit because each of the 150 rooms is actually a two-room suite. Along with 1,500 square feet of meeting space and banquet facilities for 150, the Park Inn has an indoor swimming pool, fitness center, restaurant, lounge and, of course, the beautiful beaches of the Atlantic.

CLARION RESORT & CONFERENCE CENTER
5th & Oceanfront
$$$$ *422-3186/800-345-3186*
Insiders love this part of Virginia Beach, down near Rudee Inlet where all the city's charter boat fleets congregate. The Clarion has 168 rooms, swimming pool, whirlpool, sauna, tennis court and health club.

RADISSON HOTEL VIRGINIA BEACH
1900 Pavilion Drive
$$$ *422-8900/800-333-3333*
At the foot of the Norfolk-Virginia Beach Expressway, adjacent to the Pavilion Convention Center, the Radisson offers 296 lovely rooms along with 14 luxury suites. Banquet facilities for up to 450 and 12,000 square feet of meeting space makes it a convention favorite. Although it is a few blocks to the oceanfront, it does have an indoor swimming pool, jogging track, tennis courts, popular restaurant and lounge and a cozy library, too.

For accommodations that cater to families on the run from the real world, without that "conference center" feeling, check out these friendly beachfront and beachside hotels:

THE ATRIUM RESORT HOTEL
315 21st Street
$$ *491-1400/800-443-7040*
You'll run right into The Atrium as you shoot down 21st Street off the Norfolk/Virginia Beach Expressway. There's no bad room in the 90-room house, because every one is actually a two-room suite with fully equipped kitchen, perfect for whipping up a hearty breakfast on a family vacation. Someone with a lot of class dreamed up the indoor pool and Jacuzzi, as evidenced by the

Insiders' Tips

comfy sofas in a true atrium where you can linger to watch the splashing swimmers. What's really neat is their tanning room, so you can go home glowing, even if the weatherman is not in a cooperative mood.

BOARDWALK INN
2604 Atlantic Avenue
$$ 425-5871/800-777-6070

While not perched over the ocean, the Boardwalk Inn can boast amazingly spacious rooms and efficiencies, with thick, squishy carpet that welcomes bare feet. Each of the 106 rooms is cable connected, and has balconies to check out the sunworshipers who lounge around the center court pool. There's easy access to on-site washers and dryers, and plenty of parking, too, so you can go about your vacation business without a care.

THE BREAKERS RESORT INN
16th & Oceanfront
$$$ 428-1821/800-237-7532

There's no room in the house that doesn't look out over the blue Atlantic and every room comes equipped with a coffee-maker and a fridge to chill that post-beach beverage. If you want to go first-class here, ask for the deluxe king room with Jacuzzi, a two-room efficiency or, what the heck, the bridal suite, and have a beach blast. You'll have to come out of your room sometime, so if you're weary of the lifeguarded beach with umbrella and chair rentals, request a free bicycle and pedal through the strip.

COLONIAL INN MOTEL
29th & Oceanfront
$$ 428-5370/800-344-3342

Ah heck, just go for the king suite with Jacuzzi...it's your vacation. Even if you're more practical and opt for a regular double-bed oceanfront room, you'll still get a refrigerator, private balcony hanging over the beach and TV with cable and HBO.

The indoor heated pool is kind of nifty, with bright flags hanging from the rafters, but on a glorious sunny day, you'll probably want to go for the outdoor pool and sundeck. If you're too lazy to go somewhere else to eat, Cary's Restaurant and Boardwalk Cafe will treat you just fine for breakfast, lunch or dinner.

DAYS INN OCEANFRONT
32nd & Oceanfront
$$$ 428-5370/800-344-3342

This is a handsome hotel, where every oceanfront room comes equipped with a private balcony. Each of the 120 rooms is surprisingly spacious and you can zip down the hallway to the laundry when your favorite beach outfit gets pooped. There's an indoor pool, too, for those afternoons when you're not quite in the mood for the beach crunch, and the '50s diner and lounge called Happy Days is a swell place to wind up a sun-filled day.

DUNES LODGE/DUNES MOTOR INN
9th & 10th & Oceanfront
$$/$$$ 460-2205/800-634-0709

You can squeeze out a lot of Coppertone on the 425 feet of oceanfront that stretches out in front of the Dunes. It's right on the boardwalk with a broad grassed ocean terrace enveloping a super outdoor pool. For more privacy, you can head up to the third and fourth levels and plant your bod on the tanning deck with whirlpool spa standing by to soothe. When you're burnt to a crisp, rent a bike or head indoors to their oceanfront game room sporting two pool tables, a ping-pong table and even more tables for a heated game of bridge or gin rummy. For the hungries, there's the Snack Shop or the Pancake House – PLUS, serving from morning 'til night.

NEWCASTLE MOTEL

12th & Oceanfront
$$ *428-3981/800-346-3176*

You know you're going to like this place when you first pull up. Every one of the 83 rooms has an oceanfront vista from private balcony, along with refrigerator, microwave and whirlpool tub. If you opt for a two-room suite, you'll get a full kitchen as well as a large master bedroom with a king size bed, a super option for a longer stay. Start out on the ocean view sundeck or indoor heated pool, then warm those lazy muscles with a free bicycle and pedal down the boardwalk to check out the action.

OCEANFRONT INN

29th & Oceanfront
$$$ *422-0445/800-548-3879*

Sprawling along primo beachfront, the Oceanfront Inn is just that...oceanfront. From your private balcony, you can eavesdrop on all the beach activity, and then maybe dog-paddle a few lazy laps in the heated indoor or outdoor pools. There's a nifty canopied Beachfront Cafe for a leisurely lunch, and a lounge and restaurant, too. Sideview and west side rooms are less expensive, but as long as you're on vacation, why not go for a king-size oceanfront job. We would.

PRINCESS ANNE INN

25th & Oceanfront
$$$$ *428-5611/800-468-1111*

One of the long-standing beachtime favorites along the resort strip, the Princess Anne Inn is smack in the middle of all the hot night action. That means you can check in, check your car and then not worry about any transportation other than your own two feet to get you to all the best that Virginia Beach night life has to offer. Each of the 60 rooms here has an enclosed balcony, and you'll mix and mingle with fellow guests at the indoor/outdoor pool and Jacuzzi. A lounge and coffee shop are here, too, just in case you don't want to venture beyond the Princess Anne's territory.

WINDJAMMER HOTEL

19th & Oceanfront
$$ *428-0060/800-695-0035*

Early morning beach joggers can just roll out of bed into their Nikes and hit the sand running. Choose from regular or deluxe variety accommodations, or maybe go for an efficiency fully equipped with dishes, utensils and cookware. You'll enjoy the same benefits like private balconies, L-shaped oceanfront outdoor pool, guest laundry and cable TV with HBO, CNN and ESPN. Since it's on the boardwalk, you can slide out of your room and into the beach's night action with no trouble at all.

Chesapeake Bay

VIRGINIA BEACH RESORT HOTEL & TENNIS CLUB
2800 Shore Drive
$$$ 481-9000 1800-468-2722

Rising dramatically over the Chesapeake Bay, each of the 295 luxuriously appointed two-room suites overlooks the private beach from its own balcony. Relax in the indoor/outdoor swimming pool, try out the health club, or dine in the two restaurants. Affiliation with the nearby tennis club brings you 30 outdoor and six indoor tennis courts. There's banquet facilities for up to 300, and over 14,000 square feet of meeting space.

Suburban

OMNI-VIRGINIA BEACH
4453 Bonney Road
$$ 473-1700

Just off the Norfolk-Virginia Beach Expressway, mid-way between Norfolk and the Beach, is this popular Omni with 149 guest rooms, health club, indoor pool and restaurant. The nightclub here is especially popular with locals and visitors alike, and stays hopping with the night-owl crowd until the wee hours.

HOLIDAY INN EXECUTIVE CENTER
5655 Greenwich Road
$$ 499-4400

The "anchor" of the Newtown Road corridor hotel cluster, you can't miss its six-story green roof from the Norfolk-Virginia Beach Expressway. It's pretty much green inside, too, with it's miles of green carpeting and lavish indoor plantings. The 336 rooms are quite comfortable, and most come with hairdryers in the bathrooms, a nice touch. If you travel heavy, you'll appreciate their seven parlor/meeting suites, which include two parlor suites with adjoining king bedrooms. You'll also find both indoor and outdoor pools, whirlpool, sauna and health club, along with the popular Ashley's restaurant that's always busy with local business people for breakfast, lunch and after-work drinks.

COURTYARD BY MARRIOTT
5700 Greenwich Road
$$ 490-2002

What appears to be a charming apartment complex is really a 146-room hotel that sprawls across four acres. Most of the rooms face a beautifully landscaped courtyard with swimming pool and garden gazebo, plus exercise room and a Jacuzzi. Business travelers in town for several days really love this place that accommodates them with large desks. There is a restaurant on the premises, but we hear that taking food back to the room from the pick-up counter is a favorite choice for the bone-tired executive.

DAYS INN
4564 Bonney Road
$$ *497-4488*

Convenient to the Pembroke area of Virginia Beach which we call "the central business district," this 144-room inn is a popular stop-over that's close to office complexes and shopping. There is a swimming pool and cable TV with movies, as well as a restaurant for a quick bite for breakfast.

THE FOUNDERS INN AND CONFERENCE CENTER
5641 Indian River Road
$$$ *366-5718*

Still sporting its original shine, this gorgeous new facility, tastefully furnished in the colonial manner, is located close to the Christian Broadcasting Network (CBN) and Regent University. Overlooking English gardens surrounding a small lake where swans swim, the Inn offers 249 beautifully appointed rooms, with common areas and sitting areas that have a true resort feeling. Amenities include fitness center, tennis and racquetball courts, indoor and outdoor swimming pools, sand volleyball court and playground. Award-winning chefs serve sumptuous gourmet specialties in the Swan Terrace Restaurant, and banquet facilities for 1,000 are available. Meeting space covers over 22,000 square feet and includes a 132-seat amphitheater. No alcoholic beverages are served, and smoking is prohibited throughout the complex.

Resort Rentals

For a home away from home for a family vacation, it's hard to beat the many condominium and cottage rentals available in Virginia Beach. All are fully furnished and appointed with all the right appliances and kitchen gadgets, although some may require packing your own bed linens and towels. For a week or two, even a month, all you need to do is to slide your bathing suits and shorts in a duffle and hit the road.

As with hotel and motel reservations, plan early for a summer or holiday stay, and remember that cash, credit cards and traveler's checks (not personal checks) are the accepted currency. When making reservations, make certain you request the specific cancellation, early/late checkout and refund policies as they do vary from property to property.

Condominiums

You'll literally be living high on the hog when you check into one of Virginia Beach's condominium rentals, as most are of the high-rise flavor. As a general rule, you can expect a swimming pool outside and full kitchens inside, along with balconies and beachfront either at your door or a few short blocks away. Most are two bedroom/ two bath units that sleep two to ten adults. Do check specifics, especially the availability of linens, when making reservations. Summer rates run from $500 to $1500 weekly, depending on the amenities, size and location of the property.

Beach Breeze Condos, 208 57th Street, 422-0579. Three 2BR/2BA, one block to ocean.

Colony Condominiums, 13th & Oceanfront, 425-8689. Thirty-eight 2BR/2BA, on the ocean.

Dolphin Run Condominium, 3rd & Oceanfront, 425-6166. One hundred and ten 1, 2, & 3-BR, 2BA, on the ocean.

Edgewater Condominium, 37th & Oceanfront, 425-6298. Thirty-five 2BR/2BA, on the ocean.

Mai Kai Condo Resort Apts, 56/57th & Atlantic, 428-1096. Thirty-eight studio, 1 & 2BR, 2BA, on the ocean.

Oceans II Studio Condominiums, 40th & Oceanfront, 1-800-845-4786. Forty-two studio units, on the ocean.

Oceanfront Rentals, 2408 Artic Avenue, 428-7473. 2 BR/1 BA, 2 blocks to the ocean.

Seacrest Condominiums, 21st & Artic, 428-4441. Eight 2BR, 2 blocks to the ocean.

The Seasons, 109-111 52nd Street, 428-4441. Four 4BR/3 1/2BA units, a few steps from the ocean.

Cottages

For one of the beachiest vacations you'll ever have, head to the southernmost part of Virginia Beach and hit lands' end at Sandbridge. You won't find any glitz, glamour or hopping night life in this secluded community, just the pleasure of rolling dunes, clean beaches and the salt-water surf of the Atlantic Ocean.

If it's a getaway to total peace and lazy relaxation you're after, this is the place to come. But not to worry about those creature comforts you can't live without. There's a well-stocked grocery (Ben & Jerry's, anyone?), gas station and a few great boutiques for that wayward cloudy day.

Architecture of the Sandbridge rentals varies wildly, from ye olde cottage to high tech contemporary...with rental rates that are in sync with the luxury offered. Most owners have named their homes, and for natives, the moniker is a better handle on location than the actual address. All sleep at least six quite comfortably, and come with everything you need but bed linens and towels. In summer months, expect to pay from about $900 to $2,500 for a week of the pleasure of sleeping in a real live house rather than a hotel room.

Those who know what's available, when and for how much, are very helpful in matching your particular family and budget to a rental property in Sandbridge. One quick call will win you a brochure with photos of all possibilities and their particulars.

Siebert Realty-Sandbridge Beach, 601 Sandbridge Road 1-800-231-3037.

Affordable Properties, 613 21st Street, 428-0432.

Atkinson Realty, 5307 Atlantic Avenue, 428-4441.

Hudgins Real Estate, 3701 Pacific Avenue, 422-6741.

Properties are also available for rent in the heat of the resort action, with a wide swing in style, proximity to the ocean and rental rates. Any of the above Realtors can provide detailed information on cottages in the main resort area.

Campgrounds

For those whose pulses race at the mere thought of sleeping among the bugs under the stars, the backwoods and campgrounds of Hampton Roads have a patch of shaded dirt ready for the thrill. Since most of the Insiders we know consider serious camping out an overnight at a Holiday Inn, it's hard to understand the attraction of any accommodation with a three-foot high ceiling and a bathroom with trees rather than white ceramic tile and fluorescent lights. But, if camping is your thing, we feel it's our duty to point your canoe in the right direction.

You'll find overnight camping sites clustered primarily in rural Virginia Beach, the Hampton Roads city that still has pioneer spaces to accommodate L.L. Bean types. Lest you think we're totally primitive, most facilities do offer comfort zone amenities, like swimming pools, restrooms and showers, playgrounds and camp stores for those basic necessities.

Rates vary with the season and the hookup requested (water, electrical, sewage, etc.), and reservations are recommended to secure your spot. Most also allow pets on leash, so don't keep Rover away from all the fun.

Virginia Beach

BEST HOLIDAY TRAV-L-PARK
1075 General Booth Blvd.   1-800-548-0223

Convenient to Croatan Beach, this 1,100-site park welcomes tents and recreational vehicles. Pools, laundry facilities, bathhouses, stores and restaurant are on-site or nearby. Cabins are also available.

KOA CAMPGROUND
1240 General Booth Blvd.   428-1444

This popular spot is open March through November with 165 sites plus cabins. Pools, bathhouses, and a store are added attractions.

NORTH BAY SHORE CAMPGROUND
3257 Colechester Road   426-7911

This Sandbridge campground offers 165 sites with a pool, bathhouse and store. Its open April 15 through October 1.

SEASHORE STATE PARK
2500 Shore Drive   490-3939

This is our most popular camping destination, so even with 235 sites, you'd best reserve early through Virginia State Parks or Ticketmaster. There's no water or electricity, but there are bathhouses and a store. Cabins are also available. They're open March 30 through November.

SENECA CAMPGROUND
144 S. Princess Anne Road   426-6241

There are 230 sites here plus cabins, with a pool, bathhouses, boat ramp and store to add to your good time.

SURFSIDE AT SANDBRIDGE
3665 Sandpiper Road   *1-800-568-7873*

One block from the ocean, there are 150 sites with access to bathhouses, a game room and store. Surfside is open April 1 through October 31.

Chesapeake

NORTHWEST RIVER PARK
Indian River Road   *421-7151*

Nestled in the center of this 763-acre park are campsites serviced by a camp store and bathhouses. The park itself offers a wealth of goodies for the outdoorsman, including extensive hiking trails, boat and canoe rentals, an equestrian center and a gorgeous lake that stretches almost the entire length of the park.

Portsmouth

SLEEPY HOLE PARK
Sleepy Hole Road   *393-5056*

Overlooking the Nansemond River in Suffolk, this Portsmouth-operated park plays host to 50 campsites with your pick of provided utilities. Also available: bathhouses, laundry, fire rings and sports fields with recreation equipment checkout.

Photo: Richmond Newspapers

A couple takes a romantic walk on the shores of Virginia Beach.

Inside
Night Life

We have come to the conclusion that there must be something in the water in Hampton Roads that gives us the stamina to stay up all night and boogie. And, judging from the sheer numbers of hot places where you can exercise your right to pop, rock, bluegrass and jazz yourself into a wee-hours frenzy, we must be drinking from that well every night of the week.

Which brings us to a word on drinking. The legal age to enjoy alcoholic beverages in the Commonwealth of Virginia is 21 – no ifs, buts or fake IDs. Patrons who are at least 18 may be allowed into most nighttime hot spots, but are usually burdened with a hand stamp that indicates that their money's no good at the bar. Bouncers and bartenders alike find no joke in any underage shenanigans. After all, their jobs and reputations are at stake. So, while taking teenagers to dinner in our region is encouraged and appreciated, please park them in a safe place before taking off to a night of festivities at any local night spot.

Now that we have the attention of all you adults in the audience, let's crowd in the car and take a trip to some of the area's most lively late night happenings. Most revolve around the music du jour, and so we've chosen to separate your destination choices by "the beat." Whether your rhythm of choice is pop, beach, jazz, acoustic or just plain loud, you won't have far to go to find night owls who share your tastes. Since it's not humanly possible for your Insiders' hosts to have frequented every hot spot in town, we'll give you our best shot at those we know are the places to see – and be seen – on tips from wired friends and associates who require minimal sleep.

The social architecture of the area is such that many places that rate highest marks for the evening meal are also transformed into the hottest nightspots in town. This is especially true for the primo eateries at the Beach, like Bogie's and Five 01 City Grill, where a pre-planned linger after dessert can mean entry into a whole new tidal wave of late nite party-people and fantastic entertainment. If you're just out for a delectable dinner, hang around. You never know what's going to happen when the ten o'clock curtain rises.

Pop/Rock

Norfolk

KING'S HEAD INN
4220 Hampton Boulevard   *489-3224*

A university hot spot, the King's Head packs them in for pop, rock, funk and rap. The crowd is real young, the music's real loud and the beer is ice cold. Parking to get here, or to Friar Tuck's down the street for similar stimulation with the college crowd, is pretty tight, so plan on walking a block or two. Name-brand headliners require a cover charge, usually around five bucks.

LEWIS'
4012 Colley Avenue   *489-9420*

There was a time when you went with your family to a very special seafood dinner at Lewis'. You'd savor your crabcakes served by a motherly-type waitress and then relax over coffee while you watched them close the place down. Boy, have times changed! Now, starting at 10 PM almost every evening, the dinner crowd is gone and the party-makers stream in...for pop, rock, reggae and more, from national recording artists and college-town bands brought in from all over the country. While some shows are 18+, most require you produce an I.D. proving you're 21 or older. Cover charges vary with the preeminence of the performers, but average about five dollars a head.

CHEVY'S
249 York Street, Downtown   *623-2000*

This is the new guy on the block with a history of success from their flagship location in Chesapeake. When they opened recently, they pledged themselves as the place to come "after"...after the movie, after the play, after the game. And throngs of people have taken them up on their offer, crowding in to carve out a square inch on the center stage dance floor that sways to the beats blasted by the deejay. This is oldies and top-40 territory with full bar and a pretty tasty "stuffed burger" on the menu. (They put all the goodies inside the burger, rather than on top.) It's a fun place to check out, and there's never a cover charge.

CABARET VOLTAIRE
114 Freemason Street   *No Phone*

Remember the beatnik cafes of the late '50s? The owners of this newest bid for the late night crowd not only remember, they've recreated it, spiffed up with oversized local artwork, giant scrap-metal light fixtures that hang from the vaulted ceiling and a "Goodwill" mix of furnishings. Along with the jazz, rock, country and blues acts that rotate throughout the week, you can actually order a PBJ or dinner-waffle with SPAM. This isn't just a night-spot...it's a real happening. Uh-huh.

O'SULLIVAN'S WHARF
43rd & Colley Avenue   *423-3753*

What first appears to be a couple of weather-worn shacks tossed together by some sarcastic hurricane is actually the home of some of the tastiest food and entertainment on Norfolk's west side. After a fantastic meal of crab cakes, Alaskan crab claws or tempura shrimp, you can settle in for the nightly acoustic entertainment.

Open when weather permits is a great deck that juts out over a branch of the Elizabeth River, which always seems to catch a great breeze. The crowd's a mix of ODU students, professors and just plain locals...you'll fit right in.

Virginia Beach

ABBEY ROAD
203 22nd Street   *425-6330*

Celebrating ten years in the entertainment game, Abbey Road has been the magnet for some of the finest acoustic action in town. The oceanfront night club has built a reputation on its excellent menu, too. Usually packed tight with happy patrons, there's live entertainment seven nights a week in the summer, six in the off-season. Along with a kitchen that's open from 11 AM until 1 AM, you can drink your way around the world from the largest collection of imported beers in the area. There's ample on-premise parking, too, a real benefit for the seasonal gridlock we've come to expect during summer evenings at the Beach.

PEPPERMINT BEACH CLUB
15th & Atlantic   *491-2582*

Club Pep has had more than its share of headliners through the years, and age doesn't seem to be slowing it a bit. You'll get a good dose of pop, rock and reggae at this super-casual beach landmark. The concert schedule varies, but you can call for a calendar of upcoming performers. Tickets are free before the day of the show at TicketMasters (671-8100) or $5 at the door.

CLUB ROGUE'S
616 Virginia Beach Boulevard   *422-3344*

This is your average humongous open dance place, and it pops and rocks almost every night of the week. It really is a body-press of toned and tanned beautiful young people, but some of the headline entertainers often bring the older baby-boomers out of the closet. Tickets for entry vary with the national prominence of the performers, but average five to ten dollars per person. Be nice to the bouncers at the front door, they're not especially humorous southern gentlemen.

PASCAL'S

313 Laskin Road　　　　　425-0311

This sister to the Isle of Capri is one of the best Beach places to mingle with the jet set. The huge multi-level room has plenty of comfy spots to linger over your favorite beverage with your favorite poopsie, and a dance floor that packs them in to boogie to top '40s hits from well-known favorites like Hot Cakes and Sumpthin' Special. There's a reduced cover charge before 11 PM. Neighbor Isle of Capri has just opened the Back Room Bistro and Bar that features jazz and evening menu until 2 AM on Friday and Saturday nights.

JAMAICAN JOHNNY'S

18th & Cypress Avenue　　　422-9688

With a menu special every night of the week, from steamed shrimp to all-you-can-eat pasta, Jamaican Johnny's lights up Thursday through Sunday with live entertainment. When the acoustic sound gets too loud, you can sneak away for a little foosball. Sunday night's a good time to visit, since there's no cover charge on the day of rest.

OCEAN EDDIE'S

14th & Oceanfront, Fishing Pier　425-7742

Literally plopped out on the fishing pier close to the Peppermint is the loudest, most crowded and most absolutely fun place to hang out after the sun goes down. A generally more mature crowd – say thirty something plus – squeezes into Ocean Eddie's every night of the week. It's blistering hot in the summer, and that's both in popularity and sheer physical heat from the crowd. If you can find the elbow room to eat, try their superb crab cakes. There is a cover charge, but it varies from night to night, and well worth every penny.

PEABODY'S

17th & Pacific　　　　　422-6212

When you head upstairs at Peabody's, there's no return until you've danced your socks off. It's a fairly young and trim crowd, which translates to high decibel music, but there's lots of contagious energy for the small cover charge. Food-wise, head for the killer taco bar open all night long.

RIVER HOUSE

530 Winston Salem Avenue
Rudee Inlet　　　　　425-8188

When you hear "valet parking," you know that this is a place you could love. And you will. Upstairs is a fine window-walled dining room serving one of the tastiest lobsters in the area. Downstairs, you can stay inside in the comfy glass-front casual dining lounge and bar, or stroll outside to the huge deck that catches the cool evening breezes off Rudee Inlet. Music wise, find acoustic upstairs and pop down...plus lots of happy patrons no matter on which level you land. They even offer a V.I.P. card for locals that bestows privileges, like no cover charge and invitations to private parties. This rates as one of our all-time favorite places for a Beach evening out.

MITTY'S
Omni Virginia Beach Hotel
4453 Bonney Road   473-1700

It's amazing how a "hotel" bar can be so very popular, but Mitty's ranks among the top places for live entertainment where the area's premiere bands for acoustic sound take the stage. Festivities begin at five nightly, and they get everything spiced up with an all-you-can-eat "Mexican Fiesta" buffet from 5 PM until 11PM.

SUNSET GRILLE
2973 Shore Drive
Lynnhaven Colony Shoppes   481-9815

Head on to Chesapeake Beach and take in the action at Sunset Grille. This is music like it should be...good old '50s and '60s rock and roll from popular local bands like Snuff and the Barflys. Don't plan on sitting in your comfy chair to nibble on those ten cent wings or shrimp...the music will have you swaying on the dance floor and enjoying every minute of it.

Chesapeake

WINSTON'S CAFE
1412 Greenbrier Parkway   420-1751

It's got that Jewish Mother kind of atmosphere, what with all the local lounge lizards that stream in to Winston's, especially on Friday and Saturday nights when they roll back the carpets for the crowds of pasta hungry patrons. There's live entertainment on Thursday and Saturday nights, but the casual come-as-you-are (or want-to-be) feeling prevails all week long, from 11 AM until 2 AM every day except Sunday.

Portsmouth

TOWNE POINT PUB
3558 Towne Point Road   483-2500

This is a Western Branch destination for hordes of regulars, who pop in for one of the Pub's enormous club sandwiches. Live bands grab the mikes on Wednesday, Friday and Saturday nights, and the rock and roll gets even the shyest guest out on the dance floor. A real friendly, neighborhood place where there's not a stranger in the crowd.

BOGIES
975 Hodges Ferry Road   488-1195

There are two sides to Bogies in Portsmouth....not to be confused with the Bogie's at the Beach. Their restaurant, On the Green, makes one of the most wicked racks of lamb in a fine dining atmosphere. On the other hand, there's the nightclub, that is shoulder-to-shoulder practically every night of the week, both seated and on the crowded dance floor. If the waitress can hear you above the deejay, you can order a hefty sandwich and a brew. Tuesdays here are especially boisterous, with the featured "Battle of the Bands."

Jazz

Norfolk

BIENVILLE GRILL
723 West 21st Street   *625-5427*

Late night at the Grill has some wicked tunes coming your way, thanks to the live jazz every Friday and Saturday nights from 9 PM until 12:30 AM. For more about this divine gem of a restaurant, see the "Restaurants" section for all the info.

Virginia Beach

THE JEWISH MOTHER
3108 Pacific Avenue   *422-5430*

Self-billed as the premier blues club in town, the Jewish Mother tops their corned beef with a blues jam every Wednesday night, with live blues performers every other night of the week. It's a pretty popular stopover on an all-night Beach hop, especially if you get the hungries. Their excellent food and generous portions are legendary, and you can even slide into Mom's new Deli Section and brown bag some fresh-sliced meats, cheeses and sinful desserts.

HOUSE OF JAZZ
314-A Constitution Avenue
Pembroke East Shopping Center   *456-0884*

Anyplace called the House of Jazz better be! And it is. Jazz fans pack the place Thursday through Sunday nights (Thursday is Ladies Night and there's an 8:30 PM jam session every Sunday). There is a $10 minimum, but locals who are members of the Tidewater Jazz Society can sneak in free. If you're a newcomer who would like to find out all you can about jazz in the area, call the Society at 499-3157.

Country/ Bluegrass

Norfolk

THE BANQUE
1849 East Little Creek Road   *480-3600*

I'm in a Garth Brooks kind of mood. Take me to The Banque for the cure. We are now talking country...real country...and you'd better know your two-step before you put your boots on the dance floor. Seating 500 people (most of whom are on the huge dance floor), The Banque has live toe-tapping music, super food and you can even get free dance lessons Tuesday, Wednesday and Thursday nights at 7:45 PM. If you get country fever, you can do a little late night shopping at Belle's Dry Goods located inside. Open Tuesday through Sunday from 6 PM until 2 AM.

THE LIDO INN
839 E. Little Creek Road   *480-1953*

A lot of people we know go to The Lido just for the steamed shrimp, some of the best in the region. Many of these people are the same folks that don't admit to hanging around to get into the country rhythm frenzy that picks up when the live entertainment begins, and patrons are known to leave half-finished plates to hit the dance floor. It's really a fun place, with the broadest range of guests, older and younger, and they're truly kind in teaching you how to move around the dance floor without looking too much like city-folk. There's no cover, so give it a try for a real good time.

Virginia Beach

THE COUNTY LINE
717 S. Military Highway
The Executive Inn   420-2120

We've got your dinner specials, your door prizes, your dance lessons every Sunday night. We've got a ride to the County Line and we've got country music loud and clear. Monday's there's no cover, Tuesdays are Ladies Nights and Thursdays there's a talent contest for the bravest among us. Country-western is the County Line, and if you want to hear the best twangs and see the most proficient two-steppers in town, here's the place to show up seven nights a week.

SUSI'S NASHVILLE EAST
1724 Potters Road   491-9950

How would you like your Loretta Lynn served tonight? Nashville East books all the must-hear country bands, and gets you moving without too much of a shove. Music's loud, food OK, but the friendly folks who call this place "home away from home" can make you feel mighty daw-gone comfortable. If you don't know the latest dance step (we hear Horse'n

Around is the latest 32-count craze), this is the place to come. Wear your boots and your ten-gallon, or at least fake it.

DESPERADO'S
315 17th Street   425-5566

"We're not snooty...we're rooty tooty." That's what they say, so we guess that's what they mean. Home to the only mechanical bull in the area, and perhaps the state, Desperado's rocks with country seven nights a week. Food's pretty good, too, we hear – Tex-Mex style with some pretty mean jumbo nachos and a taco plate that will set you on fire on Saturday nights. Our spies tell us that the jam session on Sunday from 8 PM until midnight is a hoot. Better check it out, with or without us.

Portsmouth

BILLY BOB'S
3960 Turnpike Road   397-4681

When you start with a 70-foot bar, you can only go uphill. So here we are at Billy Bob's with the largest dance floor in town and ever-patient Greg and Tracy are giving dance lessons to a couple who are almost as behind the corral as we are. But somehow the music, and the good-old-folks who have packed in, have that encouraging look in their eyes. You stake out a dark corner of the floor and go for it. You're moving with the beat and, hey, it's not as hard as you thought it was! Doesn't matter that you're not doing it like a pro...you're having a blast. And, that's what Billy

Bob's is all about. Even if you're a country-western want-to-be, this is the place to put your toes in the water. The staff and regular patrons are very forgiving.

And, there's more???

Two categories for after sundown entertainment that we haven't covered are comedy clubs and movies. The former has deep roots in two local spots, **The Comedy Club** at the Thoroughgood Inn in Pembroke Meadows Shopping Center and **The Comedy Zone** at Magoo's in the Day's Inn Airport, both in Virginia Beach. Here you can catch some national talent on the rise on Friday and Saturday nights.

When it comes to movie theaters, we've got them playing first run flicks from one end of the region to the other. As Insiders, however, we feel it's our duty to point out three of the many theaters that have as much personality as the reels they run up in the projector room.

The Naro Expanded Cinema in Norfolk's Ghent is an old-fashioned, big 70MM screen armed with Dolby stereo, comfy seat-type place, with the added benefit of baklava and Quibel for sale in the lobby. Along with current hits, you'll likely find those academy award winners you missed during the first run, along with some arty, off-the-wall offerings. If the movie is a dud, pop out to the concession counter for brownies or a giant cookie.

The Commodore in Portsmouth is what a movie theater experience is all about. A grand art-deco theater with a huge 42-foot screen, squishy carpet, murals and chandeliers, you plop in a stuffed chair at your own private table. Got a hunger twinge? Just pick up the phone on your table and order in some carrot cake or hot chocolate with tiny floating marshmallows. Even with the super THX sound system, the home-like atmosphere gives you that kick-your-shoes-off and enjoy the movie feeling.

In Virginia Beach, there's the **Cinema and Drafthouse**, where you also are assigned a table with comfortable chairs for the feature film.

Don't be in the dark about upcoming concerts and local best bets. Call the Virginian Pilot and Ledger Star's INFOLINE at 640-5555, then punch in 2555 to hear a recording about all the hip happenings. The call is free, but you must have a touch tone phone.

Insiders' Tips

This is one theater where you can go straight from the office (or the beach) because the menu includes heftier fare, like a pretty good chicken sandwich, fries and an ice cold beer.

As long as we're on the night prowl, we would be negligent if we didn't mention the newest Hampton Roads' craze, even if we think it's a little close to the edge. It's the current club fad called "karaoke." In brief, this means that a mildly intoxicated patron takes the stage of the nightclub, grabs a microphone and tries desperately to sing the lyrics (in tune) to a popular song played in the background. This in front of the entire evening's crowd...and they tell us it's really fun. If you're an exhibitionist, you can give this Japanese-inspired trend a shot nightly with The Comedy Zone's "Singing Machine." More power and rhythm to ya.

And, lastly, another debatable fad that's strictly for the young and strong of heart is the hyper-beat techno-rave that we hate to say is taking hold of young night owls in Hampton Roads. It started with the Tidal Rave held a while back at the old seaside amusement park from 10 PM until 6 AM, yes, 6 AM. Now other night-spots are trying to become dance-til-dawn spots with a similar theme. Mitty's has launched its way-cool version of the rave with techno-dance parties every Saturday night. And the Kings Head Inn near Old Dominion University goes semi-techno on Monday nights for dancers 18 years of age and older who can stay awake through the whole ecstatic line dancing thing for only one buck. We Insiders would have definitely gone to personally check out the latest techno/electro-rave, but our skin-tight dayglo polyester jumpsuits were at the cleaners. Darn it.

Photo: Richmond Newspapers

Located on Norfolk's waterfront, Waterside offers restaurants, shops and daily entertainment.

Inside
Shopping

*S*ome of us were born to shop. Others were born to drive us from mall to mall. That's the undeniable truth of life, and one burden (of shopping bags and boxes) we must somehow learn to bear.

The one really good thing about Hampton Roads is that we missed that lecture preaching that conspicuous consumption was out...just try to find a parking place close to any mall entrance on a rainy day. Indeed, it is a sign of today's new perspective on accumulation that we must all carefully study the most advanced extracurricular activity of shopping, and hone our expertise on field trips taken weekly to meticulously examine all the stuff we couldn't afford even if we did have loads of money.

If you're a visitor to our fair land of outlet malls and outrageous boutiques, we'll not keep those precious little plastic cards bottled up for long. You owe it to yourself, your country and our local economy to arm yourself with padded Air-Nikes and shop, shop, shop. We Insiders would give almost anything to go along with each and every one of you for a personally guided tour, but we know full well that we would be the first to succumb to the world of temptation that lies just behind

those glass double-doors. Therefore, we accept the responsibility, and the duty, to point you in the direction of our favorite shopping haunts, and hope you leave the really-marked-down size eight's behind for us.

Other than knowing where the major malls and specialty shopping places are, there are no magical skills or creative insights that we can share with you. Because we know how much it can hurt to go home empty-handed, we've taken great care to aim you to places where you're certain to fall madly and inseparably in love with something that your conscious brain won't admit that you don't really need. Not to thank us now. It's only your complete customer satisfaction that we strive for.

Let's shop!

Da Malls

Norfolk

THE WATERSIDE
Waterside Drive, Downtown Norfolk

Is it a mall? Is it a restaurant place? Is it a night spot? Yes to all the above and more. With over 120

Shopping is popular along Atlantic Avenue in Virginia Beach.

shops, kiosks and pushcarts, six international restaurants and over twenty-five specialty food shops, The Waterside is one of our favorite places to waste a lazy afternoon. There's always activity, and very often live entertainment, on the lower level where most of the "fast-food" type restaurants are located. Upstairs, there's the broadest spectrum of shops like Barr-ee Station Catalogue Outlet where you'll not be able to resist bargains from J. Crew, Clifford & Willis and, on occasion, Polo. Queen Anne's Lace has dropdead lingerie and lovely gifts; The Lodge has a great collection of industrial strength Gap-style casual wear; and The Flag Stand waves with flags of every nation, plus some adorable seasonal house flags. In Your Image is packed to the rafters with art prints, figurines, books, cards and jewelry. And you most pop in for a quick spritz at La Perfumerie (no, we are *never* able to leave without a purchase), to touch everything at Ray's Jungle, discover all things Virginia at The Virginia Shop, and check out the wonderful handmade crafts at Annabarbara. For restaurants, there's the seafood adventure at Phillips Waterside, a bit of Brit at Reggie's British Pub, golden chopsticks at Shine Shine Palace and northern Italian specialities at Il Porto, that we swear uses more garlic than allowed by law. Sporting a magnificent copper and brass grill is Harbor Grill, where you'll be served some of the best BBQ ribs, chicken and steak in town. Weather permitting, most restaurants offer outdoor dining, overlooking the busy Elizabeth River. As far as parking, there's the huge city lot directly across the street that you access by a pedestrian bridge over Waterside Drive. Take your parking ticket inside for validation with purchase...it will save you in parking fees.

SELDEN ARCADE
212 East Main Street, Downtown Norfolk

Thanks to the rebirth of our downtown waterfront, this charming antique has been restored to its former glory, and is a popular spot for workers in the financial district. J.M. Prince has one of the finest selections of collectible books, and Beecroft & Bull, Ltd. is the ultimate for men's clothing and accessories. Goldman's Salon Shoes carries all those designer brands you'd never wear in the rain, and both Facets and etceteras are great for browsing singular jewelry and gifts. Food wise, JP's SmokeHouse Restaurant is the place for a hearty helping of good old American favorites, and just opened is Gio's Pizza and Ristorante offering up garlic-laced specialties with a Sicilian touch. Another promising new Arcade eatery is Yorgo's Bagledashery with umpteen kinds of bagels and sandwiches.

GHENT SHOPPING
Colley Avenue, Ghent

While not really a mall, the time you can spend sauntering in and out of the many shops and restaurants in Ghent puts it in the park-and-shop category. If you're a parallel parking pro, you can whip into Bouillabaisse, the ultimate chef's shop for kitchen goodies, Gale Goss Country French Antiques for

THE WATERSIDE

THE WATERSIDE

★ 333 Waterside Drive, Norfolk, Virginia 23510 ★

absolutely divine furnishings, china and accessories, Harbor Gallery for original art by local artists and Breit Crafts for the most whimsical objets d'art that are truly functional. If you need a card or gift for someone you've left at home, try The Entertainers. Around the bend on 21st Street, you can browse through Turn The Page Book Shop, Decorum for exquisitely affordable home furnishings and then pop into Lili's of Ghent for that must-have ensemble. Tucked away further down 21st Street is an all-hands-alert shop-stop...Fox Glove Ltd. While they claim it's a place for gifts for home and garden, it's a homey fill of all kinds of European-flavored accessories and au courant knickknacks you just can't resist. Throw those bags over your shoulder and head a bit further down the road to more great shopping finds like NYFO Boutique for designer clothing like nothing in your closet and Presents of Mine, with fine gifts and Godiva chocolates. Besides these wonderful places, there are restaurants galore, antiques shops and even the Naro, a good old-fashioned movie theater.

Insiders' Tips

Many of the region's museums and some of its churches have gift shops that sell unusual items. Spending your money at these nonprofit organizations lets you help them while checking off your gift list. The shops with the widest variety include those at The Chrysler Museum, the Norfolk Botanical Garden and the Virginia Zoo in Norfolk, the Virginia Marine Science Museum and the Virginia Beach Center for the Arts in Virginia Beach, and Riddick's Folly in Suffolk. Churches with interesting gift shops include The Church of the Good Shepherd, 1520 N. Shore Rd. (423-3230), Christ & St. Luke's Church, Olney Road and Stockley Gardens (627-5665) and St. Andrews Episcopal Church, 1004 Graydon Ave. (622-5530). All are in Norfolk.
The Norfolk Senior Center, 924 W. 21st St., Norfolk (625-5857) runs a gift shop with mostly handmade items. For a hostess or housewarming gift, there's nowhere we'd rather shop than the Sugar Plum Bakery at 1353 Laskin Road in Virginia Beach. (422-3913). This nonprofit bakery trains and hires disabled workers. A box of Sugar Plum's cookies or pastries is a real treat.

MILITARY CIRCLE
Military Highway at Virginia Beach Boulevard

One of the original mall experiences in the area, Military Circle has undergone some major renovation in the past years. So now it looks like every other mega-mall around, and houses basically the same kind of mall-flavored shops. Of course, we're partial to The Gap, The Limited and Waldenbooks, but for department-store atmosphere, Hecht's and Leggett certainly hold their own as anchors. JC Penney's here, too, along with six movie theaters and a plethora of shoe stores and clothing shops. For the younger crowd, Legends is a favorite, with all the right name-brand sports shoes and sports gear.

JANAF SHOPPING CENTER
Military Circle at Virginia Beach Boulevard

Ok, so this isn't a "real" mall. But if you're out to bargain shop, don't drive past without a quick swing through. You pop into TJ Maxx while Dad and Junior swoon over the latest in audio-video at Circuit City. Teenagers find A&N a magnet for sweats and tennies, seamstresses and craftswomen can touch all the new bolts and patterns at Piece Goods Shop and The Sports Authority offers up more sports stuff than humankind could ever play with in a lifetime. If you need a reality shock, stroll through Portfolio, the JC Penny furnishings showcase. You'll see absolutely top-rate furniture and accessories that will make you go home and rip up every room in the house. A great B. Dalton Bookseller floats out on the perimeter of Janaf, along with Montgom-ery Ward and Hooters, a restaurant known for their great Buffalo wings and skimpily clad servers. Navy newcomers will appreciate the handy Navy Information Center in Janaf. There's also a post office as well as a city library in this shopping center.

Virginia Beach

PEMBROKE MALL
Virginia Beach Boulevard at Independence

Right in the hub of what is called Virginia Beach's Central Business District, Pembroke Mall has sprawled larger and larger to accommodate both new stores and stalwart shoppers. The tool department at Sears is where we usually park our menfolk while we head straight to Pembroke's newest shopping experience, Stein Mart. Here you'll find all the latest apparel for every member of the family, plus a grand shoe, accessory and domestics department...all discount priced. S&K, one of the best menswear discounters is here, too, plus Waldenbooks, Hit or Miss and Mother's Records and Tapes. Sports-minded kids head for the Athlete's Foot and Foot Locker and, when you need a break, you can head over to the cinema for a new release. Across from the movies, there's Boardwalk Golf & Games, boasting an indoor miniature golf course, plus all the popular arcade games.

LYNNHAVEN MALL
Lynnhaven Parkway

Many of us go to Lynnhaven just to take a "trip out of town." While it isn't very far away in miles, once inside, you can leave your worries in the parking lot and drift aimlessly inside all day long.

Two major book stores, endless women's & men's apparel (including the Gap, Shulman's, a gorgeous new Lerner's and cosmopolitan-sized Limited), jewelry stores and an out-of-this world Disney Store await. On the upper level is a food court to soothe whatever taste you have, from burgers to Chinese to pizza. Two separate Hecht's (one for men and home furnishings, the other for women and children), JC Penney, Montgomery Ward and Leggett are the big anchors, but some of our favorite shops are of the smallish variety, like The Bombay Company, Crabtree & Evelyn, Victoria's Secret and Deck the Walls (great posters!). For movie buffs, there are eleven theaters. A special note to newcomers: inside the mall is a Division of Motor Vehicles office (DMV Express) which is a blessing for simple registrations and driver's license renewals.

COUNTRYSIDE SHOPS
Landstown Road

This is an absolutely darling place, and just ten minutes from the oceanfront next to the Farmer's Market. The Countryside Shops are weathered and purposely worn-looking on the outside, but inside is a hallway of boutiques with many one-of-a-kind collectibles. Heart & Hand Gallery offers antiques, pottery and jewelry; Mike's Place has handmade woodcrafts and The Spotted Cow has a charming hodge-podge of collectibles and gifts. We especially like Countless Keepsakes, a cross stitch and stencil shop, and Just Imagine, with its dollhouses and miniatures. The Countryside Deli has wonderful homemade soups and desserts, with great overstuffed sandwiches for your middle course.

CRAFTERS MALL
4740 Baxter Road, One Block off Independence Boulevard

If you're in a crafty kind of mood, this is the only place that will

satisfy your hobby hunger. The Crafters Mall in the Baxter Run Shopping Center is 10,000 square feet of handmade art, dolls, pottery, jewelry, floral designs and wood crafts. There are more bunnies, bears, kittens and cows, in painted, stuffed and patchworked varieties, than you can even imagine. Plus some pretty interesting southwestern art and country crafts from over 300 talented crafters, selling direct to you. If you want to snag a delightful, one-of-a-kind gift, this is definitely one place you won't leave empty handed.

THE GREAT AMERICAN OUTLET MALL
3750 Virginia Beach Boulevard

OshKosh B'Gosh, you can find a lot of neat stuff at neat discount prices at the Great American Outlet Mall! Once you survive the kamikze parking lot, you can hoof through stores galore like Famous Footwear, Banister Shoes, Gitano, Dress Barn, Fieldcrest Cannon and Bugle

Insiders' Tips

If you want to take home typical Virginia souvenirs, try some of the Commonwealth's highly acclaimed food products. Peanuts, wine, jams, pound cakes and hams are the logical choices. You'll also find well-done cookbooks and the Blue Crab Bay Co. line of seafood-related products from the Eastern Shore.

For one of the biggest selection of all kinds of Virginia products stop by the Virginia Shop in The Waterside in downtown Norfolk (623-4547). In Suffolk there are two choices for peanuts. The Planters Peanut Center at 308 W. Washington St. (539-4411) sells Planters' products, many of them made in the company's Suffolk plant. Store employees create a wonderful aroma by cooking peanuts in an antique roaster. The Nutcracker Peanut and Gift Shop, also in Suffolk, is inside the Producers Peanut Co. peanut butter plant at 337 Moore Ave. (539-7496). It sells peanut products in gift packages and has a mail-order business.

For hams try the Old Virginia Ham Shop, 217 E. Little Creek Rd., Norfolk (583-0014). This shop looks like a red barn and is in the Wards Corner area. In Suffolk the Pruden Packing Co. at 1201 N. Main St. (539-6261) has a retail shop that sells hams cured in the plant.

One delightful place is Rowena's at 758 W. 22nd St. in Norfolk (627-8699). This Ghent business has gained international acclaim for its homemade pound cakes -- especially when topped with Rowena's lemon curd sauce. Rowena's sells an innovative line of jams, sauces and other tasty food products. The business is run by its founder Rowena Fullinwider, and her products are made right here. For many locals Rowena's is their first stop for out-of-town holiday presents.

Another culinary treat is coffee from the First Colony Coffee House at 2000-1 Colonial Ave. in Norfolk. All types of gourmet coffee is roasted in a Norfolk plant built in 1902 (622-0149).

Insiders' Tips

Boy...all outlets with savings up to 70% off retail. Country and western folk will go ga-ga in the Acme Boot Outlet, and you can snag a sexy slip or nightie at Bare Necessities. Connected to the Mall is B.J.'s Wholesale Club, packed to the unadorned rafters with everything from toys to computers, books to power tools and lots of food in between. While you do have to be a member to get the very best lowest price, guests can get a pass to wheel a cart through the aisles, and pay just 5% over the marked price. Those with a foot fetish should check out Lottie's in the small strip center in front of the Mall. They've got in-style designer shoes for men and women at can't-pass-up reduced prices.

HILLTOP SHOPPING CENTER
Laskin and First Colonial roads

Covering the compass points, there's Hilltop East, North, West and South. Each is a fine collection of stores, restaurants and specialty shops that cater to the Beach's picky residents and our many resort guests. Not to pass-by places include Dan Ryan's for Men, Barnett's Lighting and Gifts, Lily's Fashions and Penn's for luggage, handbags and gifts. Blue Ridge Mountain Sports is a great place for rugged outdoor wear, and The Dolling Toy Shop is teddy bear heaven. Along with popular Shoney's and Morrison's Cafeteria, try out Bella Monte and Taste Unlimited on the food trail. Just across the street is the place for all you K Mart shoppers, along with grocery stores and drug chains.

LA PROMENADE
1860 Laskin Road

This is one center of distinctive shops where the shoppers look as rich as the merchandise offered. From the exquisite linens at Arcana to designer fashions at Madison (Anne Klein, Donna Karan, Michael Kors, DKNY and others), you can pop from one boutique to another just swooning over the lushness of it all. There's NYFO and Dakota for exceptional women's clothing, Suzanne Jacobson Stationary for fine writing papers, along with Facets Jewelry, Kids Kids Kids, Victorian Charm, My Doll House and Talbots. For sophisticated dining that matches the upscale taste of the center, slip into Aldo's Ristorante for some designer pasta.

REGENCY HILLTOP
1900 Laskin Road

If you have any pennies left over from La Promenade, head a short hop down the road to the bargain shopping at Regency Hilltop. Here's off-price heaven, with Burlington Coat Factory, Dress Barn, Leeward's Arts and Crafts, Only One Dollar, Phar-Mor, Tracks Music & Video and Rack Room Shoes. Satisfy the hungries in the popular Old Country Buffet or at Sal's Italian Restaurant.

LOEHMANN'S PLAZA
4000 Virginia Beach Boulevard

World famous Loehmann's is center stage at this plaza that also tempts you with two Lillian Vernon Outlet Stores, Linens & Things, Marc Lance Mens, the Baby Superstore and the mega Herman's World of Sporting Goods. Egghead Software is also here for you computer nerds, and home decorators will go zonkers in Calico Corners with their huge selection of decorator fabrics and trims. Not to go hungry, you can slide into Arty's Deli or really pig out at Rockola Cafe.

Chesapeake

GREENBRIER MALL
Greenbrier Parkway

Rising like a modern monument on a huge berm is Greenbrier Mall, where Chesapeake shoppers travel to spend their paychecks. Run amuck through two levels of temptation, with popular anchors, Sears and Leggett. On the top level of the mall is a particularly inviting food court, with your choice of pizza, Chinese or good old American hamburger. Right across the street is Crossways Shopping Center. There's good bargain hunting here with Marshall's and the Rack Room, along with Builder's Square for the home fixer-upper. In between the two shopping meccas is a great place to grab a hearty meal and a brewsky...Cheers. It's real pub-like forest green and brass, and the servers are some of the most obliging in the area.

CHESAPEAKE SQUARE
Portsmouth Boulevard and Taylor Road

Our newest mall, Chesapeake Square grew out of a far-away pasture and suddenly traffic was ferocious. Sparkling new, modern and spit-polished, it's a replay of your favorite places, like anchors Leggett,

Montgomery Ward and JC Penney. Inside are the book stores you expect to find, plus some special places like Tuerkes Luggage, American Eagle Outfitters, Sea Dream Leather and Ingle's Nook (super kitchen stuff). If you're feeling a little frisky, there's a Frederick's of Hollywood and to pull you back home to earth, there's Country Seat, home of the Levis. A brand new Limited and Limited Express cover a zillion square feet. There's little way you won't find everything you like here, but if not, pop across the street to The Crossroads and run amuck in TJ Maxx, Circuit City and Wal Mart.

Portsmouth

TOWER MALL
Airline Boulevard

This is an older mall that's holding its own, especially with Portsmouth residents. It's a friendly sort of place that's usually pretty quiet except on payday weekends, so if you seriously need to have a mall-fix, it's a recommended destination. Quite a few stores have come and gone since it's inception, but still going strong are Montgomery Ward outlet store, Waldenbooks and World Bazaar, a hodge-podge of imported wicker and inexpensive china. The movies are here, too, and that brings a lot of folks out just before and after showtime.

Suffolk

Suffolk maintains a traditional downtown whose ongoing Main Street revitalization program is giving a facelift to the city's storefronts.

There is plenty of metered parking along downtown streets so get out of your car and go for a stroll. There are several upscale clothing and shoe stores downtown. Denison's at 177 N. Main specializes in women's clothing. Holmes Ltd. at 139 N. Main sells both women's clothing and shoes while The Shoetique at 147 N. Main is strictly a shoe store. G.S. Hobbs Ltd. at 126 N. Main specializes in men's clothing.

If you're ready for a coffee break you'll find two busy soda fountains on Main Street that turn out old-fashioned milk shakes, lemonade and grilled cheese sandwiches. Try either the counter at the Nansemond Drug Co. at 115 N. Main or the one at the Woolworth's at 134 N. Main. You may also want to stop by Ye Ole Pastry Shop at 153 W. Washington St. for a treat or pick up some peanuts fresh from the antique roaster at the Planters Peanut Center at 308 W. Washington.

There are no malls in Suffolk but there are several shopping centers with grocery stores, discount stores and smaller businesses. You'll find them on Holland Road, Constance Road and on North Main Street.

Specialty Shops

While you'll find a good variety in the region's malls and shopping centers, there are plenty of other jewels waiting to be discovered on side streets and specialty shops. We love to wander through antique stores, used book shops and other out-of-the-way spots when we visit other cities. We've included some tidbits about some of our favorite places here at home. Have fun exploring them.

Antiques

There are numerous small shops to tempt you if you're interested in antique furniture, glassware and bric-a-brac. In fact, there are more than 125 dealers in the region and several flea markets or antique malls with multiple vendors. Shops range from those filled with rare antiques to the ones selling the Mrs. Butterworth bottle you unloaded at your last garage sale. The thrill of antiquing is in the hunt for that perfect oak filing cabinet or piece of Depression glass, so grab your checkbook and start prowling around.

Since we can't cover all the shops, we'll steer you in the direction of areas that have a concentration of stores. That way you can hit a bunch of shops on the same trip. For other suggestions check the Yellow Pages. *The Virginian-Pilot/Led-ger-Stars's* classified sections are the place to watch if you are interested in auctions and estate sales. For household goods, baby furniture, antiques and just about anything else you want, buy a copy of the *Trading Post*. The shopper is published each week and is filled with merchandise for sale by private owners.

In Norfolk one must-see area for antiques is along 21st Street between Manteo and Granby and in the 2600 block of Granby Street. There are about 25 antique shops in Norfolk, and the bulk of them are along these two streets. You'll need to drive from 21st Street to Granby Street since its antique district is across the railroad tracks. The merchants have produced a brochure on antique shops in Norfolk so try to pick up a copy to guide you.

Some shops you may want to check out are the Norfolk Antique Company at 537 W. 21st St. (627-6199), the Palace Antiques Gallery at 21st and Lewellyn (622-2733) and the Ghent Antiques Consignment Emporium at 110 W. 21st (627-1900). All have several dealers in them.

One of the neatest things about living here is that you can still get fresh milk delivered to your door in glass bottles. This little perk makes us feel like we're living in an Ozzie and Harriet family. Both Bergey's Dairy Farm (482-4711) and Yoder Dairies have home delivery (497-3518) to many neighborhoods.

Insiders' Tips

There also are dealers on Colonial Avenue and in the Freemason area of the city. Nero's Antiques & Appraisals at 1101 Colonial Ave. (627-1111) bills itself as Ghent's oldest antique shop.

In Chesapeake, you'll want to hit the shops along Canal Drive. To get there take Military Highway south and go for miles. There are several shops along Military Highway you may want to plunder along the way. By the time you cross over the Gilmerton Bridge you'll be convinced you're hopelessly lost. Keep going, and you'll find shop after shop that has been doing business for years. Most are in the 900 block of Canal Drive. One place to stop is Strick's Auction Center at 917 Canal Dr. (487-5925), which has a small antique mall with about 10 dealers.

In Virginia Beach, there are several large dealers. British-European Antique Importers Ltd. (491-1001) is near the oceanfront at 606 Norfolk Ave. It has a 10,000-square-foot warehouse. Eddie's Antique Mall (486-0702) at 3352 Virginia Beach Blvd. is a large operation in the Celebration Station. This former outlet mall has numerous antique and flea-market vendors in it. On weekends the parking lot is filled with fair-weather vendors. Shomiers at 3205 Virginia Beach Blvd. (340-3385) has an interesting mix of antiques and reproductions.

Portsmouth has the Airline Flea Fair at Airline Boulevard and Greenwood Drive. This is definitely more flea market than antique mall but there are some vendors here with old records, vintage clothes, glassware and furniture. You may have to hunt through lots of junk to find the gems, but we've managed to scarf up some fun '40s clothes and a few collectibles here at good prices.

Suffolk has one of our favorite places to buy antiques – one we like so much we hesitate to tell you about. This is the Village Auction Barn at 101 Philhower Dr. It is on the outskirts of Suffolk as you drive into town, but it's easy to miss so call for directions (539-6296). The barn holds an auction every Saturday night that draws dealers as well as regular folks. Some weeks feature estate sales, but about twice a month veteran auctioneer Dewey Howell hauls in a load of furniture and goods from England. These English nights are the prime time to be at the auction barn, especially if you're in the market for oak furniture. Check the classifieds in the newspaper for specifics. Prepare to spend the evening at the barn and eat a sandwich and homemade dessert from the cafe. The auction barn also has a small antique mall.

There are several dealers scattered throughout Suffolk. One place to start is downtown at The Attic Trunk at 167 S. Main (934-0882). Nansemond Antique Shop at 3537 Pruden Blvd. on the outskirts of town is another possibility (539-6269).

Used Bookstores

Part of the joy in shopping in these stores is never knowing what you'll find – a cherished book from your childhood, a rare volume of poetry or a spellbinding novel for the beach. Here are some of the used bookstores we frequent:

*The Bibliopath Bookshop & Bindery, 251 W. Bute St., Norfolk (622-2665). Owners H.L. and Linda Wilson maintain one of the region's best-stocked stores. Their inventory runs from the classics to military history and paperback westerns. Besides used and out-of-print books they also sell records, CDs and tapes and do bookbinding and appraisals. Be sure to look for Wallaby and the Great Catsby, the resident cats, when you visit this Freemason area store. The Wilsons have been in this location since 1988 and previously ran another Norfolk book shop.

*A Likely Story, 738 W. 22nd St., #6, Norfolk (627-7323). Located in a small shopping center in Ghent, this tidy shop has a good selection of old children's books as well as the classics and maritime subjects. There also is a section devoted to Virginia and Norfolk. Owner Beverly McGhee runs the region's only search service, which can help you locate that hard-to-find book.

*Beacon Books of Ghent, Harrington Street and Colley Avenue, Norfolk (623-5641). This small book shop opened in 1992. It is packed with mostly nonfiction and technical books.

*Jolly Rogue's Bookshop, Kemps River Crossing Shopping Center, Virginia Beach (366-8702). Opened in 1992 along busy Indian River Road near CBN, Jolly Rogue's features all kinds of Americana. Calico Jack, the resident parrot, entertains with a limited vocabulary.

*Octavo Books, 1645 Laskin Road, Virginia Beach (491-6723). You'll find the general classics and much more in this store in the Hilltop area.

*Great Bridge Books, 404 Woodford Dr., Chesapeake (482-1666). Located in an old house in the Great Bridge area since 1975, this shop features a good selection of Virginiana, literature and children's books.

New Bookstores

In addition to the usual national chains, there are local stores with great selections run by people who adore books. Two of the largest general book stores are J.M. Prince in Norfolk's Selden Arcade (622-9223) and Turn the Page at 331 W. 21st St. in Norfolk (623-3030). The best variety of children's books is at Once Upon a Time in The Willis Wayside shopping center at 4220 Virginia Beach Blvd. (498-4111). In Virginia Beach, Riverbend Books' eclectic selection appeals to public radio fans as well as children and other readers. The shop is in the Great Neck Village Shopping Center on Great Neck Road (496-2758). For religious books try Dolphin Tales at 2955 Virginia Beach Blvd. (498-7909) or Dudley's Christian Books. Dudley's has two locations: 7501 Granby St. in Norfolk (423-7456) and 4314 Virginia Beach Blvd. in Virginia Beach (340-8581).

Gourmet and Wine Shops

All-purpose gourmet shops let you pick up unusual spices, grab a sandwich and select a special wine. Stores to visit include Grape & Grain, The West Side Wine Shop and Taste Unlimited. Grape & Grain is at 2973 Shore Dr. in Virginia Beach (481-5958). West Side Wine is at 4702 Hampton Blvd. in Norfolk (440-7600). There are four Taste Unlimiteds. The Norfolk location is in Ghent at 1619 Colley Ave. (623-7770). Virginia Beach shops are at 638 Hilltop West (425-1858), 36th & Pacific (422-3399) and 4097 Shore Dr. (464-1566).

Although you'll find plenty of wines and beers in grocery stores,

for a more adventuresome selection check out the stock in specialty shops. Be sure to sample some of the Virginia wines that are gaining national acclaim. East of Napa, 2224 Virginia Beach (463-0212), specializes in domestic wines. Other good selections are at Reisner's Delicatessen in the Janaf Shopping Center in Norfolk (461-8548) and in Virginia Beach at PJ Baggan, a gourmet sandwich and wine shop at 4001 Virginia Beach Blvd. (498-4748) and at Bella Monte Gourmet Italian Marketplace & Cafe, 134 Hilltop East (425-6290).

Health Foods

If you long for tofu, organic tomatoes and fresh cilantro you'll find several health food stores. The largest in Norfolk is the Whole Foods Co-Op at 119 W. 21st St. in Ghent (626-1051). The co-op, which has more than 400 members, started in 1973. You don't have to be a member to shop there, but you'll get a discount if you join.

There is a good selection of bulk grains, nuts and seeds. You'll also find olive oil and tahini for Mediterranean cooking. There are more than 200 fresh spices and herbs and many foods for diabetics and others needing special diets.

The biggest shop in Virginia Beach is Heritage Health Food Store at 314 Laskin Rd. (428-0500). It has been in business since the late '70s. There is a big selection of organic and health foods. The store has the region's only organic deli, which features all wheat-free and sugar-free products. Affiliated businesses include a bookstore and holistic health services.

Consignment Stores

Since becoming a parent, used-clothing stores have become our favorite haunt. Besides snaring some terrific duds for our fast-growing child, we've also picked up some designer labels for ourself. To get the bargains, you need to frequent the shops, be open-minded about what you're looking for and have an eye for quality. There are plenty of wealthy people in the region with expensive cast-offs that have hardly been worn. These shops are the perfect places to snare special-occasion clothes. Here are some of our best shopping spots.

*The White Rabbitt, 310 W. 21st St., Norfolk (627-4169), has all kinds of children's clothes. Its women's section also is worth checking out. This Ghent shop is a great place to buy gifts since it features jewelry and crafts created by local artists.

*Banbury Cross, 738 W. 22nd St., Norfolk (625-8372), has both new and gently used children's clothes. You'll find some delightful smocked outfits among the new clothes.

*Act II, 816 A 21st St., Norfolk (622-1533) and 3411 Virginia Beach Blvd., Virginia Beach (486-6734). These shops are run by the Organization Through Rehabilitation and Training (ORT). Act II specializes in women's clothes and has a big selection of party clothes.

*Deja-Vu, 4604 Pembroke Lake Circle, Virginia Beach (671-1692), has mostly designer women's clothes with a few things available for children and men. There are furs, evening wear, bridal gowns, work clothes and shoes in here.

*Sand Bucket, 3006 Arctic Ave., Virginia Beach (425-6016), specializes in quality children's clothes and accessories.

*Elephants Galore, 3900 Bonney Road, Virginia Beach (463-2823), is a two-story store with a little bit of everything – baby items, furniture and lots of clothes for the entire family.

* 2nd Time Around, 3772 Virginia Beach Blvd., Virginia Beach (498-3927), has clothes for adults and children as well as a good selection of jewelry. There's usually a variety of party clothes.

*Things Unlimited, 501 Virginia Beach Blvd., Virginia Beach (428-7841), is a big store with all kinds of clothes and household goods. It has a wonderful costume department that does a big business before Halloween. Proceeds benefit the Virginia Beach Friends School.

*Encore Consignment Department Store, 3535 Virginia Beach Blvd., Virginia Beach (431-6941). This two-story shop has men's and women's clothes, jewelry, furniture, books and household goods.

*Side Show, 1414 Colley Ave., Norfolk (625-2264) has both vintage and newer clothes for women and men. It also has a lot of unusual jewelry and accessories.

*Echoes of Time, 320B Laskin Rd., Virginia Beach (428-2332) is strictly a vintage clothing store with garments and jewelry from the 1800s to the 1950s.

In addition to these shops, you can find bargains among goods donated to local charities that operate thrift shops. Many organizations have loyal supporters who would rather give away their old stuff than sell it. There are five Children's Hospital of The King's Daughters Thrift Stores, five Goodwill stores, three Salvation Army stores, three Union Mission stores, two Hope House Foundation shops, one Disabled American Veteran store and one Trinity Mission shop.

Collectible Shops

We have friends always on the prowl for that special baseball card, comic book or old record. Here are a few suggestions for them.

Baseball card and comic book collectors will find about 40 shops listed in the Yellow Pages. Some places to check out include:

*Emerald City, 748 Shirley Ave, Norfolk. (627-2489) Opened in 1992, this shop quickly gained a reputation for its collectible sports cards and comic books. It is on a side street in Ghent near a laundry so you may have to hunt for it.

*Trilogy Comics, 857 Lynnhaven Rd. and 5773 Princess Anne Rd., Virginia Beach (468-0412, 490-2205), 700 E. Little Creek Dr., Norfolk (587-2540) and 3916 Portsmouth Blvd., Chesapeake (488-6578). This local chain of comic book stores also has a booth at the Airline Flea Fair in Portsmouth at 3535 Airline Blvd. Besides comics, Trilogy sells baseball cards, games and science fiction merchandise.

*Comics & Things, Holland Plaza Shopping Center, Virginia Beach (486-5870) sells new and collectible comics, collector cards, Star Trek items and related paraphernalia.

*D&D Sports Cards, 5660 D Portsmouth Blvd., Portsmouth (488-4961) sells new and used cards.

*Home Run Sports Cards, 2148 Great Neck Square Shopping Center and 981 Providence Square Shopping Center, Virginia Beach (496-2220, 461-2220) has a large selection of all types of sports cards.

*Downtown Sports Cards, 425 W. Washington St., Suffolk (539-1144) sells collector cards and is only open Wednesday-Saturday.

For collectible records, rummage through the oldies but goodies at Skinnies Records & Tapes at 814 W. 21st St. in Norfolk's Ghent area (622-2241) and Electric Smiles at 101 S. Witchduck Rd. in Virginia Beach (456-0695).

You'll find more than 30 shops specializing in new compact discs and tapes. The largest is Tracks Record Bar with seven locations, including Lynnhaven Mall, Greenbrier Mall and the outskirts of Military Mall. For jazz try Birdland Records Tapes & Compact Discs at 957 Providence Rd., Virginia Beach (495-0961). For folk, bluegrass and Scottish and Irish music the place to go is Ramblin' Conrad's Guitar Shop at 871 N. Military Hwy., Norfolk (461-3655).

Quilt Shops

This is a big interest of ours, and we love to search these shops for the perfect fabric to add to our stash at home. There are some well-respected shops here. All are well stocked, offer excellent classes and have helpful staffs.

*What's Your Stitch 'n Stuff at 4249-B Little Creek Rd., Norfolk (583-5219) is our favorite places for fabric and supplies. It's in Little Creek East shopping center at the intersection of Little Creek and Shore Drive.

*Quilt Works at 3101 Virginia Beach Blvd., Virginia Beach (463-4843) is one of the most established shops and has a full line of supplies and fabrics. It's in the Rose Hall Shops.

*Sis 'n Me, 5941 Churchland Blvd., Portsmouth (484-2647) is just off High Street. However, you may get turned around trying to find this cozy shop so call for directions. It sells fabric and all types of supplies.

*Quilt With Me Inc., 5350 Kemps River Dr., Virginia Beach (424-6345) is a full-service shop behind the Kemps River Crossing Shopping Center near CBN.

*Fabric Hut, 3520 N. Military Hwy., Norfolk (853-4609). This shop has the region's best selection of all kinds of fabric – from wools to bridal satin. It maintains a fully stocked quilting department.

Just for Children

Although you'll find several Toys R Us and Kids R Us outlets here, you may want to shop at some specialty toy and children's clothing stores. One favorite place is The Dolling Toy Shop at 761-A Boush St. in Norfolk (627-3319) and 1556 Laskin Rd. in Virginia Beach (425-5617). The shops sell educational but fun toys and some exquisite dolls. The Dolling Shop owner also is the regional expert on doll repair and appraisals.

Other fun toy stores include England's Dolls & Toys at 4355 Portsmouth Blvd. in Portsmouth (488-3655) and 701-C N. Battlefield Blvd. in Chesapeake (548-2999), and the Teachers & Parents Store in Loehmann's Plaza and Kemps River Crossing Shopping Center in Virginia Beach (463-1068, 523-0296). The biggest selection of stuffed animals is at the Embraceable Zoo in The Waterside in Norfolk (625-4360) while the best toy train selection is at Mike's Trainland at 5661 Shoulder Hill Rd. in Suffolk (484-4224). Tomorrow's World, an environmental store at 5978 E. Virginia Beach Blvd. in Norfolk, has some unusual games and toys with an ecological slant (461-4739). Lynnhaven Mall has become a hot spot since it recently added a Disney Store (486-3188).

Our child's dream merchants are the dollar stores where his buck from Grandma will buy anything from earrings for mom's birthday to a bag of plastic cowboys and Indians. There are two different dollar store chains in area malls and shopping centers – Everything's A Dollar and Dollar Tree. Both have gone national after getting their start in Hampton Roads.

There are more than 20 specialty clothing shops for children. Some to check out are: The Zoo at 1900 Colley Ave. in Norfolk (627-4192), Kids Kids Kids at 222 W. 21st St. in Norfolk and 1860 Laskin Rd. in Virginia Beach (622-4760, 422-0101), Honey Tree for Children at 4218 Virginia Beach Blvd. and 1043 Independence Blvd. in Virginia Beach (498-4797, 464-0504) and Evelyn's Small World in the Suffolk Shopping Center (934-7784). Kid's Wearhouse at the Great American Outlet Mall in Virginia Beach has a good selection and reasonable prices (498-3705). Of area department stores, Upton's has the best-stocked children's department.

For shoes for growing feet, we rely on Hirschler's Shoe Stores, which have been around since the '40s. Stores are at 7534 Granby St. in Norfolk (587-5581) and Providence Square Shopping Center in Virginia Beach (495-0967).

Unusual Stores

Two unusual stores we've never seen anywhere else are Grande Junquetion and Wine & Cake Hobbies. Both are fun to wander through and are the favorite places for many hobbyists.

Grande Junquetion, 100 S. Lynn Shores Dr. in Virginia Beach, is the kind of place that defies description. People who like to tinker with projects love this surplus store crammed with all kinds of gadgets, tools and electronic equipment. The merchandise is unpredictable and comes mostly from military surplus and bankrupt businesses. The store is just off Virginia Beach Blvd. (498-0404).

We're still amazed that wine-making and cake decorating are big enough hobbies to justify this huge store. But it's a busy place stocked with every type of cake pan and decorating paraphernalia as well as everything you need to make wine. There's also a large party supply department. Wine & Cake Hobbies is at 6527 Tidewater Dr. in Norfolk. The road curves around a viaduct at this point so call for directions (857-0245).

Photo: Virginia Division of Tourism

The Norwegian Lady, a bronze statue donated by the people of Moss, Norway, is a landmark paying tribute to the Norwegian ship "Dictator" which sank in a storm off what is now Virginia Beach in 1891 — and to the local lifesaving crew, which managed to save 10 sailors.

LIGHTS.
CAMERA. ACTION.

Join our studio audience for a *700 Club* production, and you'll see just what it takes to put a television show on the air. And if our cameras should single you out, you may even find yourself on national TV.

Whatever day you come, our lineup may include special guests from around the world, interviews with the latest newsmakers, and one-of-a-kind features. Plus, you'll get to see hosts Pat Robertson and Ben Kinchlow in action. This popular and enduring TV team combines Pat's nationally-recognized news perspective with Ben's compassionate behind-the-news look at human drama. After the show, you can go on a tour of our studio complex, the elegant Founders Inn and Conference Center, and the lovely Regent University campus and library. Last, but not least, you can join us for a modestly priced lunch.

Don't miss this chance to get in on the action. For show, tour and lunch reservations, call 804-523-7123.

CBN Center, I-64 and East Indian River Road, Virginia Beach, VA 23464

Inside
Attractions

*T*here is so much to do in Hampton Roads that you can live here for years and never get to everything. But there are three good ways to get motivated to take in all the varied attractions:

*Be a tourist determined to make the most of your visit.

*Be a new resident eager to explore your new environs.

*Have out-of-town visitors.

We're long past relying on the first two excuses, so we're always grateful to have guests come and get us out of our rut. If you need a stash of brochures about area attractions there are several places to check. The Hampton Roads Chamber of Commerce, which has offices in each city, has some pamphlets. But for the best selections, contact city convention and visitor bureaus.

For information on Norfolk call the Norfolk Convention & Visitors Bureau and order a visitor's guide (1-800-368-3097). Once in town, there are several places to pick up information:

*Norfolk's Convention & Visitor's Bureau is downtown at 236 E. Plume St. It is open from 8:30 AM to 5PM Monday through Friday. (441-5266)

*The Bureau operates a Visitor Information Center just off Interstate 64 (exit 273) in the Ocean View area. It is open from 9 AM to 5 PM daily (441-1852). It has brochures, a staff to answer questions and a hotel reservation service.

*The Bureau also runs an information center downtown in The Waterside festival marketplace. For years it has been in a kiosk on the second floor. This spring the center is scheduled to move downstairs to a storefront that will give it more space.

To learn more about Virginia Beach call 1-800-VABEACH and order a visitor's packet of information. If you're in the city and want immediate information, stop by the Visitor Information Center at 2100 Parks Ave. (437-4888). You can't miss it if you are entering the city on the Virginia Beach-Norfolk Expressway (Route 44) since the center sits in the middle of the divided road. The center, operated by the city's Department of Convention and Visitor Development, opened in 1990 as a gateway to the resort. It is open 9 AM to 5 PM daily with longer hours during the summer. Besides having a staff to answer questions and hundreds of brochures, the center has a short video to watch. It also can help with hotel reservations.

For information on Portsmouth call the Portsmouth Convention and Visitors Bureau at 1-800-338-8822 or 393-8481. To pick up brochures check the Portside Visitor Center on the banks of the Elizabeth River in downtown. It is operated by the tourism bureau at the corner of Water Street and North Street. It is open from 9:30 AM to 5:30 PM daily (393-5111). Information also is available weekdays from 8:30 AM to 5 PM at the city tourism bureau in the city hall complex at 801 Crawford Street, third floor.

Neither Suffolk or Chesapeake has tourism bureaus. Your best bets are to contact local Hampton Roads Chamber of Commerce offices. They are at 1001 W. Washington St. in Suffolk (539-2111) and

400 Volvo Parkway in Chesapeake (547-2118).

Museums

Norfolk

THE CHRYSLER MUSEUM
245 W. Olney Rd.   622-1211
Hours: Tuesday-Saturday, 10 AM-4PM; Sunday, 1-5 PM
Admission: Free with $3 donation suggested

This is the region's premier art museum. With more than 30,000 pieces from every time period, this museum is considered one of the top 20 art museums in the country. The Chrysler's 8,000-piece glass collection is one of the world's largest. Holdings include works by Renoir, Matisse and Gauguin. (For detailed information see the Arts section.)

HAMPTON ROADS NAVAL MUSEUM
Norfolk Naval Base
Pennsylvania House   **444-3827**
Hours: 9 AM-4 PM daily
Admission: Free

This museum focuses on more than 200 years of naval activity in the Hampton Roads harbor. Its collection includes ship models, artwork and artifacts retrieved from sunken ships. Exhibits cover the 1781 Battle off the Virginia Capes as well as the Civil War and today's nuclear Navy. There is a research library on the region's naval history that is open by appointment.

By spring 1994 the museum will have moved its holdings to the National Maritime Center (NAUTICUS) now under construction in downtown Norfolk. Until then it remains housed at Norfolk Naval Base in the historic Pennsylvania House, which was built for the 1906 Jamestown Exhibition. Getting on base requires a Department of Defense sticker on your car or a visitor's pass from the base's Tour and Information Center at 9808 Hampton Blvd. (adjacent to Gate 5). The museum also is a stop on Tidewater Regional Transit's Norfolk Naval Base Tour.

THE DOUGLAS MACARTHUR MEMORIAL
MacArthur Square   **441-2965**
Hours: 10 AM-5 PM Monday-Saturday; 11 AM-5 PM Sunday
Admission: Free

This is the burial spot for Gen. Douglas MacArthur, whose main link with Norfolk was that it was his mother's childhood home. Since 1964 the museum's extensive holdings have detailed the life of the famous general. It is in downtown Norfolk on the corner of Bank Street and City Hall Avenue. The main building was Norfolk's 19th-century courthouse. There are three other buildings on the grounds, including a library, gift shop and theater.

To begin your visit, stop in the theater building to see a 22-minute film on MacArthur that features newsreel footage. Inside the main building, the first thing you will see is MacArthur's resting spot in the rotunda. There are 11 galleries on two floors that take MacArthur's life from boyhood to his glory years as General of the Army. Don't miss the gift shop outside. That's where MacArthur's gleaming 1950 Chrysler Imperial limousine is displayed. Out front of the memorial is a bronze statue of the general that is a popular photo spot.

THE NATIONAL MARITIME CENTER (NAUTICUS)
One Waterside Drive   **623-9084**
Opening: Spring 1994
Admission: Adults, $8.25; Children 4-11, $5.50

This attraction is so new it isn't finished. But as it rises upon a pier along the Elizabeth River in downtown Norfolk, word is spreading that NAUTICUS will be something special. This public-private endeavor is a $52 million project whose goal is to be Norfolk's No. 1 attraction.

Nauticus will be a three-level, 120,000-square-foot structure that looks like a hybrid aircraft carrier/

futuristic ship. The center will explore maritime technology through innovative exhibits being designed by a company that helped shape Disney's Epcot Center. Visitors will be able to watch a storm arrive in the Hurricane Theatre, observe a marine biology laboratory and visit a life-sized oil drilling rig.

The entire Hampton Roads Naval Museum will move to NAUTICUS, which also will have a movie theater. Outside the center, research and Navy ships will dock so visitors can come on board.

Virginia Beach

LIFE-SAVING MUSEUM OF VIRGINIA
24th Street & Oceanfront   422-1587
Hours: Tuesday-Saturday, 10 AM-5 PM; Sunday, Noon-5 PM. Open Mondays during the summer with longer daily hours
Admission: Free

The museum is housed in a former U.S. Life-Saving/Coast Guard Station built in 1903. The simple clapboard structure gives a hint of simpler pre-condo days at the oceanfront. Two galleries highlight the history of those who risked their lives to save others during shipwrecks. A permanent display focuses on the impact of World War I and II on Virginia Beach.

ROYAL LONDON WAX MUSEUM
1606 Atlantic Ave.   425-3823
Hours: Open daily in summer and on weekends in fall and spring

This museum has been around for about a decade but changed owners in late 1992. Admission is charged, but at press time the museum's new owners had not finalized the amount. The museum's 100 wax figures range from the Beatles and Pinnochio to Dr. Martin Luther King Jr. and Joan of Arc. There also is a chamber of horrors that is easy to avoid if you're squeamish or have children with you.

VIRGINIA MARINE SCIENCE MUSEUM
717 General Booth Blvd. 437-4949 or 425-FISH
Hours: 9 AM-5PM off season; longer hours during summer
Admission: $4.25, $3.50 for children

This is one of the most popular museums in Virginia, and its ever-changing exhibits keep local residents coming back. The native fish swimming in the museum's 50,000-gallon aquarium mesmerize all ages. There are 60 hands-on exhibits exploring Virginia marine life that let visitors tong for oysters or create waves. Children especially like the touch-tank where they can get their hands on crabs, turtles and starfish with the help of museum docents. The museum frequently features a decoy carver and other demonstrations. Outside, a boardwalk takes you on a peaceful walk through a salt marsh. Educational boat trips are featured occasionally, and reservations fill up fast. In 1992 the museum took more than 5,000 people whale watching off the coast.

Popular activities include SCUBA demonstrations at 11 AM on Saturdays, Sundays and holidays, fish feedings at 10 AM and 3 PM and an interpreted marsh walk at 11:30 AM daily.

DISCOVERY YACHT CRUISES

⚓ Sightseeing Cruises
⚓ Lunch Cruises
⚓ Dinner Cruises
⚓ Bar Service Available on all Cruises
⚓ We Cruise Rain or Shine!

Come cruise on our 80', climate-controlled luxury yacht Discovery. Our 2 - 2 1/2 hour tour will take you by many local points of interest en route to the Lynnhaven Inlet and then back to Browning's Landing.

Advanced Reservations Required:
491-8090 • 422-2900

DEEP SEA FISHING
SIGHTSEEING
Ocean Front Cruise
Full and Half Day Trips - Year Round

VA. BEACH FISHING CENTER
Rudee Inlet on the Oceanfront
422-5700

See our coupon in back of book.

Portsmouth

AUTOMOBILE MUSEUM OF HAMPTON ROADS

3535 Airline Blvd.   *465-0533*
Hours: 10 AM-6 PM daily
Admission: $3.50, $2.75 for children 6 and up

Don't be put off by this museum's odd location. It shares a building with the Airline Flea Fair flea market. Inside are more than 50 vintage automobiles and a variety of automobile memorabilia such as license plates and advertisements. The restored cars represent all eras of the automobile industry and are displayed so that visitors can get a good look at the interiors.

CHILDREN'S MUSEUM OF VIRGINIA

High and Court streets   *393-8393*
Hours: 10 AM-5 PM Tuesday-Saturday; 1-5 PM Sunday
Admission: $1.50, which includes two other museums

Although it has less than 3,000 square feet, this charming museum attracts 60,000 visitors a year – one of the country's highest ratios of visitors per square foot. By April 1994 the museum, which formerly was called the Portsmouth Children's Museum, will relocate to an abandoned department store down the street. There it will have 27,000 square feet that will include 14 major displays. The current museum has three main displays – a bubble room, a make-believe room where children can dress up, and a Lego room filled with building blocks. Late afternoons are ideal times to avoid the crowds at the museum, which is housed in Portsmouth's historic 1846 Courthouse.

A ticket also buys you admission to two other city-owned museums – the Lightship Museum and the Portsmouth Naval Shipyard Museum – as well as the Arts Center of the Portsmouth Museums that is in the same building.

Popular programs at the museum include Wonderful Wednesdays – hour-long morning programs starting at 10 AM. They cost $1 a child and include such topics as Pizza Fun Time and Meet Mr. Fireman. Special workshops are held on some Saturday mornings. Call 393-8983 for information on either program.

LIGHTSHIP MUSEUM

Water Street and London Blvd.   *393-8741*
Hours: 10 AM-5 PM Tuesday-Saturday; 1-5 PM Sunday
Admission: $1.50, which includes two other museums

This is a restored lightship that was commissioned in 1915 to help mariners navigate through treacherous waters. It was once anchored at strategic locations to guide ships. Today it's a tourist attraction on the banks of the Elizabeth River. In 1989 the lightship became Portsmouth's second National Historic Landmark. The bright red ship has been restored to its early 20th-century appearance and includes the captain's quarters, officer's head and officer's mess. Ticket holders also can visit the Children's Museum of Virginia and the Portsmouth Naval Shipyard Museum on the same day with no extra charge.

PORTSMOUTH NAVAL SHIPYARD MUSEUM

2 High St.   393-8591
Hours: 10 AM-5 PM Tuesday-Saturday; 1-5 PM Sunday
Admission: $1.50, which includes two other museums

Housed in an old machine shop for the Portsmouth-Norfolk ferry, the museum pays tribute to the Norfolk Naval Shipyard. The government-owned shipyard, which is in Portsmouth, is the oldest shipyard in the country. The museum displays models of ships constructed at the yard as well as uniforms, swords, cannon balls and other memorabilia. The museum, which was founded in 1949, also has a piece of the USS *Merrimac*, which was built at the yard and had its historic battle with the *Monitor* in nearby waters. Ticket holders also can visit the Children's Museum of Virginia and Lightship Museum.

Suffolk

LANCASTER TRAIN AND TOY MUSEUM

5661 Shoulder Hill Rd.   484-4224
Hours: 10 AM-6 PM daily; 10AM-9 PM November-December 24
Admission: Donation

This museum is part of Mike's Trainland, one of Virginia's biggest model railroad stores. Mike's opened in 1983 and bills itself as the largest combined museum and train shop between Pennsylvania and Florida. The museum showcases the collection of A.J. Lancaster, an area nursery owner and train buff. It includes the mid-Atlantic's largest indoor Gauge 1 layout. It

also features Lionel, LGB and other trains in various gauges. Both children and adults are fascinated by the elaborate train displays as well as numerous Buddy L trucks and antique tin mechanical toys.

The museum is in the country on the outskirts of Suffolk and is close to Portsmouth. Call for directions.

THE SUFFOLK MUSEUM

118 Bosley Ave.   925-6311
Hours: 10 AM-5 PM Tuesday-Saturday; 1-5 PM Sunday
Admission: Free

The city-owned museum is housed in a former library near downtown. It opened in 1986 to emphasize art and features changing exhibits. Some are created by regional artists. Others are traveling exhibits from the Virginia Museum of Fine Arts in Richmond. The museum also has periodic arts and crafts, theatrical and children's programs. It is home to the Suffolk Art League.

T.J. (TED) LoCASCIO PLANTERS MUSEUM

200 Johnson Ave.   934-6200
Hours: 8 AM-4:30 PM weekdays
Admission: Free

This is one of the smallest and most obscure museums in the region. But for fans of Mr. Peanut or corporate America, it's a neat place to visit. The museum opened in 1991 to pay tribute to Planters Peanuts, which moved its headquarters to Suffolk in 1913. It is inside the factory Planters built upon its arrival in Suffolk. A new plant is under construction nearby, and it's unclear what will happen to the museum.

The museum honors former plant manager Ted LoCascio and shows off his Mr. Peanut collectibles. Included are a giant Mr. Peanut, roasting machines, peanut jars and containers, scrapbooks of clippings, and advertisements.

To see the museum, park in the visitors area across the street and check in with the receptionist who will unlock the one-room museum and let you browse through it. Be sure to note the 14 dapper cast-iron Mr. Peanut statues that sit on the fence outside the plant.

Historic Houses and Sites

Norfolk

FORT NORFOLK
803 Front St., Norfolk
Hours: Usually open Sunday afternoons
Admission: Free

You may have trouble finding Fort Norfolk, but it is worth the hunt. The fort along the Elizabeth River near downtown was authorized by President George Washington in 1794 to protect the Norfolk harbor. Most of the buildings you see date from 1810. Since then the fort has hardly changed. Its arched gateway, double oak doors, gunpowder magazine, guardhouse and other buildings remain. Surrounding the fort are a wall and ramparts built to protect against British invasion.

Today the fort is property of the U.S. Army Corps of Engineers, whose glassy regional headquarters dwarfs this historic site. After being closed to the public for years, the fort is gradually being renovated with the help of the Norfolk Historical Society. The society has its headquarters in the fort. To get there, take Brambleton Ave. to Colley Ave. and head south. Go a few blocks until the road dead ends at Front St. You will think you've made a mistake by now since you appear to be in a warehouse district. But, go right on Front Street and the road will end at the fort.

HERMITAGE FOUNDATION MUSEUM
7637 North Shore Road   423-2052
Hours: 10 AM-5 PM Monday-Saturday; 1-5 PM Sunday
Admission $4, $1 for ages 6-18

This English Tudor-style home is in Lochaven, one of Norfolk's loveliest neighborhoods. It was built in 1908 on 12 acres along the Lafayette River as a summer home for art patrons William and Florence Sloane. They established the Hermitage Foundation in 1937 to promote the arts. Today both the house and its contents are a treat to see. The house features intricate woodcarving while its holdings range from paintings, glass and textiles to carvings and other art works.

The Hermitage grounds are a terrific spot for picnics or strolling. There is no charge to enter the yard, which has picnic tables. In front of the house is a large, shady playground.

HUNTER HOUSE VICTORIAN MUSEUM
240 W. Freemason St.   623-9814
Hours: Wednesday-Saturday, 10 AM-4 PM;
Sunday, Noon-4 PM
Admission: $3, $1 for children

Built in 1894, this is a Victorian jewel that showcases the furnishings and household goods of the James Wilson Hunter family – whose children never married and appear to have never thrown any-thing away. The house is in Norfolk's oldest neighborhood, the cobblestoned Freemason district near downtown.

The three-story home is in the Richardsonian Romanesque style and has gorgeous stained-glass windows. Inside are a nursery filled with delightful toys, a bed covered with a crazy quilt and all kinds of Victorian bric-a-brac and furniture.

Historic Homes

ADAM THOROUGHGOOD HOUSE

Located on the banks of the Lynnhaven River, the Adam Thoroughgood House (circa 1680) is a modified hall and parlor structure reminiscent of English cottage architecture. It contains a spectacular 17th Century decorative arts collection and features a garden restored by the Garden Club of Virginia. 804-460-0007.

OLD CAPE· HENRY LIGHTHOUSE

One of George Washington's first official acts as the first President of the United States was, "..that a lighthouse be built near the entrance to the Chesapeake Bay." Completed in 1792, it guided mariners entering the Virginia Capes until 1881. Old Cape Henry's Lighthouse serves us still as the official symbol for the City of Virginia Beach. 804-648-1889.

FRANCIS LAND HOUSE

This gentry class lifestyle enjoyed by the land family is represented in their large Georgian style plantation home. Period rooms, temporary exhibits, a display on flax production, and special programs are featured year-round. 804-340-1732.

# of Virginia Beach

One room preserves the medical office of one son who was a physician. Tours begin on the hour and half hour.

Although this is a narrow house filled with breakable items, the museum welcomes children and has a children's membership for ages 4 to 8. On some Saturdays the museum sponsors a Victorian children's hour with crafts, games and other activities.

MOSES MYERS HOUSE
323 E. Freemason St. 627-2737, 622-1211, ext. 283
Hours: Noon-5 PM Tuesday-Saturday; Noon-5 PM Sunday. Closed Sunday and Monday from January through March; opens at Noon on Tuesday-Saturday during winter
Admission: $2, $1 for children over 6; $4 combination ticket available for three homes

This is one of three historic homes operated by The Chrysler Museum. It was the home of the Moses Myers family, the region's first Jewish residents. Myers was a merchant who moved to Norfolk in 1787, ran a successful import-export business and served on the city council. He also was known as the last man in Norfolk to continue wearing a colonial-style ponytail. The Myers family raised nine children in the Georgian townhouse built in 1792. The home stayed in the family for six generations. Many original furnishings and artifacts are in the house, which is in downtown Norfolk. This is the only historic house in the country to feature programs on Jewish practices in colonial times.

ST. PAUL'S CHURCH
201 St. Paul's Blvd.   627-4353
Hours: 10-AM-4PM Tuesday-Saturday; Sunday during worship services
Admission: Donation

This was the only building to survive the burning of Norfolk that started on New Year's Day 1776 by the British. Its war wounds include a British cannonball stuck in its southeastern wall. The building features several Tiffany windows and its original box pews. Outside is a traditional burial ground that is undergoing a historic restoration.

WILLOUGHBY-BAYLOR HOUSE
601 E. Freemason St. 627-2737, 622-1211, ext. 283
Hours: 10 AM-5 PM Tuesday-Saturday; Noon-5 PM Sunday. Closed Sunday and Monday from January through March; opens at Noon on Tuesday-Saturday during winter
Admission: $2, $1 for children over 6; $4 combination ticket available for three homes

This 18th-century home is one of three operated by The Chrysler Museum. It was built in 1794 by Capt. William Willoughby, and its style is a blend of Georgian and Federal. Period furnishings reflect the inventory made in 1800 when Willoughby died. The grounds of this downtown Norfolk home includes a lovely garden.

Virginia Beach

ADAM THOROUGHGOOD HOUSE
1636 Parish Rd. 460-0007, 622-1211, ext. 238
Hours: 10 AM-5 PM Tuesday-Saturday; Noon-5 PM Sunday. Closed Sunday and Monday from January through March; opens at Noon on Tuesday-Saturday during winter.
Admission: $2, $1 for children over 6; $4 combination ticket available for three homes

Photo: Norfolk Visitors and Convention Bureau

The Douglas McArthur Memorial pays tribute to this general's life and the era in which he lived.

Operated by The Chrysler Museum, this home was built by Adam Thoroughgood who came to Virginia in 1621 as an indentured servant. He performed the first survey of the region and started the first ferry service across the Elizabeth River. King Charles I rewarded Thoroughgood with 5,350 acres. The home that bears his name was built by a descendant around 1680. About three acres of the original grounds remain with the home, one of the oldest brick houses in the country. Its style resembles an English cottage. Outside are herb and flower gardens.

BATTLE OFF THE CAPES MONUMENT
Fort Story

A monument, overlook and plaques help visitors understand the important Revolutionary War battle that took place near this spot. In 1781 the French victory over the British at this spot helped pave the way for the British surrender at Yorktown. This site is in Fort Story near the Old Cape Henry Lighthouse and First Landing Cross.

FIRST LANDING CROSS
Fort Story

This large cross marks the spot where it's believed America's first English settlers landed when they arrived in the New World in 1607. The cross is in Fort Story near Old Cape Henry Lighthouse and an overlook where the Battle off the Capes took place.

FRANCIS LAND HOUSE HISTORIC SITE
3131 Virginia Beach Blvd.   *340-1732*
Hours: 9 AM-5 PM Wednesday-Saturday; Noon-5 PM Sunday
Admission: $2, $1 for children over 6

This home was built around 1732 for one of the first settlers in Princess Anne County. It was home to four generations of the Land family and later was an exclusive dress shop. Today the house is sandwiched among a busy strip of stopping centers and other businesses. The City of Virginia Beach saved it from demolition by buying it and the surrounding 35 acres of land in 1975. The house is in the midst of ongoing restoration but remains open for tours. It features a Dutch gambrel roof and period furnishings.

LYNNHAVEN HOUSE
4405 Wishart Rd.   *460-1688*
Hours: Noon-4 PM Tuesday-Sunday from mid-April through November
Admission: $2, $1 for children

Built around 1725 by the Thellaball family, this is one of the best preserved 18th-century buildings in the country. It is owned by the Association for the Preservation of Virginia Antiquities. The brick house features period furnishing and frequently has cooking and crafts programs that showcase the lifestyle of 18th-century residents. Costumed docents lead tours.

OLD CAPE HENRY LIGHTHOUSE
Fort Story   *422-9421*
Hours: 10 AM-5 PM daily mid-March through October
Admission: $2, $1 for students

Completed in 1791, the lighthouse guided mariners until it was replaced in 1881. Its construction was authorized by President George Washington, making the lighthouse the first federal public works project. The stone used in the structure came from the same Virginia quarry that supplied the White House, Capitol and Mount Vernon. Construction of the lighthouse cost $17,500.

Since 1930 the lighthouse has been owned by the Association for the Preservation of Virginia Antiquities. Kids particularly like climbing to the top of the 75-foot tower and looking out the windows. The lighthouse is the official symbol of Virginia Beach.

Even when the lighthouse isn't open, you can drive onto Fort Story, usually by showing a drivers license, and look at it from outside. Nearby is the newer lighthouse that replaced this one as well as the First Landing Cross and the site of the Battle Off the Capes.

UPPER WOLFSNARE

2040 Potters Road   491-0127
Hours: 10 AM-4 PM Wednesday and Thursday in summer
Admission: $2, $1 for children

This historic house is out in the country so call for directions ahead of time. Its location gives you a real feel for Colonial life in 1759 when this plantation home was built by Thomas Walke III, whose son was a ratifier of the U.S. Constitution. The two-story frame home has period furnishings and is owned by Princess Anne County and Virginia Beach Historical Society whose members help as costumed docents. Visitors will find the house prepared for a typically muggy 18th-century summer with rugs put away, gauze covering chandeliers and slipcovers on the dining room chairs. Herbs from the garden are used throughout the house to repel bugs.

Cruising

The best way to get a feel for this coastal region is to take a look at it from the water. While you're here you might want to take a leisurely sightseeing cruise so you can check out the largest natural harbor in the world. You have a variety of options.

Spirit Cruises operates the *Spirit of Norfolk*, which has lunch, brunch, dinner and moonlight cruises. Spirit Cruises is a Norfolk-based company that initiated the idea of local dinner cruises and now operates boats in Boston, New York and other major cities. *The Spirit*, which was completed in 1992 and resembles a cruise ship, has room for 550 guests. The ship leaves from The Waterside and cruises along the Elizabeth River from downtown Norfolk to the Norfolk Naval Base. Cruises last two to three hours and cost $20.53 at lunch and $33.57 at dinner with weekend rates slightly higher. The price includes a buffet, bands and a musical revue starring talented waiters and waitresses. Discounts are available for children, retired people, military personnel and groups. Call 625-1748.

The *Carrie B* is a replica of a 19th-century riverboat that has been plying the Hampton Roads harbor since 1959. The *Carrie B* offers 90-minute cruises that take in the downtown harbor and Norfolk Naval Shipyard. The boat holds 300 and runs from April through October with up to four trips a day during summer. There also are 2 1/2-hour cruises that also take visitors to the Norfolk Naval Base and site of the *Monitor* and *Merrimac* battle during the War Between the States. The *Carrie B* picks up passengers both at The Waterside in Norfolk and Portside in Portsmouth. Reservations aren't necessary. The cost is $12 for the shorter cruise, $14 for the longer one with children over 6 half price. Group rates are available. Hamburgers, hot dogs and drinks are sold on board. Call 393-4735.

The *American Rover* bills itself as the "largest three-masted topsail passenger schooner under U.S. Flag." The 135-foot ship was designed and built by a local naval architect in the 1980s and resembles a 19th-century tall ship. When the *Rover's* massive sails are at full mast, it is a breathtaking sight. The *Rover* sails through the Hampton Roads harbor from late April through October usually twice a day in the afternoon and evenings. Cruises last two or three hours and leave from The Waterside in downtown Norfolk. Costs range from $12.50 for the shorter trips to $16. Children under 12 sail for $6 or $8. Group rates are available. Snacks, sandwiches and drinks are sold on board. The *Rover's* operator also has six-passenger sailboats available for charter. Call 627-SAIL.

The Elizabeth River Ferry offers the quickest and most economical way to take in the downtown harbor. It is a paddlewheel boat that regularly runs from The Waterside in Norfolk to Portside in Portsmouth.

It makes an occasional extra stop at High Street near Portsmouth's museums. The ride lasts about five minutes and costs 75 cents each way; 50 cents for children. The ferry is operated by Tidewater Regional Transit, the regional bus company. Call 627-9291 or 623-3222.

Discovery Cruises offer a different water view. Its yacht takes passengers through the secluded bays and inlets of Virginia Beach. The sights include luxury homes costing up to several million dollars as well as marinas for both pleasure craft and commercial fishing boats. Both lunch and dinner cruises are available from May through October. Lunch lasts about 1 1/2 hours; dinner cruises go for 2 1/2 hours. The cost is $15 for lunch, $28 for dinner. The yacht, which seats 92, leaves from 550 Laskin Road in Virginia Beach. Its operator also has 19-foot runabouts and pontoon boats for rent. Call 422-2900.

For another option, check with the Virginia Marine Science Museum (437-4949) to see if it is running any boat tours. The museum periodically sponsors interesting programs that take participants out on the water. In 1992 the museum's popular whale-watching expeditions attracted 5,000 adventurers.

There's no need to pull in the sheets on *Skookum Lady,* the 36-foot sailing yacht that docks at Taylor's Landing Marina at Little Creek. This fine ship is fully crewed, and the highlight is the gourmet spread at the noon hour, served under sail on the Chesapeake Bay. You and five friends can charter the *Skookum Lady* for $300 per day, and advance bookings are definitely required. Call Capt. Fred at 340-2310.

If you're interested in seeing the Great Dismal Swamp, the *Carrie B* makes a few weekend excursions down the swamp's canal to Elizabeth City, N.C. in the spring and fall. The first trips were offered in the spring of 1993. For information call Travel Designers, the tour organizer, at 399-0111 or 800-642-8991.

Portsmouth

HILL HOUSE

221 North St.   *393-0241*
Hours: 1-5 PM Wednesday, Saturday and Sunday from April through December
Admission: $2, 50 cents for children

This circa 1825 home is headquarters for the Portsmouth Historical Association. It is in the heart of historic Olde Towne and is the only residence there open to the public. The home was given to the association in 1961 by the last of the six Hill children, none of whom ever married. The four-story English basement home is furnished entirely with Hill family furnishings.

While in the neighborhood be sure to allow time to stroll through Olde Towne, which has the largest collection of Virginia homes on the National Historic Register.

Suffolk

RIDDICK'S FOLLY

510 N. Main St.   *934-1390*
Hours: 10 AM-5 PM Tuesday-Friday; 1-5 PM Sunday
Admission: Free

This is a massive Greek Revival home with 21 rooms, 16 fireplaces and four floors. It was built in 1837 by Mills Riddick, who had 14 children, and is dubbed his folly because the house is so big. In 1967 the city of Suffolk purchased the home to save it from demolition. It had a major restoration in 1988 and work is continuing on the top floor. There is only one original piece of Riddick furniture – a butler's desk. But other period furnishings show off the graceful lines of the house, which has elaborate plaster moldings and ceiling medallions. On the third floor are penciled messages from the family who fled the Union occupation during the War Between the States. Riddick's Folly was used as a hospital during the war, and the walls also bear messages from Union soldiers recuperating there.

Military Bases

Norfolk

NORFOLK NAVAL BASE

9809 Hampton Blvd.   *444-7955*
Hours: Daily tours; weekend ship visitation
Admission: Free except for guided tours

The world's largest Navy base is a big draw for area visitors. Even people not normally interested in military affairs are intrigued by the sight of mammoth aircraft carriers and stealthy submarines. The base encompasses thousands of acres.

While on base save time for the Hampton Roads Naval Museum at the corner of Farragut Avenue and Dillingham Street. Besides clueing you into Hampton Roads' naval heritage, you'll get to take a peek at Admiral's Row – an exquisite grouping of houses built during the Jamestown Exposition of 1907 and now used as homes for the base's upper echelon. In early 1994 the museum will move to downtown Norfolk and be incorporated into the National Maritime Center (NAUTICUS).

There are several ways to get on the base: through a guided tour, by riding in a car with a Department of Defense sticker on it or by obtaining a visitor's pass. Unless your host is a real Navy insider, you'll learn the most by taking the guided tour offered through Tidewater Regional Transit (TRT). Tickets and transportation are available at The Waterside in downtown Norfolk and at the Naval Base Tour Office at 9079 Hampton Blvd. Tours last about one hour and cost $4.50, $2.25 for children.

During the summer naval base tours depart hourly from 9 AM-2:30 PM from both Waterside and the Naval Base Tour Office. Their schedules vary during other times of the year with 10 daily tours offered in the fall, four a day in early winter, one a day in January, two in February and five a day in the spring. For times and details you can consult a TRT trolley and tours brochure. But just to be sure you don't miss the bus, call the Naval Base Tour Office (444-7955) or TRT (623-3222).

Naval base tours take passengers past the piers where they can ogle at ships and submarines. They also ride by the air station, heliport and Marine security battalion. The only time visitors get off the buses is to see the Hampton Roads Naval Museum, which will move off base in early 1994. Your guide will be either the bus driver or a sailor assigned to tourist duty for having a broken leg or another physical ailment that prevents sea duty.

If you decide to venture onto the base on your own and you don't have a DOD sticker on your car, stop by the Naval Base Pass Office on Hampton Boulevard near Gate 5. You'll be issued a pass that will let you drive through the base.

On Saturdays and Sundays from 1-4:30 PM there usually are several ships open for visitation. Children especially like to clamber up and down ladders and check out the captain's bridge. You'll find the sailors on board eager to answer your questions. In the summer, arm yourself with hats, sunscreen and snacks for children. The wait to get on board can be long, and you'll swelter standing on the hot tarmac.

If you're in the area during December, it's worth driving onto the base at night to see the lighted ships.

Virginia Beach

FORT STORY
Atlantic Avenue   422-7164
This World War I-era Army base is at the extreme north end of Atlantic Avenue. There also is an entrance off Shore Drive to the Fort, which is affiliated with Newport News' Fort Eustis, a major Army transportation center. Fort Story's whitewashed buildings give it an appealing look, and it has a great beach that is open to the public on weekends during late spring and summer. There are also several historical sites on the base – First Landing Cross, the Old Cape Henry Lighthouse and the site of the Battle Off the Capes during the Revolutionary War. To get on base either show your driver's license to the guard on duty or have a Department of Defense sticker on your car.

NAVAL AMPHIBIOUS BASE LITTLE CREEK
Shore Drive   464-7923
This is the Navy's major amphibious base. It's where the elite Navy SEALS do their training. It is not normally open to the public except during December to see holiday lights. You do not need a pass to enter then. Drivers with a Department of Defense sticker on their car are allowed on base.

OCEANA NAVAL AIR STATION
Oceana Boulevard   433-3131
This is one of the Navy's four master jet bases, and you can see traces of it as F-15 Tomcats and A-6 Intruders streak across the sky. It's one of the busiest airfields in the world with a plane landing or taking off every few seconds. Oceana is home to 22 aviation squadrons. It is not normally open to the public but

drivers with Department of Defense stickers on their cars can enter. However, in the summer there usually are Saturday morning bus tours. To find out about them call the Virginia Beach Visitor Center at 437-4700.

Miscellaneous Attractions

Some of the region's major attractions are unique and defy easy categorization. But they are definitely worth seeing while you're in town.

Norfolk

d'ART CENTER

125 College Place   624-4211
Hours: Tuesday-Saturday, 10 AM-5 PM; Sunday, Noon-5 PM
Admission: Free

This is a fun place to wander through because you never know what you will find. It's a cooperative center for about 40 area artists who have their studios here. You'll find sculptors, jewelry makers and painters at work. If you find something to your liking, the artist will be happy to sell it to you. The center opened in the late 1980s in downtown Norfolk.

NORFOLK BOTANICAL GARDEN

Azalea Garden and Airport roads   441-5831
Hours: 8:30 AM-sunset daily
Admission: $2

The 175-acre garden has more than 12 miles of pathways and is a wonderful oasis in the middle of

Norfolk. With its location adjacent to Norfolk International Airport, it gives airport arrivals an impressive first look at the city.

The botanical garden was started in 1938 as a Work Project Administration Grant. Since then it has gained status as one of the country's top 10 gardens and is renowned for its rose garden. The botanical garden is in the midst of a multi-year improvement plan that will further enhance it.

Although spring is the peak time to see the garden when thousands of azaleas are in bloom, it's a treat any time of year. Among the highlights are the Renaissance Garden, the Japanese Garden and a pathway lined with statues. Climbing up the NATO Tower gives a vista of the garden while another overlook lets visitors watch planes land at the neighboring airport. Despite all the aviation activity, the botanical garden remains a secluded spot.

To get a better view of the gardens, take either a relaxing tram or boat ride. Each lasts about 30 minutes and costs $2 with young children riding for free. If you have time, enjoy a picnic overlooking Lake Whitehurst or bring along a pole (and the appropriate license) for fishing.

THE VIRGINIA ZOO

3500 Granby St.   441-2706
Hours: 10 AM-5 PM daily
Admission: $2, $1 for children

The 55-acre zoo is a favorite spot for all ages, but children particularly get a kick out of it. Although you won't find any giant pandas, lions or gorillas, the zoo has a charm of its own. In recent years it has reduced the number of animals to ensure that it has the proper environment for those in its care. One popular exhibit features two elephants who amuse visitors by getting baths from zookeepers or splashing each other with water. Other zoo favorites: the primates, llamas and ostriches.

New in 1992 were two Siberian tiger cubs confiscated from a private owner. They were housed temporarily in the zoo and won the hearts of local residents who started a fund-raising campaign to build an area for them. The cubs quickly became the zoo's star attractions.

While in the zoo be sure to take a walk through the barnyard, the reptile and small mammal house, the gazebo where injured birds recuperate, and the turn-of-the-century botanical conservatory. Kids love getting a handful of food from a dispenser to feed ducks in the pond. They also like stopping by The Beastro restaurant and eating a reasonably-priced lunch that comes in a box decorated with animals. Outside the zoo grounds are a playground and picnic area.

THE WATERSIDE

333 Waterside Dr.   627-3300
Hours: Monday-Saturday, 10 AM-9 PM; Sunday, Noon-6 PM. Longer hours during summer
Admission: Free

This is Norfolk's festival marketplace – the city's version of Boston's Fanueil Hall. It has a lively mix of shops, restaurants and entertainment and is on the "must-do list" of most visitors. The Waterside opened in the mid-1980s to revital-ize the downtown Norfolk waterfront along the Elizabeth River. Waterside has had one expansion that brought the total number of shops and dining spots to 120.

Waterside includes a food court with vendors offering tasty treats from Greece, Japan and the Mexico as well as typically American fare. There are also several full-service restaurants. Shops feature gifts, clothing and souvenirs. There frequently are musicians performing on the stage in the food court.

Outside entertainment ranges from Sunday night ballroom dancing in the summer to the never-ending parade of tugs, sailboats and Navy ships moving along the Elizabeth River. A boardwalk takes visitors past some huge yachts anchored at a marina. There are numerous benches for relaxing. Neighboring Town Point Park is the site of festivals on most weekends.

Waterside is also the place to catch the ferry to Portsmouth, embark on a harbor tour or take a trolley tour of the city. There is a parking deck across the street.

Virginia Beach

ARTISTS AT WORK: GALLERY AND STUDIO

2407 Pacific Ave.   425-6671
Hours: 10 AM-5 PM Tuesday-Saturday
Admission: Free

This is a cooperative of 30 area artists that opened in 1991. About 10 artists have their studios here while the rest rent walls to display their works. All art is for sale. Artists working on site include marble sculptors as well as painters and weavers.

ASSOCIATION FOR RESEARCH AND ENLIGHTENMENT (A.R.E.)

67th Street and Atlantic Avenue   428-3588
Hours: 9 AM-8 PM Monday-Saturday; 11 AM-8 PM Sunday
Admission: Free

The A.R.E. is one of Virginia Beach's more intriguing attractions. This organization is dedicated to Edgar Cayce, a psychic who resided in Virginia Beach and was known for falling into a trance and being able to diagnose and prescribe treatment for medical ailments. Cayce, who died in 1945, built the Edgar Cayce Hospital in Virginia Beach in the late 1920s. The hospital, which focused on holistic healing, failed to survive the Great Depression and closed in 1931.

Today the white frame building is headquarters for A.R.E., whose conferences draw participants from around the world. Adjacent to it are the A.R.E. Visitor and Conference Center. Stop by and you can view videotapes about Cayce's life, hear free lectures and see exhibits on Cayce's work. There also are a meditation room overlooking the ocean and a well-stocked bookstore. Outside is a Japanese-style meditation garden. In the summer there are guided tours of the Cayce headquarters at 11:15 AM and 2 PM.

Try to sit in on the group ESP testing if you can. It starts at 1 PM during the summer. Visiting relatives of ours who attended a session proclaimed it to be one of the most fun things they did on their vacation. During the testing, a leader asks volunteers to send messages to each other by using an electric box that flashes shapes at one person. Another volunteer and the audience try to pick up on the vibes from the sender. The leader also administers other ESP tests and answers questions about psychic phenomenon.

THE CHRISTIAN BROADCASTING NETWORK

1000 Centerville Tnpk. 523-7123 or 424-7777
Hours: Daytime, Monday-Friday
Admission: Free

Virginia Beach is headquarters for The Christian Broadcasting Network and its affiliated Family Channel, one of the fastest-growing cable TV channels. CBN's 685-acre complex features attractive Georgian-style buildings, including the home of founder Rev. M.G. "Pat" Robertson.

Tours are available Monday through Friday during the day. You can take your chances that you'll be there at the right time for a tour, but it's best to call ahead (523-7123). Guided tours take visitors behind the scenes of this international TV network and its ministry. If you want to sit in on a television show, call ahead and get reservations for the "700 Club" or "Big Brother Jake." The "700 Club" is CBN's flagship program featuring Robertson as host. It is usually produced five mornings a week. Try to call at least a day or two in advance for reservations (523-7123). "Big Brother Jake" is a Family Channel situation comedy. It stars body builder Jake Steinfeld and is taped at 4 PM and 7 PM on most Fridays. Call 523-7343 for reservations.

OCEAN BREEZE
849 General Booth Blvd.422-4444, 340-1616 (off-season)
Hours: 10 AM-10PM daily Memorial Day-Labor Day; open weekends in spring and fall
Admission: $14.95 for Wild Water Rapids or Motor World; $19.95 for both; free for ages 3 and under

This amusement park is less than two miles from the oceanfront. It has four components: Wild Water Rapids, Motor World, Shipwreck Golf and Strike Zone. Guests can choose to spend a day and take in all attractions or concentrate on one or two parts.

Wild Water Rapids is the only water park around. Its six acres include eight slides, a half-acre wave pool and a big activity pool. Young children can ride down slides and get in the pools with their parents.

Motor World has nine acres of mini-race tracks. The most popular is the Grand Prix track with 3/4-size race cars. Drivers race against a clock and hit speeds up to 35 MPH as they loop around a track. The cost is $2 a lap. There are four other race tracks, bumper boats and an activity area for younger children. Visitors have the choice of buying tickets for individual rides or $14.95 wristbands that give unlimited rides on everything but the Grand Prix track.

For $19.95 visitors can hit Wild Water Rapids during the heat of the day, walk over to Motor World, then go back to the water when they get hot again.

Shipwreck Golf is a 36-hole miniature golf course that challenges golfers with sunken ships, caves and other special effects. The cost is $4 for 18 holes, $7 for 36 holes.

Strike Zone has nine batting cages that cater to all ages. Batters can choose to hit either softballs or baseballs. Pitches can go from slow to lightning fast. The cost is $1 for 10 pitches.

TIDEWATER VETERANS MEMORIAL
1000 19th St.

Dedicated in 1988 this memorial is dedicated to all military veterans from the area who served in all wars from the Revolutionary War to more current ones. The memorial's concept came from area students and was carried out by a local architect. The symbolic structure includes a waterfall, flags and a series of split spheres. The project was built with both city and private support.

VIRGINIA BEACH CENTER FOR THE ARTS
2200 Parks Ave.   425-0000
Hours: 10 AM-4 PM Tuesday-Saturday; Noon-4 PM Sunday
Admission: Free

This is the only arts center in the region to focus on 20th-century art. It was formed in 1952, and in 1989 completed a new center whose architecture touches on Oriental and Southern styles. The center is near Virginia Beach's Visitor Center and is one of the most attractive buildings in the city. Featured are changing exhibits as well as classes and programs for all ages.

VIRGINIA BEACH FARMER'S MARKET
1989 Landstown Road   427-4395
Hours: Open daily, weather permitting
Admission: Free

This is a fun place to wander. The market is in the rural part of

Virginia Beach so it's best to call for directions and hours. It has 17,000 square feet of rough-hewn stalls that house about 19 permanent vendors. Produce is seasonal, making this is a great place to pick up a pumpkin or buy peaches, apples or whatever is in season. Some vendors specialize in meats, baked goods, dairy products, plants and outdoor furniture. Some weekends you may catch a flea market, craft show or other special event.

Portsmouth

PORTSIDE
6 Crawford Parkway   *393-5111*

The festive blue-and-white-striped tent that covers Portside gives a distinct look to the Portsmouth waterfront. The Portside Visitor Information Center is open year round. Portside is a docking point for the Portsmouth-Norfolk Ferry. From April through the fall it also has six restaurants dishing out crabcakes, sandwiches and other casual foods. There also are several places to buy frozen yogurt or ice cream. During warmer months Portside frequently has weekend entertainment.

VIRGINIA SPORTS HALL OF FAME
420 High St.   *393-8031*
Hours: 10 AM-5 PM Tuesday-Saturday; 1-5 PM Sunday
Admission: Free

Organized in 1966 the Hall of Fame honors Virginia sports heroes, including basketball player Cy Young, golfer Sam Snead and tennis star Arthur Ashe. Inductees include well-known names in football, basketball, golf, baseball, auto racing, horseback riding, speedboat racing, wrestling, bowling, swimming. sail boat racing, track, tennis and coaching. Displays include uniforms, photos and other memorabilia.

Chesapeake

CHESAPEAKE PLANETARIUM
300 Cedar Road   *547-0153*
Hours: 8 PM Thursdays
Admission: Free

The region's only planetarium opened in 1963 and was the first in Virginia to be built by a school district. The Chesapeake School District continues to operate the planetarium, which attracts 40,000 visitors a year. Program topics change monthly and recently have included the summer sky, falling stars and the Christmas star.

Photo: Virginia Division of Tourism

Building sand castles has always been a favorite family activity.

Inside
Kidstuff

While thumbing through this book you'll find dozens of ideas for entertaining your children. But just in case you miss them – or we couldn't find the right category to place them – here are 30 suggestions to keep kids of all ages on the go.:

1. Make them think they've been to sea by taking a jaunt on the Norfolk-Portsmouth Ferry. The trip lasts only about five minutes, but it's fun to ride across the Elizabeth River on a paddlewheel boat. The cost each way is 75 cents for adults, 50 cents for children 12 and under. Catch the boat at The Waterside festival marketplace in Norfolk or at Portside in Portsmouth. You can wander around at either end and explore the shops. Once an hour the ferry stops at the foot of High Street in Portsmouth where it's a quick walk to see three Portsmouth museums. You also can walk to the museums from Portside.

2. Go to the Children's Museum of Virginia in downtown Portsmouth (393-8393). This small museum is tucked away in the basement of the 1846 Courthouse at 400 High Street. It may be tiny but it's packed with fun. City officials plan to complete a $3 million expansion to a nearby location by April 1994. A former department store will be transformed into a 27,000-square-foot children's museum with 14 major display areas. In the meantime the current 2,700-square-foot museum will do. It has one room where kids can blow giant soap bubbles, step inside them or try different bubble experiments. A second room stretches imaginations as children dress up as fire fighters, run a grocery store or hop on a real police motorcycle. Another room is filled with buckets of Legos and space to build a child-sized city. The museum has special theme programs on Wednesday mornings and some Saturday mornings.

Another possibility is the Children's Art Discovery Museum at 2210 Commerce Parkway in Virginia Beach (463-8848). It features all kinds of art activities for ages 3 through 12.

3. If it's December, check out the holiday lights in downtown Norfolk. Since 1985 the city has strung its tallest office buildings with thousands of white lights. From a distance Norfolk looks like a giant gingerbread village. To get perspective go to Portsmouth and look across the water. To kick off the season, the city sponsors a lighted Christmas parade, usually on the Saturday

evening before Thanksgiving. There is a whole roster of Holidays in the City activities that goes along with the lights.

The ships at the Norfolk Naval Base and the Naval Amphibious Base in Virginia Beach also are lighted at this time of the year. For one of the best displays of gaudy but great Christmas lights, head to Commodore Park in Norfolk. This neighborhood is just off Granby Street across from Northside Junior High. Just follow the line of cars, and you'll be amazed at how each neighbor tries to outdo the other with elaborate Christmas scenes and lights.

4. Another long-time favorite Christmas activity is a trip to Coleman Nursery at 4934 High Street in Portsmouth (484-3426). Since 1966 the plant nursery has played Christmas to the hilt with its Christmas Wonderland. Two buildings feature dozens of animated Christmas scenes of animals, Santa and elves, and even a circus. For many area families, visiting Coleman's is a holiday ritual. Admission costs 25 cents for children and 50 cents for adults. Arm your kids with a handful of pennies to toss in the elaborate displays. All donations go to charity. There also are well-stocked selling candy, Christmas decorations, plants and Virginia food products.

5. To get in the Christmas spirit, spend a few hours at the annual Holly Festival at Scope in Norfolk. It is usually held on the first weekend in December and is sponsored by The Children's Hospital of The Kings Daughters. The festival typically has the area's best Santa, a kindly gentleman with a real beard and a jaunty candy-striped cane. By arranging ahead children can have breakfast with Mr. and Mrs. Santa. Even if you miss breakfast, there are plenty of other things to occupy children – games, face painting, a giant toy train display, clowns, gingerbread houses and continual entertainment.

6. Let your kids talk to Santa or Mrs. Claus on the Hillhaven Ho Ho Hotline. It operates in December with the help of residents of area Hillhaven nursing centers. Children can call and talk to either Santa or Mrs. Claus (623-HOHO, 481-HOHO, 463-1707). If they'd rather write Santa, an elf at the Retail Merchants Association of Tidewater helps Santa answer all letters addressed to him and dropped in local mailboxes.

7. At Halloween go with your older children to the Haunted Forest at the Norfolk Botanical Garden. You'll ride a tram through the woods where high school students will make you scream as you travel through spooky scenes. This is not recommended for children under 6 or those who easily frighten. The Haunted Forest is open during the weekends preceding Halloween. Another possibility is the annual Ghost Walk that points out the spooky highlights of historic Olde Towne in Portsmouth. It is usually held on the weekend before Halloween.

8. Visit Bergey's Dairy Farm at 2221 Mount Pleasant Road in Chesapeake. This is a working dairy farm that produces and delivers milk to residences. It's way out

in the country so call for directions (482-4711). The kids can see cows and horses and pet some calves. Best of all, you can go in Bergey's store and eat homemade ice cream. During one weekend in the spring, the farm sponsors back-to-the-farm days with hayrides and other entertainment.

9. Head to Pungo to pick whatever's in season in this rural section of Virginia Beach. If it's summer you'll find strawberries, blueberries and blackberries. If it's fall you can pull a pumpkin out of the patch. To keep up with what's in season look in *The Virginian-Pilot/Ledger-Star* classifieds under the section called Good Things to Eat. Be sure to call and get directions. Once you're in Pungo, you may want to keep going a few miles to Knotts Island, N.C. If it's late summer there is a peach orchard just ripe for the picking.

10. Go to the Virginia Marine Science Museum, 717 General Booth Blvd. in Virginia Beach (437-4949). One Virginia Beach grandfather marvels that his visiting grandchildren never tire of this museum. It's a hands-on place that lets kids touch turtles and crabs and other hardy sea creatures. They can watch a woodcarver create duck decoys, and they can tong for oysters. A 50,000-gallon fish tank will amaze them.

11. Visit The Virginia Zoo, 3500 Granby St., Norfolk (624-9938). This small zoo has room for kids to run around and some of their favorite animals. To get to know the zoo better, sign up preschoolers for the Zoo Tot or Early Bloomers programs. These are held on Saturday mornings to give children and parents a behind-the-scenes look at the zoo. They meet animals up close or work with plants. Sessions include crafts, games and songs. Students who have finished kindergarten can participate in summer zoo camps. There also are occasional weekend campouts in the zoo for kids and parents.

12. Attend the Children's Fantasy Fest in October at Town Point Park in Norfolk. This popular weekend festival is sponsored by The Children's Hospital of The King's Daughters. There are many activities and booths designed for children of all ages. The festival generally brings in well-known national performers for concerts. If you miss this festival, there are plenty of other weekend extravaganzas going on throughout the year that your family will enjoy.

13. Go crabbing. Take a chicken neck or other piece of meat. Tie it on a string and dangle it off a pier or riverbank. If you're lucky a crab will latch onto it. If not, your kids will still have fun trying.

14. Take a day trip and go to Fort Fun in Newport News. This is a terrific playground built by volunteers in 1992. It is a gigantic wooden structure in Huntington Park off Warwick Boulevard (near Mercury Boulevard). Children can play in the fort for hours, and there are comfortable benches overlooking the James River for weary parents. The playground has many nooks and crannies and places for climbing and pretending. There also are picnic tables. In the spring of 1993

volunteers were slated to add a 40-foot fishing pier and gazebo.

15. Not to be outdone by the Peninsula, Southside volunteers are planning to build their own elaborate playground at Mount Trashmore in Virginia Beach. The Virginia Beach Junior Woman's Club is spearheading the drive to build Kids Cove. The playground will have a nautical theme and is set to go up in May 1993 with the help of 2,000 volunteers.

16. Sign up for a class with your child. If you have a newborn, Sentara Norfolk General Hospital offers single-session infant stimulation classes for babies 6 weeks to 6 months of age (628-3428). For older children try a parent-child session of Gymboree (623-2244), and you'll both have fun. Area YMCAs and other pools often have swimming classes for children. Younger ones attend with a parent.

17. Ride the Pokey Smokey in Portsmouth's City Park. This is a real coal-fired miniature train that puffs through a lovely 93-acre park from April through November. Rides are daily during the summer and on the weekends. Otherwise, call 393-5162.

18. Go to the Norfolk Botanical Garden (855-7460). Kids can run around and look at whatever is in bloom. Be sure to leave time for either a tram ride or a boat ride. Either one costs $2 with young children riding for free. Kids will love the rides, and you get to see parts of the gardens you didn't know were there. Pack a picnic lunch because there is a playground with picnic tables overlooking Lake Whitehurst.

If your kids aren't into nature, they may like the overlook that lets them watch planes take off from neighboring Norfolk International Airport.

19. Visit Mike's Trainland at 5661 Shoulder Hill Rd. in Suffolk (484-4224). It bills itself as the largest combined train shop and museum between Pennsylvania and Florida. This is out in the country on the edge of Suffolk and Portsmouth, and it's a great place for a weekend outing. The front part is an excellent train store. In the back is the Lancaster Train & Toy Museum filled with tiny trains racing around the tracks and other antique toys.

20. Attend a Family Fun Day activity at The Chrysler Museum, 245 W. Olney Road, Norfolk (622-1211, ext. 268). These are usually held twice a month on Sunday afternoons. The free events are designed to get families into the museum, and they truly are fun. Most events have a theme. Sometimes it ties in with an exhibition or a holiday. The series has included storytellers, bands, crafts, scavenger hunts and even a family circus.

21. Head to the beach for a day. It's hard for out-of-town friends to imagine living this close to the beach and not going there all the time. But that's what tends to happen. So drag out all the paraphernalia, pack a picnic lunch and head on down for some fun. Insiders are particularly fond of the beach during the spring and fall when it's less crowded. In the summer, going in early morning or late afternoon will help you avoid throngs of people.

22. If you're a mother looking for companionship for you and your children sign up for a mother's group or start your own. The Virginia Beach YMCA has the Mother's Center, which has groups designed for mothers of infants, toddlers, preschoolers and school-aged children (456-9622). The Y provides child care while the mothers meet. The Moms Group also is based in Virginia Beach and publishes a monthly calendar jammed with activities for mothers and children (430-0527). The Young Moms Church Group meets one morning a week at a chapel at Little Creek Naval Base in Norfolk (471-1087). Child care is provided.

23. If it's warm weather, spend an afternoon at Ocean Breeze. This amusement park has Wild Water Rapids with eight giant slides, Motor World with its race tracks, Shipwreck Golf for miniature golf and Strike Zone with nine batting cages. It is open weekends in spring and fall and open daily during the summer (422-4444).

24. Take your children to

Youngsters watch the sun rise on Virginia Beach.

some spectator sports. Both Old Dominion University and Norfolk State University field some fine teams. Kids also love Norfolk Tides baseball games in the summer and Hampton Roads Admirals hockey games in the winter.

25. Go see some performances geared toward children. The Hurrah Players features talented children in its productions (627-5437). Willett Hall sponsors the Portsmouth Storybook Theater Children's Series, which brings traveling productions to town (393-5144). The Virginia Symphony has occasional Peanut Butter and Jam concerts (623-8590). There are several puppet troupes that regularly perform in the area, the Wappadoodle Puppets (481-6658), Spectrum Puppets (491-2873) and Fuzz & Stuffing Puppets (480-2991). Each December the Old Dominion University Ballet produces "The Nutcracker," a treat for children of all ages.

26. Go to some of the free weekly story hours sponsored by area libraries. Besides reading stories, innovative librarians often have seasonal crafts and other activities to occupy children.

27. Buy your child a membership to the Hunter House Victorian Museum, 240 W. Freemason St., Norfolk (623-9814). It costs $7 and is for ages 4 through 8. This entitles them to a newsletter that includes games and stories. They also get a gift and discounts on monthly programs scheduled for April through December. On the second Saturday of the month the Victorian Children's Hour offers programs ranging from croquet on the lawn to turn-of-the-century crafts.

28. Plan some day trips to Williamsburg, Yorktown, Jamestown, Hampton and Newport News to soak up history that spans from the settling of the country right through the Revolutionary War. (See Day Trips section.)

29. See some of the other attractions on the Peninsula that children love, such as the Virginia Air and Space Center and the restored carousel next door in Hampton or the Virginia Living Museum and Mariners Museum in Newport News. Another possibility is the petting zoo and menagerie of exotic animals maintained by the Newport News SPCA.

30. To keep up with children's activities pick up a copy of *Tidewater Parent*, which is published monthly and distributed for free to grocery stores, child-care centers, fitness centers and many other locations. Each issue features a comprehensive calendar of events (426-2595),

Photo: Richmond Newspapers

Fireworks at Harborfest fill the sky.

Inside
Festivals &
Annual Events

*D*eep inside every mild-man-nered citizen of Hampton Roads beats the soul of a party animal. And, on any given weekend in any given month, there's a celebration to feed that passion. From mega-blasts like Norfolk's Harborfest, to food-fetes like the Pungo Strawberry Festival, to social soirees like Norfolk's Holly Festival, there's a party going on...and you're invited!

The region literally rocks with activity from March through December, setting the most hectic pace for fanfare and pageantry. Plus, along with the following calendar of annual events and festivals, there are hundreds of smaller community generated events, including Chamber of Commerce outings, juried art shows and various organization's fundraising galas. For sports lovers, we've included the highlights of major runs and tournaments in the sports section of the guide. Our media is pretty responsive to all events, regardless of size, so you're sure to have advance warning of any upcoming party that is open to the public.

Before you become a card-carrying Hampton Roads party-goer, you should know the rules. First, come hungry. Food vendors literally come out of the back kitchen with the best finger-lickins for every taste. While prices are normally a bit higher than your local fast food drive-through, the thrill of eating a steaming hot pit-cooked bar-b-que sandwich while juggling an ice cold beer is an adventure not to be missed.

Second, if you want quiet, stay home. Practically all events feature live entertainment super enhanced by gargantuan speakers. The decibel level is something previously considered unattainable by mortal man, but actually adds to the ambiance of reckless abandon that a REAL party should exhibit.

And, lastly, all the real biggie events have instituted a transportation system to help ease traffic congestion. So don't even think about driving to the heart of Harborfest, the Chesapeake Jubilee or the Neptune Festival at the Beach. From convenient pick-up locations, you can be zipped to partyland for a very reasonable charge and with very little gridlock.

One special note for newcomers to our great region. Every event listed here is the brainchild of a volunteer group, and executed by scores of equally dedicated, unpaid, overworked volunteers. If you're new to the area and want to meet some fine people, offering to jump into the party-making spirit will gain you not only the opportunity to have a hands-on experience (and a VIP parking pass!), but also the chance to work with business people and community leaders whom you might otherwise not have the good fortune to meet. Major sponsoring organizations are listed following the events calendar. Get the spirit. Get involved!

(Unless otherwise noted, all events listed are free and open to the public.)

Springtime Revelry

March

St. Patrick's Day Celebration

'Tis a fine party under the Big Top Tent in downtown Norfolk's Town Point Park. Sponsored for over a decade by Goodman Segar Hogan, one of the region's premiere real estate corporations, green beer and Irish specialties are the order of the evening. Expect live music, zany contests and a bit of jiggin' for the big day for wearing o' the green. 627-7809.

St. Patrick's Day Parade

A family favorite in the area's largest "Irish" stronghold, the shamrock shenanigans wind their way through Ocean View on the weekend before St. Patrick's Day. A real treat for the little leprechauns in

your family. 622-2312. Norfolk.

Crawford Bay Crew Classic

Rowing teams from water-worthy colleges and universities converge on the Elizabeth River to row to victory. 393-9933. Portsmouth.

April

Downtown Doo Dah Parade

No one can claim that Hampton Roads residents don't have one heck of a sense of humor! This April Fools Day folly of a parade turns high powered business people, charitable organizations and clubs of distinction into out-of-sync units that march to a different drummer through the streets of downtown Norfolk. 627-7809.

Annual Easter Sunrise Service

With the Elizabeth River as the background, join all denominations for this annual outdoor Easter Sunrise Service in Town Point Park on the downtown Norfolk waterfront. 627-7809.

Annual Children's Easter Egg-Stravaganza

Scramble the kids together for one of the largest Easter Egg Hunts in Hampton Roads. A full day for fun, games and kid's crafts at Town Point Park in downtown Norfolk. 627-7809.

International Azalea Festival

Paying tribute to the North Atlantic Treaty Organization (NATO), the Supreme Allied Command Atlantic (SACLANT), and the military community of Hampton Roads, this, the oldest ongoing festival in the region, is the only festival in the country to honor the international command. NATO countries from all over the world select one young woman to represent their country in the Festival's court, with the candidate of the Most Honored Nation serving as Queen. Packed with pomp and circumstance, highlights include the flag raising at SACLANT headquarters, Saturday's Grand Parade through downtown Norfolk, coronation of the Queen and her court in Norfolk's beautiful Botanical Gardens and the City of Norfolk Azalea Ball on Saturday evening. Complementing these events is a weekend of entertainment at Town Point Park and a super spectacular Air Show held Saturday and Sunday at the Naval Air Station Norfolk. Cosponsored by the City of Norfolk and Chamber of Commerce. 622-2312.

BRITISH & IRISH FESTIVAL

The culture and cuisine of England, Scotland, Wales, Northern Ireland and the Republic of Ireland take center stage at Town Point Park in downtown Norfolk. You can count on more than 100 attractions, including music, dancing, arts and crafts, children's activities and, of course, dart throwing contests. 627-7809.

HISTORIC GARDEN WEEK

Peek into the homes of the rich and famous during this week when both historic homes and ex-

quisite private residences are open for touring. Initiated in April of 1929, this annual event attracts thousands of visitors to the meticulously maintained homes and gardens that reach their peak beauty during this spring month. Proceeds from the event make possible the restoration of gardens throughout the Commonwealth of Virginia. To receive a guidebook for all homes included in this year's Garden Tour, contact Historic Garden Week Headquarters, 12 E. Franklin Street, Richmond, VA 23219.

May

T.G.I.F. CONCERTS

May signals the annual kickoff for the T.G.I.F. After Work Concerts in downtown Norfolk's Town Point Park. Entering its eleventh year, these Friday night get-togethers are the place to see and be seen for workaholics of every age. Each event, with hot music and cold beer, benefits a local charity...and is definitely the place to start your weekend!

OCEAN VIEW FESTIVAL

Celebrate along the shores of the Chesapeake Bay with food, entertainment and arts and crafts. Hosted by the residents of Ocean View and Willoughby Spit, this is the first official beach blast of the year. 420-7400. Norfolk.

THE GREEK FESTIVAL

Talk about good things to eat! Every year, this annual celebration of the rich heritage of our Greek community draws throngs of Hampton Roaders who set aside their diet-for-summer plans just to smell and sample the divine dishes prepared by some of our community's best cooks. After you're full, roll out to see works of Greek artists and many handmade arts and crafts. At the Greek Orthodox Church on Granby Street in Norfolk. 440-0500.

THE GHENT ARTS FESTIVAL

Contemporary oils to photographs, ceramics to watercolors...if it's art, it's here at the annual Ghent Arts Festival, celebrating over 20 years of success. More than 200 artists are on hand displaying their work, with food and entertainment right alongside at Town Point Park in Norfolk. 627-7809.

AFR'AM FEST

An African marketplace, foods and music bring out thousands to celebrate African-American heritage. At Town Point Park in Norfolk. 627-7809.

SEAWALL ART SHOW

The perfect weekend to snap up an original piece of art while enjoying a stroll through the lovely Veteran's Riverfront park in Portsmouth. Every year, more professional and amateur artists join the respected list of artists on hand to discuss their work with show visitors. 393-8481.

SALT WATER FISHING TOURNAMENT

Not many get away from these anglers who come from all over the country to compete in this annual tournament, held in Virginia Beach. 491-5160.

PUNGO STRAWBERRY FESTIVAL

Be tickled pink with the variety of strawberry cuisine offered in this rural Virginia Beach harvest celebration. Live entertainment is always on hand so you can dance away the calories. 721-6001.

THE CHESAPEAKE JUBILEE

Not to be outdone by neighboring cities, Chesapeake pulls out all the stops for this annual free-for-all in Chesapeake Park. Top name entertainment, carnival rides, food of every description and more is the order of the weekend. This is one event to check into shuttle service to the festival site. Sponsored by The City of Chesapeake and Chamber of Commerce. 547-2118.

Summer Spectaculars

June

HARBORFEST

If most of Hampton Roads festivals are whirlwinds of activity, Harborfest is a tornado. The star of the East Coast annual waterfront spectaculars, Harborfest is a non-stop flurry of live entertainment, sailing ships, water and air shows, more food than you could possibly sample in a weekend and capped by the most singular display of fireworks you'll witness all year. Visitors number in the trillions, so use the efficient shuttle service available from a multitude of convenient locations. 627-7809. Norfolk.

SEAWALL FESTIVAL

To mirror the activity on Norfolk's waterfront during Harborfest, Portsmouth answers with its own festival. Live entertainment, food galore and a children's park compete for your attention just across the Elizabeth River. 393-9933.

BAYOU BOOGALOO AND CAJUN FOOD FESTIVAL

This one is hot...literally! Spicy foods and equally spicy music by nationally known entertainers is found here. If zydeco music and New Orleans flair get you swaying, move on in to this one. 627-7809. Norfolk.

SCOTTISH FESTIVAL

In the beauty of Norfolk's Botanical Gardens comes this major Scottish Festival and Clan Gathering. Highland games, bagpiping and the Southern Highland Dancing Competition are wonderful to see. For admission charges, contact the Chamber of Commerce, 622-2312.

BOARDWALK ART SHOW

The grandaddy of local art shows, this juried show draws artists of every medium from all over the country to set up their masterpieces

Photo: Richmond Newspapers

The Neptune Festival, held every September, draws thousands to Virginia Beach for its parades and other festivities.

on the boardwalk in Virginia Beach along the Atlantic Ocean. From paintings to photography to pottery, this is your chance to stroll through the area's largest outdoor art gallery. 425-0000.

Fall Festivities

September

THE NEPTUNE FESTIVAL

Virginia Beach's premiere festival, this five-day family affair includes activities that range from the Sand Castle Classic to a spectacular Air Show. Not to mention tons of fresh seafood and top billed entertainment. King Neptune, chosen from the city's business and civic leaders, leads his court of young outstanding women through the festivities, right up to the royal fireworks display. King Neptune's Ball, a formal affair, is one of the highlights of the Beach's social season. 498-0215.

BLACKBEARD PIRATE JAMBOREE

Revelry for the rogue in you! Pirate's garb is the norm for this annual scalawag of an affair, featuring a parade of sail, children's events, costume contests and the Pirate's Ball. Bring all your little scoundrels to Norfolk's Town Point Park for this one. 627-7809.

ELIZABETH RIVER BLUES FESTIVAL

You can get the blues nonstop from the best regional and national blues performers. At Norfolk's Town Point Park. 627-7809.

October

OKTOBERFEST

Lederhosen Alert! With a Ger-

July

GREAT AMERICAN MUSIC FESTIVAL

What began as a one-day family picnic has turned into a three-day Sousa-fest to celebrate the Fourth of July. Down-home food and big-name entertainment, plus, of course, an all-American fireworks display are par for the scene. 627-7809.

DECLARATION CELEBRATION

Ditto food, entertainment and fireworks to celebrate the Fourth. At Portsmouth's Veterans Riverfront Park. 393-8481.

August

TOWN POINT JAZZ FESTIVAL

You get to see the hottest jazz artists around for free! It's a hot, jazzy weekend on Norfolk's downtown Waterfront. 627-7809.

BLUEGRASS FESTIVAL & BAR-B-Q COOK-OFF

A fierce bar-b-q cook-off accompanies foot-tapping music all weekend long. Great fun for the entire family. 627-7809.

man beer in one hand, knockwurst in the other, you can oompah through the best of German food, dancing and music. A fantastic Festhaus weekend at Town Point Park in Norfolk. 627-7809.

CHILDREN'S FANTASY FEST

If anyone under four feet tall lives in your home, get them to Town Point Park in Norfolk for this magical day! Kids on Parade, costumed characters, nationally known children's entertainers, giant puppets and more attract kids of all ages for this all day event. 627-7809.

VIRGINIA WINE FESTIVAL

Whether you fancy a cabernet sauvignon blanc from the heart of the Shenandoah or a rich burgundy from Williamsburg, this palate pleasing event is for you. Sample products from almost 20 premium wineries throughout the Commonwealth, along with the most gourmet of foods. It's one of the largest outdoor wine festivals in the state, and it's right here at Norfolk's Town Point Park. 627-7809.

OLDE TOWNE GHOST WALK

Be spooked out of your trick or treat as actors dressed for the ghoulish occasion tell tales of ghosts and goblins while you tour through Portsmouth's historic district. 399-5487.

PEANUT FESTIVAL

It's really worth the drive to the area's "nuttiest" festival, held at Suffolk's Municipal Airport. There's entertainment, a parade, the phenomenal Shrimp Feast and so much more...all to celebrate the area's top crop. 539-2111.

Winter Wonders

November

HOLIDAYS IN THE CITY

Miles of tiny white lights outline the skyline of Norfolk's downtown as a beacon to the holiday season. A month-long celebration, there are parades on land and sea, fireworks plus a multitude of family events that run through the end of December. 627-1757.

December

HOLLY FESTIVAL

This annual Norfolk event to benefit The Children's Hospital of The Kings Daughters brings out the very best of the season, from the "Festival of Trees" to a plethora of handmade goodies and gifts. For an insider's look at very special private residences, there's the Holly Homes Tour; for all-out glitz and glamour, there's the Holly Ball. 628-7070.

HOLIDAY FESTIVITIES

Grand illuminations, yuletide carols and good cheer can be found in every city in Hampton Roads. Yule logs are stoked to the max by the spirit of the season. For those who prefer their holiday with 18th-century ambiance, Colonial Williamsburg's Grand Illumination is really a spectacular, and humbling, experience. Watch local papers for specific dates and times for all these special events.

NEW YEAR'S EVE PARTY

Make merry under the heated tent as Town Point Park in Norfolk becomes the biggest party in town. The fireworks at the stroke of midnight are spectacular! 627-7809.

Who's Putting On The Show?

For more details and schedules of the events listed here, you may contact:

NORFOLK

Festevents, 120 West Main Street, Norfolk, Virginia 23510, 627-7809

PORTSMOUTH

PortsEvents, 355 Crawford Street, Portsmouth, Virginia 23704, 393-9933

VIRGINIA BEACH

Virginia Beach Ocean Occasions, 265 Kings Grant Road, Virginia Beach, Virginia 23452, 422-0035

Photo: Norfolk Convention and Visitors Bureau

The d'Art center is the ideal place to witness the creation of art.

Alice and Sol B.Frank Photography Gallery
Adam Throughgood Historic House
The Jean Outland Chrysler Library
Blues at the Chrysler Music Series
Highlights of the Collection Tours
Willoughby-Baylor Historic House
Animals in Art Children's Tour
Palettes Cafe at the Chrysler
Chrysler Summer Music Series
Moses Myers Historic House
Jaune Quick-to-See Smith
American Sandwich Glass
Theatrical Performances
Travel with the Chrysler
Chrysler Museum Shop
Parameter's Galleries
Spring Concert Series
Changing Exhibitions
Worcester Porcelain
Ancient Civilizations
Contemporary Art
Beverly Buchanan
Memorial Garden
Family Fun Events
Crafts Workshops
Artist Receptions
20th Century Art
Louise Nevelson
Decorative Arts
Museum Trails
Norfolk Mace
Pablo Picasso
American Art
European Art
Mary Cassatt
Henri Matisse
Andy Warhol
Coach Tours
Tiffany Glass
Storytelling
African Art
Art Camp
Sculpture
Concerts
Gauguin
Lectures
Chardin
Brunch
Bernini
Videos
Renoir
Lunch
Tours
Films

there's Always something happening at the Chrysler!

Find out what's happening this week... Call us! 622-ARTS

THE CHRYSLER MUSEUM
245 West Olney Road, Norfolk, Virginia

Inside
The Arts

*I*f you're from New York, Boston or some other metropolis, you may not expect Hampton Roads to have much to offer in the way of arts. But open your eyes, ears and mind, and you will be pleasantly surprised.

Arts aficionado will find their calendars crammed from October through May with operas, ballets, concerts, lectures and exhibits. Even during summer, there are plenty of performances and shows to entertain all ages.

South Hampton Roads has nearly 100 arts groups that regularly perform and exhibit here. Since it's only three hours from Washington, D.C. the region is a regular stop on the traveling circuit that buses in talent ranging from the Bolshoi Ballet to the Sesame Street characters. Local arts groups include large, professional organizations as well as shoestring operations glued together by enthusiastic volunteers. Norfolk has traditionally been the region's cultural center, but in recent years arts groups have sprung up in area cities. The symphony and other performing artists frequently alternate performances between Norfolk and Virginia Beach.

For performing arts the main stages in Norfolk are Chrysler Hall, the Wells Theatre and the Norfolk Center Theater. Chrysler Hall, with 2,043 seats, is adjacent to the Scope arena. It is Norfolk's all-purpose hall used for everything from the symphony to ballet and lectures. The Wells Theatre, with 677 seats, is home to the Virginia Stage Company but also welcomes other groups. The Harrison Opera House (formerly the Center Theater) is home base for the Virginia Opera but also shares its stage with other organizations. In 1992 the city-owned theater was vacated and renamed so it could get a $10 million facelift that will transform it into an elegant opera house by late 1993. It will have 1,680 seats. Norfolk also has a 300-seat auditorium in The Chrysler Museum.

Concerts in Portsmouth frequently are at 2,000-seat Willett Hall, which sponsors a season of traveling Broadway shows and children's plays. Virginia Beach has the 1,000-seat Pavilion Theater in the Pavilion Convention Center. Across the street the Virginia Beach Center for the Arts also has a 262-seat auditorium. Performing groups also frequent stages at area colleges and schools.

Keeping tabs on all the arts groups can be a tough job. Each

September both *The Virginian-Pilot/ Ledger-Star* and *Port Folio* magazine publish annual arts calendars. These comprehensive listings are worth saving since they detail the entire season for most arts groups. To stay current on arts events, check the daily papers' Friday and Sunday sections and the weekly *Port Folio*. The publications do a good job of profiling arts groups and performances. The Cultural Alliance of Greater Hampton Roads publishes an annual resource directory called "Sketches" that gives details on most arts groups. It costs $10 but also is in most area libraries. To obtain a copy of the directory call 440-6628 or write the Cultural Alliance at Box 3605, Norfolk, 23514-3605.

Once you get a feel for the arts here, you may want to hook up with one or more organizations. Since volunteers are the lifeblood of these groups, they will be happy to see you. Most of the larger groups sell memberships or season tickets. These usually entitle you to newsletters, invitations to special events and gift shop discounts. Many groups have guilds that let you do hands-on work.

If you're between 22 and 45 years old you can join an affiliated organization for young adults. Membership fees are very reasonable, and this can be a great way to meet people and learn more about the arts. The Virginia Beach Center for the Arts sponsors Art & Co. The Chrysler Museum has For Art's Sake. The Virginia Opera sponsors the Operatunists. The Virginia Symphony has Bravo. These popular groups give you an inside look at the arts. They serve both educational and social functions, and get you invited to posh members-only previews and parties.

While all performing arts groups sell season tickets, feel free to sample their offerings by purchasing tickets to single performances. Some groups have two-for-one tickets in the annual Entertainment coupon books that are sold each December by various charities.

Insiders' Tips

There are two fun places to go to see artists in action. In Norfolk more than 40 artists work out of the d'Art Center downtown at 125 College Place (open 10AM-5PM Tuesday-Saturday and noon-5 PM Sunday). In Virginia Beach there are 10 artists with studio space in Artists at Work: Gallery and Studio, 2407 Pacific Ave. (open 10 AM-5 PM Tuesday-Saturday). Another 20 artists rent walls to display their works. At both places you'll find everything from sculptors to oil painters and jewelry makers. Admission is free, and art works are for sale.

The Big Four

There are four dominant arts organizations in the region: The Chrysler Museum, the Virginia Opera, the Virginia Stage Company and the Virginia Symphony. All are professional organizations with long histories and reputations that extend far beyond the region.

THE CHRYSLER MUSEUM

Olney Road and Mowbray Arch
Norfolk 622-1211
Hours: 10 AM-4 PM Tuesday-Saturday; 1-4 PM Sunday.
Admission free; $3 donation suggested

The Museum is one of our favorite spots. There is so much to see that you can go time after time and not feel like you're peering at the same art works. Founded in 1933 as the Norfolk Museum of Arts and Sciences, the museum changed its name in 1971 to honor the late Walter P. Chrysler, Jr. Chrysler, the automobile heir and avid art collector, married a Norfolk native and made his home in the city. Many of the 30,000 pieces in the museum belonged to Chrysler.

The museum has one of the largest art collections south of Washington, D.C. and is considered one of the top 20 art museums in the country. Its art library is the largest in the southeastern United States. In 1989 the museum completed an expansion and renovation of its building, which overlooks The Hague in the historic Ghent area.

The museum's permanent collection is an eclectic one with pieces dating from 2700 B.C. to the present. The museum is renowned for its glass collection, whose 8,000 pieces include the works of Tiffany, Lalique and other masters. The museum is known for its French and Italian paintings. It displays the Norfolk Mace, the silver symbol of the city created in 1753. Besides the permanent collection, there are always special exhibitions that stay for several months. An elegant cafe, Palettes, is located within the museum and serves lunch.

The museum, with its solemn guards and subdued lighting, seems like an adults-only place. However, it does welcome children, and on many Sunday afternoons it goes all out with free family activities that range from scavenger hunts to crafts and storytellers. The museum also operates three historic houses: the Adam Thoroughgood House in Virginia Beach and the Moses Myers House and Willoughby-Baylor House in Norfolk.

THE VIRGINIA OPERA

Box 2580
Norfolk 627-9545

This is a professional opera company that is gaining national acclaim. In the summer of 1992 it took "Porgy and Bess" on the road for two months with performances in Argentina, Uruguay and Brazil. The Norfolk-based opera company was formed in 1975 and performs in Norfolk, Richmond and Northern Virginia. Its typical season produces four major operas that star professional New York and regional singers. In 1992-93 the Virginia Opera presented "Carmen," "Pasquale," "The Not Mikado" and "Tosca." In the past, the opera has premiered three Thea Musgrave works: "A Woman Called Moses," "A Christmas Carol" and "Mary Queen of Scots."

This year the opera has been without a permanent home while Norfolk Center Theater is overhauled and transformed into the Harrison Opera House. In 1992 it was renamed for two local residents – the late Stanley Harrison and his wife Edythe, the opera's founding board president. Plans call for moving back into the theater by late 1993. In the meantime, the opera is performing at Chrysler Hall and the Pavilion Theater.

VIRGINIA STAGE COMPANY

Wells Theatre
Monticello & Tazewell streets
Norfolk   *627-6988*

Founded in 1978, this is a professional, nonprofit regional theater company. It puts on a dynamite season with the help of actors drawn primarily from New York and Los Angeles. When the stage company nearly folded in 1991 because of financial problems, 8,000 area residents came to its rescue by purchasing season tickets. Since then the company has been on solid footing. Its 1992-93 season included "The Lion in Winter," "From the Mississippi Delta," "The Immigrant," and "Pump Boys and Dinettes."

It's worth a trip to the theater just to see its home, the venerable Wells Theatre. This elaborate Beaux Arts structure was built in 1912 and is a National Historic Landmark. A 1985 renovation returned the 680-seat auditorium to its original splendor and erased any signs of its stint

as an X-rated movie theater in the 1960s.

VIRGINIA SYMPHONY

Box 26
Norfolk   *623-8590*

This is one of the busiest performing arts groups around with more than 100 concerts a year. The symphony, which was founded in 1919, has a core group of 50 professional musicians and about 40 others who play as needed. The group performs at Chrysler Hall, the Pavilion Theatre in Virginia Beach, Ogdon Hall in Hampton and Phi Beta Kappa Hall in Williamsburg.

Besides its classical series, the symphony produces pops, dance and Mozart series. It periodically puts on Peanut Butter and Jam concerts for children. You can also catch its players at free outdoor concerts at some area festivals. In 1992 the symphony sponsored a performance by the Bolshoi Ballet. The previous year it brought the Kirov Ballet to the area. Both the classical and pops series feature prominent guest artists. In 1992-93 they included "Doc" Severinsen on trumpet, Roger Williams on piano and singers Mel Torme and Judy Collins.

Other Organizations

Other arts groups may not be as large as the four listed above, but they have plenty to offer the region in the way of talent and diversity. The following is a sampling of area arts organizations.

Photo: Kathy Keeney

Virginia Opera's production of Carmen, October, 1992.

Dance

Dance Theatre of Norfolk – 627-2281. Classes and performances feature a variety of styles aimed at developing minority youth in theater arts.

Old Dominion Ballet – 683-4486. Offers classes in various dance styles and has several annual performances. Each December it produces "The Nutcracker."

Virginia Ballet Theater – 622-4822. This is a regional, semi-professional company that performs regularly and offers a variety of classes.

Virginia Beach Ballet – 495-0989. This is an amateur ballet organization that offers productions featuring classical ballet and modern dance.

Lectures

The Norfolk Forum – 627-8672. This popular Chrysler Hall series sells out early and has recently brought such notable speakers as Margaret Thatcher and Tom Brokaw.

Old Dominion University President's Lecture Series – 683-3115. This free series started in 1992 to bring diverse speakers to campus. Recent lecturers include Dr. C. Everett Koop and Rep. Newt Gingrich.

Tidewater Jewish Forum – 489-1371. Sponsored by the Jewish Community Center, this series brings a variety of interesting speakers. Recently they've included former United Nations Ambassador Jeane Kirkpatrick and broadcaster Nina Totenberg.

Virginia Wesleyan College Series – 455-3200. This covers a variety of topics from storytelling to the presidential election.

Music

Bay Youth Symphony Orchestra – 461-8834. Sponsors youth concerts throughout the region and also has a string group.

Cantata Chorus of Norfolk – 627-5665. Amateur chorus specializes in sacred works during concerts at Christ and St. Luke's Episcopal Church in Norfolk.

Capriole – 1-804-220-1248. This professional Williamsburg-based group has several performances in South Hampton Roads. It is a vocal and instrumental ensemble specializing in 17th-century music.

Chesapeake Civic Chorus – 421-9784. Amateur chorus presents a variety of music during annual concerts.

Eastern Virginia Brass Society – 340-6406. Chamber music ensemble features trumpets, trombone, horn and tuba.

Evensong Chorale and Chamber Ensemble – 363-1981. Performs classical music.

Feldman Chamber Music Society – 627-1077. Sponsors concerts by outstanding chamber musicians.

I. Sherman Greene Chorale - - 467-8971. African-American community chorus performs traditional music as well as the works of contemporary composers.

Norfolk Chamber Consort – 440-1803. Chamber music group features winds, strings, keyboard instruments and vocalists.

Tidewater Area Musicians Orchestra – 393-9064. Local musicians present a variety of works.

Tidewater Classical Guitar Society – 255-2304. Brings internationally known and regional guitarists to the area.

Tidewater Winds – 464-9290. Concert band performs in the Sousa band tradition.

Virginia Beach Chorale – 467-3420. Vocalists present a variety of music.

Virginia Beach Symphonic Band – 463-1166. Presents a series of theme band concerts.

Virginia Beach Symphony Orchestra – 471-2225. Community group has a series of concerts with featured soloists.

Virginia Pro Musica – 627-8375. Chamber chorus presents music of the Renaissance and Baroque periods.

Virginia Symphonic Chorus - - 427-1486. Performs several concerts a year of classical music.

Theater

Commonwealth Musical Stage – 340-5446. Theater company uses regional talent to produce musicals.

Encore Players – 460-5152. Amateur group features actors who are in the military.

Founders Inn Dinner Theater – 366-5749. Started in 1992, it uses local actors in such productions as "The Fantisticks" and "Arsenic and Old Lace."

Gallery Dinner Theatre – 461-5570. Professional dinner theater.

Generic Theater – 441-2160. Innovative theater that's part of the Norfolk Department of Parks and Recreation does only works not previously seen in the region.

The Hurrah Players – 627-5437. Features highly trained local children in plays geared toward young audiences.

Little Theatre of Norfolk – 627-8551. This is the country's oldest continuously active little theater. It was formed in 1926 and specializes in light comedies and musicals.

Little Theatre of Virginia Beach – 428-9233. Amateur theater produces a variety of plays.

Norfolk Musical Theater – 588-1072. Some musicals are presented as dinner theater productions; others are in area auditoriums.

Norfolk Savoyards -- 484-6920. Specializes in the works of Gilbert and Sullivan.

Old Dominion University Actor's Regional Theatre – 683-5305. Performances feature both students and actors from the community.

Old Dominion University Shakespeare Ensemble – 683-3991. Local actors and ODU's English department team up to give a new twist to Shakespeare's works.

University Players – 683-3828. Productions feature ODU students.

Virginia Wesleyan College – 455-3200. Productions feature Virginia Wesleyan students.

Willett Hall – 393-5144. Touring groups bring Broadway musicals and children's performances to Portsmouth hall.

Mixed Series

Norfolk Society of Arts – 622-ARTS. Presents a variety of performances by guest artists.

Portsmouth Community Concerts – 393-5144. Subscription-only concerts at Willett Hall bring professional artists to the region.

Tidewater Performing Arts Society – 627-2314. Provides some of the most innovative programs in the region by bringing nationally known dance groups, singers and other artists.

Uhuru African-American Cultural Society – 461-7975. Performances highlight songs, dances, drumming and literature from Africa.

Visual Art Museums

Arts Center of the Portsmouth Museums – 393-8393. This is part of the city-operated Portsmouth Museums and is housed in the 1846 Courthouse. It brings traveling exhibits ranging from quilts to miniatures.

The Suffolk Museum – 925-6311. City-run arts center presents a variety of art exhibits.

Virginia Beach Center for the Arts – 425-0000. Regional arts center showcases 20th-century art with changing exhibits.

Galleries

Ann Nicole Gallery, 1747 Parkview Dr., Chesapeake (424-2936).

Art America, 141 Granby St., Norfolk (625-1888).

Art Images, 312 Laskin Rd., Virginia Beach (428-3535).

Art Works Gallery & Frame Shop, 312 Bute St., Norfolk (625-3004).

Artist Frame Shop and Gallery, 3216 High St., Portsmouth (397-4233).

Artists at Work: Gallery and

Insiders' Tips

Several arts programs are targeted toward youthful audiences. The Hurrah Players and Willett Hall's Storybook Theater Children's Series present excellent theatrical productions. The Virginia Beach Center for the Arts offers occasional crafts programs while The Chrysler Museum has frequent Sunday afternoon family programs. There are several area puppet troupes that perform: Wappadoodle Puppets (481-6658), Spectrum Puppets (491-2873) and Fuzz & Stuffing Puppets (480-2991). The Virginia Symphony also periodically offers Peanut Butter & Jam Concerts.

Studios, 2407 Pacific Ave., Virginia Beach (425-6671).

Auslew Gallery, 5548 Sajo Farm Rd., Virginia Beach (464-4405).

Beach Gallery, 310 30th St., Virginia Beach (428-3726).

Breit Functional Crafts, 1701 Colley Ave., Norfolk (640-1012).

Commons Gallery, Church of the Ascension, 4853 Princess Anne Rd., Virginia Beach (425-6671).

Crestar Bank Gallery, 500 Main St., Norfolk (583-3586).

d'Art Center, 125 College Pl., Norfolk (625-4211).

Dominion Bank Gallery, Dominion Tower, 999 Waterside Dr., Norfolk (583-3586).

Eastern Virginia Medical School Galleries, Lewis Hall, 700 Olney Rd., Norfolk (446-6050).

Great Dismal Swamp Galleries, 358 N. George Washington Highway, Chesapeake (485-1114).

Harbor Gallery, 1508 Colley Ave., Norfolk (627-2787).

Hartung Gallery & Art Supplies, 4367 Portsmouth Blvd., Portsmouth, 1200 N. Battlefield Blvd., Chesapeake (488-3042, 436-7691).

Imperial Gallery & Frame Shop, 540 Taldan Ave. and 1328 N. Great Neck Rd., Virginia Beach, and 316 S. Battlefield Blvd., Chesapeake (497-2324, 481-2752, 482-1771).

Jewish Community Center's Lobby Art Gallery, 7300 Newport Ave., Norfolk (489-1371).

Ocean Art Gallery, 614 21st St., Virginia Beach (425-1666)

Old Dominion University Gallery, 765 Granby St., Norfolk (683-2843, 683-4047)

Olde Towne Gallery, 330 High St., Portsmouth (397-ARTS).

Palmer-Rae Gallery, 112 Granby St., Norfolk (627-0081).

Plume Street Design, Monticello Arcade, Norfolk (627-0301).

Potter's Wheel, 21st St. Pavilion Shops, Norfolk (625-7208).

Primavera – The Crafts Gallery, 4216 Virginia Beach Blvd., Virginia Beach (431-9393).

Quarberg Gallery, 754 W. 22nd St., Norfolk (627-6028).

R.A. Singletary Gallery, 3600 Greenwood Dr., Portsmouth (487-7362, 393-1633).

Regent University Library Lobby, Regent University, Virginia Beach (523-7487).

Studio Gallery, 1005 Cypress Ave., Virginia Beach (428-4196).

Vance Mitchell Galleries, 2973 Shore Dr., Virginia Beach (481-7434).

Village Gallery, 5256-B Providence Rd., Virginia Beach (495-0913).

Virginia Wesleyan College Hofheimer Library, 1584 Wesleyan Dr., Norfolk/Virginia Beach (455-3222).

WHRO Fine Arts Gallery, 5200 Hampton Blvd., Norfolk (489-9476, 425-6671).

Photo: Virginia Division of Tourism

Virginia Beach is an ideal vacation spot for families.

Inside
Recreation

*O*n any sunny day, no less than half the residents of Hampton Roads pack up their bikes, bats, balls and boats and head off to one of the numerous parks and recreation meccas scattered throughout the region. And, because we are also known to have perfected the art of vicarious pleasure, the other half packs up beach chairs and picnics to tag along and watch the fun.

Couch potatoes don't get much applause around these parts. With hundreds of public tennis courts, umpteen golf courses, the Chesapeake Bay and Atlantic Ocean and their fine beaches, the fishing, biking, hiking, windsurfing and sailing...it's hard to say "no" to the call of the great outdoors. What you'll soon discover, whether you are a visitor or a newcomer, is that neither our fabulously maintained recreational facilities nor our year round temperate climate will give you much opportunity for just hanging around on the sofa.

While each of the South Hampton Roads cities is proud to boast of its own public and private facilities, we've decided to group by specific activity rather than by city. After all, we know that if you're a golfer, you want to find *all* the courses in one place. Likewise for

you nature lovers who want to compare all the possibilities for park pleasure-seeking, or tennis buffs who are itching to round robin from one end of the region to the other.

Whatever your pastime passion, you're sure to find it here. So much of it, in fact, that it would be impossible to list every recreational opportunity in this huge network of community facilities. For more in-depth information about specific cities, a quick call to the following will get you detailed brochures and newsletters listing all the scoop on facilities, leisure classes and athletic programs for all ages:

Norfolk Parks and Recreation Department   441-2149

Virginia Beach Department of Parks and Recreation   471-5884

Chesapeake Parks and Recreation Department   547-6411

Portsmouth Department of Parks and Recreation   393-8481

Parks

Norfolk

LAFAYETTE PARK
25th and Granby streets   *441-2149*
One of Norfolk's oldest parks,

Lafayette Park boasts two outdoor basketball courts, four tennis courts, an amphitheater, picnic shelters, boat ramp, well-maintained fields for softball and rugby and a grand playground, including special play equipment for the disabled. The scenic pathways that wind through the mature flora and fauna are especially appealing, and you can stop for a soft drink or snack at the nearby concession stand. What we call "City Park" sits next to the 55-acre Virginia Zoo, so plan to spend a full day to take in all this park has to offer.

TOWN POINT PARK
Waterside Drive at Boush Street   441-2149
It's simply amazing to those of us who were raised in Hampton Roads that this wonderful park sits in the very location that we were never allowed to enter after dark while we were growing up. But just look at it today! Just a footstep from Norfolk's primary downtown business district, adjacent to the Waterside festival marketplace, Town Point Park is indeed the visible tribute to Downtown Norfolk's revitalization spirit. With its meandering walkways, gay nineties street lamps, London Plane trees and comfy benches set between large expanses of incredibly lush green lawn, it is a wonderful place for a quiet stroll or to sit and watch ships gliding down the Elizabeth River.

Come any given weekend, however, this sleeping giant really roars. Norfolk Festevents, the city's premiere party-thrower, engineers events and festivals that fill even the most insatiable desire for activity, from the weekly T.G.I.F. celebrations to Harborfest to festivals in honor of countries, kids and cultures of every kind.

You'll find public parking at nearby lots and ramps, and you can even take a short ferry ride across the Elizabeth River to Portsmouth for a nominal fee. The Waterside Marina is adjacent to the park, and a favorite Sunday excursion is to walk up and down the docks checking out the visiting vessels and their ports of call. There are also frequent visits from foreign ships who dock at Otter Berth, home port to *The Spirit of Norfolk*, and the public is often invited to come aboard for tours.

OCEAN VIEW PARK
Ocean View   441-1787
The jewel of Ocean View and a landmark in this close-knit community's rejuvenation efforts, this unique 6.5 acre park was just

recently opened amidst great fanfare and festivity. Located on the site of the old Ocean View Amusement Park, it features a large gazebo for presentations and dancing, a beach that's lifeguarded during summer months, boardwalk, beach handicap access ramp and lovely lawns. Events planned for this summer include monthly fireworks, a Big Band concert/dancing series and much, much more.

NORFOLK BOTANICAL GARDEN
Airport Rd. off Azalea Garden Rd.   441-5830

Botanical splendor for the viewing along 12 miles of lush pathways awaits every day of the year in this 175 acre floral wonderland. (For more information, please see the "Attractions" section.)

NORTHSIDE PARK
8400 Tidewater Drive

Here's where many softball and tennis champs meet to defend their titles. With two lighted softball diamonds, seven tennis courts, outdoor basketball court, BMX bicycle course, skateboard ramp plus playground and picnic shelters, this place is always popping with activity of one sort or another. Especially popular is the year-round indoor pool and sun patio, staffed by certified lifeguards who offer aquatic games and classes for all ages. Seasonal tennis instruction by a part-time tennis pro is also available. There's no direct phone, so to get more information, contact the Recreation Bureau at 441-2149.

LAKEWOOD PARK
1612 Willow Wood Drive   441-5833

Headquarters to the Bureau of Recreation's Athletic and Dance/Music divisions, Lakewood Park sits in the heart of Lakewood, an exceptionally lovely residential neighborhood. Featuring nine tennis courts, two lighted softball/baseball/football/soccer fields, picnic shelters, playground, rest rooms and plenty of free parking. Moms who drop off their kids for league play have been known to slip right across the street to the Lafayette Library for a little peace and quiet.

BARRAUD PARK
Off Tidewater Dr. on Vista Dr.   441-2149

From June to September, this large, newly renovated community park is staffed to organize activities and sign out equipment. You'll find lighted softball and football/soccer fields, six tennis courts, playground, picnic shelter and amphitheater, with ample free parking. Summer months offer organized playground games for ages 6 to 12, as well as a summer food program.

TARRALTON PARK
Tarralton Drive and Millard Street   441-1765

The most recent addition to the network of parks maintained by the Rec Bureau, Tarralton features over 70 acres with three family size picnic shelters, colorful play area and tot lot, lighted tennis courts, lighted basketball court, three soccer fields and a BMX bicycle trail. There's also a Little League complex and softball field.

NEIGHBORHOOD PARKS AND SCHOOL GROUNDS

Throughout the city of Norfolk, you'll find "mini parks," beautiful little pockets of well-manicured common grounds and landscaping. In addition to the 112 such areas maintained by the Norfolk Bureau of Recreation (often located on school grounds), there are many other neighborhood quiet spots, like Stockley Gardens in Ghent. Take a look around...there's more than likely a playground or park right around the corner!

Virginia Beach

SEASHORE STATE PARK
Shore Drive   *481-4836*

Designated a Registered National Landmark in 1965, Seashore State Park is an environmental magnet for visitors and residents alike. Entering this 2,770 acre sanctuary is like stepping out of the hustle-bustle of civilization into a far away world. Much of the park is preserved as a natural area, with sights that run the gamut from semitropical forest to giant sand dunes. In just one day's visit, you're sure to catch a glimpse of a number of the 336 species of trees and plants, ranging from cypress draped with Spanish Moss to hardy Yucca trees.

Daytime visitors will find a picnic area, hiking trails, a self-guided nature trail and a Visitors Center with exhibits and book sales. Nine trails, including one for handicapped visitors, cover 17 miles and are part of the National Scenic Trails System. Bikers will find their own five-mile trail, which connects to the city's bike trails.

The Shore Drive side of the park borders on the Chesapeake Bay where you'll find an overnight camping section with 215 sites and 20 group sites, along with a camp store, mile-long beach reserved for campers, rest rooms, showers and amphitheater for interpretive programs. Twenty cabins are also available in this area, but you must reserve early. Call 481-2131.

From 64th Street, you can access the east end of the park, where there's a boat ramp that slides you into Broad Bay, to Lynnhaven Inlet and then out to the Chesapeake Bay. Near this boat ramp is a favorite place for a lover's picnic...a hill that offers a scenic view high above the water. For guided tour information, just stop in at the Visitors Center. Admission to the park is free, but there is a nominal parking fee.

BACK BAY NATIONAL WILDLIFE REFUGE
4005 Sandpiper Road   *721-2412*

If you follow the thousands of migrating geese, ducks and swans, you'll find yourself in the natural habitat of the marshy islands of shallow Back Bay. Here, on 5,000 acres of virtually untouched natural beauty, you can be witness to the splendor of beach, dunes, marsh and woodlands along with resident waterfowl, deer and other animals.

To preserve the integrity of the park, strict rules are enforced. First, the park is only open during daylight hours, from sunrise to sunset. Parking is permitted only in designated areas during open

hours, and only those with special permits are allowed motorized vehicle access to beaches and unpaved dirt roads. Other no-no's: unleashed pets, guns, horses or open fires. Likewise, the fragile dunes are off-limits to visitors, but that still leaves the beach shore and nature trails for hiking.

The Seaside Trail and Dune Trail guides you from the parking lot to the stunning beach. The north mile of the beach is closed to protect shore birds there, but the south beach is open, although swimming, sunbathing and surfing is prohibited. Just consider Back Bay to be the perfect place to bring your binoculars, a canteen of water, camera, picnic lunch and a big can of bug spray.

FALSE CAPE STATE PARK
4001 Sandpiper Road   426-7128

Five miles south of the Back Bay Refuge sits the home to migratory waterfowl, wildlife and protected marshlands. False Cape State Park is a six-mile stretch of undisturbed beach along a barrier spit that divides the ocean from Back Bay, and is accessible only by foot, bicycle or boat. If you choose to walk, you'll have to hike through five miles of Back Bay Refuge to reach the boundaries of the park. You really must have a pioneer camping spirit to overnight here, because other than pit toilets, there are absolutely no amenities, and open fires are not permitted. You'll also have to lug in your own water and anything else you might need to create an overnight comfort zone.

If you're interested in learning all about the park's diverse ecosystem, the Wash Woods Environmental Education Center, housed in a converted hunting lodge near the southern end of the park, is the place to turn. For small groups, comfortable overnight accommodations can be arranged to allow time for more intensive study of the area's natural resources.

For a day visit during peak visiting periods, any questions can be answered at the park's ranger station located just about a mile south of the northern entrance.

MOUNT TRASHMORE
Edwin Drive   473-5251

Boasting one of the city's highest elevations – 68 feet – Mount Trashmore comes by its name honestly. A brilliantly conceived solid waste management project, what was once a huge hill of 750,000 tons of trash was transformed in 1973 into

Insiders' Tips

what is now a beautifully landscaped hub of activity, and one of Virginia Beach's most popular parks.

When you're done flying kites or model airplanes from its peak, you can peer down on the action at the skateboard bowl and ramp and get a bird's eye view of the ramp used annually for the area's Soap Box Derby. Then you can climb down to one of two well-stocked lakes where you can paddle-boat away your worries or fish with bait from the on-site tackle shop. Feeling lazy? Just lie back and toss bread crumbs to the resident ducks, geese and coots that have no problem marching right over to you for a hand-out.

Also part of the complex are several playgrounds, picnic shelters, basketball and tennis courts as well as volleyball nets where pick-up games are the norm. Windsurfers are welcome, and plentiful, during peak summer months, and jon boats can be rented to row alongside.

In the works as of this writing is an all-volunteer effort to create a 25,000-square-foot park designed for children called "Kids Cove." This colossal wooden playground will incorporate slides, mazes, ramps and bridges all built around a nautical theme, and will be the largest playground in the entire region. Coordinators hope to hold a five day "barn-raising" in May of 1993 to make this children's fantasyland a reality.

PRINCESS ANNE PARK

Princess Anne Road   427-6020

Eighty acres of a sports lover's paradise sit right next to the popular Virginia Beach Farmer's Market. Along with plenty of wide open space, Princess Anne Park can be proud of its outstanding facilities, including four playgrounds, a number of baseball and softball fields, plus equipment for basketball, volleyball, croquet and horseshoes. Really special is the horse arena for horse shows and rodeos, as well as a children's garden and popular wooded picnic area.

BAYVILLE PARK

First Court Road   460-7569

Bayville has the city's only disc golf course for frisbee players, an 18-hole challenge that is considered by experts to be one of the toughest in the nation. The tree-shaded 66-acre park has features designed for the handicapped, along with facilities for basketball, shuffleboard, softball, volleyball, handball, badminton and horseshoes alongside a comfortable picnic area. For kiddies, Bayville is a veritable Garden of Eden with the neatest playground in town. Just watch their smiles as they come face to face with giant futuristic structures to climb, wood and metal towers, swinging tires and rocking metal disks.

RED WING PARK

General Booth Blvd. & Poor Farm Rd.   437-4847

Because of its proximity to some of the Beach's favorite attractions, including Croatan Beach, Wildwater Rapids and the Virginia Marine Science Museum, Red Wing Park is a super stop-off for a picnic lunch. Once here, you can't leave before you stroll through the beautiful gardens...the lovely Japanese garden and aromatic fragrance garden...along with a look at the prisoner of war memorial.

Activity-wise, Red Wing has a skateboard ramp, fitness course, playground, three ball fields plus facilities for tennis, volleyball, badminton, basketball and horseshoes. And, like most Virginia Beach parks, all you need is a valid I.D. to borrow any sports equipment you forgot at home.

LITTLE ISLAND PARK
Sandpiper Road   426-7200

Almost a secret treasure of a park, Little Island takes full advantage of its location on Sandbridge Beach as well as Back Bay, and its fishing pier makes it especially attractive for anglers.

The broad beach is lifeguarded during summer months from 9:30 AM to 6 PM, and after a swim, you can move on to the playground, tennis courts, basketball or volleyball courts. A snack bar and shaded picnic area are also here at Little Island.

MUNDEN POINT PARK
Munden Point Rd. off
Princess Anne Rd.   426-5296

Getting to Munden Park is an excursion in itself...a long ride through the rural areas of Virginia Beach to the North Landing River. Once here, the 100 scenic acres offer a multitude of choices for boaters and landlubbers alike. Since the North Landing River is a link to the Intracoastal Waterway system, you can either watch the fancy vessels powering out, rent a canoe or

paddleboat or launch your own boat from the boat ramp for a small usage fee.

Landside, there's softball, basketball, volleyball and horseshoes, along with a playground and picnic area. Noteworthy, too, is a Parcourse Fitness Circuit.

BEACH GARDEN PARK
Holly Road   471-4884

A quiet retreat from the busy Oceanfront scene, this delightful park features a playground, fitness trail and picnic tables.

Chesapeake

CHESAPEAKE CITY PARK
500 Greenbrier Parkway   547-6411

This 75-acre site features rows of reforested pine trees bordering 45 acres of open space. The open space is naturally divided by roadways into segments that can be rented for corporate or private events according to the space needed, with a network of electricity and water service in place for support. For regular daytime visitors, there's a fitness trail, play equipment, basketball courts and picnic shelter.

NORTHWEST RIVER PARK
1733 Indian River Road   421-7151

This 763-acre park has been developed as a natural recreation area incorporating camping, an extensive trail system, picnic shelters, play areas, an equestrian area, miniature golf and plenty of wide open spaces. Located in the southeastern section of Chesapeake, water abounds, including the lake that stretches almost to the southern activity area which runs along the banks of the Northwest River where canoes and boats can be rented. Of special note is the fragrance trail created for the visually handicapped, along with a ropes and initiative course, 103 campsites with camp store, two modern bath houses, laundry, picnic tables and fire rings. It's also a favorite place for horseback riding and hikes along the six-mile nature trail system.

DEEP CREEK LOCK PARK
300 Luray   487-8841
This is a 25-acre site named for the Corps of Engineers' lock which separates the salt water of Deep Creek from the fresh water of the historic Dismal Swamp Canal. The heavily wooded park includes several overlook towers, picnic shelters, play areas, a fitness trail, indoor rest rooms and a combination pedestrian bridge and elevated walkway system to traverse a tidal inlet and marsh area. Diverse foot trails wind through the woods, and a canoe launch along with fishing and crabbing are favorite Deep Creek activities.

GREAT BRIDGE LOCK PARK
Lock Road   547-6292
Located at the transition from the Southern Branch of the Elizabeth River to the Albemarle and Chesapeake Canal along the Intracoastal Waterway, this 19-acre park features a two-lane boat ramp, picnic shelters and a foot trail along the northern shoreline and through the western portion of the park.

There's also a large play area and extensive fishing and crabbing areas from the bulkheaded banks. Because one of the area's favorite activities is boat-watching, bleachers have been erected for glimpsing the many yachts that transit the lock southbound in the fall and northbound in the spring.

INDIAN RIVER PARK
Military Highway   424-4238
While the City of Norfolk actually owns the 100-acre tract known as Indian River Park, the City of Chesapeake uses 35 acres of the northern section for activities including basketball, baseball, picnicking and a playground. Discussions on joint development of the southern section, like undeveloped trail opportunities, are still underway.

WESTERN BRANCH PARK
4437 Portsmouth Blvd.   465-0211
The first phase of planned development has just been completed for this 80-acre park, with the first of the picnic areas and playgrounds already being enjoyed by Western Branch residents. As a prelude to future development, the city has constructed the park access road and one parking lot, and scouts have marked a rudimentary nature trail, while volunteers have planted thousands of wild flowers. On the boards now are softball fields, tennis and basketball courts, with additional picnic and playground areas.

LAKESIDE PARK
Byrd and Holey aves., South Norfolk 543-5721
Large lawn areas, a wooded section, picnic shelters with grills,

play areas and walkways highlight this 6 1/2 acre park. Popular here is the fishing along the bulkheaded lake.

GREENBRIER SPORTS PARK
Greenbrier Parkway   *547-6400*

When you come here, get ready to play! A 12-acre site, this sports park lives up to its name with eight tournament-quality lighted tennis courts and two tournament-quality softball fields. For spectators, there's also a picnic shelter and play equipment.

Portsmouth

CITY PARK
City Hall Avenue   *393-5162*

Tucked behind the tombstones of the Olive Branch Cemetery are 93 gorgeous acres of well-maintained golf course, six lighted tennis courts, boat docks, duck ponds, gardens and playgrounds. Voted best park in the state in 1989 by the Virginia Parks and Recreation Association, City Park borders the western branch of the Elizabeth River and Baines Creek. The highlight for little ones is the real live mini-train, a coal-fired engine called Pokey Smokey with open seating

behind, that whistles its way through a tunnel and around a pond...a real treat of an attraction that's just been recently overhauled along with the rest of the park. This is an absolutely delightful place to spend a lazy day – with or without children.

SLEEPY HOLE PARK
Sleepy Hole Road   *393-5056*

Once the plantation of Amadeo Obici, the Italian immigrant who founded the Planters Peanut Company, Sleepy Hole Park was purchased by the city of Portsmouth in 1972, and has since developed into a premiere playground for area residents. Along with the popular Sleepy Hole Golf Course, the park boasts a well-stocked lake for fishing, nature trails through the tidal marsh that surrounds the park (including one especially constructed so that the handicapped can use it with ease), picnic shelters and playgrounds. A camper's favorite spot, there are fifty camping sites available under the tall oaks – twenty-eight tent sites with water, tables and grills and another twenty-two with electric and water hookups. Campers also have access to modern rest room facilities with hot showers and a laundry area.

CHURCHLAND PARK
Cedar Lane   393-8481

This open space, 38-acre community park is home to six soccer fields, two softball fields, a BMX bicycle track, playgrounds and picnic shelters equipped with grills. There are also trails for biking, jogging and leisurely nature walks.

RIVERFRONT PARK
At the Foot of High Street   393-8481

A delightful little park that runs along the banks of the Elizabeth River, Riverfront is the place to relax and just watch the ships glide by. Nearby, you'll find the Lightship Museum, Naval Shipyard Museum, Portside and the Elizabeth River Ferry.

RECREATION AND COMMUNITY CENTERS

Got an urge to learn to tap dance? Weave an Appalachian basket? Strum a guitar? Master your swimming skills? Hampton Roads not only has the talented teachers, but the easy-to-get-to facilities where you can take classes on the cheap...and have a fantastic time while you're at it!

Special programs, classes and activities are scheduled year round in each of the area's cities, and held at their respective recreation facilities. Because programs change seasonally, we won't be able to be more specific than to say that whatever you've got the urge to do, you'll likely find it coming up in the next class session. In most cases, the following centers are open daily from 10 AM until 6 PM, with some offering various night time hours that change from winter to summer. A call to check on your nearest center's hours is recommended.

Norfolk

To use any of Norfolk's 25 recreation centers, you must obtain a facility use card. Cost of the card is $5 for youths ages 5 to 17 and $10 for adults ages 18 to 64. The cards are available at two sites:

Sherwood Recreation Center, 4537 Little John Road, 441-5824

Huntersville Recreation Center, 830 Goff Street, 441-1545

You will not need a card if you attend a fee-based class or attend a special event or meeting at any of the facilities, and both "good grade" and family discounts are available. You can also get a temporary three-day pass to give you an opportunity to check out the facility before you purchase a card.

RECREATION CENTERS

Bayview, 1434 Bayview Boulevard, 441-1768

Berkley, 89 Liberty Street, 543-1230

Southside (Seniors), 500 South Main Street, 441-1911

Bolling Green, 1319 Godfrey Avenue, 441-2746

Crossroads, 8044 Tidewater Drive, 441-1769

Diggs Town, 1401 Melon Street, 441-1975

East Ocean View, 9520 20th Bay Street, 441-1785

Fairlawn, 1132 Wade Street, 441-5670

Grandy Village, 3017 Kimball Terrace, 441-2856

Huntersville, 830 Goff Street, 441-1545

Ingleside, 940 Ingleside Road, 441-5675

Lakewood Dance/Music, 1612 Willow Wood Drive, 441-5833

Larchmont, 1167 Bolling Avenue, 441-5411

Merrimac Landing, 8809 Monitor Way, 441-1783

Northside Pool, 8400 Tidewater Drive, 441-1760

Norview, 6800 Sewells Point Road, 441-5836

Ocean View (Seniors), 600 East Ocean View Avenue, 441-1767

Park Place, 620 W. 29th Street, 441-1346

Sewells Point, 7928 Hampton Boulevard, 441-5393

Sherwood, 4537 Little John Drive, 441-5824

Tarrallton, 2100 Tarrallton Drive, 441-1765

Theater Arts, 912 21st Street, 441-2160

Therapeutic Recreation, 180 East Evans Street, 441-1764

Titustown Center for Arts & Recreation, 7545 Diven Street, 441-5394

Young Terrace, 804 Cumberland Street, 441-2754

For information concerning specific activities:

Athletics   441-2149
Senior Citizens   441-2109
Special Events   441-2140

THERAPEUTIC RECREATION

The City of Norfolk sponsors a complete year-round program for children and adults with disabilities, from clinics and workshops, sports classes (swimming, golf, tennis, horseback riding and more) to field trips. Special events are free and open to the public; class fees range from $6 to $25. For a full schedule and details, call 441-1764 (V/TDD). Note: if you are hearing impaired, press your space bar so that the staff will know you are calling on TDD.

COMMUNITY CENTERS

JEWISH COMMUNITY CENTER

Here you can back-stroke any day of the year, thanks to an indoor heated pool protected by a huge domed skylight roof. The gymnasium is almost always a noisy place, thanks to the pick-up basketball games you'll find on almost any given day. Ditto for the well-

Insiders' Tips

If you're headed for a swim in the Chesapeake Bay, pack a jar of meat tenderizer in that beach bag. It's the most effective treatment for soothing the burn of a stinging nettle (jellyfish) sting.

equipped exercise room. The center offers a wide variety of programs for all ages, and membership fees are very reasonable for the beautiful facilities. You need not be Jewish to join.

BOYS & GIRLS CLUBS OF SOUTH HAMPTON ROADS

W. W. HOUSTON MEMORIAL CLUB
3401 Azalea Garden Road   855-8908
Swimming, cheerleading, football, wrestling, cooking and crafts...all this and more is offered to kids 6 - 17 years. The large pool is the central focus year round, from lifeguard training to classes designed for babies. Annual membership is $15, with additional fees for special classes and training.

YMCA TOTAL FITNESS CENTER
312 Bute Street   622-6328
It's definitely "the thing" to belong to this outstanding facility located in the heart of Downtown Norfolk in the historic Freemason district. Businessmen and women trade in their suits for jogging shorts and hit the covered outdoor track, Nautilus exercise room or one of a zillion aerobics classes before, at lunch or after work. Swim laps in the indoor heated pool, play racquetball, basketball or volleyball...it's all here, and there's always someone to play and strain with. Extra perks are babysitting services available for some classes, along with a super summer camp program and fitness evaluations. Corporate memberships are available.

YWCA
253 West Freemason   625-4248
Right around the corner from "The Y" is a community center dedicated totally to the needs of Hampton Roads women. An exceptional hotline and shelter is offered for battered women (625-5570), along with timely programs such as "Women in Transition." The staff is small, but thoroughly knowledgeable and sympathetic to any problem, and applauded by many who have found their services invaluable.

ARMED SERVICES YMCA
500 East Ocean View Avenue   480-3744
One of 50 such facilities in this country and overseas, the purpose of the Armed Services YMCA is to serve as a bridge between the civilian and military communities of our area. The main focus is on recreation for military families, along with spiritual and social programs for all ages. Especially helpful are their special programs for military spouses on subjects ranging from job searching to aerobics to cooking and crafts.

WILLIAM A. HUNTON YMCA
1139 East Charlotte Street   622-7271
The stated purpose of this special YMCA is to "nurture positive self image, develop leadership skills and assist in fostering positive values in our youth." Established to help children and youths who might otherwise be "just hanging out" or a number in the juvenile justice system, the center gears its programs and activities to meet the special needs of these kids, many of whom

The Great Dismal Swamp

One of the most asked about attractions in Hampton Roads is also one of its most inaccessible. At area convention and visitor's bureaus, the world-renowned Great Dismal Swamp draws frequent inquiries. But unlike many attractions there are few campgrounds and hiking trails and many parts of it are accessible only by small boats. Despite its remoteness, the swamp manages to attract more than 10,000 visitors a year.

The 200,000-acre wilderness is much more than pure swamp. It is one of the most scenic spots in Virginia and North Carolina, with lush greenery, cypress trees, calm waters and an incredible variety of wildlife. Among its residents are bears, bobcats, otters, weasels, frogs, 23 fish species, bats and butterflies. More than 200 different kinds of birds have been sighted in the swamp, which also is a haven for swarms of mosquitoes and 21 varieties of snakes.

Col. William Byrd gave the swamp its gloomy name in 1728. Thirty-five years later George Washington surveyed the swamp and dreamed of draining it and cutting the timber on the 40,000 acres he and several other businessmen owned in the swamp. In 1793 slaves started digging at both ends of a 22-mile canal, which took 12 years to complete. It is still in use today, making it the oldest operating artificial waterway in the United States. The Dismal Swamp's canal, which has two sets of locks, is an alternate route for the Atlantic Intracoastal Waterway.

There are several ways to take in the beauty of the swamp, which spreads through Chesapeake and Suffolk as well as northeastern North Carolina:

*In Suffolk there is the Great Dismal Swamp Wildlife Refuge operated by the U.S. Fish and Wildlife Service (986-3705). The office there is staffed from 7 AM-3 PM Monday-Friday, and the refuge is open from a half hour before sunrise to a half hour after sunset. From the refuge you can hike or bike along a 4 1/2-mile road beside the Washington Ditch, named for George Washington who dug the first spade of dirt to create the canal. The Washington Ditch ends up at Lake Drummond, the largest natural lake in Virginia.

There is also a seven-mile road along the Jericho Ditch that leads to the lake, but it is not maintained as well as the shorter route. For the less hardy or those with small children, there is a half-mile boardwalk. Meandering along it will give you a feel for the swamp.

To get to the refuge take Route 58 to Suffolk, turn left on E. Washington St. (Route 337) and go left on White Marsh Road (Route

642). Look for the refuge signs and turn into the Washington Ditch entrance, which has a parking lot.

*In Chesapeake you can enter a 3.5-mile feeder ditch if you have a small boat or canoe. It is across the Dismal Swamp Canal on Route 17 (George Washington Highway), about three miles north of the North Carolina border. There is a city-owned boat ramp and parking lot on Route 17 a mile north of the feeder ditch entrance. You can rent a canoe from the Chesapeake KOA Campground on Route 17 (485-5686), which is located about eight miles north of the feeder ditch entrance. Canoe rental costs $2 an hour or $15 a day.

It takes about two hours to paddle down the ditch to Lake Drummond where the Corps of Engineers maintains a rustic campground. Bathrooms with toilets and sinks are on site but there are no showers or running water. You will find grills, picnic tables, places for campfires and two screened dining areas. No reservations are required, and camping is free. For information, call 421-7401. Remember that access to Lake Drummond is only by foot, bicycle or boats weighing less than 1,000 pounds.

To see the swamp, you can just drive down Route 17, also known as George Washington Highway, and look at dense woods that border the road. There are several picnic areas along the way.

*Just three miles over the state line in South Mills, N.C. is the Dismal Swamp Canal Visitor Welcome Center run by the state of North Carolina (919-771-8333). It prides itself on being the only visitor center in the country whose clients come by both boat and car. The center provides brochures and maps, has a helpful staff to answer questions and maintains a picnic area. There is a 150-foot dock at the center. Each year about 2,000 boaters tie up there for the night.

*In April 1993 visitors got a new way to absorb the beauty of the swamp. A joint venture between the Portsmouth Department of Tourism and the Elizabeth City Area Chamber of Commerce in North Carolina created cruises along the Dismal Swamp Canal. Two cruises were scheduled for April with two others set for the weekends of October 23 and 30. To start their adventure, Hampton Roads passengers ride a bus from Portsmouth to Elizabeth City, N.C. where they spend Saturday night. The next day they board the *Carrie B* paddlewheeler for an eight-hour trip up the Atlantic Intracoastal Waterway that cuts through the swamp and ends in Portsmouth. The cost is $139 for double occupancy, which includes the bus ride, boat trip, hotel and all meals. For information call Travel Designers, the tour organizer, at 399-0111 or 1-800-642-8991.

are from single parent or low income families. After school and day care, team sports, youth employment, summer camps and a number of other activities are scheduled year round.

Virginia Beach

Since you can't always go play on the beach, Virginia Beach operates excellent recreation facilities that seem to be jammed with activity almost every day of the year. The program offerings suit practically every taste, from arts and crafts, dance, music, drama and, of course, SPORTS! It almost seems as if no one dares to leave the house without some sort of ball or racquet in their hands. So, if you're a newcomer, the best way to fit right in is to get yourself over to a rec center and learn a sport. You'll meet a lot of nifty people when you do. And, if you're visiting, it's great to have the opportunity to continue your favorite sport while you're away from home.

You'll need a Facility Use Card to use any of the Virginia Beach Rec facilities. For children 6 - 17, the fee is $10; Adults 18 - 64, $25. Seniors above age 65 can snag a lifetime membership, the Golden Age Club, for $50. Want to check out the facilities for a day? Get a guest pass for just $3.

RECREATION CENTERS

KEMPSVILLE RECREATION CENTER
800 Monmouth Lane   *474-8492*
Here's a huge center serving

as headquarters for six popular city programs: Aquatic Services, Athletic Services, Youth Services, the Pre-School Program, Adult Services and the Kempsville Playhouse for the performing arts. Highlights include a 25-meter, six-lane indoor pool, a 200-seat theater, youth lounge and game room, two automatic bowling lanes, a gym and exercise room and a number of other rooms that are used for special programs and classes. Outside, there's a lot more: six lighted tennis courts, six basketball courts, a children's playground, two softball fields, three volleyball courts, two horseshoe pits, picnic area and open spaces for soccer and football. There's also a therapeutic track and field practice course.

BOW CREEK RECREATION CENTER
3427 Clubhouse Road   *431-3765*
A fairly new and attractive center – the lobby even has a fireplace – Bow Creek hosts classes and programs for children, youths, adults and seniors. Especially popular with the kids is a fully equipped game room that's open daily, with two billiard tables, table tennis, footsball, bumper pool and other games. For seniors, they can take advantage of bridge club, ballroom dance and square dancing, along with lots of special field trips.

OTHER VIRGINIA BEACH REC CENTERS:
Bayside Recreation Center, First Court Road, 460-7540

Great Neck Recreation Center, 2521 Shorehaven Drive, 496-6766

Seatack Community Center,

141 South Birdneck Road, 437-4858

THERAPEUTIC RECREATION

A number of programs are offered for children and adults who are physically, mentally or emotionally disabled, many at no fee. They include instructional classes and recreational programs to promote independence, and are found at the following locations:

Center for Effective Learning, 233 North Witchduck Road

Main Office, Dept. of Parks and Recreation, 2289 Lynnhaven Parkway

Bow Creek Recreation Center, 3427 Clubhouse Road

Kempsville Recreation Center, 800 Monmouth Lane

For detailed information and program schedules, call 471-5884.

COMMUNITY CENTERS

UNITED WAY FAMILY CENTER
4441 South Boulevard   *499-2311*

If you're travelling on the Norfolk-Virginia Beach Expressway by Mount Trashmore, you'll spot a sprawling brick building with a parking lot jammed with cars. How that many people can pack the United Way Family Center every day of the year amazes us all, but perhaps it's because the facilities and programs offered are some of the finest in the city. You can swim in the heated pool, learn a little balance beam, play tennis or work out in their fitness center. Housed here are a number of charitable organizations, including the YMCA of Virginia

Beach, The Boy's and Girl's Clubs of Virginia Beach, Big Brothers/Big Sisters, Family Services and the Retired Senior Volunteer Program. Newcomers should put this top-notch center on one of their first-to-check-out lists.

Chesapeake

It's soccer, basketball and ballet! It's volleyball, quilting and karate! It's more activities, classes, day trips and workshops than one person can squeeze into a lifetime. But, come on, give it a try. Just hook up with the City of Chesapeake's Parks and Rec facilities and it's bye-bye spare time.

Chesapeake operates six community centers that each feature a full plate of activities and classes. You'll find squeaky-clean gyms and lockers at all, along with weight rooms, kitchens and outdoor sports facilities. Membership and I.D. cards for residents are $5 per year for adults, $2 for kids 9 through 17, free for seniors. One day guest passes are available for $3.

THERAPEUTIC RECREATION

Chesapeake extends a particular welcome for children and adults with disabilities. A full schedule of programs, classes and trips is on the agenda, and many are free. Preschool and after-school programs are also offered. Volunteers are always needed to assist during activities, so if you've got some spare time, this would be a rewarding way to pass an afternoon. For information and assistance, call 547-6639. If you require a TDD, call Chesapeake's main library at 436-8300 to serve as a relay station.

RECREATION CENTERS

Deep Creek Community Center, 2901 Margaret Booker Drive, 487-8841

Great Bridge Community Center, 212 Holt Drive, 547-6292

Indian River Community Center, 2250 Old Greenbrier Road, 547-6292

River Crest Community Center, 1001 Riverwalk Parkway, 436-3100

South Norfolk Community Center, 1217 Godwin Avenue, 543-5721

Photo: Richmond Newspapers

Seashore State Park is enhanced by miles of trails, rustic cabins and campgrounds.

Western Branch Community Center, 4437 Portsmouth Boulevard, 465-0211

COMMUNITY CENTERS

CHESAPEAKE FAMILY YMCA

1033 Greenbrier Parkway　　547-8301

Adjacent to the city's sports complex, this beautiful, modern facility comes complete with all the sports trappings: a large swimming pool, complete Nautilus center, saunas, showers and locker rooms and large activity room. Take your pick of classes, from scuba diving and gymnastics to aerobics and martial arts. Working moms are particularly fond of the center's Before and After School Fun Club, available for elementary school children and a wonderful, activity-packed program for "latchkey" kids. The Y's summer day camp called Y.E.S. (Youth Experience Summer Program) is especially popular with Chesapeake children.

Portsmouth

The game's the same, only the place and people have changed. Any activity, class, workshop or program you can find in other Hampton Roads cities, you can find here at any one of the eight recreation centers operated by the City of Portsmouth. Arts and crafts, games, field trips and the real popular adult softball, basketball and volleyball leagues are par for the frantic pace.

As in other cities, the facilities vary from neighborhood to neighborhood, but all feature gym-

nasiums and lockers, exercise equipment and activity rooms.

THERAPEUTIC RECREATION

A packed calendar of activities is available for children and adults, each geared to accommodate a specific disability. For full information concerning class offerings, schedules and fees, call 393-8481.

RECREATION CENTERS

Cavalier Manor Recreation Center, 404 Viking Street, 393-8757

Craddock Recreation Center, 45 Afton Parkway, 393-8757

Hi-Landers Recreation Center, 409 McLean Street, 393-8441

Joseph E. Parker Recreation Center, 2430 Turnpike Road, 393-8340

Kingman Heights Recreation Center, 105 Utah Street, 393-8839

Neighborhood Facility, 900 Elm Street, 393-8595

Port Norfolk Recreation Center, 432 Broad Street, 393-8709

COMMUNITY CENTERS

PORTSMOUTH YMCA

527 High Street　　397-3413

One of the most popular features of the Portsmouth Y is the indoor running track, so you can deliver your laps through wind, rain or snow. Also aboard: pool, gymnasium, basketball, handball and volleyball courts, exercise/weight lifting rooms and sauna, steam room and whirlpool. A variety of classes and fitness evaluations is offered to both regular and corporate members.

EFFINGHAM STREET YMCA

1013 Effingham Street   *399-5511*

You know you're seeing pride and practice in motion when you spot the award winning special drill team from the Effingham Y march in a local parade! This is but one of the outstanding results of the leadership at this Y, which offers a family night program, youth bible class and a golden age club. Activities include everything from judo and karate to crocheting and ballet, all in a facility that houses a gymnasium, basketball court, pool tables and meeting rooms.

ARMED SERVICES YMCA

509 King Street   *397-1675*

Serving the Portsmouth Naval Shipyard, Portsmouth Naval Hospital and the Coast Guard Support Center, this Y provides recreational and social opportunities to military personnel and their families. It is part of the Armed Services branch of the national YMCA which began during the Civil War when 5,000 civilian volunteers provided aid to soldiers of both North and South. Today, it serves not only as a complement to programs offered by the military, but offers many dances, parties and social events. Men with a night off from their ships often stay over in comfortable dormitory type rooms.

NEW GOSPORT FAMILY PROGRAM CENTER

25 Stack Street   *396-2047*

This fairly new center was opened as a branch of the Armed Services YMCA to provide support for military wives. Along with their very popular support groups, the center offers aerobics and arts and crafts classes, with babysitting available for women attending these programs.

Inside
Golf

*F*rom the sting of Honey Bee to the agony of Hell's Point, if you're a golfer, you might as well admit you've come to duffer's paradise. Not only will our average 60 degree temperatures keep your bag parked at the front door almost every day of the year, but our depth of courses will call to you in your dreams. And, because Hampton Roads is such a friendly place, even if you're on your own, you can pick up a foursome at practically any time, although weekends are tougher to access popular tee times unless your golfing buddies are in place. You'll soon realize you're never alone on any of our courses. According to the National Golf Association, there are 518,000 golfers 12 and older in Virginia, a quarter of whom call Hampton Roads home. That's nearly 10 percent of our population, each and every one of whom has their favorite courses and holes yet to conquer.

Across Hampton Roads, there are beautifully maintained courses - - public and private – that will test every club in your bag. Unless you can almost qualify for the PGA tour, those in the know suggest you control your urge to play the big-time links unless you have stock in the golf ball industry and have more room on your score card to fill in those triple figures. Our area's proud to boast of some of the state's toughest advanced courses, and they got their reputation for good reason. If you're long on ambition but short of temper, it's best to wait until you can confidently break 100 before you consider shelling out greens and cart fees for the most difficult courses. Take it from the pros...wide fairways, few sand traps and little or no water hazards will make your 18 a lot more pleasurable if your clubs still have their initial shine.

To that end, we'll list all the play possibilities not only by city, but by ability to really enjoy yourself. We've also included the "Toughest Holes" as defined by some of the area's leading pros. So step up to the white tees, or blue if you dare...and ping your way into one of the most popular sports in Hampton Roads.

The Basic, Beautiful Courses

Virginia Beach

BOW CREEK GOLF COURSE
3425 Club House Road   431-3763

Thank goodness, here you'll find wide and forgiving fairways, few manmade hazards and trees. This par 72, 6,800-yard course does have small greens and sharp doglegs along some fairly ominous wooded roughs, so we're not exactly talking cake walk. Even so, it's quite a reasonable course, with greens fees to match : $14 for 18 holes and $9 for 9 holes. Ride a cart for $16, and seniors and juniors under 17 play for $8.

KEMPSVILLE GREENS MUNICIPAL GOLF COURSE
4840 Princess Anne Road   474-8441

A Russ Breeden-designed 6,200-yard, par 70, this course has the devilish habit of confiscating your ball in one of its three lakes or thick woods. There are some fine greens and excellent driving range at this city-owned facility. Plan on $10 for 18, $7.50 for nine. Seniors get a real deal for a $5 round.

Portsmouth

CITY PARK GOLF COURSE
Portsmouth City Park   393-8005

Let's start easy. This nine-hole course is really the easiest to test your clubs on in the area. It's the perfect place for juniors and others just getting their first taste of the golf bug. Matching the ease of the course are the fees: $5 for adults and $4 for juniors and seniors allows you to play unlimited golf during the week. Weekends, it's $6 to play 36.

Norfolk

LAKE WRIGHT GOLF COURSE
6280 Northampton Boulevard   461-2246

Sure, it appears easy enough, what with the practically wide open front nine. But make the turn and you'll find trees and water along the back nine – as well as nasty prevailing winds – and your glorious score may just take a downward spiral. Even so, No. 5, a testy par 3, is a 190-yard nightmare over Lake Wright, and judged the fourth toughest hole to play in the area. If you make it over the lake, you're up against a trap to the left and bunker to the right of the green. Just pray the wind's going in your direction. For extra practice, however, there is one of the best driving ranges in the area, plus a pro shop. Greens fees: $23, $17 for the cart.

OCEAN VIEW GOLF COURSE
9610 Norfolk Avenue   480-2094

Many area golfers describe this course as "flat," but the straight, if narrow, fairways, a few sharp doglegs and trap-lined greens give it a bit of a challenge. During the week you can play this 5,900-yard course for a mere $11, weekends for $13. Ride a cart for $16. After 2:30 PM, two can play unlimited golf for

$25 during the week, $34 on the weekend (that even includes a cart).

Intermediate Play

Portsmouth

SLEEPY HOLE GOLF COURSE
Sleepy Hole Road   393-5050

Even though it's long and surrounded by water, the secluded Suffolk location of this City of Portsmouth-owned course offers little distraction, or excuses, from city noise and bustle. It boasts the second toughest hole in the area, the par 4, 423-yard 18th that requires a long, slight draw off the tee to clear the rolling hill and carry down the open fairway to within 180 yards of the green. Don't even think about the marshes of the Nansemond River on the left and Clubhouse and trap on the right as you land on the green. Just lob your second shot short, chip and pray. Try this course during the week for $10, $14 on the weekend. Carts are $16 at all times.

BIDE-A-WEE GOLF COURSE
Greenwood Drive   393-5269

This par 72, 6,308-yard beauty is not only a pretty rough trip for even a fairly good shotmaker, it boasts the number one toughest hole in our area...the 405-yard No. 8. If you've got a booming tee shot, you're looking at a narrow, critical landing area flanked by sentinel oaks. Ahead there's more to outsmart you on this, one of the longer dogleg par 4's in the area...an elevated green with water hazard to the left and woods that flank the entire right side of the hole. Just try and break 73, the course record that stood for many years. Chip out $5.50 for a weekday 18, $7 on weekends. Add a cart any day for an extra $5.

Virginia Beach

HONEY BEE GOLF COURSE
5016 South Independence Blvd.   471-2768

Designed by Rees Jones, Honey Bee is a 6,700-yard challenge, what with its 80 monstrous sand traps, elevated tees and water on ten holes. Virginia Beach's newest golf course, it's privately owned but open to the public, and is home to the Virginia Beach Golf Academy, an assemblage of four of the finest teaching professionals in the area. If you walk, fees are $18 for a weekday 18, $28 if you ride. Carts are required at peak time on weekends, for $33.

OWL'S CREEK GOLF CENTER
411 South Birdneck Road   428-2800

Designed by Brook Parker, this is a great course for the golfer who wants to pack 18 into three hours or less. Dubbed "The Little Monster," this executive 4,155-yard, par 62 course, all par 4 and 5's, does offer the opportunity for extra practice on its lighted driving range and super practice putting greens. Plunk down $18 for 18, $12 for nine (both with carts); after noon, except during peak periods and weekends, you can walk it for $12 for 18, $8 for 9.

RED WING LAKE GOLF COURSE

Prosperity Road   437-4845

The greens are large and fairways are wide...but you'll still have to face water hazards on 10 holes and 84 traps along the fairways and long sloping greens. If you're adept at short iron shots, have at the par 5 No. 18, the ninth toughest hole in the area. It not only challenges your birdie with the lake in front of the heavily trapped green, but tests accuracy just getting there through a narrowing fairway. But, go ahead, knock yourself out for $23 in greens fees.

STUMPY LAKE GOLF COURSE

4797 Indian River Road   467-6119

This is one to write home about. A Robert Trent Jones designed 6,757-yard course, Stumpy Lake is surrounded by water on four sides and entered via a bridge. Amateurs and professionals alike fear the par 4, 400-yard No. 5, the tenth toughest hole in the region. The dogleg right to an elevated, gently trapped green presents a hint of the difficulty that awaits. Your choice at the tee is directly over the trees or a long fade or slice to hold the fairway. And, don't count on the green to hold a flat approach shot. At least you can enjoy the quiet tranquility of the secluded location. It's $22 for the pleasure of 18.

Suffolk

SUFFOLK GOLF COURSE

1227 Highland Road   539-6298

With wide fairways on the front nine and narrow ones on the back, Suffolk claims a birdie killer with its par 5, 450-yard No. 18, the eighteenth toughest hole in the area. A gambler's hole, it's dominated by a lake that begins on the left side of the fairway and lingers to about 20 yards short of the narrow green. If you make it through the 15-yard wide fairway, look out for the traps to the right, left and rear of the green. Greens fees: $16.

Chesapeake

SEVEN SPRINGS GOLF COURSE

1201 Club House Drive   436-2512

A relatively mild yet fairly tight course, as of this writing only 10 of 18 holes are open for play. Play weekdays for $6 for 10; $8 for 20. Weekends, $8 for 10, $12 for 20. Add a cart for $5 to $8.

Killer Courses

Virginia Beach

HELL'S POINT GOLF CLUB

2700 Atwood Road   721-3400

Designed by Rees Jones, the 6,900-yard Hell's Point has been rated one of the top 130 courses in the country by the Golf Architects of America. If you survive the three large lakes and 61 sand traps, you'll still have great stories to tell about the snake that fought you for your ball in the dangerous rough. Watch out for the 389-yard No. 2, judged the 11th toughest hole in the region. It's a long par 4 with a narrow fairway and double-trapped green.

For the thrill of defeat, you can reserve a tee-time a week in advance, and carts are required for play. It'll cost you $36 on weekdays, $40 Friday through Sunday and holidays.

CYPRESS POINT GOLF & COUNTRY CLUB
5340 Club Head Road   *490-8822*

So beautiful, the Bermuda fairways and rough and lush bent grass greens. Ha! Pack your bag heavy for this 6,740-yard, par 72 romp through a killer designed by Tom Clark of Ault Clark Associates. Just step up to the 469-yard, par 4 No. 7, judged the 14th toughest hole in the area. It's another long tee shot to a dogleg right, bunkered left and right. Before you: a huge, elevated green trapped on three sides. You could be looking at a 100-footer, and putting over a tier. Good luck. On the backside, is the picturesque 17th, a 175-yard, par 3 with water and front and a three tiered-green. You'll need $40 for greens fees for the privilege.

Private Courses

There are several private courses in Hampton Roads worth chumming up to a member to play. This is where well-heeled residents take in 18 to practice their swings...all beautiful courses with equally beautiful clubhouses waiting at the end of a round.

Portsmouth

ELIZABETH MANOR
1 Ace Parker Drive   *488-4534*

Area pros agree that Elizabeth Manor's 14th and 15th are the toughest back-to-back holes in Hampton Roads. We'll take you right to No. 14, where long off the tee is the only way to a relatively flat green with bunker and out-of-bounds left and a small knoll to the right. Then cart straight to No. 15, where a long, accurate tee shot of at least 270 or so is a prerequisite to clear the drive bunkers. This hole plays especially sinister a few days before or after the Eastern Amateur in August when the rough is longest and thickest. If you're keeping score, the 14th was judged the 16th toughest hole; the 15th right up there at the fifth toughest in the region.

Virginia Beach

CAVALIER GOLF & YACHT CLUB
1052 Cardinal Road   *428-6161*

If you crave treacherous closing holes, here's a place you'll find nirvana. Designed to decide tournaments, a thin, carrot-shaped green waits on a hole with water on three sides, not to mention the five bunkers. This, the 18th, serves to destroy any decent score up to this point. If you bailout and hit short, chip up and putt, you might hold par. This is the third toughest hole in the region, you know.

PRINCESS ANNE COUNTRY CLUB
38th Street & Pacific   *422-3360*

Rambling through primo

Gold Coast territory, this luscious course plays host to the rich and famous of Virginia Beach. The most dangerous parts are cart paths that cross roads leading to secluded private residential communities.

BROAD BAY GREENS GOLF COURSE
2120 Lord's Landing   496-9092

A beautiful course that winds its way through one of Virginia Beach's newer private residential communities, this Ault and Clark designed 6,135-yard, par 70 features unique elevated tee platforms, numerous mounds and medium-sized, well bunkered greens. The challenging second hole rated a "toughest hole" honorable mention from area pros. A treat is the handsomely appointed clubhouse, along with a tempting pro shop.

Chesapeake

GREENBRIER COUNTRY CLUB
1301 Volvo Parkway   547-7375

A fairly new course that weaves through an upwardly mobile residential community, the hole that gets attention is the long, twisting par 5 closing hole, a popular favorite among area pros. You really need to bang it here, with bunkers popping up along the fairway and a steeply elevated green. Hit short, pitch and putt on this, the 7th toughest hole in Hampton Roads. And, look out for big club...it's the par 4, 461 No. 3 with a green that's large and flat with a two-foot bowl indention in the middle left. It's the 12th toughest hole in the area.

Photo: Richmond Newspapers

Hampton Roads is a fisherman's paradise.

Inside
Fishing

Oh, to be an angler when spring hits Hampton Roads. You can tell the season is starting because all those funny, fuzzy little lures, rods and reels start taking over shelf space where footballs used to be. Fishing frenzy hits, and the throngs head to the seas...each probably looking for the one that got away last season.

The beauty of it all is that you don't have to have a lot of talent or a lot of money to enjoy this sport. The basic prerequisites are patience and a lift to the nearest pier or head boat. Whether you're inshore or offshore, the biting's grand from March through December, thanks in great part to the Chesapeake Bay, considered by some marine biologists to be the country's premier spawning ground for saltwater fish. Each spring, many fish, like striped bass, herring, shad and sturgeon, migrate to the bay's tributaries to spawn. Others, like speckled trout, flounder, spot, croaker and gray trout, call the bay home for the first stages of their lives.

Beyond the bay, the big bluefish, bluefin tuna, marlin, dolphin, yellowfin tuna and wahoo are a hook away in the Atlantic Ocean. Likewise, there's some of the hottest angling action when the big billfish, amberjack, cobia and black drum start their summer runs.

Whether you cast a line on one of hundreds of freshwater lakes, head off to a quiet cove, drag your tackle to the nearest pier or trawl for big ones on the open ocean, your chances of a big catch are better here than almost anywhere on earth. And, that may or may not be a fish story depending on your results on any given day.

No fishing license is required to fish in saltwater. Freshwater fishing requires licenses for resident anglers 16 years and older, are valid for the calendar year January 1 - December 31, and cost $12. Non-residents can purchase a five-day license for $6. You can pick one up at numerous places throughout the area, including most bait and tackle shops, marinas and department store sporting goods counters.

For avid anglers, take note of the Annual Virginia Saltwater Fishing Tournament, held April through November. It is a program that maintains state records and honors certain catches with a "citation," a laminated plaque that displays the fisherman's name, species caught, date, etc. The tournament is open to anyone, with twenty-two species eligible for citations. If you're interested, call the tournament's headquarters at 428-4360.

Freshwater Fishing, Fishing Piers

Norfolk

HARRISON BOAT HOUSE AND PIER
414 West Ocean View Avenue   587-9630

A landmark on the fishing scene, this is the place to count on the biggest spot and croaker hauls. Granted, these are little league fish, most less than 12 ounces, but their numbers are incredible. Harrison's sits in the enviable position of being the perfect location to be when Virginia's most popular inshore fishing season begins in late July or early August. The season lasts well into September, and even into October if mild weather continues.

WILLOUGHBY BAY MARINA
1651 Bayville Street   588-2663

Even if you're not a fisherman, this is a great place to wander on a summer's day, taking in the sights of sailboats and boaters. Count on more spot and croaker than you can catch all summer long.

LAKE SMITH
5381 Shell Road   464-4684

One of the largest freshwater lakes in the area, Lake Smith boasts an ample supply of largemouth bass, bluegill, crappie, catfish, stripped bass and carp. Eighty boats are available for rental, or you can just cast off from shore. A fully stocked bait and tackle shop is right there for anything a promising angler might need for a day of heavy fishing.

Portsmouth

SLEEPY HOLE PARK
Sleepy Hole Road   393-5056

Located in Suffolk, this gorgeous park with its immense mature oak trees shelters a lake well-stocked with panfish, catfish and large mouth bass. Charge is only $1 for a full day of possible frustration.

Virginia Beach

VIRGINIA BEACH FISHING PIER
15th Street and Oceanfront   428-2333

Fish, or just watch those who try, 24-hours a day all summer long. You can even rent a rod to try your own luck. Crabbing is also popular

Insider anglers unanimously agree that the best Bay fishing spot is at the Chesapeake Bay-Bridge-Tunnel at the "tubes." That's at the tunnels for all you out-of-town folk.

Insiders' Tips

from this pier, where crab cages and bait are available. Open April through October, there's a small fee to fish, even smaller fee just to watch.

LYNNHAVEN INLET FISHING PIER
Starfish Road off Shore Drive   *481-7071*

Another 24-hour fish-a-thon happens here along the Chesapeake Bay all summer. Look for spot and croaker early in the season, then cast for flounder, speckled trout and puppy drum. There's a small fee to fish or watch; rod/reels rentals are available.

SEA GULL FISHING PIER
Chesapeake Bay-Bridge-Tunnel,
South Island   *464-4641*

Perhaps one of the country's most unusual fishing piers, Sea Gull extends 600 feet into the middle of the Chesapeake Bay. Beginning in mid-June, you might reel in a cobia of 40 pounds or more. It's also the best time to catch the biggest gray trout. There's no fee to fish here, but you will have to pay the regular $10 one-way crossing fare.

LITTLE ISLAND FISHING PIER
Sandbridge, Atlantic Ocean   *426-7200*

It's possible to snag a big bluefish from this pier, along with a plethora of other choppers that come close to the shoreline. A favorite summer hang-out for Sandbridge visitors, there's a small fee to park as well as fish April through October.

Deep Sea Fishing & Marinas

How about a 1,000-pound blue marlin? Or a 50-pound white marlin? Not to mention bluefin tuna, dolphin, wahoo, false albacore, amberjack and more. They're all out in the blue waters of the Atlantic, and there are almost as many charter boats waiting to make a wake out to where they can be found.

Offshore fishing does have its price, however. Fleets sail from several sites in both Norfolk and Virginia Beach, and you can be aboard for from $300 for a day of bottom-fishing to as much as $1,000 for a jaunt out to the marlin grounds. An alternative is an outing on a headboat, so named because they charge by the person, or the "head." These headboats, which also depart from Norfolk and Virginia Beach, concentrate mainly closer to shore, with rates running from as little as

$10 for a four-hour spot fishing trip to $35 for an all-day adventure.

All these charter and headboats are very popular, especially when local angler forecasters raise the checkered flag for a big score. Call well in advance to confirm availability, amenities and fees.

Norfolk

Car Harbor Custom Charters, 863-3 Little Bay Avenue, 587-5645

Cobbs Marina, 4524 Dunning Road, 588-5401

Harrison Boat House, 414 West Ocean View Avenue, 588-9968

Willoughby Bay Marina, 1651 Bayville Street, 588-2663

Virginia Beach

Virginia Beach Fishing Center, 200 Winston-Salem Avenue, Rudee Inlet, 425-9253

D&M Marina, 3311 Shore Drive, Lynnhaven Inlet, 481-7211

Bubba's Marina, 3323 Shore Drive, Lynnhaven Inlet, 481-3513

Inlet Station Marina, Foot of Mediterranean Avenue, 422-2999

Lynnhaven Marine Center, 2150 West Great Neck Road, 481-0700

Lynnhaven Municipal Marina, Lynnhaven Inlet, 481-7137

Lynnhaven Waterway Marina, 2101 North Great neck Road, 481-7517

Fisherman's Wharf Marina, 524 Winston-Salem Avenue, Rudee Inlet, 428-2111

Inside
Tennis

*Y*ou've got the gear, you've got the serve, you've even got the backhand. But do you have a court to call your own? Yes! There are literally hundreds of free courts for the volleying throughout Hampton Roads, and one of them is sure to be lit at night for that after-work workout.

Virginia Beach alone has more than 188 public tennis courts, Norfolk, 150, most of which are lighted and may be played at no charge. The majority of these public courts can be found in the parks and schools maintained by each individual city. Here, we'll give you the locations of the most popular courts in each locale, and highlight those specific ones where classes are offered. Also note the private, indoor facilities listed for each city.

Norfolk

TIDEWATER TENNIS CENTER
1159 Lance Road   *461-3015*
Not only can you play indoors and out here, but you can also be videotaped to reveal every single flaw in your game. Instructors are forgiving, and encouraging, however, so it's a great place to winter your game in preparation for the big time.

NORTHSIDE PARK
8400 Tidewater Drive   *441-2149*
Headquarters for Norfolk tennis activity is Northside Park, where classes for all levels are offered seasonally by resident pros. Many of the city's tournaments are held here at a facility that offers lighted courts to soothe night-owl lobs.

Other city courts, most of which are lighted:
Azalea Garden Jr. High School, 7721 Azalea Garden Road
Barraud Park, Barraud Avenue
Booker T. Washington High School, 1300 Virginia Beach Boulevard
Granby High School, 7101 Granby Street
Lafayette City Park, 3500 Granby Street
Lake Taylor High School, 1380 Kempsville Road
Larchmont Elementary School, 5210 Hampton Boulevard
Little Creek Elementary School, Tarpin & Little Creek roads
Maury High School, 322 Shirley Avenue
Norview High School, Middleton Place
Ocean View Elementary School, 9501 Mason Creek Road

Ocean View Recreation Center, 600 Ocean View Avenue

St. Helena Elementary School, 903 South Main Street

Portsmouth

Classes for all skill levels and ages are offered during the summer through the Portsmouth Parks and Recreation Department at both Churchland Park and City Park, along with annual Junior and Senior Tournaments. For more information, class schedules and fees, call 393-8481.

Lighted courts available for public play:

Cavalier Manor, 404 Viking Street

Churchland Park, 5601 High Street, West

City Park, City Park Avenue

Craddock High School, 4300 George Washington Highway

I. C. Norcom High School, 2900 Turnpike Road

Manor High School, 1401 Elmhurst Lane

Park View Athletic Complex, 1401 Crawford Parkway

Tidewater Community College, Frederick Campus

Woodrow Wilson High School, 3701 Willett Drive

Virginia Beach

VIRGINIA BEACH TENNIS AND COUNTRY CLUB

1950 Thomas Bishop Lane   481-7545

If you see a car packed with tennis players in a rare severe cold snap, chances are they're headed here. Of course, you'll have to be a member, but if you're a got-to-play fanatic, this is the place to be. Six indoor courts plus 30 outdoor courts are just an appetizer for what's available, including both group and private lessons from some of the most patient, encouraging pros in the area. The vibes from all the tennis mavericks who wander around only make the experience all the more invigorating – or intimidating – depending on your skill level. Check out the excellent junior academy in the summer, as well as the swimming pool, exercise room, sauna, Jacuzzi and pro shop.

OWL'S CREEK MUNICIPAL TENNIS CENTER

928 South Birdneck Road   437-4804

Secluded, shady, well-lighted...this is just for starters. Named one of the 50 best municipal tennis centers in the country by *Tennis Magazine*, here the grandslam want-to-be's can find expert instruction from U.S.P.T.A. and U.S.P.T.R. instructors who conduct private and group lessons as well as various clinics. On hand are 12 hard-surface and two tournament courts, with seating for 1,300 spectators. Fees vary, as well as reservation requirements, so do check in advance.

LYNNHAVEN JUNIOR HIGH SCHOOL

1250 Bayne Drive

This is a super popular place to test the reaction to your new tennis outfit. There are 12 courts here that stay lit until 11 PM, with no fee to play, nor are there reservations taken. If courts are full, you can always get in a practice session at the backboard.

Find other lighted Virginia Beach courts at:

Bayside High School, 4960 Haygood Road

Bayville Farm Park, First Court Road

Center for Effective Learning, 233 North Witchduck Road

Creeds Athletic Park, Morris Neck & Campbell Landing Road

First Colonial High School, 1271 Mill Dam Road

Great Neck Junior High, 1840 North Great Neck Road

Green Run High School, 1700 Dahlia Drive

Kellam High School, 574 Kempsville Road

Kempsville Jr. High School, 860 Churchill Road

Kempsville High School, 574 Kempsville Road

Lynnhaven Park, Bayne Drive

Plaza Junior High School, 3080 South Lynnhaven

Princess Anne Park, Princess Anne Road

Princess Anne High School, 4400 Virginia Beach Boulevard

Chesapeake

The City of Chesapeake sponsors men's and women's team tennis for ages 18 and over for both spring and fall seasons. For more information on team tennis sign-up, call 547-6642.

GREENBRIER SPORTS PARK
Greenbrier   *547-6400*

Take center court on any of eight tournament-quality lighted courts...this is the big time in Chesapeake. Novices bored with ball-chasing can always sneak away to the softball fields or picnic areas.

CHESAPEAKE COUNTRY CLUB
411 Cedar Road   *547-9366*

Ten clay, two hard surface courts await you here at the club's new facility. Six of the courts will be lighted for night play, along with a stadium court for exhibition play. And, don't spend too much in the well-stocked pro shop.

Find additional lighted public courts in Chesapeake at:

Crestwood Junior High School, 1420 Great Bridge Road

Deep Creek Junior High School, 2901 Margaret Booker Drive

Deep Creek High School, 1955 Deal Drive

Great Bridge Junior High School, 301 West Hanbury Road

Hickory Elementary School, 2701 South Battlefield Boulevard

Indian River High School, 2301 Dunbarton Drive

Oscar Smith High School, 2500 Rodgers Street

Western Branch High School, 4222 Terry Drive

Photo: Richmond Newspapers

The East Coast Surfing Championships are held every August in Virginia Beach.

Photo: Richmond Newspapers

Sailing regattas are very popular in the Hampton Roads area.

Inside
Participatory and Spectator Sports

*H*ampton Roaders can create more ways to exercise and compete than you can shake a racquet at. Here, we'll give you a brief run-down of the most reasonable of the area's participation sports and who to contact if you're interested in finding out more. For you really pro-sports fanatics, an excellent reference tool is a special newspaper section called "Venture," a weekly recreation guide published as part of the sports section of the *Virginian Pilot/Ledger Star* each Thursday. It not only lists all upcoming clinics, classes and special trips, but includes the definitive fishing forecast for all you anglers.

Participatory Sports

Basketball

Each of the Hampton Roads' cities sponsors both adult and youth basketball leagues, with registration beginning in November and play continuing through mid-March. Youth leagues begin at age 10, and you must be 18 before you join the adult ranks. For complete information, contact your city's recreation department. All phone numbers are listed at the end of this section.

For casual hoopers, scads of indoor and outdoor courts are scattered throughout the region: at schools, parks and recreation facilities. You shouldn't have far to go for a quick game of one-on-one.

Baseball/Softball

Again, leave it to the cities to organize highly competitive teams for both adults and kids. Registration normally begins in early March, with the season dragging on from May through the heat and humidity of late July. Teams for males, females and co-eds are here for the joining. Call your specific city for exact registration times and locations.

Hampton Roads is home to the Amateur Softball Association, the largest amateur association in the world, that operates in each Hampton Roads city and provides playing opportunities for children and adults. In any given year, you can count as many as 150 different teams in the association, and they can play as many as 200 games on a weekend. Junior Olympic leagues are for girls ages 12 to 18, with play in the fall. Adult leagues, for ages 18 and over, are grouped according to ability, with a season that runs from April to November. For more information, 427-5219 or 428-0784.

For baseball players 18 years and older, check into The Virginia Adult Baseball League which is planning its entry into South Hampton Roads in the spring of 1993. For information, 1-800-322-6414.

Boxing

Sweet Pea-want-to-be's have it made in Hampton Roads. For starters, Claude Taylor of Norfolk's rec department has been teaching boxing for years at Barraud Park in Norfolk, and Sweet Pea Whittaker, the undisputed Lightweight Champion of the World, was one of his students. In Virginia Beach, Wareing's Gym is as good as you can get for training and a really scary sparring partner.

Cycling

Have bike, will travel. And travel Hampton Roads' cyclers do. Weekend leisure riders will find bike paths throughout Hampton Roads, and special trails reserved for bikers in most of our area's parks. Minibikers, mountain bikers and BMX aficionados will find their own

tracks, too. (See the "Parks" section for specifics.) Serious peddlers won't want for companionship, with several clubs active in planning special events, competitions and field trips. To get the full scoop, contact The Tidewater Bicycle Association (Touring & Racing), 523-2596; L'team Junque (Touring & Training), 486-1948; or, Colley Off-Road Club (Touring & Training), 622-0006.

Crew

Crewing is an up and coming sport in this region blessed with quiet waters. Novices and experienced oarsmen are welcome to join The Hampton Roads Rowing Club for both recreational and competitive thrills. Call 425-8488.

Fencing

Yes, fencing. The Tidewater Fencing Club is always looking for new targets to sign up for membership in this very active organization. Annual membership is $80, which includes instruction and equipment. Call 460-2975.

Football

Knock 'em, pop 'em, sock 'em. Pack your kids into the pads and get them off to sign up for your city's youth community football league. Registration is in August, with power play for city titles running from September through November. Volunteer coaches are widely respected, and known for teaching more than just the principles of the game. Sportsmanship, leadership and team spirit messages prevail, even if you're on the bench. Contact your city's rec department for exact registration times and locations.

Horseback Riding

Virginia Beach, Suffolk and Chesapeake are the area leaders when it comes to facilities to mount a steed and ride off into the sunset. In the still rural areas of Virginia Beach, many people still board their own, and there are many private stables where you can rent a ride. In Chesapeake, Northwest River Park offers the city's only designated horse trails, with three miles of inter-connected loops. Private stables and farms also offer mounts for lessons and rental. Suffolk offers boarding, training and lessons, but no rentals are available. Excellent sources for information to steer you in the right direction are:
Acredale Saddlery
467-3183
Hillcrest Farms Ltd.
471-4646
Sterling Meadows Farm
471-2133
Royal Meadows Stables
255-0729

Ice Skating

Even in a region of moderate temperatures, ice skating is popular...for Olympic want-to-be's as well as for one heck of a great party idea. The center for the activity is Iceland at Virginia Beach (4915 Broad Street, 490-3907), where excellent instruction is available. There's also The Tidewater Figure Skating Club that welcomes all skating abilities, 423-5411. If you've got a hankering for the game of ice hockey, check out the Virginia Beach Open Hockey League, 490-3999.

Jet Skiing

If there's a sport, there's a club for it here, with folks who share your passion. If you're into jet skiing, find out about the Tidewater Personal Watercraft Club that meets monthly at Marina Shores in Virginia Beach, 496-2325.

Rugby

There are bumper stickers around town that say " Love an Animal...Kiss a Rugby Player." Well, maybe *before* one of the games sponsored by the Virginia Beach Rugby Club, that fights it out at Princess Anne Park in Virginia Beach. Right now, they're looking for new players (makes you wonder what happened to the old ones!). Go ahead, give them a call at 497-2208.

Racquetball

A most civilized racquet sport, you won't find many public facilities to satiate the habit, but there are several membership facilities where you can happily box yourself in. In Norfolk at the Downtown Athletic Club, 625-2222 or at the

Y.M.C.A., 622-6328, or in Virginia Beach at Gymstrada, 499-9667.

Running, Jogging, Walking

Whatever your speed, you can be in a crowd – or all alone – when you put one foot in front of the other for recreation. Every park in every city has well-marked, well-shaded paths for walking and jogging, and you'll see people of all ages out in neighborhoods, on the Boardwalk at the Beach, around the Hague in Ghent, and even on covered tracks at the Y.M.C.A. in Downtown Norfolk.

If you're more serious about leaving your footprints in jogging or walking history, you might check out several clubs in the area that sponsor a multitude of competitive and recreational events:
Tidewater Striders 627-7223
Gator Volksmarching
Club 486-0664
Mount Trashmore Walking
Club   474-0460

Sailing

If you don't know the difference between a boom-vang and a spinnaker, you'll miss out on one of the most popular addictions in the area...sailing. From baby sunfish to beamy Morgans, there's a vessel just waiting to reach you out into the calm waters of the Chesapeake Bay. One great place to chart your sailing adventure is the Chesapeake Sailing Association, located at Willoughby Harbor in Norfolk. CSA offers ASA-certified sail training,

along with super five-day "Learn to Sail" vacation packages. Call them at 588-2022. At the Beach, Chick's Beach Sailing Center (481-3067) is a beehive of sailing activity, and a great place to take a lesson, rent a boat or just hang around to pick up some sailing lingo.

Skateboarding/ In-Line Skating

For those who haven't traded in their skateboards for roller blades, you can head to the bowls and ramps located in Norfolk at Northside Park and at the beach at Mount Trashmore, Lynnhaven Park and Red Wing Park. At all these facilities, proper safety equipment is required, as well as should be. In-line and roller skaters can wheel with the pack by joining the Beach Skater Club, 422-6105.

Skydiving

Beam me up, Scottie! If leaping for your life out on this air is the kind of thing that turns you on, head out to Suffolk Municipal Airport. Skydive Suffolk, Inc. offers lessons on Saturday mornings by appointment, and you can make your first jump that same day. For the experienced skydiver, an accelerated freefall program is also offered. For fees and details, call 539-3531.

Soccer

Soccer's hot here, so sign that

kid up quick. Every city and practically every neighborhood has its own team, so have your child talk to classmates about the best place to put on the cleats.

Youth soccer leagues sprout up so quickly that they can't be counted...boys and girls are not only encouraged to join up, but have a great time wearing their uniforms after the games. Contact your city's rec department for full details on spring and fall registration times and locations.

Adults don't have to miss out, either. Several soccer clubs are active and alive in Hampton Roads. To find out specifics:

Tidewater Soccer Association, at 489-2724, is a men's league and member of the USSF. It's for those experienced enough to play at collegiate level or better.

Southeastern Virginia Women's Soccer Association, 625-2414, is a regional league that's busy all year, with teams divided according to age and play ability.

Southside Soccer League, 423-3147, is for men who play well but not quite at championship speed.

Virginia Beach Soccer Club, 464-6452, has over 7,000 members. This club for both youths and adults has leagues for both neighborhood play and advanced teams. To accommodate, both spring and fall seasons are packed with play.

Surfing

Surf's up! Well, maybe it's not Hawaii, but when a Nor'easter blows, it's get-out-your-wetsuit time around the Virginia Beach oceanfront. Even if our waves might not be giant killers, we're still host to the East Coast Surfing Championships every year, with stiff competition from the best in the business.

Needless to say, Virginia Beach lays claim to all surfing rights in the area...you'd look ridiculous trying to catch a ripple at Ocean View. There are certain places you can and cannot take your board, however. Surfing areas are restricted to protect your average lazy backstokers and waders, as well as surfers themselves. If you get the urge to wax a board, head to:

Area A: Little Island Park. Stick to the north side of the pier from Memorial Day to Labor Day, 9 AM til 5 PM.

Area B: South of Little Island Park. You are allowed to catch a wave off False Cape's beach, but restricted within the boundaries of the Back Bay National Wildlife Refuge.

Area C: Between the southern line of the U.S. Naval Reservation/ Dam Neck and the northern line of Little Island Park. You can only surf here before 10 AM and after 5 PM between Memorial Day and Labor Day. Otherwise, surf's up between sunrise and sunset.

Area D: North of Camp Pendleton to 42nd Street, except for the area 300 feet north and south of the pier. Again, you're beached between 10 AM and 5 PM, May 15th through September 30th. Other times, have at it from sunrise to sunset.

Area E: Fort Story to 42nd

Street. No surfing between 10 AM and 5 PM, Memorial Day through Labor Day. Allowed sunrise to sunset at all other times.

Area F: South end of Croatan Beach (600 feet). Except for occasional military maneuvers, you can maneuver on your board from 9:30 AM until 6 PM from Memorial Day through Labor Day.

Area G: Croatan Beach for 800 feet below the southern jetty of Rudee Inlet. Open and waiting for you from sunrise to sunset.

Area H: North of Rudee Inlet's northern jetty (500 feet). Hang ten sunrise to sunset.

Swimming

Well, of course, swimming. Here we are surrounded by water. In fact, one of the hottest baby presents going is lessons for those not even old enough to walk, or even complain about the water being too cold.

It is critical, however, whether you're a newcomer or a visitor, that you not venture out into the ocean or the bay without a basic knowledge of our waters or fundamental swimming skills. Strong currents, and riptides (streams of water running under the surface that can draw you out toward sea in no time flat) that are sometimes hard to spot are an ever present menace to adults and children alike. And that goes double for rafts and swimming aides that lull you into the feeling of safety. While experienced lifeguards are on duty at the locations listed below to keep a constant eye on you,

lives have been unnecessarily lost because the excitement of white sands and blue waters overshadowed the real danger of unpredictable seas. If you are a newcomer from a dry terrain, we urge you to check into the swimming courses offered at most nominal fees through your new city's recreation department, and to take extreme safety precautions when you visit any of our wonderful beaches.

Norfolk

City Beach, East End of Ocean View

Community Beach, 601 East Ocean View Avenue

Sarah Constant Shrine, East Ocean View and Tidewater Drive

Virginia Beach

The Ocean Front, Atlantic Avenue Resort Strip

Croatan Beach, General Booth Boulevard

Fort Story, 89th Street

Sandbridge Beach Park, Sandbridge

Little Island Park, Sandbridge

Indoor Swimming

Whether you want to learn how to backstroke, or dive into the wet world of competitive freestyle, there are several options for water babies and adults alike. The TIDE Swim Team is a great connection for youth swimmers, and they travel to competitions along the East Coast. For information, call 496-3979. To perfect your stroke, call the Old Dominion Aquatic Club at 683-3403. They offer an excellent development program for novice and intermediate swimmers with an emphasis on stroke mechanics. New on the block is the Southern Amusement Pool League in Norfolk. They're looking for member swimmers right now, so call 855-2114.

For lessons or laps, here are the pools to check out when it gets a little too brisk for a bikini:

Norfolk
Huntersville Pool, 830 Geoff Street
Northside Pool, 8400 Tidewater Drive
Maury Pool, 322 Shirley Avenue
Y.M.C.A., Bute Street, Downtown Norfolk
Old Dominion University, Hampton Boulevard, Larchmont

Virginia Beach
Little Creek Pool (For military), Naval Amphibious Base, Little Creek
United Way Family Center, 441 South Boulevard
Kempsville Recreation Center, 800 Monmouth Lane

Chesapeake
Y.M.C.A., 1033 Greenbrier Parkway

Volleyball

When you're hot, you're hot. This is one old sport that's enjoying a major renewal across Hampton Roads...as evidenced by the nets strung out along the beaches and parks throughout the area. There are city leagues wherever you live, just waiting for a great spiker like you. When you get the action down pat, why not call the Tidewater Volleyball Association at 468-0527 to get the low-down on any upcoming tournaments.

Windsurfing

Looks easy. It's not. But, if you want to put that upper body strength and miracle balance to the test, here's the place to do it. You can start easy, with a smooth glide along the lake at Mount Trashmore, then graduate to the more wicked waters of the Chesapeake Bay. Why not let the experts at Chick's Beach Sailing Center give you a lesson or two before you rush out to invest in a board of your own. If you already know what you're doing, they'll rent you a board. Other great guidance counselors can be found at the Sandbridge Sailing Center and RK's Windsurf Shop. We're talking Atlantic Ocean now, so be easy on yourself.

Who Ya Gonna Call?

For up-to-the-minute info on all sporting activities offered for children and adults through city Parks and Recreation Departments, contact:

Norfolk Athletics, 441-2603
Virginia Beach Athletics, 471-5884
Chesapeake Athletics, 547-6400
Portsmouth Athletics, 393-8481

Annual Sporting Competitions

Bulk up on pasta and get ready to rumble. There are a zillion competitions for practically every sport known to humankind in Hampton Roads, and many are not only held annually for competitors who train all year, but bring out scores of spectators. While not every one will lure you to the starting gun, they are indeed annual events that are anticipated by the best in the respective fields, from the Hampton Roads area and well beyond.

Shamrock Marathon & Sports Fest

Virginia Beach
An annual March event sponsored by the Tidewater Striders, it's one of Virginia's most popular marathons averaging 2,000 runners.

Bud Light USTS Triathalon

Norfolk
Ouch! An Olympic distance event featuring a 1.5K swim, 40K bike race and 10K run. Starts at the Norfolk Botanical Garden and ends at Town Point Park, hosted by the City of Norfolk.

Sandman Triathalon

Virginia Beach

Held annually in September as part of the Neptune Festival, it draws the toughest competitors who go neck–to–neck in a 2K swim, 20 mile bike race and 10K run.

East Coast Triathalon

Fort Story, Virginia Beach
Held each June, there's a 0.9 mile swim followed by a 20 mile bike race and 10K run.

The Sentara Fitness Fest

Norfolk
This is by far Hampton Road's largest and most complete athletic and recreational event. It includes the popular Elizabeth River Run, Southeastern Cycling Classic, volleyball battles and so much more.

Virginia Beach East Coast Surfing Championships

Virginia Beach
Any local surf shop will be abuzz with the news about this August tournament that attracts the biggest names in surfing. Even if you don't know the first thing about the boards, it's a great excuse to get a lot of sun while watching the competition.

National Offshore Grand Prix

Virginia Beach
Now, we're talking boats that really fly. This EVORA Powerboat Race takes place every Labor Day

off Virginia Beach's shoreline and draws competitors from all over the country. Last year, super-star Don Johnson even brought his boat into our humble waters to take a shot at the crown.

The Chesapeake Challenge

Virginia Beach
What a sight! It's the annual Hobie/catamaran race that lasts a long, grueling 27 miles.

The World 1000

Virginia Beach
This one always makes network news...the annual summer race that begins in Florida and ends, at last, in Virginia Beach. Only the strong of body and soul outlive this test of endurance and sailing expertise.

Low Rent Regatta

Chick's Beach
Here's one to jump into – a wild and wacky competition for boardsailing and catamarans. But, beware, there are some competitors that take the title very seriously.

Shodeo

Virginia Beach
For the horsey set, this annual September competition at Princess Anne Park gets big scores for the high level of showmanship.

Spectator and Professional Sports

Baseball

The Norfolk Tides

The Class AAA farm team of the New York Mets, the Tides are not only the biggest success story of local professional sports, but can boast of some of the biggest players who started out on the Tide's roster. Primo pitcher Dwight Gooden, super slugger Darryl Strawberry and tough-guy Lew Dystra all started with the Tides before being jettisoned up to the Met's lineup.

The Tides got their start in 1962, competing in the old Sally League at Frank D. Lawrence Stadium. In 1969, they leapfrogged to AAA status, and the following year, took up residency at the then brand new Met Park in Norfolk. They swung, they won and they made history as a winning team, and to that end, they are now waiting to move their locker gear to a brand new, state-of-the-art facility being built as we write along the waterfront in Downtown Norfolk. The new facility, Harbor Park, will feature plush skyboxes for corporate sponsors, seating for 12,000, a restaurant we all hope will be as accommodating as the old "Diamond Club," and a unique walkway constructed from paver stones embedded with the names of anyone and everyone who paid $30 to be a part of history. The new facility is promised to be ready for the opening game in April, 1993.

Ice Hockey

The Hampton Roads Admirals

You want winners? You got them! Who would've thunk that an ice hockey team in Hampton Roads would not only come out on top of the pack year after year, but draw sell-out crowds to every home game in Norfolk's Scope? In March of 1992, their season attendance record surpassed the 300,000 mark, and, as back-to-back East Coast Hockey League champions, the rough and rugged team looks to break that record this year with ease. All going to prove that "kinder and gentler" is definitely out.

Partners with the Washington Capitals, who have supplied some of the team's leading scorers,

the Admirals' season starts in October and face-offs continue through March. You can catch all the action at Scope for the single ticket price of $6 and $7, but buy in advance to ensure you've got a seat to cheer from.

Football

Wrapping up and packing off to a local high school football game has turned into one of the most popular social events of the fall season. Even if you don't have a child in the school, you'll be missing a lot if you don't huddle in blankets on the bleachers to cheer on your neighborhood team. The same spirit prevails for college ball, and following the stats for Norfolk State University and Hampton University, both of whom compete in the highly competitive CIAA, is a local pastime. Old Dominion University's efforts to jump start a football team have failed in the past years, despite substantial local support, both emo-

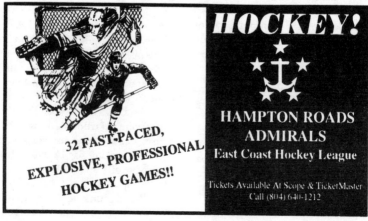

tional and financial.

For semi-pro action, The Tidewater Sharks take the field each fall in the up-and-coming Mason Dixon football league.

For another twist on football, take in a game of rugby, played to the fullest by the Norfolk Blues. And, while rugby is still a much understood and unappreciated sport in the region, the sheer ferocity and stamina of this winning team has brought attention, if not small fame, to its stars.

Basketball

Some of us can remember the old Virginia Squires, with Charlie Scott, George Gervin and Julius "Dr. J" Erving taking center court back in the olden days of the 1970s. The Squires were the first major league sporting franchise in Hampton Roads, and died a slow, painful death due to lack of spectator support just before the NBA-ABA merger.

Support is not the problem for the Monarchs of Old Dominion –men and women's teams. Buy your tickets early (or better yet, season's tickets) for games played at Norfolk's Scope for both the Monarchs and Lady Monarchs. Across town, the Spartans and Lady Spartans of Norfolk State University pose an annual threat to the title-grabbing in the CIAA.

There's no cure for hoop fever at the high school level, either. Fans pack gymnasiums all over town to cheer on their favorites. We grow them good, too, like J. R. Reid from Kempsville High School and Alonzo Morning, straight from Chesapeake's Indian River High.

Professional Wrestling

Boy, we really debated whether to include this under "sports" or "theater." Mid-Atlantic Wrestling is a big-time spectator sport for Hampton Roads kids of all ages, just hankering to see that big throw across the turnbuckle. It all happens every year at Norfolk Scope, and the crowds of seemingly timid, well-dressed patrons turn into vicious, make-him-suffer lunatics. Well, it's not for everyone, but the release of frustrations here can be cheaper than a therapist. Go figure.

Photo: Richmond Newspapers

A waterman docks his boat after a long day working on the Chesapeake Bay.

Inside
The Chesapeake Bay

When you're in Hampton Roads it's impossible to ignore the Chesapeake Bay, the region's most important feature. Even when you're not in direct view of the bay, you're near one of the many rivers and creeks that flow into it.

Besides creating some breathtaking scenery, the Chesapeake Bay influences countless aspects of daily life:

*It is the main reason Hampton Roads excels as a port and a popular tourism destination. It is the engine that drives much of the region's industry – from shipbuilding and repair to manufacturing and distribution.

*It provides the livelihood for hundreds of hardy watermen whose families have plied the waters for generations. The crabs and finfish they harvest make Virginia the third largest seafood producing state.

*The type of fish pulled from the bay has a direct impact on what's on the menu when you go out to eat. If rockfish or softshell crabs are in season, they'll be hot items at area restaurants.

*The bay and the deep Hampton Roads harbor were the main reasons the Navy built its largest installation here.

*The bay enticed the first permanent English settlers in the New World to stay in the area after they landed here in 1607. One of the bay's tributaries led them to Jamestown where they began colonizing this country. As a result, Hampton Roads has a treasure trove of historical sites.

*Because of the bay and its tributaries, getting from here to there can be tricky in this coastal region. Bridges and underwater tunnels are vital links between cities divided by the bay and other waterways.

With its 200-mile length, the Chesapeake Bay is the United States' largest estuary, and Hampton Roads is where it starts its journey northward to Havre de Grace, Md.

Although the Chesapeake Bay is physically surrounded by only Virginia and Maryland, its watershed reaches as far as Cooperstown, N.Y. and Pendleton County, W.Va. In this drainage area nearly 50 rivers and thousands of streams, creeks and ditches empty into the Bay, making it vulnerable to any pollutants they carry. The largest tributary is the Susquehanna River in Pennsylvania, which is why that inland state is a key player in keeping the Bay healthy. All the rainfall that drops on the 64,000 square miles between North Carolina and Vermont ends up in the Bay.

For most people, the Bay's special meaning comes from watching a glorious sunrise, spending the day fishing in its waters or strolling along one of its many beaches. Every city in South Hampton Roads is situated on hundreds of miles of coastline along the Bay and its tributaries. Portsmouth alone has 185 miles of shoreline with Norfolk stretching along 140 miles of waterfront.

For environmentalists, the bay is revered as one of the most productive places on the earth. Its waters, marshes and wetlands shelter an incredible variety of life – from blue crabs and flounder to egrets and whistling swans. More than 2,700 species of plants and animals depend on the bay for life.

The Chesapeake Bay is where

Chesapeake Bay Facts
(From the Chesapeake Bay Foundation)

• The Chesapeake Bay is the largest and most biologically productive estuary in North America. More seafood is harvested from the bay than from any of the 840 other estuaries in the United States.

• It is 200 miles long and averages 15 miles in width. Its depth averages 21 feet.

• It has 49 rivers with 102 branches and tributaries that flow into it. They are navigable for 1,750 miles

• It has more than 15 million people living in its watershed, which includes Virginia, Maryland, West Virginia, Pennsylvania, Delaware and New York.

• It is home to more than 2,700 species of plants and animals.

• It has an oyster catch representing one-fourth of the total U.S. harvest and a blue crab harvest that is more than half of the country's total catch.

• It is the winter home for about 500,000 Canada geese and 40,000 whistling swans

• It is the nesting area of choice for 1,600 pairs of ospreys – the largest population in the U.S. It also is the nesting area for about 125 pairs of bald eagles – one of the largest populations in the lower 48 states.

salt water from the ocean meets and mingles with fresh river water. Geologists believe it was created at the end of the last Ice Age approximately 12,000 to 18,000 years ago. The Indians who were Virginia's first inhabitants called the bay various names that paid tribute to its majesty: "Great Waters," "Mother of Waters" and "Great Shellfish Bay." In the 1600s, British colonists named it "Chesapeake" from the Indian word "Tschiswapeki."

Although the Chesapeake Bay is renowned for its oysters, crabs and finfish, their population has dropped drastically in the past 100 years. Pollution, over-harvesting and the stress put on the Bay by development have reduced the oyster population to only one percent of what it was in the late 20th century. Rockfish, once one of the bay's most prolific fish, nearly disappeared until a multi-state ban on catching them was implemented in 1986. Now the rockfish have rebounded to the point that there are limited fishing seasons.

A 1983 Environmental Protection Agency study showed the bay was ailing from too many nutrients, toxic substances and sediment. This helped created a public awareness that the bay is a fragile resource that must be protected. A ban on phosphate detergents, restrictions on wetland destruction and other coordinated efforts are helping turn the tide for the bay.

You'll still spot blue "Save the Bay" bumper stickers on cars, but there are some hopeful signs that the bay's health is on the mend. One improvement is the growth of underwater grasses, which are vital to filtering pollutants. Grass fields have increased from a low of 35,000 acres in 1984 to more than 50,000 acres today. This is still nowhere near the 300,000 acres that were growing in the early '60s, but it is a step in the right direction.

To soak up the beauty of the bay there are several places to go. Norfolk has its Ocean View beaches. The Cape Henry area inside Fort Story in Virginia Beach has a good stretch of undeveloped beaches. You can admire the bay from the Chesapeake Bay Bridge-Tunnel, which connects Virginia Beach with the Eastern Shore and has an overlook on a manmade island. And, there are all the rivers and inlets that run into the bay. To really appreciate the Chesapeake Bay, you must get out on the water. There are many fishing boats and tour boats that take groups out daily.

To get involved in improving the bay, join the Chesapeake Bay Foundation. It was founded in 1966 and has grown to more than 83,000 members. The foundation is headquartered in Annapolis, Md., but has a field office in Norfolk at 100 W. Plume St. (622-1964). The foundation is the country's largest regional environmental organization and a powerful voice for the bay.

Other organizations with an interest in the bay are the Southeastern Association for the Virginia Environment, or SAVE (426-7501). There is a local chapter of the Sierra Club (855-5896) and two Audubon Society chapters (428-5962). There also are numerous clubs for anglers. On the first Saturday of every month the environmental community gathers at Morrison's Cafeteria near Norfolk's Military Circle mall for an informative breakfast meeting. It starts at 9 AM and often draws more than 100 guests.

Another event that attracts a huge response is the annual Clean the Bay Day on the first Saturday in June. The effort started in this region in 1989 when volunteers joined forces for three hours to clean 52 miles of local waterways. Their reward was the satisfaction of hauling away 60,000 pounds of trash. Since 1989, Clean the Bay Day's momentum has swelled. In 1992 more than 3,000 volunteers combed 223 miles of shoreline and collected 150,000 pounds (77 tons) of aluminum cans, old tires and other junk.

As Clean the Bay Day approaches each spring you'll see and hear a barrage of publicity that brings out families (including ours), Scout troops and individuals. But in case you miss the media messages, call 427-6606 for information.

This photo of the Chesapeake Bay Bridge-Tunnel was taken from the Eastern Shore of Virginia, northern terminus of the bridge-tunnel. The mainland of Virginia is the far horizon with the Atlantic Ocean on the left.

A life-size Benjamin Franklin ponders the U.S. Constitution along Main Street in Smithfield.

Inside
Daytrips

*N*o matter how stimutating our great region is, there comes a time when you've just got to get out of dodge...to flee the static scenery to freshen your perspective and boost your mental attitude. These mini-escapes from reality can be made even more fulfilling when you can reach your destination within a few hours and within the comfort of your own sedan. You're the pilot, and you can steer towards a big dose of history, a wild and wonderful shopping excursion, an out-of-this-city dining experience, or just to spread-eagle on an empty plot of sand along some rolling surf with a good pulp paperback.

What we call Daytrips, we might as well call "head-trips," because they give us, and you, the primo opportunity to break the everyday pattern and run away with the not-so-rich and famous to renew our spirit while we snoop around in someone else's backyard. Whether you head out over the Chesapeake Bay Bridge-Tunnel to the charming Eastern Shore, don your tri-cornered hat for a stroll through Colonial Williamsburg, or pack up your sand chair and bikini for the broad beaches of the Outer Banks, you can be in what will seem to be a far away place in no time, all on one tank of gas.

So, fasten your seat belt, please. Come with us on a whirlwind tour of the cities and sights that are right around the corner in miles, but galaxies away in exploration opportunities for the entire family. Ready? Let's go!

Hampton/Newport News

You've noticed, we're sure, that we constantly refer to our fair community as "southside Hampton Roads." Where, do you ask, is the northside? Well, it's right up there on the other side of the James River and Hampton Roads, and it's called the cities of Hampton and Newport News.

Not that we're competitive, or anything like that, but those folks on the opposite end of the Hampton Roads Bridge-Tunnel insist on having their own newspaper, the *Daily Press*, their own convention dome, the Hampton Coliseum, their own beaches, like the refurbished Buckroe, and even their own superstar attractions. Why, they can even claim the state's largest private employer, Newport News Shipbuilding.

Yet, friendly enemies that we are, we're obliged to give you a quick tour of our northern neighbors. We'll combine our topics for both cities, since they geographically blend from one to the other, and you can choose which places to visit based on your personal preferences.

A quick history lesson is in order, too. Hampton was born in 1610 when the first settlers landed on the beach to the utter amazement of the quite content native Kecoughtan Indians. The city lays claim to the beginnings of free education, the downfall of Blackbeard the pirate (though there is, we must admit, a competing claim from Ocracoke Island, NC), and the training of America's first astronauts. If that's not enough, they can also claim a rich military history tracing back to the Civil War.

Newport News got its start in 1607 when the Virginia Company of London gave Captain Christopher Newport the assignment to scope out a nifty spot for a new settlement on the James River. Newport and his crew from the ships *Susan Constant,* the *Godspeed* and the *Discovery* liked the looks of the sandy point at the mouth of the river, set up camp and called their settlement Jamestown. Over the years, because everyone would rush out to the point to spread the word that big boss Newport would be coming in with news from home, by 1619 the name that stuck was Newportes Newes, the oldest English place name of any city in the New World.

Together, Hampton and Newport News are referred to as The Peninsula, and the places to go and things to see will whisk you from the long-ago past to the space age future. We'll give you phone numbers for the attractions you might want to visit, but be advised that calling from southside is a nominal long-distance call.

Getting there: Getting to the Peninsula is a snap, unless you see the flashing light on the Interstate indicating traffic congestion at the Hampton Roads Bridge-Tunnel. If the lights are on hold and you get the all-clear signal, just zip down I-64 West and in less than 30 minutes you can be inside a museum. An alternate route is the spanking new Monitor-Merrimac Bridge-Tunnel (locally referred to as the M&M), accessed through I-664 in Suffolk.

Attractions: Peninsula museums are a visual and rich experience for all ages. Starting in Newport News, you'll want to visit the world-renowned Mariner's Museum (595-0368), which explores our relationship with the sea. You should start with the film "Mariner," narrated by James Earl Jones, and then set off to examine exquisite miniature ship models, carved figureheads, unbelievable scrimshaw, working steam engines and an Antique Boats Gallery. Alongside the museum is the 550-acre Mariner's Museum Park with nature and bike trails as well as boat rentals for fishing on Lake Maury. Open Monday through Saturday from 9 AM-5 PM and Sundays from noon -5 PM, there is a nominal admission charge to the museum.

Just across the street from the Mariner's Museum is the Peninsula Fine Arts Center (596-8175) which has just recently tripled its size. Changing exhibits by living artists along with contemporary art from museum collections and private sources are on display. The gift shop is a treasure house of gifts, books, cards and unique decorative objects, so while admission to the museum is free, plan on spending a few dollars anyway. Don't try to visit on Mondays, they're closed, but come Tuesday through Saturday, 10 AM- 5 PM and Sundays, noon-5PM.

On J. Clyde Morris Boulevard is the Museum created for kids of all ages, The Virginia Living Museum (595-1900). Part zoo, part botanical gardens, part observatory and planetarium, there's also an aviary and massive aquarium. Especially popular is the Touch Tank for hands-on learning. Here you can reach out and touch something fishy. Outside there are animals, like skunks and even a bald eagle, that you can observe in their natural wooded habitats. There are nominal admission fees that vary with the parts of the museum you want to explore. We, heavy with children, say go for it all.

Leave terra firma and head to Hampton, to the Virginia Air and Space Center (727-0800), designated the official NASA Langley Visitor Center. On Freeman and Ames roads and open every day of the week, here you'll see moon rocks and space capsules, more than a dozen aircraft, the Hampton Roads History Center and the only IMAX theater in Southeastern Virginia. There's a nominal admission charge for the Center and the theater. Right

next door on the downtown waterfront is the Hampton Carousel, built in 1920 and completely restored to it's original beauty. For just fifty cents, from April through October you can climb aboard history and take a twirl on an original horse or chariot.

Other sight-seeing possibilities include The War Memorial Museum in Newport News and Casemate Museum, Air Power Park, Bluebird Gap Farm (pet an animal you would never allow in your home) and Fort Wool/Fort Monroe in Hampton.

Restaurants: On the Peninsula, you can take your pick of brand-name burger and fast-food places, but here are a few culinary gems that we favor. Bon Appetit (11710 Jefferson Avenue, 873-0644) is a charmer, with a scrumptious French/Vietnamese menu. They do wonderful and strange things with chicken, along with some grand stir-fry entrees. Port Arthur near the Mariner's Museum (11137 Warwick Boulevard, 599-6474) is a very popular Chinese place; Das Waldcafe (12529 Warwick Boulevard, 930-1781) is authentic German, with sauerbraten, spatzle and the most divine hazelnut cake. A new eatery on the scene is Buckroe's Island Grill at Salt Ponds Marina in Hampton (850-5757). In the octagonal white dining room you can munch on fresh seafood prepared grilled, blackened or broiled with a multitude of toppings like roasted red pepper sauce, jerk seasonings or salsa. For lighter fare, order a platter of raw or steamed seafood or an appetizer of their delicious crab dip.

A sweetheart of a place is under the green awning at the Grey Goose in Old Hampton across from the Air and Space Museum (723-7978), with its intimate country ambiance and wonderful homemade soups, Brunswick stew and ham biscuits. It's a shame they're only open for lunch Monday through Saturday. For more of a resort-feel – "I'm out of town so why not go for it" – atmosphere, we recommend The Restaurants at Kiln Creek Country Club (874-2600), off Jefferson Avenue in the delightful Kiln Creek Golf Course Community. Here you can be satisfied according to your hunger, from a wonderful club sandwich to a fine dinner of prime rib.

Shopping: A little bit of old, a little bit of new...shopping is a mixed-bag on the Peninsula. In Old Hampton, with its quaint brick and tree-lined streets, you'll see some wonderful little shops spotlighted by antique English street lamps. Harrogate's, Ltd. is a Peninsula tradition, with its fine china, crystal, Faberge eggs and pewter collection. If you need to buy a lovely gift for someone that you feel guilty leaving back at home, this is the place to come. The Old Hampton Bookstore is filled to the rafters with a phenomenal selection of great tomes; Kitty & Co. on Queens Way is a must when you just really must have a fashionable new ensemble or that just-right accessory to complete your power outfit.

For mall lovers, there's Coliseum Mall in Hampton, with our favorite Hecht's as one anchor, along with your favorites like The Gap, The Limited and so much more. Patrick Henry Mall and Newmarket Mall are Newport News' shopping haunts with much of the same mall-flavored department stores and specialty shops. The up-and-comers of this area have staked out the Denbigh area of Newport News as the place to build houses and raise kids and pets. Naturally, stores galore have followed the homesteaders, so the area in every compass point from Jefferson Avenue at Denbigh Boulevard has birthed a wide variety of options, like a Wal Mart and Sam's Club, TJ Maxx, Bootlegger's Shoes and a broad stretch of drug stores and home centers.

Accommodations: If you choose to stay overnight, there are two primary hubs we'll point out. One is in Hampton in the Coliseum area off Mercury Boulevard. Because of the proximity to mega-shopping and the convention center, you'll find all the name brands spiffed up to their finest. Our vote goes to the Sheraton Inn Coliseum. Not only are their rooms spacious and comfy, and indoor swimming pool a real all-weather treat, but the front desk personnel are some of the most knowledgeable and friendly in the region.

In Newport News, the Oyster Point corridor houses not only the nucleus of the city's business brains, but some fine overnight accommodations. The Omni Newport News is in the heart of the action, along with Days Inn Oyster Point and Governor's Inn. Any of these hotels can offer a pleasant night's sleep in clean and comfortable surroundings.

Phoebus: Phoebus is cute. This small pocket of cuteness is actually a tightly-knit Hampton community you can find when you take the Mallory Street exit off I-64 (the first exit you come to after the tunnel) and head towards Fort Monroe. Along Mallory are some of the best eats and most unique shopping experiences just waiting to happen, and a stopover there is similar to being whisked back in history to a time when people were friendly, life was slower and love was always in the air. See what we mean with a browse through the incredible Benders Books and Cards, Phoebus Needleworks and Crafts and the Electric Glass Company where you'll find hand-blown goblets, Tiffany glass and etched glass for your front door. Locals are hard-pressed to reveal the secret that Clyde's serves up the coldest beer and best burger this side of Kansas; Victorian Station, in a charming Victorian home, not only offers a silky smooth quiche or chunky chicken salad, but is one of the last remaining places on the face of the earth where you can linger over afternoon tea along with jam lathered scones, tea cakes and open faced sandwiches. Even hard-nosed Insiders know that an afternoon in Phoebus is better than a month with a therapist. Don't even think about leaving town until you've been here.

For more information: As in all Hampton Roads cities, an army of knowledgeable patriots stand ready to swamp you with information about their respective cities. In

Hampton, you can reach the Visitor Center (710 Settlers landing Road) at 727-1102 or 1-800-800-2202. In Newport News, the number to call for the Tourist Information Center (13560 Jefferson Avenue) is 886-2737.

Smithfield

Renowned for its hams, Smithfield is a traditional Virginia town that proudly preserves its historic past. Smithfield, in Isle of Wight County, has been producing distinctive hams since 1779. By then the town along the Pagan River was a busy port for tobacco and peanuts that flourished in the rich soil. The town's world-famous hams are produced from pigs fattened on native peanuts. They also get their taste from curing over slow hickory fires. To be called a Smithfield ham, the product must come from Smithfield and nowhere else.

Getting there: From Norfolk, Virginia Beach, Chesapeake and Portsmouth, get on Route 17 in Portsmouth (High Street) and stay on it until it intersects Route 10. Turn left and follow the signs to downtown Smithfield. The trip will take no more than an hour. From Suffolk, take Route 258 and you'll be in Smithfield in about 30 minutes.

Attractions: The town itself is charming and is a National Historic District. Its main street is lined with restored homes, many of them large, ornate Victorians. There are 15 pre-Revolutionary War homes. Many of the back yards run right down to the

Pagan River.

To get oriented, stop by the Old Isle of Wight Courthouse, which houses the county tourism bureau (357-5182), and pick up brochures and a walking tour map. The courthouse is at Main and Mason streets.

On your way into town, you'll see a sign for Saint Luke's Church on Route 10. Built in 1632, it is the country's only original Gothic church and the oldest church of English foundation in America. This Episcopal church, nicknamed "Old Brick," is still in use and has lovely wooded grounds. Its Jacobean interior features gables, buttresses and traceried windows. St. Luke's, a National Shrine, is open daily except during January (357-3367). It sits back from the parking lot, so plan on a short, pleasant walk to reach the church. Admission is free.

The Isle of Wight County Museum, at Main and Church streets, is housed in a turn-of-the-century bank building and has archeological displays highlighting county history. Exhibits include a country store and Civil War displays (357-7459). Admission is free.

The Old Isle of Wight Courthouse dates from the mid-18th century. Its clerk's office and county jail are restored. The courthouse is owned by the Association for the Preservation of Virginia Antiquities. It is usually open Wednesday through Friday (357-5182).

Out in the country is Fort Boykins State Park, a Civil War fort on the banks of the James River, which still has its earthworks. There is a gazebo overlooking the river and a picnic area.

Restaurants: For a small town, Smithfield has many choices. Both the Smithfield Station and the Smithfield Inn and Tavern have fine menus. Many Hampton Roads' residents drive over here just to pig out at these restaurants. The Smithfield Station at 415 S. Church St., on the banks of the Pagan River, serves seafood, pork, pasta and other local favorites during lunch and dinner daily (357-7700). The Smithfield Inn and Tavern, 112 Main St., was built as a tavern in 1752. It serves dinner on Friday and Saturday and lunch on Sunday. As soon as a restoration is completed, the inn plans to expand its meal service. The menu features Smithfield ham, Brunswick stew and other regional foods (357-0244)

Angelo's Seafood and Steak House, 1804 S. Church St., serves mainly steak and seafood for lunch and dinner (357-3104). It is open daily. Smithfield Confectionery and Ice Cream Parlor, 208 Main St., has a menu of sandwiches as well as ice cream. It is open daily (357-3166).

Another possibility is the Twins Old Town Inn at 220 Main St., a cafe frequented by locals. It is run by twin sisters who whip up good country cooking for breakfast and lunch. The restaurant closes on Sunday and serves only breakfast on Saturday (357-3031).

Accommodations: The Isle of Wight Inn, 1607 S. Church St., has 12 guest rooms, including honeymoon suites with Jacuzzis and fireplaces. It has a charming historic feel (357-3176). The Smithfield Station also has guest 15 rooms, most of which overlook boats moored at the inn's marina. The Smithfield Inn and Tavern is undergoing a renovation that will transform it into a bed and breakfast.

Shopping: For antiques try the Isle of Wight Inn at 1607 Church St. Its gift shop has some unusual pieces and is where we go to buy restored antique clocks. Wharf Hill Antiques, 218 Main St., is a general antique store with furniture, glassware and prints (357-9524). Smithfield Rare Books, Main and Underwood, specializes in Virginiana, history and science (357-2189). For brass, sterling or porcelain items, visit Southern Accent's Cards and Gifts, 913 S. Church (357-2724). If you want a Smithfield souvenir, try Simpson's Pharmacy, 221 Main St. (357-4361).

Recreation: The Smithfield Downs Golf Course is an 18-hole private course open daily to the public. It is on Highway 258 just outside town. Although it is only 5,200 yards long, this course is a challenging one for all golfers. (357-3101).

Williamsburg

Martha Stewart would just be tickled pink with this place. To visit Williamsburg, for a woman, is like the supreme mother's guilt, what with all the perfectly spotless, perfectly decorated and appointed rooms, from hotel suites to the restored Governor's Mansion, along with a scatter and panic attack through the miles of aisles at the Williamsburg Pottery. For a man, however, a visit to Williamsburg means being thankful for your V-8 horsepower, electric screwdriver and a macho perusal of the Brooks Bros. and Polo outlets.

If you're seeking the perfect hodge-podge of Colonial ambiance tossed with a little contemporary bargain shopping, turn your cruise control towards mecca...to Williamsburg. In fact, you can work up into a full-blown sight-seeing/shopping frenzy in the mere 45 minutes on speedy interstate that it will take you to get there from Southside Hampton Roads.

Because this is intended to be a daytrip guide, we won't even begin to tell you about all the teeth-gritting rides, fabulous architecture and wonderful food that you'll find at Busch Gardens on the fringes of Williamsburg. That alone is a daytrip unto itself. If you're so inclined to stretch your Williamsburg visit into more than one day, there are numerous motels and hotels with open registers, ranging from the sublime Williamsburg Inn to brand-name sleep-places like Econo Lodge, Ramada and Holiday Inn. If you plan to stay over during peak summer season or on a holiday, definitely make reservations in advance.

A few notes about conduct in the Historic Area. While touring any restored building, even thinking about fondling the priceless furnishings and accessories is prohibited, as is smoking, drinking or eating. No pets, strollers or baby carriages are allowed either. You may bring a camera or camcorder into the buildings and shops, but you will be asked to put them away in their cases during any program or tour lecture. Cranky children will have to be likewise stowed, preferably beyond earshot of your fellow visitors.

Getting there: From southside Hampton Roads, Williamsburg is a fairly quick shot north on Interstate 64, and the only congestion you're likely to encounter is at the Hampton Roads Bridge-Tunnel that connects Norfolk to Hampton. Once you've spurted through the tube, it's a pleasant 45 minute drive. Interstate exit signs are clearly marked. Take the Busch Gardens exit for that destination, or follow the signs a few more miles north pointing you to the College of William & Mary to

Photo: Richmond Newspapers

Visit nearby Williamsburg and discover Colonial America.

reach the Historic Area.

Attractions: Wherever do we begin? The 173 acres occupied by Williamsburg's Historic Area is chocka-block with 18th-century public buildings, homes, crafts shops and over 90 acres of gardens and greens. If you're a true history buff, we suggest you first go to the Visitors Center, which is located on Rt. 132Y off the Colonial Parkway. Here you can see the film "Williamsburg – The Story of a Patriot," which is shown continually throughout the day. Shuttle buses also leave every few minutes from the lower level that will take you directly to the Historic Area so you'll not have any parking headaches. For a full tour, you will need to purchase an admission ticket, available at the Visitors Center.

We'll start at the Governor's Palace, the place where everyone wants to have their picture taken. The residence of seven royal governors and the first two governors of the Commonwealth of Virginia, the restored interiors and formal gardens are simply gorgeous. Walking down Palace Green will take you to Duke of Gloucester Street (Dog Street in local language), where Colonial milliners, silversmiths, wigmakers, bakers, blacksmiths and more set up shop three hundred years ago. All are staffed by contemporary craftspeople donned in authentic wardrobe, who will be pleased to answer any of your questions, and sell you a few wares priced at today's dollar. Don't neglect to stop in at the Dora Armistead House that sits midway down Duke of Gloucester. It's a Victorian jewel of

a home that holds the original Armistead family furnishings and was decorated by the late Laura Ashley.

The trail down Duke of Gloucester ends at the front steps of the Capitol, where the principles of self-government, individual liberty and responsible leadership were developed by Virginia's patriots. If you hike across the green on the pedestrian pathway, you'll come to a popular photo opportunity...the Public Gaol on Nicholson Street. Here you can fling your arms into the wooden shackles while your partner snaps away.

Two fine museums are also located within walking distance. The DeWitt Wallace Decorative Arts Gallery houses over 8,000 objects from Colonial Williamsburg's permanent collection of 18th-century ceramics, furniture, metals, maps, prints and textiles. The Abbey Aldrich Rockefeller Folk Art Center offers changing exhibits of American Folk art. Both museums require a separate ticket for admission.

On the opposite end of Duke of Gloucester from the Capitol, you'll be able to stroll through Merchant's Square and then onto the campus of the College of William & Mary. You'll feel smarter just touching the weathered brick walls of these truly handsome buildings, home to the second oldest college in the country.

Restaurants: You can dine or eat-on-the-run. The choice is yours. We prefer the Colonial taverns for their warm, fuzzy feeling and consistently excellent menus. There are three in the Historic Area.

Christiana Campbell's Tavern was one of George Washington's favorites, with skillet fried chicken, pecan waffles and Southern spoon bread. Josiah Chownings Tavern, adjacent to the Courthouse, is a typical Colonial alehouse, favored for its sandwiches, Brunswick stew and Welsh rabbit. At night take in the Gambols – colonial games, entertainment and "diversions." Lastly, there's King's Arms Tavern on Duke of Gloucester Street where peanut soup with Sally Lunn bread is a must to start, followed by Virginia ham or prime rib.

For contemporary dining with all the graciousness of Southern hospitality, our unanimous vote goes to a tie. First, we highly recommend The Regency Room at the Williamsburg Inn. Divine breads, prime rib, seafood and veal match beautifully with the extensive wine list. Sunday brunch here is one you'll talk about for weeks. Reservations are definitely required for dinner, 229-2141. Next is the Trellis, located in Merchant's Square and the creation of renowned Executive Chef Marcel Desaulniers. The mesquite-grilled fare and regional specialities like Chesapeake Bay seafood and Smithfield ham laced with divinely delicate sauces can not be imitated. Whether you opt for a table in the intimate Vault Room, Grill Room or Garden Room, or linger in the Cafe or outdoor bistro, your meal will be a delight. Call early to reserve the room of your choice: 229-8610.

Shopping: Now we're getting warm. Williamsburg is host to some of the finest discount shopping this side of the recession. Comfy shoes are the basic entry requirement at the world-famous Williamsburg Pottery, located five miles west of Williamsburg in Lightfoot. From a roadside shed on a half-acre lot, the Pottery has sprawled to over 200 acres, with more than 30 structures including a passive solar building the size of eight football fields. This book isn't long enough for a laundry list of what goodies you can snap up for tiny prices. China, glassware and stemware, furniture, lamps, wicker and, of course, pottery is just the beginning. They also have a wonderful gourmet food section, and the largest wine selection in the state of Virginia.

Stuff those newspaper-wrapped goodies from the Pottery in your trunk and drive back towards town to the Williamsburg Outlet Mall. The one-story bargain mecca is so popular that it has just expanded to its full-blown size of over 60 factory outlet shops, all arranged in a cross pattern with the food court in the middle of the "x." For ladies, there's the Dress barn, Hit or Miss and Bruce Alan Bags, Etc. For men, head to Bugle Boy, Cape Isle Knitters and S&K Famous Brands. Join forces to browse The Kitchen Place, The Paper Factory, Book Hutch and Solid Brass of Williamsburg. Grab a sugar hit from the Fudge Factory, jump on in the car and head to...

Berkeley Commons, just a hop down Richmond Road towards town. We are now talking top-of-the-line, bottom-of-the wallet type shopping mania. Calvin Klein, J. Crew, J.G. Hook, Jones New York,

Anne Kline, Liz Claiborne, Geoffry Beene, Brooks Bros...need we say more? The entire u-shaped outlet center is charming, and especially attractive with it's savings to 70% off the original hefty price tags that designer wear demands. The only eatery here is the Pelican Cafe. They make a wonderful sandwich platter, reasonably priced, with just enough fuel to keep your motor going to one last discounter center.

Patriot Plaza Outlets, just down Richmond Road from Berkley Commons, is a show-off...not just with its handsome architecture, but with its shops and showrooms. West Point Pepperell, Lenox, Villeroy and Boch, Gorham and Dansk all have their outlets here. But don't leave without us. We'll be between Ben & Jerry's and the Ralph Lauren shop.

All along Richmond Road are other small centers with wonderful crafts and gift shops. Back in town, there's Merchant's Square in the city's center. Here are some exquisite shops offering fine apparel for women (Binn's, Casey's and Laura Ashley) and for men (Beecroft and Bull, Ltd.). For kids, don't pass up Uncommon Toys, and everyone will enjoy relaxing in the wonderful Rizzoli Bookstore. Sign of the Rooster for folk art, Quilts Unlimited and Needle-crafts of the Nicholson-White House are also on the must-see list.

On your way back to southside Hampton Roads, there are two other stops you should make...Yorktown and Jamestown, which, along with Williamsburg, define the Historic Triangle. See our next section for details.

For more information: For more than you'd even really want to know about Colonial Williamsburg and beyond, call 1-800-HISTORY. The free call will earn you a complimentary copy of the Vacation Planner, with all the details for full enjoyment of this special place. You should also pick up a copy of *The Insiders' Guide to Williamsburg, Jamestown and Yorktown*, which, as you hopefully already know from this book, will give you the true "inside" scoop on the area.

Jamestown/Yorktown

Two of the most historic sites in the country are within an easy hour's drive from the Norfolk/Virginia Beach area. If you're already planning a trip to Williamsburg, they are definitely worth working into your itinerary. However, it is feasible to zip up for a day and see both Jamestown and Yorktown.

Jamestown, founded in 1607, is the site of the country's first permanent English-speaking settlement. The early years were tough on the settlers as humid summers, cold winters, hungry mosquitoes and unfriendly Indians thwarted their settlement efforts. Jamestown endured, however, and became Virginia's first capital. After the colonial capital moved to Williamsburg in 1699, Jamestown ceased to exist as a community. Today it is the site of a painstaking restoration.

Nearby Yorktown is a scenic town on the banks of the York River. Its claim to fame is being the place where the British threw up the white flag in 1781 and ended the Revolutionary War. Yorktown was established in 1661 and is filled with history.

Getting there: Take Interstate 64 and head west. Go through the Hampton Roads Bridge-Tunnel and keep going. If you're not familiar with the area, it's easiest to head for Yorktown first and start your tour there. Take Route 17 North (J. Clyde Morris Blvd.) in Newport News. Look for signs steering you toward the Yorktown Visitor Center run by the National Park Service.

When you finish at Yorktown, take the scenic Colonial National Parkway to Jamestown. This 23-mile wooded stretch directly links the Yorktown Visitor Center with Jamestown Island. Along the way you'll see historic markers, picnic areas and magnificent views of the James and York rivers. In spring and fall the scenery is spectacular. Keep a light foot on the gas pedal; this is part of a federal park and the speed limit is only 45 m.p.h.

If you're returning to the Norfolk/Virginia Beach area from Jamestown, get on Route 5 and take it to I-64 East.

Attractions: Both the Yorktown Battlefield and Jamestown Island are part of Colonial National Historical Park, which includes the parkway that connects them.

In Yorktown, start your tour at the Yorktown Visitor Center (898-3400). Get oriented with a 15-minute film, pick up maps and check out the exhibits. Our favorites are George Washington's canvas battle tent preserved behind glass and a replica of a British warship.

Children love going through the ship. Older ones will enjoy dioramas depicting the Revolutionary War through a boy's eyes.

Be sure to take a drive through the battlefields where you'll see earthworks, a historic house and the surrender site. There are markers along the way. For $2 you can rent a tape with a narration of what you are seeing. The tape comes with its own cassette player. There are numerous places to get out of the car and inspect the battlefields. The visitor center is open daily. Admission to it and the battlefields is free.

The Yorktown Victory Center is on Old Route 238 (887-1776). It was built by the Commonwealth of Virginia and is run by the Jamestown-Yorktown Foundation. Outside is a recreation of a Continental Army camp. In spring and summer, an 18th-century farm site also comes to life. Inside the center are interesting exhibits pertaining to the Revolutionary War and the events leading up to it. There also is a short film that focuses on the people who lived during the Revolution. There is an admission fee, and you can purchase a combination ticket to the center and Jamestown Settlement in Jamestown. The center is open daily.

Another interesting site in Yorktown is the victory statue, which was ordered by the Continental Congress in 1781 but not started until 1881. The statue is downtown. Note the inscriptions in the base and the lightning rod on top.

To get completely away from the Revolutionary War stop by The Watermen's Museum on Water

Street (887-2641). It pays tribute to the crabbers, fishermen and oystermen who work the Chesapeake Bay and its tributaries. The museum is housed in a historic wooden house floated across the York River in the 1980s. It generally closes in winter.

You also may want to check out the York River beach in downtown Yorktown and also drive past some of the town's historic homes.

In Jamestown there are two main places to see. The Jamestown-Yorktown Foundation runs Jamestown Settlement. Jamestown Island is part of the Colonial National Historical Park. Start your tour at either place.

At the Jamestown Settlement, which is just off Route 31, you'll see costumed participants pretending to be settlers living in a re-created fort. Docked along the James River are full-size replicas of the three ships that brought the first settlers in 1607. There also is a museum with displays on English colonization, the Powhatan Indians and the settlement's early years. A 15-minute film gives a good overview. There is a charge to visit the Settlement, which is open daily. You can buy a joint ticket with the Yorktown Victory Center.

There also is a fee to drive onto Jamestown Island. However, if someone in your car has a Golden Age Passport from the U.S. Park Service, everyone in the car gets in for free. Once on the island you can see a 15-minute film in the visitor center and look at displays of 17th-century artifacts. Outside are three- and five-mile drives that loop through the island. Glassblowers and potters on the island represent the island's first industries.

At Jamestown you can put your car on a ferry and ride across the James River to Surry County. The trip takes about 30 minutes.

Restaurants: If you want to eat in Jamestown your only options are the snack bar at the Jamestown Settlement or the picnic lunch you hauled along. Or you can ride the ferry to Surry County and eat at the Surry House on Route 10, which is known for its country cooking (294-3389).

There are several restaurants in Yorktown. The most famous is Nick's Seafood Pavilion on Water Street (887-5269). Founded in 1940, the restaurant has an elaborate decor and excellent seafood. More informal restaurants include the Yorktown Pub at 540 Water St. (898-8793), Sammy & Nick's Family Steak House, 11806 George Washington Blvd. (898-3070) and the Beach House Restaurant, 114 Water St. (890-3804).

Shopping: There are gift shops at the various historic sites. For art try the On the Hill Creative Arts Center in Yorktown at 121 Alexander Hamilton Blvd. (898-3076). This is a cooperative gallery of local artists. Nationally known folk artist Nancy Thomas also maintains a gallery at 145 Ballard St. (898-3665). The Yorktown Shoppe on Main Street has a variety of gift items (898-2984).

Accommodations: Your best bets are the numerous motels and hotels near Williamsburg.

Richmond

There is so much to do in Richmond and surrounding counties that you could spend days here. It's one of our favorite cities to visit. With nearly 20 museums and 30 other interesting places to visit, we still haven't seen all of it yet.

Ever since PBS showed its documentary on the War Between the States several years ago, Richmond has been invaded by history buffs from around the world. But there's more to see here than the city's Civil War heritage; Richmond boasts great architecture in its historic neighborhoods, excellent museums and fine restaurants.

For tourism information check with the Richmond Visitors Center at Robin Hood Rd. and the Boulevard (358-5511) or the Metropolitan Richmond Convention and Visitors Bureau at 300 E. Main St. (782-2777). For more extensive information check out the *Insiders' Guide to Greater Richmond.*

Getting there: Head straight up Interstate 64 and keep going for about 90 minutes. To get downtown take the Fifth Street exit to Broad Street and maneuver through the city from there.

Attractions: If you are interested in history or the War Between the States, start at either the Richmond National Battlefield Park Visitor Center or the Museum and White House of the Confederacy. The center at 3215 Broad St. (226-1981) has exhibits, a film and employees to guide you toward the city's numerous battlefields. It is open daily, and admission is free.

The museum and White House (former home of Confederate President Jefferson Davis) have the world's largest collection of Confederate memorabilia. Both are fascinating so plan on spending several hours. They are at 12th and E. Clay St. (649-1861) and are open daily. There is an admission fee.

Other sites to see include the Richmond Children's Museum at 740 N. Sixth St. (643-JIDO) and the Science Museum of Virginia at 2500 W. Broad St. (371-1013). Both are hands-on places all ages will enjoy. The Virginia Museum of Fine Arts at 2800 Grove Ave. (367-0844) has a vast art collection from all periods. The science museum is open daily. The other museums close on Monday. All charge admission fees.

Two other museums that are favorites of ours are the Edgar Allan Poe Museum at 1914 E. Main St. (648-5523) and The Valentine Museum at 1015 E. Clay St. (649-0711). The Poe museum pays tribute to Richmond's native son. It is housed in Richmond's oldest building, a stone house built in 1737. The Valentine Museum focuses on the life and times of old Richmond and has one of the country's best costume collections. Both are open daily and charge admission fees.

You also might want to check out the state Capitol at Ninth and Grace streets. The building was designed by Thomas Jefferson and built in 1788. The grounds include fountains and statues of famous Virginians. The Capitol is open daily.

For outdoor activities wander along the James River downtown

Photo: Richmond Newspapers

Capitol Square in Richmond.

along Tredegar Street or along Monument Avenue named for its many historic statues. Maymont is a 100-acre Victorian state with a mansion, elaborate gardens and petting zoo. The paths along its grounds attract wildlife lovers, joggers, parents strolling babies and lots of other people. Maymont is at 1700 Hampton St. (358-7166). You also may want to wander through some of Richmond's historic neighborhoods such as The Fan, Church Hill and Jackson Ward.

One other fun event to attend in Richmond is the Bizarre Bazaar, held two times a year – The Christmas Collection show in December held at the Virginia Fairgrounds and the Spring Market show in April at The Richmond Centre. Both offer an array of unusual gifts, gourmet foods, quality craftspeople, artists, seasonal decorations and gifts, imported items...the list continues. Started in 1975, the shows now attract over 20,000 people a year. For more information, call 804-288-7555.

Restaurants: You'll find lots of restaurants in the Shockoe Bottom area, Carytown, Fan District and around Virginia Commonwealth University (VCU). Also, suburban Chesterfield and Henrico counties have many good places to eat. Recommendations from Richmond residents include ethnic dinners at the Greek Island, 10902 Hull St. in the Genito Forest shopping center in Chesterfield County (674-9199) and the Island Grill at 14 N. 18th St. (643-2222). This Shockoe Bottom restaurant cooks French food with a Caribbean flair.

Our usual stopping off place is the Texas-Wisconsin Border Cafe, 1501 W. Main near VCU (355-2907). It has a fun, funky atmosphere, fiery chili and great burgers. For fine dining we enjoy the Tobacco Company Restaurant, an elaborately renovated warehouse at 1201 E. Cary St. (782-9555). Other notable establishments include Traveller's Restaurant (707 E. Franklin St., 644-1040), which housed Robert E. Lee's family, and Blue Point Seafood in the Sixth Street Marketplace at 550 E. Grace St. (783-8138).

Shopping: For boutiques and specialty shops park your car and walk through Shockoe Slip, Carytown, Sycamore Square or the Shops of Libbie and Grove. The Sixth Street Marketplace is a festival marketplace that runs along several downtown blocks. There also are several malls in suburban areas.

Accommodations: There are many downtown and suburban hotels as well as bed and breakfasts. If you're looking for something elegant try the Jefferson Hotel, built in 1895 and splendidly restored in the 1980s. It is on Franklin and Adam streets (788-8000). Linden Row Inn at 100 E. Franklin St. was created from seven restored antebellum townhouses (783-7000) and is a lovely choice for lodging.

Outer Banks

There's a magically wonderful change in your personality as you are swept up onto the Wright Memorial Bridge and then to the downhill coast to the wonderland we call the Outer Banks. We think it might have something to do with the calming vapors rising from the Currituck Sound, those strange and wonderful mesmerizing molecules that envelope all those nasty little hyper brain cells and numb them into a peaceful little nap that lasts as long as you stay on this fragile barrier island. With its laid-back attitude, long stretches of clean beaches and acres of protected flora, fauna and wildlife, to visit the Outer Banks, from Corolla on the northern tip to Ocracoke at its southernmost extreme, is to shed the burdens of civilization without giving up any creature comforts or amenities. From accommodations to restaurants, shopping to historical sightseeing, this is a destination that has no equal on this earth.

Getting there: From southside Hampton Roads, steer the car packed with beach chairs, bikinis and coolers onto Interstate 64 East. Take the Battlefield Boulevard North exit (Rt. 168) and drive straight ahead to the 168 Bypass to Nags Head. Don't worry if you miss the bypass, it connects back to 168 on the other side of the Great Bridge area. Head on straight down 168, which will turn into Rt. 158 about 30 miles from the beach. (That's when those magic powers start taking over.) Aim for that mystical Wright Memorial Bridge and...bingo, lottery winner...you're in paradise. North Carolina's Outer Banks is only about 70 miles south of Hampton Roads, but depending on traffic, it can take you from one and one-half hours to too long to tell...but who cares? Summer weekends are especially crowded on the two-lane last stretch, so plan your time accordingly.

Attractions: The beach.

Other attractions: It does rain occasionally in the Outer banks, so here's where we would be forced to go if we couldn't splash in the Atlantic Ocean.

Use the 60-foot granite pylon on a mammoth dune as a compass as you travel down the 158 Bypass road towards Kitty Hawk. If you pretend it's December 17, 1903, you might just witness Wilbur Wright launch the world's first motorized flying machine off this dune and stay airborn for a full 12 seconds. This is where aeronautical history was birthed, and you can visit the recreated airstrip and rustic camp where Wilbur and brother Orville put the Outer Banks on the map here at the Wright Brothers Memorial. If you're here in June, you'll find yourself in the midst of modern examples of that original flying machine as they buzz through the air in the annual Wright Brothers Fly In and Airshow. There is a small entry fee at the National Park Service-run historic site, but it's well worth it for all ages.

You'll see this popular attraction even before you reach MP (Mile Post) 12 on Rt. 158 Bypass. It's the famous Jockey's Ridge...one mile long, 12,000 feet wide and rising to 140 feet above sea level. It's 140 acres of playground for the physically fit, where you can hike up to the top to catch spectacular views of the Atlantic Ocean on one side, the Roanoke Sound on the other. Kite-flying is a primo activity and you can purchase some of the zaniest kites at Kitty Hawk Kites right at the foot of Jockey's Ridge at a cute little shopping center called the Kitty Hawk Connection. The center is also where those with a death-wish can sign the release form that will give them the stomach-churning pleasure of hang-gliding, monitored by experienced instructors. You have to make a reservation for the thrill of it all, so call 441-4124 if you dare.

Traveling south on 158 towards Hatteras, you'll come to the quiet little town of Rodanthe. Here is the Chicamacomico Life Saving Station, restored to the glory it enjoyed back when it guarded the northern coast of Hatteras for 70 years. Established by the U.S. Government in 1874, a nonprofit organization has spearheaded its preservation, and every week during the summer months (usually on Thursdays, but you can stop at the information center right at the start of Highway 12 in Nags Head to ask for specifics on all NPS activities) you can watch as volunteers reenact a life-saving rescue of a shipwrecked crew.

Restaurants: Practically every restaurant on the Outer Banks offers three distinctive courses: seafood, seafood and seafood. We can almost guarantee that you will not be disappointed with any of these courses, and all you must choose is in what kind of atmosphere you want to join the clean plate club. As all Insiders, we have our favorites, and these are the three we highly recommend.

In the heat of the beach action is a quirky little place called Awful Arthur's, that sits right across from the Avalon Fishing Pier at MP 6 on the Beach Road in Kill Devil Hills. If you don't have a brimming platter of their Alaskan crab legs washed down with Bass Ale straight from the tap, you might as well not even bother to come to the Outer Banks. It's casual, it's crowded and it's the best place to dive into the world of steamed seafood to slather with full-strength melted butter. If you pass on dessert, use those dollars to buy an Awful Arthur's t-shirt. It will mean that you're part of the in-crowd.

Point your car north towards the village of Duck and wheel into Blue Point Bar and Grill in The Waterfront Shops that dangle over the Currituck Sound. The 1940s style diner will serve you unusual seafood dishes in the nouvelle manner, along with some sinful desserts whipped up fresh by Ms. Phyllis. Hosts John Power and Sam McGann pack the place seven days a week for both lunch and dinner, and if you're claustrophobic, you might make a beeline for the outdoor dining deck.

For fine dining, Outer Banks style, head to Sanderling Inn Restaurant. Here you'll be pampered with some delectable Carolina recipes, served with panache in a restored lifesaving station, Caffy's Inlet Station No. 5. The furnishings, table appointments and the cordial service all tie with the food for top-spot excellence. After dinner, you might stroll over to neighbor Sanderling Inn and check out the beautiful English country lobby and gallery. The decor and atmosphere are so very alluring that you might find yourself pleading to check into one of their gorgeous rooms for the evening.

Shopping: One of the first signs that there is definitely a shopping experience in your Outer Banks future is The Marketplace Shopping Center you'll see on your left as you travel in on 158 towards the beach. Here there's an immaculate Food Lion for all the nibbles and cold drinks you'll require, along with some nifty shops. Daniel's, a locally owned department store, has all your name-brand goodies, well-priced and well-displayed; The Mule Shed has terrific women's sportswear and pop into Paige's for one-of-a-kind garments.

Farther north in Corolla, you should visit the John de la Vega Gallery. This intriguing place houses beautiful artwork, some of our favorite done by Mr. de la Vega himself. It's a quiet, calming stop, and the perfect respite from the more hustle-bustle shopping experience. While in this area, you'll also want to visit the Corolla Light Village Shops and the Bell Tower Station. Be sure to watch for the wild horses that roam through the Corolla area. They're descendants of Spanish mustangs and the focus of a well-organized protection effort. Don't feed or pet them, please; just admire them for their beauty.

Duck Village, to the north of the main Outer Banks strip, is a shopper's heaven, with a plethora of small shops with geegaws and jimcracks you'll not likely find anywhere else. You can weave in and out of one darling shopping plaza to another, like Scarborough Faire,

with the Island Bookstore, Ocean Annie's for singular jewelry, pottery and gifts, Smash Hit, a great place for tennis and golf attire, and Elizabeth's Cafe and Winery, where you'll find the best wine selection on the Outer Banks, served with a charming menu and an equally charming atmosphere. Whip into the Duck Waterfront Shops for bargains at Barr-ee Station, handcrafted fashions at Donna's Designs and Marine Model Gallery with its wonderful model ships. A last must-stop is The Lucky Duck in Wee Winks Square. You'll not be able to resist the urge to touch every little thing in the place, including home accessories, cards, toys and games.

In Kitty Hawk, a trip to Ben Franklin's is mandatory for all the beach stuff you need that you might have forgotten, as is a stop at Gray's Department Store, one of the oldest and most favorite shops for clothing and accessories. In Kill Devil Hills, you'll find The Dare Centre, anchored by a Belks Department store with all the fine clothing, cosmetics and shoes you might want. Also located in this new center are a NY Bagels and Petrozza's, where the Italian cook in your group can find nirvana with their already-prepared dishes as well as their selection of goodies for you to do the cooking. There's also a new K Mart where, despite our conflicting feelings over seeing this type of commercialism entering the Outer Banks scene, you can find everything you might even think you need while on vacation. In Nags Head, Glenn Eure's Ghost Fleet Gallery is a fascinating art gallery where, if you're lucky, you'll find the gracious owners, Glenn and Pat, on hand to tell you all about the featured works. If you must have your mall-fix, there's the Outer Banks Mall with a Roses, The Mule Shed and Lady Dare (popular clothing stores, the latter featuring beautiful styles for the fuller figured woman) and Soundfeet Shoes for your Reeboks and Nikes. Fairly new on the shopping circuit is Soundings Factory Stores with everything for home and family at discount prices. Pfaltzgraff Collector's Center, London Fog and Rack Room Shoes are all here, among many others.

And, don't forget Manteo for shopping – or for a great break from the beach scene. Our absolutely favorite stop in this small town is Manteo Booksellers, one of the best book stores we have even seen. You'll want to browse here all day (which is encouraged by the friendly and knowledgeable manager, Steve Brumfield), and your only problem will be not blowing your entire vacation budget on books. When you're finished here, spend the rest of the day ambling around town. You'll find a wonderful woman's clothing store, Shallowbags, several gift shops with quality merchandise, and eateries like Clara's Seafood and Grill, Poor Richard's sandwich shop, and Darwin's, a natural foods restaurant. Don't leave Manteo without visiting the famous Christmas Shop. Its rooms are filled with tinkling lights,

ornaments, and gifts of every description. Right next door is the Weeping Radish, where authentic German beer is brewed right on the premises. If there is a heaven after a hard day of shopping, it's sipping this nectar of the gods.

As in any resort climate, there are also zillions of souvenir and beachy type shops that line both the Beach and Bypass roads, along with other shopping centers that seem to spring overnight right out of the sand. Strolling through any of them will earn you the right to bag a t-shirt, bathing suit or a new pair of flip-flops. Most of these pocket centers have places where you can grab a burger, sandwich or platter of shrimp for the stamina to get on to the next shopping adventure.

For more information: There are so many other fascinating places to wander on the Outer Banks that to discover every one you will need *The Insiders' Guide to North Carolina's Outer Banks*. In it you can get a full rundown of places like Manteo, Hatteras Island, Ocracoke Island, Oregon Inlet and Corolla, along with so many other wonderful hidden treasures just waiting for you to uncover. The Chamber of Commerce will also send you its helpful Vacation Guide, just by calling 1-800-446-6262.

Photo: Richmond Newspapers

A visitor explores the marshland on the Eastern Shore.

Inside
The Eastern Shore

*T*his remote peninsula between the Chesapeake Bay and Atlantic Ocean is one of Virginia's best-kept secrets. "God's country" is what one person we know affectionately calls the Eastern Shore.

The 70-mile-long shore is the southernmost part of the Delmarva Peninsula that encompasses parts of Delaware, Maryland and Virginia. Physically it is linked to the commonwealth only by the Chesapeake Bay Bridge-Tunnel that runs from Virginia Beach to Cape Charles. But historically the Eastern Shore has been an important part of Virginia since the early 1600s. The shore, which has nearly 45,000 residents, is primarily an agricultural area renowned for its sweet potatoes, azaleas and tomatoes. Its abundant seafood harvest includes cherrystone clams and flounder.

There are numerous attractions on the shore, but the most prominent are the Chincoteague National Wildlife Refuge and the Assateague Island National Seashore. Both are on Assateague Island, a barrier island that harbors wild horses and deer and is a birdlover's paradise. There numerous other draws besides Assateague – outstanding hunting and fishing, historic homes and even a NASA museum. Many visitors come to chow down on fresh clams and flounder, unwind at country inns and just get away from it all. Summer is when beach-bound tourists flock to the Eastern Shore but don't rule out the other seasons. Even in winter the shore has its own special beauty, and mild weather lets you enjoy everything but swimming and sunbathing.

The best source for tourism information is Virginia's Eastern Shore Tourism Commission, P.O. Drawer R, Melfa, VA 23410 (804) 787-2460. The commission produces a comprehensive travel guide for the entire region. It shares quarters with the Eastern Shore of Virginia Chamber of Commerce. Their offices are near Melfa on Route 13. Stop by on weekdays from 8:30 AM-5 PM and arm yourself with a slew of tourism brochures. Another resource is the Chincoteague Chamber of Commerce, P.O. Box 258, Chincoteague, VA 23336 (804) 336-6161. The Chincoteague Chamber offers information on its island community and has an office on Maddox Boulevard near the entrance to Assateague Island. It is open on weekdays.

To guide you on your trip, buy a copy of *Off 13 – The Eastern*

Visit Virginia's Eastern Shore

THE CHESAPEAKE BAY BRIDGE-TUNNEL, a 17.6-mile link in U.S. Highway 13, is an "engineering marvel," travel convenience and tourist attraction that connects Virginia's Eastern Shore with Virginia Beach/Norfolk, Virginia. For more information write:
Chesapeake Bay Bridge-Tunnel
Dept. IS-93, P.O. Box 111
Cape Charles, VA 23310

Shore of Virginia Guidebook. Kirk Mariner, a minister and Eastern Shore native, wrote this excellent book in 1987 to provide insight into the approximately 40 communities that make up the shore. The book gives specific directions to steer you off Route 13, the shore's boring main drag. On backroads you'll discover quaint fishing villages and historic towns with white clapboard homes.

Because there is so much to see and do on the Eastern Shore, try to spend several days here. We've included some suggestions to send you on your way. Look for an expanded section on the Eastern Shore in the next edition of the *Insiders' Guide to Virginia Beach/Norfolk.*

Getting there: There's only one way to go from Virginia – up Route 13 and over the Chesapeake Bay Bridge-Tunnel. You get on it in Virginia Beach off of Northampton Boulevard. The tunnel toll is $10 each way, but don't sweat it and consider the trip part of your adventure.

Also known as the Lucius J. Kellam Jr. Bridge-Tunnel, this 17.6-mile structure divides the Chesapeake Bay from the body of water known as Hampton Roads. It was completed in 1964 after 3 1/2 years of rigorous construction. The American Society of Civil Engineers was awed enough to name the bay bridge-tunnel the outstanding engineering achievement of the year. It is the longest bridge-tunnel in existence and is one of the seven wonders of the modern world.

With traffic on the bridge-tunnel swelling by 7 percent a year, plans are in the works to start building parallel bridges by 1996 that would share the two tunnels already in use.

When traveling along the current three bridges and two tunnels, take a break and fish from a 625-foot fishing pier along the way. Or just admire the Chesapeake Bay from the overlook on the manmade island. The rest stop includes a restaurant and gift shop. For bridge-tunnel information call 331-2960 or 624-3511.

Once you're on the Eastern Shore, Route 13 leads you up the middle of the peninsula and into Maryland. Although this is the quickest route, it speeds you right by some of the most scenic parts of the Eastern Shore. And, you'll never see water unless you get off the highway. Except for stately manor houses, along Route 13 you'll mostly pass fireworks stands, small homes and a few McDonald's or gas stations. Pull off Route 13 toward towns such as Wachapreague, Cape Charles, Accomac, Onley and Parksley and you'll be treated to charming downtowns, fishing villages and restored houses several centuries old.

Don't hesitate to wander off the main road. The Eastern Shore is so narrow that you can't get too lost. And, if you do, your jaunt is likely to take you past creeks and notable architecture. You'll have no trouble finding a helpful resident to guide you back on course.

In Chincoteague, there's only one way onto the island – over a causeway that takes you right to Main Street. Turn left and then go

right on Maddox Boulevard and you'll head right to Assateague Island. Most of the island's businesses are on these two streets.

Attractions: Chincoteague and Assateague islands are the hands-down winners as major attractions with their 40 miles of beaches. Assateague, an uninhabited barrier island, is in both Virginia and Maryland but all of it is in the public domain. The U.S. Fish and Wildlife Service manages the Chincoteague National Wildlife Refuge. This was established in 1943 as a wintering area for migratory birds. The refuge is on the Virginia end of Assateague. Also on the Virginia side is Assateague Island National Seashore, managed by the National Park Service. The island's undeveloped seashore is the only place on the Eastern Shore to actually plunge into the Atlantic Ocean. Most of the other shoreline has marsh grasses and barrier islands dividing the mainland from the ocean. On the Maryland side of the island there is a state park that has the only camping spots on Assateague.

Admission onto Assateague from Virginia costs $3 a carload. Get there by driving over a short causeway from Chincoteague. Once on the island you can hike, swim, picnic and birdwatch. You can also ride your bike onto Assateague along a path that runs by the main road. There are numerous trails so be adventurous and tromp through marshes to look for waterfowl or hike the quarter mile to the island's red-and-white 19th-century lighthouse. Most of the island is accessible only by foot or bike. Drag along your binoculars and camera. On one recent visit we saw deer, herons, pelicans, ducks, swans, geese and the wild horses that are Assateague's most famous inhabitants.

Two visitor centers on the Virginia side of the island provide maps, information and occasional guided walks and talks. To contact them call 336-6122 or 336-6577. From spring through fall, Island Cruises, Inc. of Chincoteague shows off Assateague's wildlife with guided tours on either a boat or a tram. Reservations can be made at the Chincoteague Refuge Visitor Center, at the nearby Refuge Motor Inn or by calling 336-5593 or 336-5511. Assateague Adventures, another local company, provides lectures and tours on Chincoteague and Assateague islands. Topics include ecology, decoy carving and wildlife photography. Participants can opt for package programs that come with lodging by calling (800) 221-7490.

Chincoteague Island bills itself as Virginia's only resort island. It's filled with motels, gift and craft shops, bed and breakfasts and seafood restaurants. Main Street is a fun place to wander with its stores selling decoys, T-shirts and souvenirs. There are two museums here, the Oyster and Maritime Museum (336-6117) and the Refuge Waterfowl Museum (336-5800). Both are on Beach Road just before the Assateague entrance.

Just five miles outside Chincoteague on Route 175 is the NASA/Wallops Visitor Center (824-1344, 824-2298). This high-tech mu-

Bed & Breakfasts
of Virginia's Eastern Shore

Maryland

Virginia

New Church •

• Atlantic

Chincoteague

CHESAPEAKE BAY

13

• Accomac

• Locustville

Onancock •

Pungoteague •
Harborton

• Wachapreague

Davis Wharf •

Nassawadox •
Franktown •

• Willis Wharf

ATLANTIC OCEAN

Eastville •

• Cape Charles

• Townsend

Chesapeake Bay Bridge Tunnel
To Norfolk, Williamsburg, Virginia Beach

Ballard House Bed & Breakfast · 804/442-2206
Route 660, Willis Wharf, Va 23486
Old fashioned hospitality at Grandma Jo's. Pets and children are welcomed with well behaved parents. Nature trail, entrance ramp, hot tub, attic playroom, bottomless cookie jar and more.

Stillmeadow · 804/442-2431
P.O. Box 144, Franktown, Va 23354
Restored Victorian in historic town near nature conservancy. Hiking- biking- pool-library. Piano. Charter fishing, rental boats and scheduled hunting nearby. Full breakfast, afternoon tea or coffee. Private baths.

Holly Brook Plantation · 804/678-7853
P.O. Box 1136, Eastville, Va 23347-1136
Eighteenth century Eastern Shore architecture- big house, little house, colonnade & kitchen, with 18th century charm- old floors, old fireplaces, old garden, many birds.

Sea Gate Bed & Breakfast · 804/331-2206
9 Tazwell Ave., Cape Charles, Va 23310
In town setting, steps from beach, our restored home is your perfect get-away. Full breakfast, afternoon tea, porches, glorious sunsets, bikes, swimming, compose a restful escape.

Sunset Inn Bed & Breakfast · 804/331-2424
108 Bay Ave., Cape Charles, Va 23310
Romantic getaways, relaxation, hot tub, bird watching. Charter fishing available. Continental breakfast, plus suites and private baths.

In the Land
of Pleasant Living

seum highlights the U.S. space program, particularly the balloon and rocket experiments carried out across the road at the Wallops Flight Facility. Wallops is affiliated with NASA's Goddard Space Flight Center. Displays include space suits, a moon rock and rocket-launching films. Admission is free.

Just off Route 13 is Parksley, a nicely restored Victorian town with the Eastern Shore Railway Museum (665-RAIL). Opened in 1989 in a restored 1906 train depot, this small museum has 3,000 artifacts and showcases the old New York, Philadelphia and Norfolk line that ran through town. Outside are several train cars, including a 1927 observation car and a 1933 lounge car. The museum closes on Mondays. It is planning to add an adjacent antique car museum.

Affiliated with the Railway Museum is the Worcester Accomack Northampton Daycoach (W.A.N.D.), which hooks up the antique train cars several times a year and hauls passengers from Parksley to other Eastern Shore towns. For information call 800-852-0335 or 665-6271.

For a dose of history stop by Accomac and walk through the downtown area where you'll see a 1784 Debtor's Prison and more restored colonial architecture than anywhere except Williamsburg. There is a walking tour map available.

Onancock is another picturesque village. There are many restored homes here, including Kerr Place (787-8012). This Federal mansion was built in 1799 and is owned by the Eastern Shore of Virginia Historical Society, which opens it to the public every day but Monday. The house is under restoration and is being returned to its original colors, many of them surprisingly bright. It costs $3 to tour Kerr Place (which is pronounced Carr Place). Also in Onancock is Hopkins and Brother Store, one of the oldest general stores on the East Coast. Its merchandise includes dry goods as well as arts and crafts.

In Locustville you can see Locustville Academy, the shore's only surviving school of higher education from the 1800s. It's usually closed. To go inside call 787-7480.

In Willis Wharf during midfall and early spring visitors can visit an oyster house to learn the fine art of shucking. In Wachapreague they can watch fishing fleets come in or arrange their own fishing trip. History and genealogy buffs will enjoy Eastville, where the courthouse holds the oldest continuous court records in America. The records date from 1632. Cape Charles is a Victorian town created as a railroad terminus along the Chesapeake Bay. Its downtown features several antique shops. A walking tour map will guide you along attractive residential streets.

At the southern end of the Eastern Shore are Kiptopeke State Park and the Eastern Shore National Wildlife Refuge. Kiptopeke, which opened in 1992 at an old ferry stop, is Virginia's newest state park. Its 375 acres on the Chesapeake Bay include areas for swimming, picnicking and camping. There also is a boat ramp. For infor-

Restaurants

mation call 331-2267. The wildlife refuge is a haven for all types of birds. It has a museum featuring a waterfowl carving collection. (331-2760).

In the spring of 1993 longtime farmers Phil and Barbara Custis began welcoming city slickers to their sprawling farm near Willis Wharf. Visits include a hayride, lunch and the chance to watch the Custis' cultivating potatoes, planting azaleas or doing other seasonal work. Call 800-428-6361 or 442-4121 to arrange group tours.

While driving around the Eastern Shore, be sure to admire its unique historic architecture. There are more than 400 buildings that date from before 1865. The Eastern Shore has its own indigenous architecture – the big house, little house, colonnade kitchen style that was common by the end of the 1700s. These houses evolved when someone built a home, added on another part and then another until there was a long house with varying roof lines.

To tour some of the Eastern Shore's landmark homes, time your visit with Historic Garden Week. Usually on the fourth Saturday in April, owners of some of the shore's oldest homes fling open their doors for visitors. The Eastern Shore day is part of a week of historic home tours throughout Virginia sponsored by garden clubs. For details call 787-4118 or 442-9322.

Eastern Shore residents are big on festivals and go all out with native foods like fried sweet potatoes and steamed clams. You'll get a bonus if your visit coincides with

one of them. The biggest crowds come for the Eastern Shore Chamber of Commerce's May seafood festival in Chincoteague, which is by advanced tickets only, and the Volunteer Firemen's Carnival in Chincoteague in July. This is when Assateague horses are rounded up to swim over to Chincoteague for a benefit auction. Other fun events are a harvest festival in October at Kiptopeke Beach, a marlin tournament in Wachapreague in July and the spring and fall festivals in Parksley in June and October.

One part of the Eastern Shore you can't get to in your car is Tangier Island in the Chesapeake Bay. This island is inhabited mainly by watermen. To get there hop on the daily mail boat at Crisfield, Md. (891-2240 in Tangier) or another boat that goes from Reedville, Va. (333-4656). Or, if you have access, there is a landing strip for small planes.

Restaurants: As you can guess, seafood is the cuisine of choice on the Eastern Shore. You won't find it any fresher so take advantage of it and eat your fill of steamed clams, soft-shell crabs and flounder. Your restaurant options include:

AJ's on the Creek, 6586 Maddox Blvd., Chincoteague (336-5888) serves seafood, steaks, pasta and veal in one of the Shore's most elegant atmospheres.

Armando's, 10 North St., Onancock (787-8044) is the trendiest place on the Shore. Its Argentine owner specializes in homemade pasta, seafood and divine desserts. On weekends Armando's has entertainment.

Beachway Restaurant, 6455

Maddox Blvd., Chincoteague (336-5590) gives seafood a different twist by serving it in crepes or bouillabaisse. The Beachway has a reputation for luscious desserts.

Cape Center Restaurant, Route 13, Cape Charles (331-2505). This may look like a truck stop, but it offers a full menu of crab, flounder and is famous for its fiery chili.

Formy's Barbecue, Route 13, Painter (442-2426) serves excellent Carolina-style barbecue with all the fixings.

Someplace Else, Route 13, Cape Charles (331-8430) is known for its fresh seafood and prime rib dinners.

Steamer's Seafood Restaurant, 6251 Maddox Blvd., Chincoteague (336-5478) opened in 1992 and serves mainly steamed crabs, clams and shrimp.

The Trawler, Rt. 13, Exmore (442-2092) has excellent seafood and is renowned for its she-crab soup and sweet potato biscuits. Four times a year the Trawler transforms itself into a dinner theater.

Wolff's Sandwich Shoppe, Route 679, Atlantic (824-6466). Located in an old market, Wolff's old-timey charm is highlighted by Oscar the cockatiel. Sandwiches range from fresh-ground burgers to crab cakes and meaty subs. Wolff's also has clam strips and fish platters and serves both breakfast and lunch. It's a popular hangout for nearby NASA workers.

Wright's Seafood Restaurant, Atlantic (824-4012). Located just a few miles outside Chincoteague, Wright's sits right on the shore of Watts Bay. Its large seafood selection runs from flounder to clams. Wright's popular all-you-can-eat specials team up steamed crabs with fried chicken, ribs or other entrees. Although Wright's is in the country, there are big billboards to guide you.

Accommodations: Whether you prefer family motels with a pool, country B&Bs or exclusive inns, you'll find many options on the Eastern Shore. The greatest concentration is in Chincoteague but accommodations are scattered all along the shore. Some are in small towns, others in rural areas. In the past few years there has been a profusion of new B&Bs in restored historic homes. Many open year round; some only operate from April through October. If you're traveling with children, be sure to admit this fact right off the bat. Some B&Bs and inns welcome children only over the age of 10 or 12.

The following are some B&Bs and inns to consider:

Ballard House Bed & Breakfast, Route 660, Willis Wharf (442-2206). The owners of this Victorian home welcome families. Children can explore grandma's attic filled with toys and books, crab off a wharf, play on a tree swing and walk along a nature path. Guests also can watch movies on cable TV or a VCR and sing together around a piano. They enjoy a full breakfast, afternoon tea and midnight snack. The cookie jar also is filled and waiting. There are four guest rooms with shared bathrooms. Pets are accepted. The Ballard House is accessible to handicapped guests.

Bay View, 35350 Copes Dr.,

Davis Wharf (442-6963). If you're fascinated by country living and Eastern Shore architecture, consider this bed and breakfast. Its main house was built in the early 1800s and has been added on in the big house, little house, colonnade, kitchen style known only on the Eastern Shore. Bay View sits on the banks of the Occohannock Creek in view of the Chesapeake Bay. It is in the country outside Exmore and Belle Haven. The innkeepers have had the house in their family for several generations and first opened it to guests in 1992. There are two guest rooms. Amenities include a swimming pool, a dock for crabbing and woods for hiking as well as a full breakfast.

Burton House, 11 Brooklyn St., Wachapreague (787-4560). The owners of this bed and breakfast also run the adjacent Hart Harbor House. The restored homes are the only B&Bs in Wachapreague, a fishing village. Both look out on the marshes leading to the Atlantic Ocean. The inns serve full breakfasts and have bicycles available.

Channel Bass Inn, 100 Church St., Chincoteague (336-6148). Built in the 1880s, this home has been an inn since the 1920s. For more than 20 years it's been under the ownership of James S. Hanretta, who is both innkeeper and chef. Hanretta's continental cuisine and impeccable style have earned the inn a Mobil four-star rating and made it a favored getaway for the Washington, D.C. crowd. This is the most exclusive and expensive inn on the Eastern Shore. Its restaurant seats fewer than 20 and is open to the public for dinner if space is available. The inn has 10 guest rooms with private baths and operates on the European plan.

Drummond Town Inn, 23208 Lilliston Ave., Accomac (787-3679). Built in 1892, the inn is a Queen Anne Victorian that bears Accomac's original name. It is located in one of the Eastern Shore's most historic towns and has three guest rooms. Guests can relax over a full breakfast served on a screened-in porch. In addition to traditional parlors there is a separate TV room.

Evergreen Inn, Pungoteague (442-3375). This is an 18th-century Georgian manor house on the Chesapeake Bay. The inn has two guest rooms with private baths and fireplaces. There are 25 acres of grounds, including a beach and dock for crabbing or fishing. Guests can borrow a paddle boat, canoe or bike. A full breakfast is served.

The Garden and the Sea Inn, New Church (824-0672). Two Washington, D.C. expatriates opened this elegant country inn in 1989 after studying inns and restaurants in the south of France. The inn was built in 1802 as Bloxom's Tavern and is 15 minutes from Chincoteague. There are five guest rooms with private baths. Guests enjoy complimentary beverages, hearty continental breakfasts and afternoon tea. The elegant dining room, which is open to the public for dinner, features country French cuisine. The inn has earned a three-star Mobil rating. It usually closes in winter.

Holly Brook Plantation, Route 13, north of Eastville (678-5057). Built in the early 1700s, this vener-

Accommodations

Channel Bass Inn
And Restaurant

100 Church Street
Chincoteague Island, VA 23336

For Dinner, Lodging or Cooking Vacations
CALL 804 -336 - 6148

Four Star Cuisine And Comfortable Lodging

Discover the Difference

WATERSIDE MOTOR INN

Luxury Waterfront Accommodations
featuring the finest amenities

- Solar Health Spa with Jacuzzi
- Tennis Court
- Waterfront Pool
- Fishing and Crabbing Pier
- Marina
- Conference and Hospitality Room
- Refrigerators
- In-room Coffee
- Elevator

WATERSIDE MOTOR INN

3761 South Main Street
P.O. Box 347
Chincoteague, VA 23336

(804) 336-3434
FAX (804) 336-1878

able home is owned by the Association for the Preservation of Virginia Antiquities. It is built in the big house, little house, colonnade, kitchen style. It started accepting overnight guests in the fall of 1992.

The Little Traveller Inn by the Sea, Main Street, Chincoteague (336-7853). This home in the heart of Chincoteague has an interesting history. It was built before the Civil War by two men who later married sisters. To accommodate both families they split the house in half and moved the front part next door. The restoration that created the Little Traveller Inn reunited the two houses with an airy garden room. There are eight guest rooms, some with private baths. A full breakfast and afternoon tea are served.

The Main Street House, Main Street, Chincoteague (336-6030 or 800-491-2027). This Victorian B&B is right on Chincoteague Channel. Its screened-in porch offers spectacular sunset views, and there are several guest rooms. Nature lovers will enjoy the owner, a retired manager of the Chincoteague National Wildlife Refuge. Big country breakfasts are served on Sunday. It's Continental-plus otherwise.

Miss Molly's Inn, 113 N. Main St., Chincoteague (336-6686) The claim-to-fame for this Victorian bed and breakfast is that it is where Marguerite Henry stayed while writing part of *Misty of Chincoteague*, which was published in 1947. Miss Molly, the daughter of J.T. Roweley who built the house in 1886, lived here until the age of 84. The house is in the heart of Chincoteague and is open from Easter through Thanks-

giving. Guests can enjoy full breakfasts on the back porch and afternoon tea in the gazebo.

Pungoteague Junction Bed & Breakfast, 30230 Bobtown Rd., Pungoteague (442-3581). This 1869 house with a wrap-around porch has two guest rooms. The B&B serves a full breakfast and offers dinners upon request. Children are welcome and will find toys waiting for them.

Sea Gate, 9 Tazewell Ave., Cape Charles (331-2206). Built in 1861 this home is near the Chesapeake Bay beach in historic Cape Charles. The bed and breakfast offers porches for relaxing, bikes for touring the town, full breakfasts and afternoon tea.

The Spinning Wheel Bed & Breakfast, 31 North St., Onancock. (787-7311) This 1890s home opened in the spring of 1993 after extensive restoration. It is just off the main street of historic Onancock. Among its antique furnishings are several spinning wheels, which give the inn its name. All rooms have private baths. Guests enjoy wine and hors d'oeuvres when they arrive as well as full breakfasts.

Stillmeadow, 7423 Bayside Rd. (Rt. 618), Franktown (442-2431 or 800-772-8397) Built in 1895, the restored house has three guest rooms with private baths. The home is near Nature Conservancy property and Nassawadox. It has a well-stocked library for visitors as well as a piano. Bicycles also are available. Full breakfasts and afternoon tea are served.

Sunset Inn, 106 Bay Ave., Cape Charles (331-2424). This vintage

Accommodations

home overlooks the Chesapeake Bay and offers guests the chance to unwind on the porch, bicycle and swim. It has two guest rooms and two suites and serves a heavy continental breakfast.

The Watson House, 4240 Main St., Chincoteague (336-1564). This Victorian home in the heart of Chincoteague has six guest rooms with private baths and provides full breakfasts served in the dining room or on the veranda. The inn offers afternoon tea and equips guests with free bicycles and beach chairs.

Wynne Tref, Locustville (787-2356). This is a traditional 18th-century Eastern Shore home one mile from the Atlantic Ocean. Its name means "White House" in Welsh. There is one suite for rent. Guests are served a hearty continental breakfast.

Year of the Horse Inn, 600 S. Main St., Chincoteague (336-3221). This Colonial-style inn was built in the 1940s. It is right on Chincoteague Sound, and several guests rooms have balconies overlooking the water. The three guest room have private baths. One has a kitchenette, and there is a two-bedroom apartment available. Guests renting rooms are served a continental breakfast.

Other beds and breakfast to consider are:

Chesapeake House, Tangier Island (891-2331). Comfortable rooms, full breakfasts and a family-style seafood dinners are designed for island visitors. Prices are downright cheap. The dining room is also open to the public. Guests are

welcome April through October.

Colonial Manor Inn, 84 Market St., Onancock (787-3521). Built in 1882, the inn has welcomed guests since 1936, longer than any other Eastern Shore establishment. It has 14 guest rooms and is on the main street of historic Onancock.

Nottingham Ridge, Cape Charles (331-1010). With 100 acres bordering the Chesapeake Bay, this Colonial home has its own beach. Guest rooms have private baths. Breakfast is served on the porch overlooking the bay.

Picketts Harbor Bed & Breakfast, Cape Charles (331-2212). This B&B is near Cape Charles' Chesapeake Bay beach. It offers full country breakfasts, and some guest rooms have private baths.

Winder House, Atlantic (824-4090). This turn-of-the-century home is eight miles from Chincoteague. Its hosts serve a full country breakfast.

Woodbourne, Accomac (787-3114). This is a farmhouse just outside Accomac. The house was a Union hospital during the War Between the States. Guests are served a continental breakfast.

There are many nice motels to choose from on the Eastern Shore. The following are some to consider.

Driftwood Motor Lodge, Beach Road, Chincoteague (336-6557, 800-553-6117, ext. 11). Located at the causeway to Assateague Island, the Driftwood has 52 rooms with balconies and patios. Rooms come with free HBO and refrigerators. There is an outdoor swimming

Hotels & Attractions

pool. The motel is handicapped accessible and has an elevator to upper-level rooms.

Holiday Motel, Route 13, Cape Charles (331-1000, 800-331-4000). This is one of the nearest motels to the Chesapeake Bay Bridge-Tunnel. It has 103 rooms, a swimming pool and accepts pets. There also is a meeting room.

Island Belle Motor Lodge, Beach Road, Chincoteague (336-3600) is one of the island's newest motels and is located just before the causeway to Assateague Island. There are 50 rooms, including some that are handicapped-accessible. There is an outdoor pool and a meeting room. The lobby has an interesting display of more than 600 handbells.

Island Motor Inn, 4391 Main St., Chincoteague (336-3141 or 800-832-2925). All 48 rooms here have a view of Chincoteague Bay as well as small refrigerators. There is an outdoor swimming pool and a fitness center with a hot tub. Amenities include a meeting room, heliport, fishing and crabbing pier, deepwater docking and an elevator.

The Mariner Motel, 6273 Maddox Blvd., Chincoteague (336-6565 or 800-221-7490, ext. 4). Located between downtown Chincoteague and Assateague Island, the Mariner has 92 rooms and an outdoor pool. It has a meeting room, is handicapped accessible, has a laundry facility and refrigerators in some rooms. Outside are picnic tables and a pony.

Refuge Motor Inn, Beach Road, Chincoteague. (336-3141 or 800-544-8469, ext. 14) This 68-room

motel is near the causeway to Assateague Island. It has an indoor/outdoor swimming pool, fitness center and hot tub. Outside are several Chincoteague ponies. There are bicycles for rent, a playground, grills and picnic tables. Rooms have small refrigerators and some are handicapped accessible. There is a meeting room, laundry facilities and a gift shop.

Other motels you may want to check out are:

Anchor Inn, 534 S. Main St., Chincoteague (336-6313). There are 40 rooms, some of them efficiency apartments. The motel has a boat harbor, launching ramp and fish cleaning and storage areas. There is a pool. Rooms have refrigerators and some are handicapped accessible.

Anchor Motel, Route 13 in Nassawadox and Onley, (442-6363, 787-8000 or 800-283-4678). The Nassawadox location has 36 rooms and the Captain's Deck restaurant. The Onley location has 32 rooms and four efficiency apartments. The motels accept pets.

Comfort Inn, Route 13, Onley (787-7787). There are 80 rooms, some of which are handicapped accessible. In addition, you'll find a swimming pool and meeting room.

Cape Motel, Route 13, Cape Charles (331-2461) There are 16 rooms at this hotel six miles from the bridge-tunnel. It has free HBO, an outdoor swimming pool and a picnic area with grills.

Captain's Quarters, Route 13, Melfa (787-4545). There are 22 rooms, some with kitchenettes and handicapped accessibility here. Pets are accepted.

The Lighthouse Motel, 224 N. Main St., Chincoteague (336-5091). There are 25 rooms, some with refrigerators and microwaves. There are handicapped facilities and an outdoor pool as well as a screened picnic area.

The Owl Motel & Restaurant, Route 13, Parksley (665-5191). This 40-room motel has a restaurant known for its country cooking and homemade pies.

The Sea Hawk Motel, Maddox Boulevard, Chincoteague (336-6527). There are 28 rooms, some of them efficiency apartments, as well as two cottages. Amenities include an outdoor pool, playground and picnic area.

Sea Shell Motel, 3720 Willow St., Chincoteague (336-6589, ext. 3). This 40-room motel has several efficiencies and apartments. All rooms have refrigerators. There is an outdoor pool and a screened-kitchen and eating area. A play area has picnic tables and grills.

Waterside Motor Inn, 544 S. Main St., Chincoteague (336-3434). Guests at this 45-room motel can use a private pier for crabbing or fishing. Rooms have small refrigerators, coffee makers and HBO. There is an outdoor pool. Some rooms are handicapped accessible.

Wachapreague Motel & Marina, Wachapreague (787-2105). This 30-room motel sits along the marsh that leads to the Atlantic Ocean. It is a popular spot for fishermen, since the marina is right across the road. Rooms come with a small refrigerator and coffee maker. Some rooms have kitchenettes. Pets are welcome, and some rooms are handicapped accessible.

If you really want to spread out and stay awhile, rent a house. Chincoteague Island Vacation Cottages (336-3720 or 800-457-6643) handles all types of rental property that you can have for a weekend or all week. Many homes have great waterfront locations.

Shopping: Chincoteague's Main Street is lined with all kinds of crafts and gift shops. You'll find work by many local artisans, including decoy carvers whose talents are known nationwide. Most Eastern Shore towns have traditional downtowns with interesting antique and

On the Eastern Shore directions are based on two things - - whether you're going bayside or seaside. Bayside is west toward the Chesapeake Bay. Seaside is east toward the Atlantic Ocean. Bayside is characterized by numerous creeks that lead to the Chesapeake Bay. Seaside is outlined by marshes and barrier islands that protect the Eastern Shore from harsh ocean waves.

Insiders' Tips

gift shops. For basic necessities, there are two strip shopping centers along Route 13 at the Four Corners area near Onley.

To take home a taste of the Eastern Shore visit the Blue Crab Bay Co. at 108 Market St. in Onancock. This company creates a variety of specialty foods and runs a booming mail-order business. Its customers include Macy's, Marshall Field's and Disney World. Blue Crab Bay has a retail store on Onancock's main street that sells gift baskets, seasonings, canned clams and other Eastern Shore delicacies. (787-3602).

Two other shops also could be considered attractions. Near Melfa on Route 13 is Turner Sculpture (787-2818), where artists William and David Turner cast bronze animal sculptures. Their work is world-renowned and housed at such places as the Brookfield Zoo in Chicago and Philadelphia Zoo. Prices in the shop range from $25 to $35,000. Browsers are welcome.

In Oak Hall check out the Decoy Factory (824-5621), the world's largest maker of decoys. Visitors can watch woodworkers carving native waterfowl. They also can purchase their own decoys.

Recreation: The great outdoors beckons on the Eastern Shore. Hunters enjoy seasons for deer, dove, duck and 12 other animals. Fishermen can go bayside or seaside for their catch. There are many charter boats as well as small boat rentals. Wachapreague, the flounder capital of the world, has the greatest number of charter boats. However, Cape Charles, Chincoteague and other coastal towns also have boats available. The Eastern Shore of Virginia Chamber of Commerce publishes a helpful hunting and fishing guide.

Bird watching, hiking and bicycling are other popular outdoor pastimes. Camping is available at Kiptopeke State Park and several private campgrounds. Recently Occohannock on the Bay, a Methodist summer camp for children, started welcoming adult groups and individual campers to its grounds along the Occohannock River, (665-6295).

Inside
Real Estate

What you're certain to discover when you enter the wonderful world of Hampton Roads real estate is the voracity of neighborhood spirit, a spirit that can reach the level of territorial supremacy previously attributed solely to the primitive tribes of Mongolia. City dwellers, ocean-front habitants and rural pioneers all claim their hometime lifestyle to be the ultimate in residential superiority. Which puts new homebuyers in our market in a delightful quandry...what would you like in your backyard? The Atlantic Ocean or Chesapeake Bay? A manicured golf course? How about acres with a stable, or maybe the urban hustle-bustle of late-night restaurants and cultural centers?

After you've answered that question, the next decision is style. New construction or resale, townhome, ranch, high-rise condo or Southern Colonial...pick your favorite and you're sure to find it at

Photo: Richmond Newspapers

Just one of the many beautiful homes overlooking the water in Hampton Roads.

the right price. So right, in fact, that if you hail from the West Coast, New England or Washington, D.C., you'll be pleased to learn that the median price of homes in Hampton Roads averages close to half of what you're used to. So, not only will you find a lot more house for your homebuying dollar, you'll also save loads of time in your work commute. No matter where in which city you choose to live, thirty minutes in rush hour is about all the time it will take to get from your pajamas to your desk.

There are a few general rules of real estate in Hampton Roads. First, the closer to water, the more expensive the property. Because we've been blessed with not only the ocean and the bay, but zillions of rivers, tributaries, creeks, inlets and lakes, your chance to land a waterfront property is fairly good. The price of the property rises proportionately with the size of the body of water it overlooks. So a home on the Atlantic Ocean might carry a price tag of $500,000 to over a million dollars; a cedar-shake contemporary on the Chesapeake Bay, around $200,000; a resale rancher on a marshy creek averages $150,000.

The second rule is that a resale home in an older, established neighborhood generally sells at a lower square foot cost than a new construction home in a new, planned community. A recent comparison of homes sold in Virginia Beach reveals a median price of $85,000 for resale and $105,000 for new construction. What you get for that extra $20,000 is brand new everything, well worth the investment if you're not an adept do-it-yourselfer. Yet, plenty of people feel the trade-off in terms of knowing the "personality" of the neighborhood is well worth the cans of paint and elbow grease that might be required.

The final rule is that you really should have a definite focus on the style, community lifestyle and price of the home you're looking for. Faced with the alternatives of restored period homes, slick condo high-rises, beachy cottages, tract houses, city townhomes and country farmettes, the best advice is to first take a couple of days for a "just looking" tour through our different communities and neighborhoods. By contacting a relocation specialist within any of our major realty companies, you can be inundated with brochures, magazines, maps, city-by-city information and market details to confuse you even further. These relo specialists are used to your confusion, however, and are expert at helping point you in the direction of your new home-to-be, as well as being fountains of information for rentals, day care, job referrals for spouses, school systems, recreational opportunities and anything else that will help your family settle in to your new community. (Of course, this book will answer many of those questions, too!)

While nothing can really beat the advice and counsel of a well-informed human being, there are a slew of homebuying magazines that can serve as a wish list in narrowing your search. *Home Search, Harmon Homes, Homes & Land of Greater Tidewater, Real Estate Digest* and *For Sale By Owner* are the leaders in resale properties, and are all available free at local grocery and convenience chains. For new home construction, *New Home*, published by the Tidewater Builders Association, is the definitive volume for those interested in a brand new home in a new community. Our local newspaper, *The Virginian-Pilot and Ledger-Star*, publishes "Real Estate Weekly" each Saturday. This tabloid-sized edition is a wealth of information, covering both resale and new construction, along with weekly updates on area lenders' mortgage rates and helpful editorial content.

All in all, real estate is big business in Hampton Roads. Home to numerous regional headquarters and, of course, the world's largest military base, people are constantly packing the vans for moves in and out of our market. To serve them, nearly 5,000 Realtors are at work around the clock, shifting folks between neighborhoods and between cities, across town, across country and even across the world. Because of the competition, any one of these go-getters you choose will more than likely bend over backwards to ensure your satisfaction. And, whether your chosen Realtor hails from a small, independent firm, or a nationally affiliated company like ERA, Century 21, The Prudential or Re/Max, you can trust each one knows the business, and the market he or she represents. If you do need assistance in making that Realtor choice, contact the Tidewater Board of Realtors, serving Norfolk and Virginia Beach (340-9700), or the Portsmouth-Chesapeake Board of Realtors, serving Portsmouth, Chesapeake, Suffolk and Franklin (397-4613).

Real Estate Companies

To make your initial search a bit quicker, here's a sampling of the major real estate firms serving Hampton Roads:

WILLIAM E. WOOD & ASSOCIATES
16 Offices   *Relocation: 464-0022*
         TDD (Hearing Impaired): 363-2557
The region's largest real estate company, you'll find a William E. Wood & Associates Sales Office in practically every popular neighborhood in Hampton Roads. Boasting a sales force of over 400, it began as, and remains, a locally

owned and operated firm, with specialists in resale, new construction, relocation, commercial and bank-owned properties. They also have a strong property management division that handles a wide variety of rental properties.

GSH REAL ESTATE

12 Offices   *Relocation: 490-6530*
TDD (Hearing Impaired) 1-800-828-1120

An equally strong independent firm, GSH Real Estate has just celebrated 40 years of service to the community. Four hundred sales associates strong, GSH offers resale and new construction sales, relocation services and property management, including resort rental properties. Each of their offices has a book with color pictures of every VA/HUD property available, updated daily. The firm also offers escrow and title services. It is a member of The Dozen, a selective and prestigious group of independent Realtors across the country who meets annually to share new ideas and service innovations.

LONG & FOSTER

8 Offices   *Relocation: 420-0000*

This largest real estate company in Virginia is a relative newcomer to the Hampton Roads market, but its hometown agents are both well known and respected. Help for resale and new construction, along with relocation services, is available at any of the Long & Foster offices.

CENTURY 21

District Office   *499-0164*

Over 20 independently owned and operated Century 21 offices are at work in Hampton Roads, offering top-notch advice on resale, new construction, investment and property management services. You can even shop for a house in Greenbrier, Pembroke and Lynnhaven malls at the Century 21 At The Mall offices that are staffed during mall hours. Because of their national affiliation, any of this network of Century 21 offices can provide excellent relocation information for moving in or out of the area.

ROSE & KRUETH REALTY CORP.

6 Offices   *Relocation: 499-3330*

One of the strongest companies around for new construction, Rose & Krueth is known for its excellent marketing materials, and can provide one of the most comprehensive relocation packages around these parts, including a video. An efficiently run organization, it also offers resale and rentals.

WOMBLE REALTY

6 Offices   *Relocation: 486-8052*

For nearly 30 years, Womble Realty signs have been seen in Hampton Roads' finer neighborhoods. While not as large as some of the major hitters in the market, Womble agents are considerate and helpful to a fault, and excel in resale, new construction, commercial properties and property management.

THE PRUDENTIAL/DECKER REALTY

3 Offices   *Relocation: 486-4500*

Known for their representation of some of Virginia Beach's

most exclusive properties, The Prudential/Decker Realty holds its own with the "big boys," especially in higher-end sales. It is an especially friendly firm, with well-respected agents and an excellent reputation for resale and new construction sales as well as relocation services.

NANCY CHANDLER ASSOCIATES

1 Office   *Relocation: 623-2382*

If you're interested in Norfolk's West Side, this is the company to hook up with. While their listings cover the entire market (due to some long-term agents who have strong roots in the upper-end marketplace), the neighborhoods of Ghent, Larchmont and Lochaven are Chandler strongholds. An exclusive affiliate of Sotheby International, this close-knit group of real estate professionals offers excellent service for resale, new construction (especially downtown townhomes), property management and relocation services.

COLDWELL BANKER

Garman Real Estate	436-5500
Gifford Realty	583-1000
Harbor Group Real Estate	484-4400
Helfant Realty Inc.	463-1212
Jeanne West & Associates	481-6181

All five of the Caldwell Banker affiliates in Hampton Roads were strong independent companies before changing banners. Joan Gifford's company excels in medium priced housing and rental properties. Gifford, a past president of the Norfolk Division of the Hampton Roads Chamber of Commerce and a past director of the National Association of Realtors, is herself a real estate landmark in the community. Dorcas Helfant, who just finished her term as the first woman to serve as president of The National Association of Realtors, has long been respected for her commitment to the advancement of integrity in the industry, and Jeanne West is synonymous with the sales and marketing of finer homes in Virginia Beach. Bill Garman is a Chesapeake fixture for both resale and new construction, and is as well known for his involvement with the marketing of commercial properties in the area. Harbor Group claims Portsmouth as home, and is one of the most knowledgeable firms for home buyers in this Hampton Roads city.

RE/MAX

Advantage	436-4500
Associates	498-7000
Central	490-7300

The independently owned and operated offices of the Re/Max network are known for their aggressive marketing of properties, and the longevity of their experienced agents. Naturally, their relocation specialists are excellent, as are their resale and new construction agents.

Other selected independent real estate firms include:
Realty Consultants, 499-5911. New construction and resale in Virginia Beach.
Leading Edge Realty, 671-3343. New construction experts.
Realty Executives, 456-9500. New construction and resale in Virginia Beach.
Marshall-Ewald Realty, 463-2600. Personable firm specializing

in Virginia Beach resales.

Judy Boone Realty, 587-2800. A family owned and managed company headquartered in Norfolk's Ocean View.

Pyle Realty, 491-1600. A Landmark company specializing in Virginia Beach properties.

Cooke & Neff Realtors, 622-5075. Known for representation of higher-end properties, the firm is most widely recognized for their rental and insurance divisions.

Mary Lee Harris Realty, 498-7775. The leader for primo properties at Virginia Beach, if you're looking for top-of-the-line, Mary Lee is your connection.

Builders

If you want to direct the moving van to a never-been-lived-in new construction single family home, townhome or condominium, here's the basic scoop on the builders who have made their mark in Hampton Roads. Together, they have literally changed the face of our area, developing innovative communities and neighborhoods that incorporate some of the most novel features of homes being built all over the country, adapted to the tastes of Hampton Roads homebuyers. The reason for their success is their commitment not only to the highest standards in the building industry, but to buyer satisfaction as evidenced by their competent customer service divisions. A purchase from any of these fine companies is a sure bet.

While flipping through the pages of any local real estate publication, you'll see these names again and again:

THE FRANCISCUS COMPANY
620 Village Drive   *425-8391*

Frank Spadea is the captain of this huge ship, one that is known primarily for their innovative townhome communities. He's a hands-on kind of builder, involved in every detail, from master-planning to window detail, and it shows. Franciscus is recognized for demanding the most picky property management teams to watchdog their properties, meaning that all common grounds are meticulously maintained and repairs are promptly attended to. Current developments include Fairway Villas and Club 2 Condominiums, both in Chesapeake's Greenbrier Golf Community.

NAPOLITANO ENTERPRISES
3012 Scarlett Oak Court   *340-8847*

Vince Napolitano continues his family's tradition of building homes and condominium communities that dovetail with the needs of local buyers. A past president of the Tidewater Builders Association, Napolitano himself is one of the most visible and vocal advocates for excellence in building design, and has steered his company to be voted one of the top five builders in Virginia by *Builder Magazine*. Napolitano products are known for their contemporary architecture and volume. Check out Beacon Point in Riverwalk and single family homes in Greenwood at Greenbrier, both in Chesapeake.

R.G. MOORE
4480 Holland Office Park   *499-8501*

The granddaddy of builders and developers in Hampton Roads, R.G. Moore has touched practically every new community built in this area for the past forty years. His single family homes stick to the traditional on the outside, but incorporate open, contemporary floor plans inside. There's no wall in his office wide enough to accommodate all the awards he's won from area building organizations, and there's no sign that his quest to be the biggest and best has any chance of slowing. He's a feisty kind of guy who wants things done the way he knows will give his buyers the most bang for their buck. If you're looking for real value, check out an R.G. Moore home in Willow Ridge at Redmill Farms East or Ocean Lakes in Virginia Beach.

DONALD L. MOORE
4480 Holland Office Park   *499-8501*

While he shares an office with dad, R.G., Donald Moore is a card-carrying member of the new age of builder, creating intimate communities that each have a personality that physically and emotionally sets them apart from the norm. The first local developer to introduce the three-story townhome concept in his applauded Aeries By The Bay, he continues to introduce innovative interior space-planning features and unique exterior designs that wow from first sight. A young man with a golden touch, both for industry awards and customer satisfaction, you can find his exceptional single family homes in Wedgewood

Estates on the Greenbrier Golf Course in Chesapeake; condominium communities in the drop-dead gorgeous Royal Court Estate Condominiums, and in the frisky Grand Bay Condominiums, both in Virginia Beach.

HEARNDON CONSTRUCTION CORP.
2010 Old Greenbrier Road   *523-2569*

Chesapeake is home turf for Hearndon Construction, who has taken Hampton Roads by storm in recent years with their superior single family developments on some of their home city's prime real estate. Primarily known as developers, the organization was listed a few years back as one of the "Giant 400" builders in the nation in a list compiled by *Professional Builder Magazine*. To see their work, check out the Chesapeake communities of Wellington and Cedarwood.

Custom Builders

For one-on-one builders, Hampton Roads can boast some of the best custom crafters in the business. These guys – and, proudly, women too – take your ideas, a few bricks and Palladian windows and turn out one beautiful product on whatever homesite you've been lucky enough to snap up. While space does not permit listing all the custom builders in our market, these few are the most well known by peers and clients, and each is a vital force in the Tidewater Builders Association, our most powerful trade organization dedicated to the highest standards of professionalism and craftsmanship in the building industry.

LARRY HILL, L.R. HILL CUSTOM BUILDERS
481-6748
Two-time chairman for this area's ultimate home show, Homearama, Larry Hill does it all, from design to financing, using the best subs and materials around.

BOB JOHNSON, RESIDENTIAL CONCEPTS LTD.
363-9050
A third-generation builder, Bob Johnson has a handle on wide open spaces within a traditional exterior. He takes on only 25-30 super custom home projects a year, so reserve his time early.

CLIFF BERNARD, BERNARD BUILDERS LTD.
547-9549
This man knows style and how to build it. And, along with wife, Carolyn, they make a fantastic dream team in the design and meticulous construction of every home they touch.

JOE ROBINSON, JOE ROBINSON CUSTOM CONSTRUCTION CO.
547-2772
For more than 20 years, Joe Robinson has won enough design and quality construction awards to fill every wall he's built. His kitchen designs are to die for.

STAN EURE, STAN EURE CUSTOM BUILDER
424-3616
Here's a man who, along with

wife and partner Jan, dares to take a risk in presenting the newest, most innovative products available in the home building industry. Their "Environmental House" entry in this area's recent Homearama met with rave reviews, combining transitional design with the highest technology in energy efficiency and recycling innovations.

The list of highly qualified and respected custom builders goes on and on. If you're tossing the idea of a home built just-for-you around, a call to the Tidewater Builders Association will give you the background info on your many qualified builder choices in our marketplace. Call them at 420-2434.

Hampton Roads Neighborhoods

Remember that territorial thing? It would be total suicide to even attempt to pick and present the best places to live in Hampton Roads, given the diversity of lifestyle alternatives the region has to offer. All we can do is to give you a general lay-of-the-land, pointing out some of the most popular communities, new and established, and then you're on your own. The neighborhoods that we'll address specifically are those that have a distinctive flavor, either sophisticated urbanite or country chic, that sets them apart from the rest. Your final neighborhood decision will most probably be based on your family's requirements, like school systems, proximity to the workplace and budget. Let's take the Insiders' armchair tour from one end of the region to the other.

Norfolk

THE WEST SIDE

While it's no longer appropriate to call this the "Land of the Yuppies," deep down we know it's true. Running almost the full length of the city on the side where the sun sets, Norfolk's West Side is home to older, established neighborhoods with true old-fashioned neighbor-helping-neighbor spirit.

FREEMASON DISTRICT/GHENT/ GHENT SQUARE

This is where the "Downtowners" migrate and mingle. The Freemason district is as close to city living as you'll find in the area, what with cobblestone streets and the Hampton Roads version of row houses. New affluence meets old money in the condominiums enveloping the area, like Harborplace, the Tazewell complex, the Pier and Archer's Walk. There's not much turnover in this deep-rooted neighborhood, so you'll need a lot of luck to snag one of these properties.

Ghent and West Ghent are two other older, well-established neighborhoods, the former sprinkled liberally with spacious apartment buildings and rehabbed condominiums. West Ghent is where you'll find many of the grand old houses...three-story jobs that can accommodate young, professional families with kids and pets to spare.

For new construction with that old-timey feel, Ghent Square is the place, a planned urban development with a mix of traditionally styled townhomes and single family residences. The 65-acre urban pocket features large expanses of brilliant green common areas, so while homes may be packed tight, the feeling of spaciousness pervades. It is definitely an address you'll be proud to claim.

LARCHMONT/EDGEWATER

Within walking distance to the ever-sprawling Old Dominion University, these two back-to-back neighborhoods are where you'll find a congenial mix of professors, young business folk, students and, along the bordering Elizabeth River, corporate presidents. The older homes are shaded by huge, mature trees, and the quiet streets are usually packed with kids on rollerblades, with mom and dad biking alongside. With homes priced from the low $100s, it's a great place to relocate if you want to find yourself surrounded by friendly, well-educated residents who take pride in maintaining the integrity of one of Norfolk's most coveted neighborhoods.

LOCHAVEN/MEADOWBROOK/ NORTH SHORE POINT

We'll be moving on up when we tour through these premiere neighborhoods, home to gracious Colonials, Georgians and Cape Cods, many of which hug the banks of the Elizabeth and Lafayette Rivers.

Many of these superb residences are known by the families who built them, and you'll pay the average price of $250,000 to even consider these addresses. What you get in return, however, is an exceptionally stable neighborhood, with a large, manicured lot and, if you're lucky, a backyard with a river view.

TALBOT PARK/BELVEDERE

These neighborhoods have Granby Street as their dividing line, with the more moderately priced Belvedere on the east. More and more younger people are finding jewels in the rough in many of these older homes, and choosing these neighborhoods over the Ghent sisters for convenience and value. Many of the Talbot Park residents claim the Elizabeth River as a neighbor; Belvedere's border ends on the ever-calm Lafayette River.

LAKEWOOD/LAFAYETTE SHORES

Across the river you can get a glimpse of the docks that belong to the residents of Lakewood, a relatively small pocket of lovely and oh-

Ghent, An Insiders' History

While there certainly is a lot that's new in Ghent, there's a whole lot more that's old. This popular community in Norfolk's west side can boast almost more historical roots than anyplace else in the territory.

While there's heated debate as to where the name Ghent actually originated, most agree it was to commemorate the Treaty of Ghent that formally ended the War of 1812 when it was signed in Belgium. Version one traces the name to Jasper Morgan, a plantation owner that gave his home the name in 1821. Version two gives all the credit to Commodore Drummond, who carried a copy of the Treaty of Ghent on his ship to Norfolk and so named his plantation in 1830.

Whomever started it all, little did they know what was to follow. In 1890, the publication *Norfolk's Industrial Advantages* reported that Ghent property was sold at $1,400 an acre, and no homes could be built that cost less than $7,500... a mega-home in that time. John Graham accepted the challenge and erected Ghent's first home at 502 Pembroke Avenue, and by 1892 was paying welcome calls to neighbors Horace Hardy (442 Mowbray Arch), Richard Tunstall (530 Pembroke), Fergus Reid (502 Pembroke) and William H. White (434 Pembroke Avenue).

The majority of the streets in Ghent were named in honor of principals in the Ghent-Norfolk Company, a subcorporation of three syndicates formed abroad after the Civil War to develop Virginia's rich resources. Today you can stroll down Bossevain Avenue (after a Dutch banker), Stockley Gardens (after the same Dutch banker's birthplace

so-exclusive Colonial and Tudor homes set among quiet, heavily treed streets. Across Willow Wood Drive is a brand new executive community of exceptional custom homes called Lafayette Shores. This gated 66-acre community boasts the last remaining waterfront homesites available in the city, and many corporate leaders have snapped up the offer and are now in the process of building their dream homes.

OCEAN VIEW

Until a few years ago, the only thing Ocean View could offer was the beauty of the Chesapeake Bay and rickety old beach cottages. Today, it's starting to be another story, as sparkling new condominium and single family communities are taking advantage of the valuable, if previously neglected, real estate. Of particular note is Pinewell By The Bay, a new neighborhood of single family homes that rests on the bayfront. While prices average in the $250s, you'll get a lot more home for the dollar than any you could find on the oceanfront in

in Northampton County) and Onley Road (for Richard Onley, who later became secretary of state for President Cleveland).

In the heart of Ghent Square, sits the Terminal on the Square that houses the Fred Huette Foundation, a horticultural society. The charming building first knew life more than a century ago as the Norfolk-Portsmouth ferry terminal concession building. While the terminal building itself was torn down in 1964, the concession building was taken apart, piece by piece, each one carefully numbered and matched to a diagram. In 1974, the Housing Authority took all the pieces out of the warehouse and set upon solving the most difficult jig-saw puzzle ever created...somewhere along the line, somebody lost the carefully diagrammed plans for the building's reconstruction. But here it is today, restored to better than its former glory, and serving as a central landmark in this vibrant community.

Ghent also claims a few of our country's firsts in the wonderful world of food. Bosman & Lohman, liquidated in 1924, was the largest peanut company in the world in its earliest days, and is credited with introducing commercially sold peanut butter to the United States. James G. Gill added a two-bag coffee roaster to his wholesale grocery store in 1902 and begat the Norfolk-based First Colony Coffee and Tea Company, and Abe Doumar is said to have invented the very first ice cream cone, introduced at the St. Louis Fair in 1904. Abe must have loved ice cream, because he created a machine to make the cones, and kept it at Doumar's, the restaurant that bears his name, where it is still operational today.

Virginia Beach. For a less expensive investment with a built-in marina, Bay Point offers townhomes and condominiums starting in the $60s. At the end of Pretty Lake Avenue, Bay Point takes advantage of its magnificent views of both the Chesapeake Bay and Little Creek Inlet.

Portsmouth

OLDE TOWNE

With the largest number of authentic homes dating from the Colonial period between Charleston, South Carolina and Alexandria, Virginia, Olde Towne residents share the spirit of renovation along with a sense of history. While prices average in the low $200s, these homes are less expensive than their Norfolk counterparts, even though they are just a quick tunnel ride under the Elizabeth River apart. The 62-acre residential area supports its heritage with a passion, and a stroll down the clean, quiet rebricked streets illuminated by antique electrified gas lamps proves that no neighborhood can ever be too old to restore to its past glory.

STERLING POINT/GREEN ACRES

From the Elizabeth River, you can see the docks of the residents of Sterling Point, and the river's tributaries will take you to many Green Acres backyards. Both neighborhoods were developed in the 1950s and have that rancher type feeling, but lots are large and well-treed and streets are remarkably litter-free. Green Acres borders on the Elizabeth Manor Country Club, and hubs around Green Lake in its center. Homes here hover around the $150,000 mark, with waterfront prices at $300,000.

CHURCHLAND

Where Portsmouth's up-and-comers call home, Churchland is almost like a small city unto itself, served by a flotilla of shopping strips, groceries and movie theaters. One of its neighborhoods, River Shore, is a neat-as-a-pin brick rancher community, blessed with heavily wooded lots. If you can snag a waterfront property here, you'll have a breathtaking view all the way to Newport News.

Along Carney Creek, a small Western Branch of the Elizabeth River, is Hatton Point, with fairly new homes that each have their distinctive personality. While most of the interior homes are ranches, some of those that border the water are truly magnificent. Home resale prices in both neighborhoods begin around $100,000.

For luxury condominium living, Churchland has Cypress Cove that offers residents their own boat slip on the Elizabeth River and Carney Creek. Credited with being the first condominium development in Portsmouth, prices average $140,000.

Chesapeake

Chesapeake has a split personality. One face is that of old-line, deeply entrenched Chesapeake natives like those of the Great Bridge area. Flip the coin and you'll see the youthful expression of newly developed neighborhoods like River Walk and Greenbrier. Together they make for a city bulging at the waist from too many good meals...of incoming industry, migrating families and the retailers who serve them.

Because homes in this awakening city are simply more affordable than their comparable counterparts in Virginia Beach, the call of the once-rural Chesapeake has reached deafening proportions, especially to builders who firmly believed that the outskirts of Virginia Beach was the true mecca. But, throw in an acclaimed golf course, over-sized homesites and developers who know how to squeeze a great home out of a tiny dollar, and you've got one of the hottest real estate markets in the region.

GREENBRIER

Twenty years ago, a group of investors had the vision to turn what was once fertile farmland into one of the fastest-growing commercial and residential areas on the East Coast. Today, it's a community of 3,500 homes and growing, along with a championship golf course, gorgeous shopping mall, numerous spanking-new strip centers and hundreds of offices and industrial plants.

Just 15 minutes from Norfolk via Interstate, the Greenbrier corridor, especially along the golf course, offers single family homes where young families can spread out and grow. One of the newest and last communities to be built here is Emerald Greens, with homes constructed by some of the area's premiere builders. While prices are somewhat hefty, plan on $250,000 average, what you'll move into is scads of square footage with a backyard view of a manicured fairway or green. Smaller pockets of prime golf course real estate are also in the final development stages, like Wedgewood Estates, with custom built homes starting in the $170s.

RIVER WALK

Another Chesapeake phenomenon, River Walk on the Elizabeth spans 300 acres between Great Bridge Boulevard and the Intracoastal Waterway. While it seems light years away, it's only 10 minutes from the business district in Downtown Norfolk. Here you'll find private enclaves of custom homes, like Mystic Isle, Quiet Cove, Laurel Haven and Watch Island. Those seeking a more streamlined way of life will delight at the varied condominium alternatives, from Inlet Quay to Beacon Point to Creek Side, all set in heavily wooded sites. Condos start at around $120,000 with remaining custom home sites from $40,000 before the house. You can stop at River Walk's Information Center to pick up some exquisite marketing propaganda, and browse through their library of available home plans.

GREAT BRIDGE

The school system is superb, the people downright neighborly. This is Great Bridge, the granddaddy of Chesapeake neighborhoods. Sprinkled with solid ranchers and farmhouse Colonials, the many individual neighborhoods that make up this corridor are blessed with large, heavily treed lots and super out-in-the-country smells. But, if you're thinking "rural," you're wrong. Here's where you'll find Chesapeake General Hospital, financial branches and food places of every description, and shopping strips galore. If you're thinking on settling in a neighborhood that has a handle on mixing the old with the new-fangled, Great Bridge is the place.

"OUT THERE"

Those of us who grew up in the big city still find it hard to believe that people would actually want to live "out there" in Chesapeake. But we're not who some very savvy builders and developers were targeting. Past Great Bridge, in one direction you'll drive into the new communities of Forest Lakes, Cheshire Forest and Cedarwood, all master-planned neighborhoods with varying levels of single family custom homes. Do a U-turn and drive in another direction to Etheridge Manor and Dominion Boulevards and run into Country Mill, Mill Run and River Pines, all offering exceptional, if similar in architecture, single-family homes at remarkably low prices, from the low $100s. If you want to start off big while still preserving your pocketbook, here's where to look.

Virginia Beach

THE GOLD COAST

There's but so much Atlantic Ocean, and all of its beachfront that isn't reserved for hotels is owned by the tanned and hearty of Virginia Beach's Gold Coast, that diamond strip of golden real estate that stretches from streets numbered in the 40s north about 50 blocks to the turn at the Chesapeake Bay. Mostly, we're talking wind-weathered cottages, but there are a few sparkling contemporaries strewn about, as well as a token mansion or two. Buying one of these beach-hugging beauties is almost out of the question as turnover is almost nil, but if you're in a renting kind of mood, many go for reasonable tariffs during the winter season. At the other end of the oceanfront is Croatan, just south of Rudee Inlet, which has become more and more popular for year round residents, many of whom have erected monolithic contemporaries to worship the sun. Tres expensive (got an extra mil?), but worth the drive through.

BAY COLONY/PRINCESS ANNE HILLS

There's one "I-could-live-there!" home after another in these premiere neighborhoods that are just steps away from the Gold Coast. Many of these sprawling mini-estates border on Crystal Lake and Linkhorn Bay, and their price tags float upwards accordingly. Home to many upper middle-management and corporate executives, entry into the life of the Beach's rich and famousdom will set you back no less than $250,000 for a pleasant starter home, a hair's breath past $2 million if you're on a roll. This is a very active real estate market, however, with many old-timers fleeing to the carefree condominium lifestyle, so if this is the sort of lifestyle you crave (the garden club is a must, daahling), go for it.

THE GREAT NECK CORRIDOR

Just minutes from the ocean, close to business centers and boasting a strong school system, the Great Neck corridor lays sole claim to the most affluent per capita demographics in the city. While you can start in a condo you can move into for the $90s, count on higher end single family homes to set you back up to a mil. Along Great Neck Road, you can turn into such coveted neighborhoods as Broad Bay Point Greens (that owns one of the premiere golf courses around) to Wolfsnare Plantation to Alanton, and loads of small pockets of affluence in between. Waterfront naturally commands the highest price tag, and many of the secluded mini-mansions have been built to take advantage of the inlets of Lynnhaven and Linkhorn Bays. For single families in this prestigious area, have at least $170,000 in your back pocket.

THE LITTLE NECK CORRIDOR

Let the chips keep falling. We're talking the highly desirable neighborhoods of Kings Grant, Middle Plantation and Little Neck Cove – all upper middle class magnets for those who feel comfy in a sprawling home with lots of lawn and, perhaps, a waterfront vista of the Lynnhaven Bay or Western Branch of the Lynnhaven River. While many Realtors urge that this is an excellent opportunity to snap up a waterfront property, better have your financial ducks in a row for the $250,000 plus bucks these beauties will demand.

KEMPSVILLE

Now we're talking suburban spread. The first real Virginia Beach suburb, the Kempsville area keeps getting larger and more popular, what with neighborhood additions like Fairfield, Dunbarton and Indian Lakes, with neighbor community Salem Woods a short hop down the road. A quick zip to the interstate, you're still a ways from the oceanfront, but you are in the belly of retail heaven with strip centers galore lined up with specialty stores to serve your every indulgence. All in all, the Kempsville area is a solid market. Even Sweet Pea Whitaker, Mr. Boxing, owns a home in Bellamy Manor. To be a next door neighbor, $250,000 should do the KO.

THE PEMBROKE CORRIDOR

Leave it to Virginia Beach to toss the old with the new and come up with a dish that suits everyone's taste. For older, established and very desirable addresses, you can check out Thoroughgood, the Haygood area and Lake Smith. Whip down to mucho affordable Aragona Village and then swing the pendulum to the newest star in Virginia Beach's crown, Church Point. All you need to create a new neighborhood today is 260 acres of prime real estate, then invite the region's premiere builders and crayon out huge lots into pockets called The Mews ($200,00 and up), The Commons ($300,00 and up) and The Quays (up to $1 million). This really is one handsome private residential development, and worthy of a serious look by affluent buyers.

CHESAPEAKE BEACH

To the north of Church Point, and kissing the Chesapeake Bay, is the home to many beachcombers who prefer yards of sand, not grass. A weird architectural mix of high-tech condos, townhomes, old beach cottages and stark cedar contemporaries, both home styles and family backgrounds melt into one under the hot Hampton Roads sun. What residents share, regardless of their home's selling price ($75,000 to $200,00+), is their explicit love for the casual beach lifestyle. If you're a sand-in-your-shoes kind of person, this is one great place to hang your flag.

GREEN RUN/HOLLAND ROAD CORRIDOR

Green Run, the first PUD (Planned Urban Development) in the area, has come by hard and tough times. Single family homes, townhomes and condos share the cul-de-sacs and curved streets that were the master plan of GSH Real Estate's Oscar Ferebee in the 1960s. Today, new construction developments like Parkside Green, Woods of Piney Grove, Holland Pines, Princess Anne Crossings and Landstown Meadows call new homebuyers farther down Holland Road, and entice them more by offering solidly built, value-priced homes starting in the high $90s. While this particular area may seem way off the track for many urbanites, the area creeps right up to the Virginia Beach City Municipal Complex and is just a stone's throw from the connecting interstate system.

CYPRESS POINT/GLENWOOD

The link that connects these neighborhoods is golf – beautifully manicured championship golf courses, all encroached by single family homes and condos that beckon with their country-club, resort feeling lifestyle. Both target families on the way up (and empty-nesters on the reverse downward spiral) and offer pockets of glamour to varying degrees. Many different builders have opted on prime homesites in these two popular neighborhoods, so plan on a full day to inspect the fully decorated model homes in each.

Inside
Retirement

*T*he retirement market is a growing one for Norfolk, Virginia Beach and surrounding cities. Some older residents have lived most of their lives here. But many have returned in later years – lured by the Atlantic Ocean, Chesapeake Bay, moderate climate and reasonable taxes. Most older newcomers have relatives in the area or passed through here during their military careers and decided to make it home.

Living in the area are more than 84,000 people age 65 and older. Lifestyle options for them are varied – from totally independent living to gracious retirement communities and assisted living and nursing home care. There also are many services and activities geared toward keeping older residents active and independent.

SEVAMP Senior Services

If you're a newcomer who's over age 60, don't hesitate to learn

Photo: First Colonial Inn

A resident at First Colonial Inn in Virginia Beach enjoys the peace and quiet of her apartment.

about the Southeastern Virginia Areawide Model Program Inc., or SEVAMP Senior Services as it's commonly known. SEVAMP was incorporated in 1968 as a nonprofit organization. In 1972 it became one of 10 national programs for the aging selected for a federal grant. A year later SEVAMP became the region's Area Agency on Aging.

SEVAMP's goal is to help older residents live independently so they can be involved in the community and enjoy their lives. SEVAMP will issue a photo identification card that will get you discounts at numerous businesses. If you need transportation, SEVAMP vans can take you to doctor's appointments, geriatric day care and SEVAMP recreational programs. Rides must be arranged in advanced.

SEVAMP, a United Way agency, also operates several senior centers that provide hot lunches and all kinds of activities. It offers job counseling, training and placement for people over 55. Through its Retired Senior Volunteer Program, it matches residents with more than 225 nonprofit organizations needing help. SEVAMP has a licensed geriatric day care center as well as health screening, legal services and home care services. For information call 461-9481.

Other Services

Senior centers can provide a vital outlet for older residents. One of the largest is the Norfolk Senior Center at 924 W. 21st St., which is a SEVAMP affiliate. One of 11 senior centers in Norfolk, it opened 25 years ago in the Ghent area and recently expanded. The center has classes ranging from crafts to ballroom dancing. It brings in a variety of speakers, runs a gift and thrift store, and operates two adult day care centers for those who cannot be home alone. A van takes center participants on shopping trips, to festivals and on other outings. The center also has a Senior Wellness Center that screens for medical problems. For information call 625-5857

Virginia Beach has five senior centers providing a variety of services and activities. Call 471-5884. It also has the M.E. Cox Center for Elder Day Care. Call 340-4388. Adult day care also is available from the Beth Sholom Home of Eastern Virginia (420-2512).

Chesapeake has two senior centers. For information call 543-9211, extension 265. Suffolk has two senior centers. Call 925-6388.

Portsmouth provides three senior centers. The largest at 305 High St. is run by the city's Department of Parks and Recreation. The department sponsors a variety of senior activities, including Chesapeake Bay cruises, parties and day trips. To receive a quarterly schedule call the senior center at 398-3777.

One popular Norfolk program is The Ghent Venture, which has educational sessions for anyone age 50 and over. It started in 1982 and is sponsored by seven churches and one synagogue in the Ghent area of Norfolk. Sessions run for six weeks at First Presbyterian Church and regularly draw big crowds. Participants come between 10 AM to 2:30 PM on Thursdays to take a variety of free classes – from lap quilting and mah jongg to foreign languages and money management. The program includes interesting book reviews and lectures. A hot lunch is available for $3, or participants can brown bag it. To receive a course schedule call 640-8566.

One other option for courses are city-sponsored recreational courses (see Schools section) as well as area colleges. State-supported institutions such as Old Dominion University, Norfolk State University and Tidewater Community College let state residents over the age of 60 take one course a semester for free. To do this you must have been a Virginia resident for at least a year and pay taxes in the state. You can sign up on the day the class starts and attend the session if it isn't full. For information contact the registrars' offices at the colleges.

Virginia Wesleyan College, ODU and Atlantic University are among the local participants in Elderhostel. This popular program lets people 60 and older attend colleges around the country for a week. They live on campus and enjoy classes that range from history to music appreciation. Prices are so reasonable that some people go Elderhostel-hopping for a few weeks and make that their vacation. For a catalog write Elderhostel at 7575 Federal St., Boston, MA 02110 or call 617-426-8056 or 617-426-7788.

For local social events, there is the Memory Lane Club 50+ sponsored by Seniors Gazette. For $5 members are eligible to sign up for big band dances, day trips, contests and discounts. Call 431-2326 for information.

If you need legal assistance, one possibility is the Tidewater Legal Aid, which helps older low-income residents through its Senior Law Center. Call 627-3232.

Community Service

If you have a few hours to spare, there are many nonprofit groups that will welcome you with open arms. You may find your niche counseling business owners through the Service Corps of Retired Executives (SCORE) by calling 441-3733. Or you might lean more toward volunteering in a hospital, kindergarten, museum or literacy program. The Retired Senior Volunteer Program keeps tabs on these opportunities. Call 393-9333 in Portsmouth, 539-6385 in Suffolk, 622-6666 in Norfolk, 436-8178 in Chesapeake and 473-5238 in Virginia Beach.

Other clearinghouses for volunteers include the Volunteer Action Center at 624-2400 and the volunteer program of the City of Norfolk at 441-2584. Feel free to directly contact any organization that interests you. Chances are good the staff can find a job to suit your time and talents.

Local chapters of the American Association of Retired Persons also keep up with volunteer possibilities as well as providing other services to anyone over age 50. There are chapters in Chesapeake, Norfolk, Portsmouth, Suffolk and Virginia Beach. To find out about local AARP chapters call 481-7438. For information on AARP's Senior Community Services Employment Program call 625-7001. This service helps find part-time jobs for people over age 55 who need additional income.

Wellness Programs

Some area hospitals have programs geared toward older adults. Chesapeake General Hospital has the Seniors Health Resource Center, which has fitness, recreational and educational programs. Call 482-6132. The Chesapeake hospital also has an Older Adult Mental Health Program that includes in-patient services. Call 482-6143.

DePaul Medical Center in Norfolk has the Gerontology Institute, which does assessments and peer counseling and has a resource center. DePaul's Classic Care Program offers health screenings, support groups and help in filing insurance claims for members over age 55. One popular program is Friday night dinner at the hospital. Meals cost $3 and there usually is a piano player or other entertainment. Call 889-5976.

In Portsmouth Maryview Medical Center has a Senior Advantage Program that includes wellness workshops, help with insurance claims and social events. Call 398-2273. Its affiliated Maryview Psychiatric Hospital has a Senior Day Program that provides activities and respite care for older adults. Call 398-2537.

Obici Memorial Hospital in Suffolk has a Lifeline Unit that provides devices to use to summon help in case of emergency. Call 934-4847.

Sentara Leigh Hospital operates the Sentara Select Plus program for the Sentara Health System hospitals in the region. The program includes free classes, health screenings, educational programs and social activities. Call 1-800-736-8272.

If you're into fitness, check with area malls. Many have mall walking groups who meet regularly to stride through the climate-controlled environments. Some malls also have occasional breakfasts and programs for their walkers.

Lifestyles

Housing options range from total independence to varying degrees of assistance. Buying a single-family home, a condominium or townhouse certainly is an option. Throughout the region you'll find a variety of prices and neighborhoods that ranges from historic to brand new. If you like a great view – and don't mind paying for the privilege – scout out some of the possibilities along the Chesapeake Bay, the Atlantic Ocean and the Elizabeth River.

Apartments are also worth considering. You'll find some that particularly appeal to older residents, including the Hague Towers and Pembroke Towers in Norfolk and many apartment buildings in the Wards Corner area of the city.

There also are numerous subsidized apartments that rent for reasonable fees. However, many of these require lengthy waits to get in and have strict guidelines on income levels. Among the apartments designed for people on limited incomes are John Knox Towers and Stonebridge Manor in Norfolk and Chesapeake Crossing in Chesapeake.

If you prefer a retirement community that lets you live independently but offers numerous amenities, there are three to choose from in South Hampton Roads. And, if you don't mind traveling a little farther there are others in Williamsburg and Newport News.

Before settling on a retirement community, take time to explore the facility and get to know residents and staff. Eat a meal or two to see if you like the food. Check out the recreational activities and learn what your options are should your health suddenly decline. If you are considering a continuing-care community that charges a large entrance fee, make sure you know what is covered and what percentage is refundable if you decide to leave.

WESTMINSTER-CANTERBURY IN VIRGINIA BEACH

3100 Shore Dr., Virginia Beach   496-1100

Westminster-Canterbury is the hands-down winner for the best location of any area retirement community. It is built right on a beach overlooking the Chesapeake Bay and has 16 acres of grounds. This 14-story complex has 335 apartments as well as a health care center. Westminster-Canterbury opened in 1981 as a joint venture of the Presbytery of Eastern Virginia and the Episcopal Diocese of Southern Virginia.

It is open to any person age 65 or older who can live independently. Apartments range in size from studios to two-bedroom apartments. Most have full-sized kitchens. The smallest studio apartments sometimes are available immediately. Expect to wait from one to five years for larger apartments – the bigger the apartment the longer the wait.

Amenities include one prepaid meal a day, weekly maid service, bed and bath linens, 24-hour security, indoor swimming pool, whirlpool, steam room, gardening areas and a full roster of activities.

To tap into the wealth of community services available to help you, call the Information Center of Hampton Roads. This nonprofit group provides information on everything from adult day care to child care. Call its hotline at 625-4543. The number for deaf residents is 626-0675.

Insiders' Tips

As residents need more help, they can move to assisted living and a nursing home that are part of the facility.

Admission to Westminster-Canterbury requires paying an entrance fee that ranges from $72,831 to $190,485 for one person. For two people entrance fees start at $109,781 and go to $210,985. Paying this fee guarantees lifetime occupancy in an apartment, the Assisted Living Center or Health Care Center. In addition, a single resident pays monthly fees ranging from $893 to $1,654. The amount of both the entrance fee and monthly fees depends on the size of the apartment. There is a limited amount of financial assistance available.

First Colonial Inn
845 First Colonial Rd., Virginia Beach 428-2884

If you're interested in an independent retirement community but don't want to pay an up-front fee, First Colonial Inn is a definite option. It is strictly a rental community for retired people. The 185 apartments in this three-story building in the Hilltop area range in size from studios to two-bedroom models. There sometimes is a short wait to move in, especially if you want a larger unit.

Besides independent living, First Colonial Inn also has 21 personal care apartments that provide assistance with bathing, dressing and medications.

First Colonial Inn opened in 1985 and is managed by Excel Retirement Communities of Fort Worth, Texas. Amenities include three meals a day in the dining room, twice monthly maid service and laundering of linens and towels as well as transportation to nearby shopping centers, banks and doctor's offices. Most apartments include full-sized kitchens. There are many recreational activities from which to choose.

Monthly rent for a single resident ranges from $1,160 to $1,625, depending on the size of the apartment. Some units are available immediately, others sometimes require a wait of a few months.

Atlantic Shores
1398 Gibraltar Court, Virginia Beach 426-0000
800-2774

This retirement community is so new, it's not even open. It is under construction, however, and has a model complex available for inspection. Even though the first occupants won't arrive until early 1995, some have already paid 10 percent of their entrance fee to guarantee them room at Atlantic Shores.

Atlantic Shores is being developed by Rauch & Co. of Chicago for Horizons Retirement Community Inc., a not-for-profit organization of retired military officers from Virginia Beach. Although Atlantic Shores is targeting retired military officers and their spouses, anyone who is retired is eligible to live here. The community is on 200 acres near the Dam Neck Navy base and its beach. It is adjacent to Red Wing Lake Municipal Golf Course.

Plans call for two four-story buildings, each with 100 units, plus additional detached villas with garages. The first phase will have 243 units, including 140 of the villas. For residents who later need more care, Atlantic Shores will have assisted living and intermediate and skilled nursing services.

Amenities will include a fitness center, indoor swimming pool, tennis courts and Atlantic Shores' version of an officer's club.

Enrollment fees for one person range from $84,650 to $306,020 based on the size apartment or villa as well as the refund plan selected. A spouse can enroll for an additional $5,000. In addition monthly service fees for one person range from $1,327 to $2,260.

Continuing Care

There are more than 60 nursing homes in the area – far too many to discuss here. In the past couple of years there has been a boom in assisted living facilities. These can bridge the gap between independent living and nursing home care by providing gracious surroundings

and supplemental help for older residents.

The staff of assisted living facilities typically help with bathing and dressing, transportation to doctor's offices, dispensing medicine and recreation. All meals are served in the dining room, and residents are expected to dress in street clothes. Elegant common areas are brightened by chintz curtains and potted plants while residents' rooms are personalized with furniture from home.

After spending months exploring this assisted living option for an ailing parent, we can forewarn you that you will be confused. Licensing varies from facility to facility, and you must be careful you're not comparing apples and oranges. It's crucial you know how ambulatory the resident must be. Some centers are licensed only for residents who walk independently or with a walker. Others will allow residents to be in wheelchairs. However, at some centers residents must

get into wheelchairs by themselves. At other centers employees can assist them into wheelchairs.

Among the possibilities to consider are Brighton Gardens in Virginia Beach, Marian Manor Retirement Community in Virginia Beach, and Ghent Arms and Leigh Hall in Norfolk. All are privately owned except Marian Manor, which is affiliated with a Catholic church. Sentara Health System has Sentara Villages in Norfolk, Virginia Beach and Chesapeake as well as several nursing homes. Sentara provides a Senior Assessment Center to help determine what type assistance – from meal delivery to nursing home care – older residents need. It recently opened an Alzheimer's unit in one of its nursing homes. Call 463-0100.

Another helpful option is the Hillhaven Rehabilitation and Convalescent Center, located at 100 Hampton Blvd. in Norfolk. It has short-term care with intensive therapy, as well as long-term nursing care. Call 623-5602.

Publications

There are several free publications geared toward the senior market. The most extensive is the monthly *Senior Times* published by *Port Folio* magazine. Look around, and you'll see stacks of it in grocery stores, YMCAs and other gathering places. Included are profiles on older residents and interesting articles on health care, restaurants, financial planning and other topics. Call 363-2400.

Another publication is *Seniors Gazette*, published by Universal Publishers. It's basically a monthly "shopper" geared toward older residents with an emphasis on entertainment. You can pick one up at area grocery stores. Call 431-2326.

During the past several years a local company called Selective Concepts has published the annual *Silver Service* directory. This carries listings of helpful services for older adults. It is available at area senior centers and from businesses that advertise in the directory. Call 640-1105.

Inside
Child Care

Child care became a big topic in this area when *The Virginian-Pilot/Ledger-Star* ran a lengthy series on day care abuses in the fall of 1992. Although the articles took a statewide focus, since they were written by local reporters, residents have taken their advice to heart.

If you're from out of state, you may be surprised to see how loosely some day care providers are regulated. Virginia is one of only three states that completely exempts a care-giver from regulation if she keeps no more than five unrelated children in her home. In addition, she can also tend to her own children and any number of others who come only before and after school. Virginia also is one of only 10 states that does not regulate church-sponsored day care centers.

That's not to say you won't find some excellent family day care homes or church centers. It just means parents must do their homework. Pretend you're Sgt. Columbo when grilling potential providers. Once you select a care-giver be constantly on the lookout for potential problems. From experience, we know that child care can work smoothly one day and fall apart the next. Try to keep an option in the back of your mind and be ready to

move quickly if your instincts say you need to make a switch.

When it comes to child care, your best sources of information are other parents. Hunt them down and ask for suggestions on who to call. Be sure to jot down the names of any providers they recommend avoiding.

There are numerous licensed child care centers in the area that meet state standards on staffing, curriculum, safety and nutrition. To find out about them contact the Virginia Social Services Department. Its Eastern Regional Office is in Virginia Beach. Call 473-2100.

Another good resource is the Child Care Resource and Referral Center of The Planning Council. This Norfolk-based nonprofit program has its own Child Care Assurance Program (CCAP) that involves on-site inspections of family day care homes. For a nominal fee, parents can receive a listing of CCAP- and state-approved providers. Before paying the fee, check to see if your employer has arranged with the center to provide information to workers for free. Call 627-3993.

In the region, 70 day care centers and 400 home providers belong to the Tidewater Child Care Association. This nonprofit group was formed in 1974 to upgrade child care. The Portsmouth-based association offers on-going training to child care providers. It also conducts inspections to make sure homes and centers meet standards for health, safety and nutrition. Call 397-2981.

Seven area child-care centers and preschools are certified by the National Association for the Education of Young Children. The association has standards that are stricter than the state's. For a listing of area members call 1-800-424-2460.

Military families can help solve their child care dilemmas by calling the Navy Family Service Center. The center can steer you toward child care centers affiliated with area bases. You also can find out about military-approved providers who can accept only military or Department of Defense dependents. Call 444-4359.

Some parents have had luck locating good child care through the classified section of *The Virginian-Pilot/Ledger-Star.* So many family day care providers advertise here, that there is a separate Babysitting/Child Care section in the classifieds (category 5085).

For suggestions on child care centers pick up a copy of *Tidewater Parent,* a monthly tabloid newspaper. This free, locally produced newspaper is loaded with ads from care givers. And, it frequently runs helpful articles on child care. You can usually grab a copy at grocery stores, child care centers, consignment stores and just about anywhere else parents gather. For more information call 426-2595.

Extended Care

For before- and after-school care, try the YMCA of South Hampton Roads. It offers on-site service in many public schools complete with snacks and homework assistance. Fees average $30 to $40 a week. The YMCA also has a well-respected summer camp program for school-age children that suits many working parents' schedules. It starts right at the end of school and offers 11 weeks of swimming, crafts and other activities. Call 547-YMCA in Chesapeake, 622-YMCA in Norfolk, 398-9348 in Portsmouth, 934-YMCA in Suffolk, and 456-YMCA in Virginia Beach.

In Norfolk the YWCA of South Hampton Roads provides extended care from September through May in several schools. Fees are based on income. Call 625-4248.

You'll also find before- and after-school care at many private schools (see the Schools chapter). Some private schools also have fun summer programs that make life easier for parents whose work continues year round.

There are several popular summer programs that let your children explore nature and art. One of the most popular is the summer Zoo Camp run by the Virginia Zoo in Norfolk for elementary students. There are six one-week sessions. Younger students stay half a day while those in fifth and sixth grade can participate in full-day programs. Campers explore such topics as rain forests, insects and animal care. Call 624-9938.

Students age 8 through 16 can focus on marine life during one-week camps sponsored by the Virginia Marine Science Museum in Virginia Beach. For information call 437-4949.

The Virginia Beach Center for the Arts runs one-week camps that last either a half day or a full day. Most classes are for ages six to 12 but there usually is one session for preschoolers. Typical courses range from photography to painting and cartooning. Call 425-0000. The d'Art center in Norfolk also runs art camps for children aged 6 through 10. During one-week sessions students focus on such activities as painting or working with clay. Call 625-4211.

Another possibility for summer camp is the Jewish Community Center in Norfolk whose Shalom Children's Center runs two four-week summer camps for ages 2 through 13. Older children can choose from drama and sports camps while younger ones explore activities ranging from art to swimming. Call 489-1371.

Preschools

As far as preschools go, there are many excellent ones. Again, your best bet in finding the one that is right for you is to talk to other parents. Look around your neighborhood – or the area near your office – to see what schools are nearby. Many preschools are in churches. Others operate independently. Numerous private schools for older children also have a pre-

school program (again, check the Schools section).

Although some preschools stick to the traditional half-day program, many are melting under pressure from two-career parents. You'll find a number of schools that have started extended-day programs. Some also have summer fun days or camps that go beyond the September to May school year.

Even at preschools with half-day programs, working parents may be able to find another parent to keep their child after hours. There are care givers whose main business is caring for children after preschool ends at noon. Ask the schools for recommendations and try to hook up with other parents for carpooling.

Once you've come up with a list of preschool possibilities, call for brochures and tuition schedules. Then take your time visiting the schools and getting to know the teachers and directors. You may want to go without children at first so you can concentrate on asking key questions. Once you narrow your list down, take your child and spend some time soaking up the surroundings. If you're like us, you and your child may go to the same schools two or three times before making a final decision.

For some of the most popular and prestigious preschools the wait to get in can be long. So start your search as early as you can – at least a year ahead of time is not unreasonable. Be aware that some locals register their children at birth for a couple of the most prestigious preschools. Of course, there are plenty of newcomers who've lucked into a slot when a family suddenly moved from the area. So don't give up hope.

Hint: Among the preschools with the longest waiting lists are the Child Study Center run by Old Dominion University in Norfolk (683-4117), the Stratford Preschool in Virginia Beach (460-0659) and the First Presbyterian Church Preschool in Norfolk (625-0667).

Nannies

Finding in-home child care is a definite option. If you place a classified ad in the Help Wanted section of *The Virginian-Pilot/Ledger-Star*, you'd better have a telephone answering machine. The one time we tried it, the calls easily topped 100 and only a few of those sounded like anyone you'd want to hire.

Although there are parents who've found excellent care-givers through the classifieds, many prefer to use a service to do the screening. There are several that are active in the area.

Au Pair in America is a national program run by the American Institute for Foreign Study Scholarship Foundation of Greenwich, Ct. Au Pair in America matches families with European au pairs ranging in age from 18 to 25. Au pairs live with families and work an average of 45 hours a week. They can stay in the United States only 12 months. The program has a local counselor who helps match families with au pairs, makes sure everything works smoothly and arranges activities for au pairs. The weekly cost averages $170 no matter the number of children. Call 1-800-727-2437 or 623-7321.

We've had good personal experience with another service, AuPairCare. It is headquartered in San Francisco and also provides European nannies ages 18 to 25. The au pairs, both young women *and* men, work an average of 45 hours a week, live with families as family members, and can stay in this country 13 months. Since AuPairCare is the largest au pair provider in the area, it has several local counselors to work with families and au pairs. The weekly cost averages $170 for any number of children. Call 1-800-288-7786 or 393-9484.

If you prefer to hire someone who is local, possibly older than 25, and making a career of child care, then you may want to contact the Nanny Career Center. It is a program of the Summit School and Montessori Centers in Virginia Beach and Chesapeake. The center offers an eight-week training course for nanny certification and operates a placement agency. Nannies can either live in your home or come there daily. Call 467-1644.

Babysitting

If you're new to the neighborhood, right now is the time to start cultivating that teenager or college student down the street. There seems to be a dearth of people in that age group, and finding reliable babysitters can be a ruthless business. In fact, don't be shocked if that friendly neighbor next door who welcomed you with brownies refuses to reveal the name of her sitter.

We've had great success hiring workers at our child care center for occasional babysitting. But since we once called 12 people before snaring a sitter for a Saturday night, we try to keep a long list of prospects. Soon, you too may be asking any responsible teen or college student you meet whether they babysit. The going rate for sitters is about $3 an hour.

One resource is students at Old Dominion University's excellent Child Study Center. If you send a written notice of what type of help you are looking for (regular, occasional, weekend), it will be posted on a bulletin board. Be sure to specify where you live. Send the information to Child Study Center, Old Dominion University, Norfolk 23519-0136. You also can put notices in Webb Center, ODU's student center, as well as at other local colleges. Tidewater Community College in Virginia Beach recently opened a Child Development Lab.

Since 1949, Baby Sitters of Tidewater Inc. has come to the rescue of countless newcomers. Many of them come to rely on the service for their babysitting needs. The business has passed from its founder, Emma Johnson, to her daughter-in-law, Clarice Johnson. This is a word-of-mouth service that hires mainly retired teachers and nurses as well as grandmothers. You can hire a sitter for a day, evening, weekend or while you go on vacation. For one or two children the charge is $4 an hour, with a minimum of four hours. Plus there is a $4 transportation fee if you live within 30 miles of the sitter. It costs $4.75 an hour for three to five children and slightly more for two

families or groups of kids. Although there are nearly 75 sitters on call, to make sure you get one try to phone several days ahead. Call 489-1622.

Many churches, especially those with preschools, have mother's-morning-out service available. This is usually a drop-in service for toddlers and lasts only a couple of hours one or two mornings a week. It can be a great sanity saver for stay-at-home moms and provide valuable interaction for children.

Another resource for occasional care is Sentara Child Care Center at 5232 Providence Road in Virginia Beach. It has been around since 1983 and is affiliated with Sentara Health System, the region's largest health-care organization. The center keeps children from infants to age 12. It is open until 9 PM on most days and charges about $2.50 an hour. On Fridays and Saturdays the center remains open until 1 AM. This is strictly for temporary child care since no child can be there more than 20 hours a week. Children must have medical records to be registered. Call 467-9105

For sick children, Sentara Home Care Services will send a nursing assistant to care for your children at home as long as their fevers are under 101 degrees. This is a definite option for working parents facing a lengthy siege of the chicken pox. Children must be registered in advance of illness. Fees are $6.50 an hour between 7 AM and 3 PM and slightly more at other times. You can get a jump on chicken pox season by preregistering your children without paying any enrollment fees. Call 461-5649.

Inside
Schools

Whether you are searching for a kindergarten or a high school for your children, Hampton Roads has an abundance of choices. Each of the five cities in this area has its own public school system. In addition, there are numerous private and parochial schools. Many of them also offer preschool and extended care programs.

Public Schools

All public schools in the re-

gion are governed by school boards appointed by city councils. There is a movement in Virginia toward voter-elected school boards. But so far none of the region's cities has approved this measure.

In Virginia all eighth graders must pass the Virginia Literacy Passport Test, which is first administered in sixth grade. The test focuses on reading, writing and math basics. Students who fail the test receive special instruction. However, if they don't pass all three parts of the test by the eighth grade

Students pose at Cape Henry Collegiate, a private school founded in 1924.

Photo: Cape Henry Collegiate

they cannot be promoted. Special education students are exempt from the test.

To enroll a student in a school district for the first time, you will need the child's Social Security number, a certified birth certificate, a completed physical examination form, an immunization record and a report card from the child's last school, if the child has attended one.

Kindergarten students must be 5 years old by September 30 to enroll. However, several districts let parents enroll students whose birthdays fall within a month or two after that cutoff. The exact date varies with the school district. Kindergarten is not mandatory in Virginia, although we're hard-pressed to think of any parents who don't send their children to kindergarten. However, the state legislature is considering changing the law to require kindergarten attendance.

Public schools throughout the region tend to draw students from nearby neighborhoods. Bus service is provided for students living too far to walk to school.

All public schools offer a wide range of academics, sports and extra-curricular activities. Programs for gifted and talented students and those with special educational needs are provided. In the region, there are strong links with the business and military communities. Some organizations adopt entire schools and channel a lot of energy into improving them. Others occasionally provide lecturers and tutors.

The school districts receive federal money to help education-

ally disadvantaged students. Head Start programs also are available. For information on them call 623-6974.

Virginia Beach Public Schools

Virginia Beach has the largest public school district in the region and the second largest in Virginia. It has more than 72,000 students and 4,600 teachers. The school district has a dropout rate of about 5 percent.

In 1992 the school district opened a new middle school and Tallwood High School – the ninth in the city. There are 12 middle schools, 52 elementary schools and six specialized centers. Since the city's population boom in the mid- to late-1980s, the school district has worked to alleviate overcrowding by building new schools throughout the city.

Kindergarten in Virginia Beach operates in two shifts. Students are assigned to either morning or afternoon sessions. Students in first grade and beyond attend school all day.

For students with special needs, the school district offers several programs. Gifted first graders can participate in school-based programs that challenge them. Those in grades 2 through 6 can attend the Old Donation Center for the Gifted and Talented one day a week. The center also has additional programs for those in grades 4 through 6 with talent in visual arts and dance.

Students needing additional

help are assisted by reading resource teachers and other remedial instruction. Some schools offer special instruction for students who speak English as a second language.

By the end of the 1993-94 school year the Virginia Beach district will have converted all its junior highs to middle schools for sixth, seventh and eighth graders. A variety of programs is offered for gifted and special education students.

Virginia Beach's high schools offer both regular and advanced studies. Those in advanced studies take high-level classes in math, science and language. They also are required to complete more courses to graduate. Advanced placement classes are offered in art, biology, calculus, chemistry, computer science, English, foreign languages, physics and United States history. High schools offer instruction in French, German, Latin, Russian and Spanish.

Alternative schools include the Career Development Center, which offers a core curriculum and vocational courses, and the Vocational-Technical Educational Center, which teaches numerous trades and job-training courses.

Adults 17 and older can attend evening classes at the Open Campus High School to earn their high school diploma or GED certificate.

They also can study at the Adult Learning Center, which has some basic courses as well as more recreational ones.

Virginia Beach numbers to note:
Superintendent's Office – 427-4373

Office of Pupil Services – 427-4791
Gifted/Talented Center – 473-5043
Adult Learning Center – 473-5091
Career Development – 473-5058
Vo-Tech Ed. Center – 427-5300
Open Campus
High School – 473-5200
Recreational Classes – 473-5091

Norfolk Public Schools

With more than 37,000 students, Norfolk has the second largest school district in the region. There are five high schools, eight middle schools and 36 elementary schools. The district has 2,500 teachers and a dropout rate of 6 percent.

The Norfolk school district offers a number of special programs. More than 6,000 students participate in gifted courses. For students in kindergarten through the fifth grade, there is the Field Lighthouse Program. One day a week gifted students travel to Stuart Gifted School for specialized studies. The center is also where foreign-speaking children spend part of the day learning English.

Gifted sixth graders can challenge their creativity once a week with an in-school program designed for them. Students in grades seven through 12 can take gifted alternative classes in math, science, social studies, communication skills and foreign language. Students eager for more learning can stay late or come on Saturday for the Arts & Sciences Gifted Extended Day Program. The curriculum includes Russian language, problem solving and architecture/engineering. Students whose interests lean towards high technology, can get practical training at the NORSTAR Student Research Institute, which conducts space shuttle experiments and robotics projects. Those learning toward health careers can participate in the Magnet High School for the Sciences and Health Professions through Eastern Virginia Medical School.

Many programs are designed for special education students. The district runs St. Mary's Infant Home for severely disabled children and toddlers. The school district has a program for disabled preschoolers. Students kindergarten age and above are mainstreamed, if possible, with the help of resource rooms.

The Willard Model Elementary School is the school district's only model school. Since 1985 Willard has been a laboratory school designed to prepare students for the 21st century. It uses a lot of computers and a flexible staff to introduce innovative educational programs.

There are several specialized centers run by the school district. The Coronado School is for pregnant students. The Norfolk Technical Vocational Center helps students prepare for careers. The Madison Career Center also provides vocational training as well as adult basic education.

In Norfolk adult education courses, which run the gamut from quilting to computers, are administered by the city's parks and recreation department. The reasonably priced classes are scheduled year round at the city's recreation centers and are some of the better bargains in town.

Norfolk numbers to note:
Superintendent's Office – 441-2107
Adult/Vocational Ed. – 441-2957
Gifted Programs – 441-2638
Special Ed. Services – 441-2491
Recreational Classes – 441-2149

Chesapeake Public Schools

The Chesapeake Public School District gained acclaim in 1990 when it put a warranty on all its graduates. The gimmick guarantees that any employer can "return" a Chesapeake graduate to the school district if he or she fails to have mastery of basic skills. So far no one has taken the school district up on its offer to re-educate any deficient graduate.

The Chesapeake School District operates five high schools, seven middle schools and 26 elementary schools. It has more than 30,000 students and 3,068 teachers.

Gifted and talented programs are available for those in grades kindergarten through 12. Younger students have in-school programs while fifth and sixth graders go once a week to the Laboratory School for the Academically Gifted. There they do problem solving and learn more about math, science and computers. Middle school students can participate in gifted programs in most subject areas while senior high students have advanced placement and honors courses.

Special education students attend their assigned schools. Those who can be mainstreamed are included in regular classes. Resource rooms and teaching assistance are available along with some self-contained classes. The Preschool Education Center is designed to help disabled children ages 2 to 5.

Among the school district's special centers are the Adult Education Center, which offers preparation for the GED as well as career-oriented classes for working adults; the Chesapeake Center for Science and Technology, which offers vocational courses training in such fields as engine repair and nursing; and the Alternative School for students whose discipline problems prevent them from attending their assigned high schools.

Chesapeake numbers to note:
Superintendent's Office – 547-4114
Gifted Programs – 494-7640
Vocational Ed. Programs – 547-6013
Adult Education Program – 548-6001
Special Ed. Programs – 547-1321
Recreational Classes – 547-6411

Portsmouth Public Schools

There are more than 18,000 students attending Portsmouth Public Schools. The district has five high schools, four middle schools and 16 elementary schools. In 1992 the new Churchland High School opened. Plans are under way to replace I.C. Norcom High School with a new school within several years. The school district has 1,207 teachers and a dropout rate of 5 percent.

Gifted and talented programs run from kindergarten through grade 12. Through the Spectrum Program for the Gifted and Talented, students can participate in a variety of programs. This year the district started a Potential National Merit Scholars program for high-achieving fifth graders. They are offered supplementary Saturday and evening sessions. The program will take the students through graduation and each year bring in a new group of fifth graders.

Kindergarten through second grade students are offered the Explorer program that supplements everyday studies. Twice a month gifted and talented instructors also come to the schools for special programs. Grades three through five have the Search program, which takes students to one of the district's five gifted and talented labs for a full day of studies once a week. The Discover program takes middle school students to a weekly lab and supplements their program with workshops and seminars. High school students have both honors and advanced placement labs and can participate in a special program in conjunction with the College of William & Mary in Williamsburg.

The school district offers a variety of special education programs. Some are based in regular classrooms. Others involve resource rooms or special education centers. Preschools and early elementary students can get special help at the DAC Center for Learning.

Among the school district's special centers are the Emily Spong Center, an alternative school for elementary students with discipline problems, and New Directions, a similar school for secondary students. The S.H. Clarke Vocational Training Center offers hands-on training in practical trades while the Adult Learning Center offers adults the chance to earn their GED or take computer classes or other helpful courses.

Portsmouth numbers to note:
Superintendent's Office –393-8742
Adult Ed. Program – 393-8822
Special Ed. Program – 393-8658
Vocational Ed. Program – 393-8869
Gifted Programs – 393-8483
Recreational Classes – 393-8481

Suffolk Public Schools

To keep pace with growth in Suffolk, the school district opened two new high schools in 1990 and did a massive renovation of its older schools. In the transition, three of the city's old high schools became its middle schools. Its three former middle schools became new elementary schools, giving the city a total of 10 primary schools. The school district has more than 9,000 students, 651 teachers and a dropout rate of 5.9 percent.

About 10 percent of the student body is involved in gifted programs while another 9.5 percent participates in special education services. Gifted and talented programs start in kindergarten. Through the Student Trial Enrichment Program (STEP) students in kindergarten through third grade meet once or twice a week for special creative thinking programs in their schools.

Gifted students in grades four through eight can attend the QUEST Center at John F. Kennedy Middle School once a week. Topics of study include space exploration, Japan and foreign languages. These students also can take special art

and music classes designed for gifted students. In high school teachers offer gifted students special units designed for them. Students also can take advanced placement and honors courses. They can earn college credits at Paul D. Camp Community College by taking such advanced courses as calculus and western civilization.

The school district has programs for disabled students ranging in age from 2 to 21. Offerings include the Parent Resource Center, which trains parents and educators to work with the disabled. There is a preschool program for handicapped children. Elementary and upper level programs for more severely disabled and special education students are consolidated at several schools. As many students as possible are mainstreamed.

The school district operates the P.D. Pruden Vo-Tech Center, which trains high school students during the day for careers in 16 areas, such as cosmetology, horticulture and data processing. The Pruden Center is a joint project of the Suffolk School District and neighboring Isle of Wight County School District. At the same facility the two districts also operate the Center for Lifelong Learning. Evening programs let adults earn their GED and learn skills such as welding or word processing. They also can take fun courses on decorating cakes and troubleshooting their VCR. The school district also co-sponsors a school for practical nurses at Obici Memorial Hospital.

With the help of a grant from the Planters Peanuts plant in Suffolk, the school district operates The Planters Reach-A-Parent Center. This resource center has materials and workshops that help parents improve their children's skills. It is open afternoons in Booker T. Washington Elementary School.

Suffolk numbers to note:
Superintendent's Office – 925-5000
Special Ed. Programs – 925-5579
Planters Reach-A-Parent
    Center   –   925-5727
Pruden Vocational-Technical
    Center   –   925-5590
Recreational Classes – 925-6328

Magnet Schools

There is only one regional magnet school in south Hampton Roads -- the Norfolk-based Governor's Magnet School for the Arts (451-4711). The school provides intense training in dance, music, theater, visual arts or performing arts for nearly 300 public school students. The program is sponsored by the Virginia Department of Education and public schools in Chesapeake, Norfolk, Portsmouth, Suffolk, Virginia Beach and nearby Franklin, Isle of Wight County and Southampton County.

The school, which started in 1987, is one of five magnet schools in the state and the only one focused on the arts. Graduates have gone on to such prestigious schools at Yale, Princeton and Juilliard.

Magnet school students take academic courses at their home high schools in the mornings. They then hop on buses and congregate in Norfolk for afternoon arts studies. Dancers, artists, singers, musicians and actors meet at various locations such as Old Dominion University and Norfolk State University. In 1992 the school raised funds to renovate a downtown building as the home of its theater department. Plans call for consolidating more of the Magnet School in the building as funds become available.

Norfolk Public School students can participate in the Magnet High School for the Sciences and Health Professions. It was founded in 1986 and sends 80 Norfolk high school students to study five days a week at Eastern Virginia Medical School.

If Suffolk school officials have their way, students will be eligible for a new Tidewater Governor's School for Science and Technology. The proposed school would be a three-week summer program that would serve students in Suffolk and

Isle of Wight and Southampton counties.

Private Schools

Stroll through some of the region's nicest neighborhoods on an early fall morning and you may wonder why clusters of students are gathered on different corners. Chances are they are waiting for buses headed for their various schools. Gathered in one block may be the public school students. A few streets away you may see the group waiting for buses from Norfolk Academy or Norfolk Christian School. Rounding the corner may be the parent driving the carpool for a private elementary school with no bus system.

In these neighborhoods the mix of public and private school students is pretty even. And there's not a lot of rivalry between the students. In the afternoon you're likely to see a cross-section of the older children playing street hockey. Younger ones may gather for a game of soccer in someone's yard as their parents wind down by chatting with neighbors.

If you're interested in private or parochial schools there are more than 50 to choose from. Some are only for primary school students; others can take children from pre-school through graduation. You'll find both religious and secular schools. Among the secular schools are some with private owners and others run by independent boards. There are schools with dozens of organized sports and extra-curricular activities and others with just a few offerings.

Despite these differences all schools pride themselves on their small class size and emphasis on excellence. Upper level schools all tend to have college-preparatory curriculums. Tracking down the right school for your child can be a time-consuming but rewarding process. The ideal is to start your search a year ahead of time, but when that's not possible you can jump start the process with a lot of legwork.

Your best resources are other parents who have been down the same road and settled on schools for their children. Grill as many of them as you can for their insight. Then call the schools and ask for information packets. After perusing them spend time in the schools talking to administrators, teachers and students. Be aware that admission policies vary greatly. Some schools have open admissions but others are very selective, and there may be competition for a limited number of slots.

Be sure to check into accreditation since it varies widely. Some schools have no accreditation. Others are accredited by the selective Virginia Council for Private Education and the Virginia Association of Independent Schools. Schools with these designations also are recognized by the state Board of Education. Other schools are accredited by the Association of Christian Schools International, the Southern Association of Colleges and Schools, the Virginia Catholic Educational Association and the American Montessori Society.

To get you started, we have

included a sampling of private schools that is by no means all-inclusive. All tuitions reflect 1992-93 rates. Remember that transportation, before-school care and other special services cost extra. And, most schools charge applicants an enrollment fee. When comparing schools, be sure you know exactly what the tuition covers. To avoid throwing your budget out of whack, find out if there are any mandatory funds or fees.

Some schools offer a tuition discount for families enrolling more than one student. A few have some financial aid available for financially strapped families.

Among the area private schools are:

ATLANTIC SHORES CHRISTIAN SCHOOLS

1861 Kempsville Rd., Va. Beach   479-1125
1219 N. Centerville Turnpike,
Chesapeake   479-9598

This Christ-centered school was organized in 1985 and has a preschool through high school program that includes a college-preparatory curriculum along with training in music and sports. There are two campuses -- one in the Kempsville area for elementary student and an 18-acre complex a mile away for secondary students. Enrollment in the preschool and elementary program is 315. There are 170 secondary students. Besides Virginia Beach, students come from Chesapeake, Portsmouth, Suffolk and nearby parts of North Carolina. Extended care is available for grades K-6, and there are both half-day and full-day kindergartens. Annual tu-

ition ranges from $1,065 for a half-day kindergarten to $2,570 for students in grades 7-12.

BAYLAKE PINES PRIVATE SCHOOL

2204 Treasure Island Rd., Va. Beach 464-4636

Started as a preschool in 1951, this school now also takes students through the seventh grade. It is located at the entrance to the upscale Baylake Pines neighborhood but draws some of its 445 students from as far away as Norfolk and Chesapeake. The academically oriented school features a traditional curriculum grounded in phonics, reading, math and science that also promotes creativity. Students begin French lessons in kindergarten and science labs in second grade. There are both all-day and half-day kindergartens. Annual tuition ranges from $3,212 for first graders to $3,652 for seventh graders. Discounts are available for paying the year's tuition in full and enrolling two or more children.

BAYVIEW CHRISTIAN SCHOOL AND DAYCARE

707 E. Bayview Blvd., Norfolk   588-5687

This Christian school was founded in 1979 by Bayview Baptist Church and is adjacent to the church in the Ocean View area. The school's 100 students run the gamut from preschoolers to eighth graders. Although most are from Norfolk, many live in outlying cities and have parents working at the nearby Norfolk Navy Base. Before- and after-school care is available. For working parents there's also a summer program and child care available on non-school days. The

Bible and Christian teachings are integrated into all areas of study. Annual tuition ranges from $1,006 for preschoolers to $1,994 for students in grades one through eight. Discounts are offered to church members, military personnel and those with two or more children enrolled.

CAPE HENRY COLLEGIATE SCHOOL
1320 Mill Dam Rd., Va. Beach   481-2446

With nearly 600 students, this is the largest private school in Virginia Beach. Cape Henry was started in 1924 and has a 30-acre campus. Its individualized learning programs are for preschoolers as well as high school seniors. Middle school and upper school students are required to complete some community service work. There are both half-day and full-day kindergartens. The upper school focuses heavily on college preparatory studies with some honors and advanced placement classes available. Younger students also have some accelerated classes. The Academic Enrichment Program helps students who may have trouble maintaining the academic pace. There is before- and after-school care for younger students and an all-day summer program. Buses bring students from Virginia Beach and parts of Norfolk and Chesapeake. Annual tuition ranges from $4,150 for half-day preschool, to $5,800 for grades one and two, and $6,650 for middle- and upper-school students. Discounts are offered for multiple enrollments.

CHESAPEAKE BAY ACADEMY
5721 Sellger Dr., Norfolk   459-2300

The academy has a specialized curriculum for students with learning disabilities, attention deficit disorders and other special learning needs. The school was organized in 1988 and uses an individualized, multisensory approach for students in kindergarten through eighth grade. Its student body averages about 50 students who come from as far away as Williamsburg. Annual tuition costs $6,400.

COURT STREET ACADEMY
447 Court St., Portsmouth   393-2312

Founded in 1966, this academy offers a traditional curriculum for preschool through eighth grade. For the academy's nearly 200 students, the emphasis is on the mastery of basic skills. The kindergarten program lasts a full day. Before- and after-school care is available. Although the school is in Court Street Baptist Church it is not directly affiliated with the church. Monthly tuition ranges from $155 for kindergartners to $190 for elementary and intermediate student. Transportation is available for students in Portsmouth and parts of Chesapeake and Suffolk. There is a tuition discount for enrolling more than one student.

FIRST BAPTIST CHRISTIAN SCHOOL
237 N. Main St., Suffolk   925-0274

Started as a kindergarten more than 25 years ago, the school is affiliated with First Baptist Church. It has more than 100 students in preschool through fifth grade. Most come from Suffolk. The school provides a Christian-based education and has both half-day and full-day kindergarten programs. There is before- and after-school care, and vans will take children to and from public school. Tuition costs $1,440 a year for kindergarten and $2,250 for grades one through five.

GHENT MONTESSORI SCHOOL
610 Mowbray Arch, Norfolk   622-8174

Founded in 1978 this school is housed in a building designed for the Montessori approach, which lets children move freely around their rooms working on a variety of projects. Students can start as young as 2 1/2. The school has steadily expanded its program to older students and now goes through sixth grade. Enrollment is about 110, and students come from throughout the region. Classes combine several ages of students so younger ones can observe older ones, who get a chance to teach what they've learned. To appreciate the Montessori style, parents are encouraged to enroll children before they are 4 years old. On occasion, upper level slots go to students not previously in Montessori studies. Full-day and extended-day programs are available.

Annual tuition costs $2,630 for half-day students age 6 and younger. It is $4,040 for ages 6 and up. The full-day program costs $5,720.

GREENBRIER CHRISTIAN ACADEMY
311 Kempsville Road, Chesapeake 547-9595

This academy was founded in 1982 and goes from kindergarten through high school. It is situated in the fast-growing Greenbrier area on a 20-acre campus and draws its 710 students from Chesapeake, Suffolk, Portsmouth and Virginia Beach. Greenbrier has a full-day kindergarten and before- and after-school care available for younger students. The school sponsors specialized summer camp programs in sports, computers and remedial studies. Integrated with the school's basic curriculum are Bible studies. Annual tuition is $,2,150 for kindergartners, $2,375 for lower school students and $2,575 for junior and senior high students. Discounts are available for families.

HEBREW ACADEMY OF TIDEWATER
1244 Thompkins Lane, Va. Beach   424-4327

The academy, which opened in 1955, offers a general and Judaic education for students in preschool through seventh grade. Its 200 students come from throughout the region, including the Peninsula. Besides emphasizing a core curriculum of science, math and language, students take daily classes in Hebrew, the Torah, and Jewish history, laws and customs. The school has a program for students with learning difficulties. Kindergarten is a full-day program. Transportation and before- and after-school care are available. Tuition ranges from $4,500 for kindergarten to $4,800 in grades 7.

NANSEMOND-SUFFOLK ACADEMY
3373 Pruden Blvd., Suffolk   539-8789

Founded in 1966 for grades one through seven, the academy added an upper school in 1970 and now educates preschoolers through high school seniors. The academy is on a 50-acre campus and has an enrollment of about 900. Most students come from Suffolk, but the academy also attracts students from Portsmouth, Chesapeake and nearby counties. The academy stresses a college-preparatory curriculum, offers honors and advanced placement courses in high school and sponsors several athletic teams. Annual tuition ranges from $2,045 for half-day kindergartners to $3,677 for eighth graders and $3,993 for seniors. Discounts are available for families enrolling three or more children. Extended care is available for younger students.

Transportation is available.

NORFOLK ACADEMY
1585 Wesleyan Dr., Norfolk   461-6236

With a founding date of 1728 and an enrollment of 1,169, this is the region's oldest and largest private school. Students can enroll in first grade and stay until they graduate. Liberal arts and college preparatory work are stressed as well as community service and independent study. In the upper school there are advanced placement courses. There are 40 extracurricular activities, an emphasis on fine arts, and dozens of athletic teams. Buses bring students from Norfolk, Virginia Beach, Chesapeake and Portsmouth. Before- and after-school care is available for grades one through six. There is a diverse summer program for all ages that includes sports camps and sessions on archeology, theater and marine science. Annual tuition and fees are $5,863 in the lower school and $6,760 in the upper school.

NORFOLK CATHOLIC HIGH SCHOOL
6401 Granby St., Norfolk   423-2553

Established in 1950, Norfolk Catholic has a student body of 425 that comes from throughout the region. After adding a middle school several years ago when another Catholic school closed, Norfolk Catholic is phasing out the program. After 1993-94, it will be strictly for grades nine through 12. The school concentrates on a college-preparatory curriculum in a Catholic environment. Community service is emphasized, and members of the graduating class of '93 must have completed 40 hours of volunteer work. Starting with the class of '94, graduates must complete 80 hours of community service. By September 1993 the school will have moved into a new building being constructed in Virginia Beach on a 15-acre site on Princess Anne Road. Its name will then change to Catholic High School. Annual tuition ranges from $2,200 for middle school students to $4,200 for high school students who are not part of a Catholic family. For those who are Catholic, tuition is $3,100. Some financial aid is available.

NORFOLK CHRISTIAN SCHOOLS
255 Thole St., Norfolk   423-5770

From their start as a grammar school in 1952, these schools have grown into three schools in Norfolk as well as a Virginia Beach campus.

The schools are evangelical and nondenominational and go from preschool through high school. There are more than 600 students who come from throughout the region. There are both half-day and full-day kindergartens. Special programs are available for students with learning disabilities and those who need accelerated studies. The upper and lower Norfolk schools are about a block apart. The Virginia Beach school, at 1265 Laskin Rd., is limited to kindergarten and first grade. Annual tuition ranges from $1,440 for half-day kindergarten to $3,125 for elementary students and $4,200 for grades eight through 12. Discounts are available for enrolling more than one child. Transportation is available.

NORFOLK COLLEGIATE SCHOOL
5429 Tidewater Dr., Norfolk   625-0471
7336 Granby St., Norfolk   480-2885

Founded in 1948 as a kindergarten, Norfolk Collegiate has grown into a complete school system with academic programs that take students through high school. There are two campuses with about 600 students who come from throughout the region. The lower school is on nine acres on Tidewater Drive while the middle and upper schools are on five acres on Granby Street. Kindergarten is a full-day program. The school stresses a college-preparatory curriculum and advanced studies are offered to high school students. Transportation is available. Annual tuition ranges from $3,750 for kindergarten to $4,410 for grades four through six, and $4,995 for high school students. Some scholarships are offered.

PARKDALE PRIVATE SCHOOL
321 Virginian Dr., Norfolk   583-5989

Although this school only goes through second grade, we're partial to it since we have a child enrolled in preschool. Parkdale started in 1957 as Barbara Jacobs School and has nearly 100 students. Its proximity to Norfolk Naval Base draws students from throughout the region. There is before- and after-school care for students as old as 14 and transportation for them to and from nearby public schools. There also is a summer program. Kindergarten lasts a full day. Tuition is $255 monthly for ages 4 through grade two.

PORTSMOUTH CHRISTIAN SCHOOL
3214 Elliott Ave., Portsmouth   393-0725

Biltmore Baptist Church started this school in 1965 as a church ministry. It added a grade a year until it built up a Christian program for kindergarten through 12th grade. Enrollment is about 528, and students come mostly from Portsmouth, Chesapeake and Suffolk. There are both half-day and full-day kindergartens. Extended care is offered through the fourth grade. Annual tuition ranges from $1,004 for half-day kindergarten to $1,493 for elementary students and $1,737 for junior and senior high school. Family discounts are available.

RYAN ACADEMY
844 Jerome Ave., Norfolk   583-RYAN

Ryan Academy started in 1988 on the site of a former private school that dated back to the 1950s. Its 140 students include kindergartners through high school seniors. The academy has an Alternate Learning Center and resource rooms for students with learning difficulties. It has an all-day kindergarten. Transportation is available. Annual tuition ranges from $2,950 for kindergarten for $3,490 for sixth and seventh grade and $3,990 for high school.

STAR OF THE SEA CATHOLIC SCHOOL
311 Arctic Crescent, Va. Beach   428-8400

Founded in 1958 and affiliated with St. Mary's Star of the Sea Catholic Church, this school has about 300 students who come primarily from Virginia Beach. It emphasizes a Catholic education for students in preschool through eighth grade. There is a full-day kindergarten. Tuition is $1,425 for parishioners, $1,740 for a member of another parish and $2,300 for non-Catholics. Discounts are available for families, and some financial aid is available.

STONEBRIDGE SCHOOLS
4225 Portsmouth Blvd., Chesapeake 488-7586

Stonebridge was founded in 1980 to offer a Christian, non-denominational, college-preparatory curriculum. Its 220 students come primarily from Chesapeake, Portsmouth, Suffolk and Virginia Beach. There are two campuses. The lower school is on Portsmouth Boulevard in the Western Branch area while the middle and high schools are in Faith Baptist Church on Jolliff Road. There are half-day kindergarten classes for 4 year olds and a full-day program for 5 year olds. Extended care is available, and transportation is an option for students in Virginia Beach and the Great Bridge area of Chesapeake. Annual tuition ranges from $1,735 for the 4-year-old kindergarten to $2,760 for second through fourth grade and $3,360 for high school. Financial aid is available.

VIRGINIA BEACH COUNTRY DAY SCHOOL
2100 Harbor Lane, Va. Beach 481-0111

Started in 1975, the school offers classes for preschool through sixth grade. It has a four-acre campus and an enrollment of 130. Students come primarily from Virginia Beach and Chesapeake. There are both half-day and full-day kindergartens. Extended care is available, and there is a summer program. Transportation is available. Monthly tuition ranges from $359 for full-day preschoolers to $307 for kindergarten through elementary school. Fees are based on an 11-month payment plan. Other options are available.

VIRGINIA BEACH FRIENDS SCHOOL
1537 Laskin Rd., Va. Beach 428-7534

Organized in 1955, this is Virginia's only Quaker school. It promotes the values of community, equality, harmony and simplicity. The school has an 11-acre campus and is for preschool through eighth grade. There are 110 students who come from throughout the region. Before- and after-school care is offered. There are both half-day and full-day kindergartens. Annual tuition ranges from $2,420 for half-day kindergarten to $3,780 for the lower school and $3,990 for the middle school. Financial aid is available.

THE WILLIAMS SCHOOL
419 Colonial Ave., Norfolk 627-1383

Housed in a historic home in the residential Ghent area, this school was founded in 1927. It has about 115 students in kindergarten through eighth grade, with most coming from Norfolk and Portsmouth. The school prides itself on its environment, which nurtures individuals while giving them a solid grounding in basic studies. Transportation and after-school care are available. Annual tuition is $4,500.

Photo: Old Dominion University

Students at Old Dominion take a break on a sunny afternoon.

Inside
Colleges, Universities and Adult Education

*D*octor. Lawyer. Executive chef. Name almost any career you are interested in, and chances are you'll find a degree in it offered somewhere in Hampton Roads. There are six major colleges and universities based in the five-city area. In addition, the region's large military population has attracted a number of out-of-the-area colleges that offer undergraduate and graduate degree programs here. And, if that's not enough, there are four other colleges on the Peninsula within easy driving distance – Christopher Newport University, the College of William & Mary, Hampton University and Thomas Nelson Community College.

If you're holding down a job and thinking of earning a degree on the side, you'll find that easy to do here. All colleges offer evening programs, and some also have early morning and weekend sessions that cater to working students.

There also are more than 50 private career colleges and schools that train mechanics, computer technicians, cosmetologists, travel agents and chefs, to name a few of the possibilities.

For residents with a life-long love of learning, reasonably priced adult education programs can teach them to tap dance, paint or become a tennis ace. Most of these fun classes are run by city parks and recreation departments. However, some are offered through the continuing education departments of area schools and colleges. Most programs publish quarterly guides giving class times and fees. Among the city programs, Norfolk Parks and Recreation Department stands out for its Lakewood Dance and Music Center, which has an excellent curriculum for both adults and children.

Colleges and Universities

Major colleges and universities based in the area that are accredited by the Southern Association of Colleges and Schools are:

EASTERN VIRGINIA MEDICAL SCHOOL
Norfolk   *446-5600*
Established in 1973, Eastern Virginia Medical School is one of only three medical schools in Virginia. The school is operated by the Medical College of Hampton Roads

from a campus in Norfolk. However, its students and medical residents use 30 area hospitals and clinics as their training ground. From its first class of 24 medical students, the school has grown to an enrollment of about 475 students who come from Virginia as well as other states. Each year EVMS sponsors 20 residency programs, a psychology internship, and fellowship programs that attract about 300 physicians. Besides the M.D. degree, EVMS grants a doctorate in clinical psychology and biomedical sciences through cooperative programs with area universities. It also offers a master's degree in art psychotherapy.

EVMS receives some state funding but depends heavily on support from area cities and private donations. In fact, the school got its start when area residents raised $17 million in the late 1960s and early 1970s to start the school. Having a medical school in Hampton Roads has brought a full range of sophisticated medical services – including heart transplants and in vitro fertilization – to the region. The school has also greatly increased the number of physicians working in the area.

EVMS is noted for its Jones Institute for Reproductive Medicine – the first in vitro fertilization clinic in the United States. In 1981 the Institute helped produce the country's first in vitro baby. Since then more than 1,100 in vitro babies have been born with the Institute's help. It has the world's highest pregnancy rate among in vitro programs and draws patients from across the country. Housed in a $12.5 million building that opened in late 1991, the Institute has an international reputation for treating reproductive problems.

Another major program of EVMS is the Diabetes Institutes, which has dedicated itself to finding a cure for diabetes. It also operates both outpatient and inpatient treatment programs for area residents with diabetes.

NORFOLK STATE UNIVERSITY
Norfolk 683-8600

Founded in 1935 as a division of Virginia Union University, Norfolk State has grown into one of the country's five largest predominantly black colleges. It has an enrollment of more than 8,300 and about 400 faculty members. Students come from throughout the United States and 35 foreign countries.

In 1944 NSU became part of the Virginia college system and in 1979 gained university status. Today it has nine schools, 32 departments and 72 degree programs. NSU offers seven associate, 50 bachelors and 15 masters degrees. Degree programs include education, nursing, journalism and social work. There are 13 varsity sports, including football and basketball.

In 1986 NSU established the Ronald I. Dozoretz National Institute for Minorities in Applied Sciences, which recruits top high school seniors across the country to study science.

NSU is renowned for its marching band and Army ROTC program. It has the country's second largest female ROTC cadet

enrollment and its total ROTC enrollment is the largest in Virginia for a non-military school.

Besides its 130-acre campus in Norfolk, NSU operates a graduate center in Virginia Beach with Old Dominion University.

OLD DOMINION UNIVERSITY
Norfolk   683-3000

Founded in 1930 in Norfolk as a branch of the College of William and Mary, ODU became independent in 1962. In 1970 the state-supported institution gained university status. It has an enrollment of nearly 17,000 with 5,500 graduate students and more than 600 faculty members. Students come from across the United States as well as 80 foreign countries. ODU offers 85 bachelor degree programs, 53 masters programs and 16 doctoral degrees.

ODU is one of Virginia's top Ph.D. research institutions and receives about $13 million annually in research grants and contracts. ODU's proximity to NASA Langley Research Center in Hampton has helped it become the leader among Virginia universities in NASA research contracts. ODU recently formed a partnership with the Continuous Electron Beam Accelerator Facility (CEBAF), a massive nuclear physics project that should open in Newport News in 1993. The university is expanding its physics faculty to meet its goal of having one of the country's premier physics programs.

ODU already is recognized worldwide for its Department of Oceanography, which offers two graduate degrees and includes the Center for Coastal Physical Oceanography. ODU's Applied Marine Research Laboratory conducts environmental studies for regulatory agencies and private organizations.

At ODU degree programs include business, education, science and English. There are 16 varsity sports, including basketball, sailing and soccer. In 1992 both ODU's sailing and field hockey teams were ranked No. 1 in the country.

Besides its Norfolk campus on Hampton Boulevard, ODU operates the Old Dominion University Peninsula Center in Hampton and an off-campus program in Portsmouth. It is a partner in the ODU-NSU Virginia Beach Graduate Center. A variety of courses is offered at the satellite locations, which utilize both on-site instructors and teleconferencing. ODU widely uses telecommunications. Recently about 1,000 students in various areas took 36 of ODU's credit courses by using television link-ups.

REGENT UNIVERSITY
Virginia Beach   523-7400

Founded in 1977 as CBN University, this private graduate school gained a new name in 1990. Regent shares an 800-acre campus in Virginia Beach with The Christian Broadcasting Network. Its 800 students come from across the United States and 20 countries. They can earn any of eight masters degrees in business, communication, counseling, education, government, law, ministry and theology.

Regent is the only university in South Hampton Roads to offer a law degree. All its classes are taught from a Christian perspective.

Although Regent is accredited by the Southern Association of Colleges and Schools, its law school is seeking accreditation from the American Bar Association. The school currently has provisional status from the ABA.

TIDEWATER COMMUNITY COLLEGE

Chesapeake	547-9271
Portsmouth	484-2121
Virginia Beach	427-7100

Started in 1968, Tidewater Community College provides training and higher education throughout the region. It has campuses in the Green Run area of Virginia Beach, the Churchland area of Portsmouth and the Great Bridge section of Chesapeake. TCC is working to open a branch in downtown Norfolk by 1995. TCC also offers off-campus programs at area high schools, military bases and other locations.

With more than 18,000 students – the majority of them part time – TCC is the second largest public community college in Virginia. TCC offers two-year associates degrees as well as occupational training in 90 different programs. In addition to academic courses in English, math and business, TCC offers training in such fields as truck driving, landscaping and welding. Some TCC graduates transfer to four-year colleges while others launch right into their careers.

VIRGINIA WESLEYAN COLLEGE

Norfolk/Virginia Beach 455-3200

Sitting astride the Norfolk-Virginia Beach city line, Virginia Wesleyan was founded in 1966. It has a 300-acre campus and a student body of 1,440. Students come from 30 states and 13 foreign countries. The private college is affiliated with the United Methodist Church and offers a liberal arts curriculum.

Virginia Wesleyan students can earn bachelors degrees in 30 areas, including business management, communications and physics. They can participate in eight varsity sports, including basketball, baseball and tennis.

The college's adult studies program schedules classes early in the mornings, at night and on weekends. It is aimed at working adults eager to return to college and earn a degree. To keep college within working students' budgets, tuition is half-price for evening classes. One popular offering is an alternative certification program for professionals who want to become teachers. Participants must have degrees in either math, science, English, history or a foreign language. By taking three concentrated courses, student teaching for a semester and passing the national teacher's exam, they can be certified to teach.

Other Opportunities

Educational options abound in Hampton Roads. Here is a sampling of what is offered in the region:

*A masters degree in transpersonal studies from Atlantic University. The private university is affiliated with the Virginia Beach-based Association for Research and Enlightenment and the Edgar Cayce Foundation. It also offers an independent studies program. Call 428-1512.

*Courses in law enforcement, data processing, English and business at the Suffolk branch of Paul D. Camp Community College. At this public college, associate degrees are available in some fields with certificates offered in more technical fields. Call 925-2283.

*An associate of applied science degree in business management from Commonwealth College. This proprietary, two-year college has branches in Norfolk, Virginia

Beach and Portsmouth. Its programs include computer science and hotel and restaurant management. Call 626-3247.

*An associate degree from ECPI Computer Institute in Virginia Beach. The proprietary school offers training in such fields as computer programming, word processing and accounting. Call 490-9090.

*A two-year culinary arts degree from Rhode Island-based Johnson & Wales University. The University has a Norfolk branch of its College of Culinary Arts that trains chefs. It also offers a series of excellent one-night community classes for people who love to cook. Call 853-3508.

*Graduate courses at the Hampton Roads Graduate Center run jointly in Virginia Beach by the University of Virginia and Virginia Tech. Among the offerings are engineering degrees and teacher recertification. Call 552-1890

Other outside colleges and universities offering degrees here are: Central Texas College, City Colleges of Chicago, Embry Riddle Aeronautical University, Florida Institute of Technology, George Washington University, King James Bible College, Saint Leo College, Tabernacle Baptist Theological Seminary and Troy State University.

Photo: Virginia Wesleyan College

Students at Virginia Wesleyan College take a break between classes.

The sun and sea — an ageless prescription for good health.

Inside
Hospitals

*I*f you want to see what health looks like carried to its most robust level, look no further than the medical community of Hampton Roads. Apparently armed with a powerful vaccine against the symptoms of recession, hospitals throughout the region are expanding, cutting edge specialized programs have been introduced, and world renowned volunteer programs have reached new proportions.

On the expansion front in just the last year, Norfolk's Children's Hospital of The Kings Daughters broke ground for a $73.5 million, eight-story, 387,000-square-foot addition that will more than triple the hospital's size. CHKD's neighbor, Sentara Norfolk General, is in the process of building a cancer institute into its six-story addition that will also increase emergency room facilities. Eastern Virginia Medical School completed its $12.5 million Jones Institute for Reproductive Medicine, a brand new 60,000-square-foot facility that hosts the incredible in-vitro fertilization program that gave our nation the first successful birth using the in vitro technique, and has added more than 1,100 more healthy births to that record in the past 11 years.

Chesapeake General Hospi-

tal joins the expansion list with a $30 million, 50-bed addition. Maryview Medical Center is using $13.6 million to expand its emergency room and renovate a surgical suite, lobby and intensive care unit. DePaul Hospital is in the middle of a $10 million, three-year project to create a new critical care pavilion and ambulatory surgery center to complement its new laser center and renovated rehabilitation center. Portsmouth Naval Hospital is several years into an eleven-year $330 million expansion that will add an additional 550 new beds to the facility.

While all these millions prove that the medical community of Hampton Roads certainly knows how to spend a buck, it shows that they also know the humanitarian value of offering time and talent to benefit those less fortunate around the world. Headquartered here, the organization called "Operation Smile International" has donated reconstructive surgery to tens of thousands of indigent children in developing countries. Begun by local surgeon Dr. Bill Magee and his wife, Kathy, ten years ago and comprised of volunteer surgeons, physicians, nurses, dentists, social workers, psychologists, speech therapists and other good-hearted medical professionals, "Operation Smile" flies off several times a year with hundreds of these volunteers from around the country to travel in teams to Africa, South America, Vietnam and the Philippines. Here they perform life-changing operations on children who would face a future of permanent disfiguration from such things as cleft palates and lips, burn scars and club feet. When not in the operating room, they provide educational support and training to health-care professionals in these struggling countries.

Also working to educate the medical communities of far-away countries like Egypt, Greece, Israel, Jordon, Syria and Turkey is another nationally applauded volunteer organization, "Physicians for Peace." Formed in 1987, teams of U.S. physicians and health care specialists travel several times a year to the Middle East to further their mission of "international friendships and peace through medicine." Its founder, Dr. Charles Horton, was honored in 1992 by Jordon's King Hussein for the acclaimed medical missions of his organization.

And, there's more. The Children's Hospital of the Kings Daughters is not only expanding its own facilities here in Hampton Roads, but in a land many moons away. It has forged a relationship with the former Soviet Union Ministry of Health that has led to the very first officially sanctioned U.S./ Russia health-care association. A critically-needed neonatal intensive care unit at a children's hospital in Moscow is being developed through this partnership while this book is being written.

While all this information should swell the pride of any newcomer to our area, the outstanding leadership of our emergency and trauma-care network will likewise be a comfort to any short-term visitor. Considered one of the best emergency care networks on the East Coast, we are an integral provider of Virginia's number two rated trauma-care system in the nation. Sentara Norfolk General's Level I trauma center and burn/trauma units, along with the Nightingale medivac helicopter, join Level II emergency rooms throughout the region. Numerous urgent care centers for minor emergencies and emergency medical services councils that oversee the area's rescue services are all considered absolutely top-notch.

So, from a bee-sting to bypass heart surgery, influenza to in-vitro fertilization, any medical assistance that might be required is not only here, but at the highest levels available anywhere in the United States. Here are the hospitals that form one of the finest medical networks in the country.

Norfolk

CHILDREN'S HOSPITAL OF THE KINGS DAUGHTERS
601 Children's Lane   *628-7500*

Built in 1961, CHKD operates as a regional referral center for pediatric specialists including cancer, cystic fibrosis, orthopedics, craniofacial and urological recon-

structive surgery. It has 152 beds, 32 of which are in the region's only non-military Level III Neonatal Intensive Care Unit.

One of the first of its kind in the country, CHKD's Transitional Care Pavilion has 12 beds for stable, ventilator-dependent children. The Children's Outpatient Center houses 50, along with specialty clinics for genetics, comprehensive opthalmology and weight control. The Child Speech and Language Center offers a special preschool for language acquisition as well as diagnostic and therapeutic programs; Children's Home Health provides home infusion therapy for children on intravenous medication and apnea monitors for high-risk infants as well as private duty nursing services and access to necessary medical equipment.

Associated with the hospital are the Barry Robinson Center for emotionally disturbed and learning disabled children and the Discovery Care Centers in Greenbrier, Chesapeake and Ghent in Norfolk.

DePaul Medical Center
150 Kingsley Lane   *889-5000*

A 402-bed, acute-care teaching hospital for Eastern Virginia Medical School, DePaul was founded in 1855 by the Daughters of Charity of St. Vincent de Paul and is affiliated with the Charity National Health System, the nation's largest not-for-profit health care

provider.

Its "Centers of Excellence" include The Cancer Center, a 30-bed unit selected by the American College of Surgeons as a teaching hospital cancer program; The Center for Birth, offering single-room maternity care (the latest concept in family-centered maternity service); The Diabetes Center, one of the most comprehensive in the region and the inpatient component of the Diabetes Institutes of Eastern Virginia Medical School; The Heart Center; The Eye Center which offers laser procedures; and the Gerontology Institute which offers a comprehensive range of services for those 65 and over.

Just opened is DePaul MedExpress, a quick and convenient service for minor emergencies within the confines of the Center's emergency facilities. It's the place to go for colds, cuts or minor mishaps that do not require full-blown emergency room treatment.

LAKE TAYLOR HOSPITAL
1309 Kemspville Road   *461-5001*

A 332-bed, long-term care/chronic disease hospital, Lake Taylor is governed by the Hospital Authority of Norfolk and managed by Riverside Health System. The 100-year-old hospital is the only one in the state that offers chronic disease care including AIDS treatment.

Included in the facility is a

Tidewater Health Care Meets The Needs Of Hampton Roads

Tidewater Health Care provides quality health services through a comprehensive system of health care providers dedicated to the cost-effective improvement of the health status of citizens of Hampton Roads.

**VIRGINIA BEACH
GENERAL HOSPITAL**

**PORTSMOUTH
GENERAL HOSPITAL**

**TIDEWATER
HEALTH SERVICES**

**BEACH HEALTH
SERVICES**

**VIRGINIA BEACH
HEALTH FOUNDATION**

**PRIORITY
HEALTH PLAN**

**TIDEWATER
HEALTH CARE**

*1080 First Colonial Road
Virginia Beach, Virginia 23454
804.496.6260*

104-bed wing providing intensive recuperative care for patients with long-term chronic diseases and a 229-bed nursing facility for long-term residents who require either skilled or custodial care.

NORFOLK COMMUNITY HOSPITAL
2539 Corprew Avenue   *628-1400*

Opened in 1915, this 202-bed facility offers specialized services including therapeutic counseling, nuclear medicine, stress testing, outpatient surgery, peripheral vascular lab and a renal dialysis center.

NORFOLK PSYCHIATRIC CENTER
Granby Street at Kingsley Lane   489-1072

With in-patient and day treatment programs for adults and adolescents, this 62-bed psychiatric hospital provides therapy for individuals, groups and families. Along with recreation, occupational and expressive therapy, a chemical dependency recovery program, detoxification facility and rehabilitation program for those addicted to alcohol and drugs are offered by NPC.

NDC+ MEDICAL CENTER
850/880 Kempsville Road   461-5900

A well-respected independent urgent care facility with expertise in dermatology, gerontology, neurology, rheumatology and internal medicine, NDC+ also offers a full menu of occupational medicine services, including pre-employment examinations, executive physicals and Worker's Compensation treatment. A full service laboratory and x-ray facility is on-site.

SENTARA LEIGH HOSPITAL
830 Kempsville Road   466-6700

An acute care facility established in 1903, this 250-bed, all private-room hospital operates a 10-bed pediatric unit and new Family Maternity Suite featuring 16 suites for LDRP (labor/delivery/recovery/postpartum).

Special services include cardiac catherization, an expanded imaging center with nuclear medicine, C.T. scanning, MRI, telemetry, one-day surgery, breast diagnostic center and 24-hour emergency room.

The hospital's Physical Therapy Specialty Center specializes in back, orthopedic and sports medicine; the Mobile Medical Diagnostic Services Unit provides X-rays and EKG's to nursing homes and retirement communities as well as mammography to businesses. Of note is Tel-Med, a telephone tape library with information on more than 200 health-related subjects.

SENTARA NORFOLK GENERAL HOSPITAL
600 Gresham Drive   628-3000

Our largest, and considered by many to be our best, Sentara Norfolk General is a 644-bed, acute care facility and the primary teaching hospital for Eastern Virginia Medical School.

The 104-year old hospital provides the broadest spectrum of services, including a Level I trauma center, Nightingale medivac helicopter service for southeastern Virginia and northeastern North Carolina, regional burn center, The Heart Pavilion, The Sentara Cancer Institute, hospice, high-risk preg-

Around The Nation, We're Known For Our Advanced Technology. Around Town, We're Known For Our Compassion.

When people in Colorado think of DePaul, they think of our diabetes expertise. When DePaul is mentioned in Washington, D.C., so is our fully equipped laser center. But when someone in our neighborhood talks about DePaul, they talk about the friendly smiles. The tenderness. The comfortable atmosphere.

You see, DePaul is devoted to serving our local community. And when we see needs in the area, we develop health centers to address those needs.

Compassion. Respect. Concern for the people in our community. These have made DePaul the advanced medical center it is today. They are what keep us on the leading edge, as does our affiliation with the Daughters of Charity, the largest not-for-profit health care system in the country.

So if you, or someone you love, needs medical care, ask your doctor about DePaul Medical Center and receive the kind of patient care you won't find anywhere else in the region. Because before we use our technology, we use our hearts.

DePaul
Medical Center

nancy center, Women's Health Pavilion, kidney and heart transplants, renal dialysis, Kidney Stone Center of Virginia, Imaging Center, Lions Sight and Hearing Center, Eating Disorders Center of Virginia and Sleep Disorders Center of Virginia.

The hospital manages the School of Allied Health Sciences, which trains nurses and professionals in eight fields, and is affiliated with the Jones Institute for Reproductive Medicine, the Institute for Plastic and Reconstructive Surgery and Specialized Urologic Surgery.

Portsmouth

FHC OF PORTSMOUTH
301 Fort Lane   *399-3300*

FHC operates The Pines Residential Treatment Center, The Phoenix at Portsmouth Psychiatric Center and Crawford Day School. It offers specialized comprehensive mental health care programs for adults and children.

MARYVIEW MEDICAL CENTER
36 High Street   *398-2200*

Part of the Bon Secours Health Systems, Inc. of Marriottsville, Maryland, Maryview is a 267-bed, general hospital that offers a wide variety of technologically advanced diagnostic in-patient and out-patient services. It includes many "Centers," including the newly remodeled Family Birth Center, the Martha W. Davis Cancer Center, Plastic Surgery Center, MRI Center, Eye Center and Breast Center. It also operates three Maryview MedCare Centers, free-standing urgent care facilities.

Included in the current $13.6 million expansion and renovation project are a new ambulatory surgery pre-operative and recovery area, sterile processing and outpatient testing, a new Intensive Care Unit and an expanded emergency department.

Adjacent to the general hospital is Maryview Psychiatric Hospital, a 54-bed facility that provides psychiatric and chemical dependency treatment for adults and adolescents. Along with a Women's Treatment Program and a Pain Management Program, the facility offers the innovative "Turning Point" program for patients in the early to middle stages of chemical dependency.

PORTSMOUTH GENERAL HOSPITAL
850 Crawford Parkway   *398-4000*

Three hundred and eleven beds strong, nonprofit Portsmouth General provides acute care, diagnostic and educational services. It is the only Portsmouth hospital to provide full service obstetrical care featuring private rooms, birthing rooms, a new-born nursery operated by Children's Hospital of the Kings Daughters along with Lamaze classes, Stork Night/hospital tours, sibling awareness classes and other programs and support groups for parents.

Other specialty areas include the Center for Sight, a surgical center dedicated to the diagnosis and treatment of eye disease, The Cardiac Fitness Center, an in-patient rehabilitation program, and Homelife Health Care. Community outreach programs include the Dia-

betes Education Program, the Better Breathers Club (for those with chronic lung disease) and Mended Hearts (for heart surgery patients). It is affiliated with The Urgency Care Center at 2425 Taylor Road in Chesapeake.

PORTSMOUTH NAVAL HOSPITAL
Foot of Effingham Street   *398-5000*

The oldest naval hospital in the United States and the second largest naval hospital in the country, the 500-bed Portsmouth Naval Hospital offers superlative health care to the military community, including active duty, their dependents and retirees.

Suffolk

OBICI HOSPITAL
1900 N. Main Street   *934-4000*

A 243-bed medical center, Obici offers an affiliated three-year registered nursing school and one-year LPN school along with diagnostic and acute care services.

Special services include neuro-ophthalmology, a Psychiatric Care Center, a Women's Health Center, cardiac catherization lab and cardiac rehabilitation, comprehensive radiology department, mobile MRI and mobile lithotripsy, rehabilitation medicine, outpatient surgery and a 24-hour emergency department.

Virginia Beach

SENTARA BAYSIDE HOSPITAL
800 Independence Boulevard   363-6100

Obstetrics, diabetes center, intensive and coronary care, surgery, physical therapy, radiology, nuclear medicine, emergency room and community classes are offered at this 250-bed, acute care facility.

VIRGINIA BEACH GENERAL HOSPITAL
1060 First Colonial Road   481-8000

Home to the Tidewater Perinatal Center for high-risk pregnancies, Virginia Beach General is a full-service, 274-bed hospital. It provides a full range of technologically advanced services, including a Level II intensive care nursery, open-heart surgery, diagnostic cardiology, nuclear cardiology, cardiovascular therapy and coronary care. Along with intensive care and critical care units, it offers an excellent emergency room.

Special centers at VBGH include the Cardiac Fitness Center, the Sleep Disorders Clinic, the Heart Institute, the Department of Neuroscience, the Coastal Cancer Center, the Ambulatory Surgery Center and Birthing Center.

In a cooperative venture with Riverside Health System, Tidewater Health Care, parent corporation of VBGH, operates a 60-bed long-term care facility called Windermere on the hospital campus.

VIRGINIA BEACH PSYCHIATRIC CENTER
1100 First Colonial Road   496-6000

This private, 60-bed facility provides comprehensive psychiatric and substance abuse services for children, adolescents, adults and families. Among its many services are free support groups, outpatient referrals, day treatment services and in-patient services.

It also offers the Mental Health Crisis Line which has qualified professionals who provide free, confidential consultations 24 hours a day, seven days a week.

Emergency Services

Whether a Hampton Roads resident or a visitor to our medically astute community, if a crisis requires ambulance service, you can be assured of attention from the best in the business. Every member of our phenomenal ambulance crews has taken at least 125 hours of training and has been certified by the state of Virginia as an Emergency Medical Technician. Even more training can be claimed by cardiac technicians and paramedics.

Because speed of response is critical in emergency situations, you might just find a fire truck wheel up to your door. Not to worry. All Hampton Roads firefighters have been extensively trained as "first responders," and if they are the closest emergency vehicle to your given address, they will be first on the scene.

If your situation does not warrant calling out our emergency angels, you will most likely find a free-standing acute care facility or hospital emergency room close to where you are. Regardless of where you go, or who you might need to call, we advise that you take not only personal identification, such as a driver's license and medical insurance card, but a list of current prescription medicines and respective dosages for any examining physician.

Physician Matchmakers

If you are new to the area, asking co-workers or neighbors about the physicians and dentists of choice is an excellent way to make the doctor-connection. If you would like more information, however, there are several referral services that are on standby to answer any of your questions about the selection process for a physician for the members of your family. Feel free to call any of the following for no-charge, no-obligation information:

Norfolk Academy of
Medicine   622-1421

Portsmouth Academy
of Medicine   398-4100

Virginia Beach Medical
Society   481-4516

Chesapeake Medical
Society   547-7800

Sentara Norfolk General
Physician Referral
Service   628-3677

Ask A Nurse
Riverside Health
Systems   398-4454

Portsmouth General
Hospital   1-800-533-1852

Tidewater Dental
Society   627-8534

Tidewater Optometric
Society   490-4015

HEALTH DEPARTMENTS
Norfolk   683-2700
Portsmouth   393-8585
Chesapeake   547-9213
Virginia Beach   431-3500
Suffolk 925-2300

The Norfolk skyline

Inside
Business & Industry

One symptom of our country's economic roller coaster that Hampton Roads is not accustomed to dealing with is the negative G's of the downward force of recession. After all, we've always been strapped tight in our seats by the comforting power of our strong military presence. Even in the 1980s, while we watched those news clips of distraught laid-off workers, we happily skipped from one thrilling business ride to the next, and added nearly 200,000 civilian and military jobs during those years. In fact, during that dismal period, Hampton Roads grew faster than 90 percent of the nation's metropolitan statistical areas, according to the Hampton Roads Planning District Commission.

Well, the carnival has closed. By the fall of 1990, the downsizing of service businesses, construction companies, banks and shipyards had come home to our own backyards. Even our military, facing the groundswell for national defense spending cuts, found that many get-a-job/keep-a-job ticket booths were slammed shut.

While many economic ringmasters are convinced that it will continue to rain on Hampton Roads' parade, others are cautiously optimistic about the future. Even

though a worldwide 25 percent military force reduction (that's 500,000 jobs) looms heavy on the horizon, our position as host to the world's largest Navy base – and heavy concentration of other military installations – could well mean the infusion of military personnel from closed bases around the world. And, that hope is what gives us all, civilian and military, an outlook entrenched in a better tomorrow.

With all that discussion of gloom out of the way, we flip the page to the good news about the Hampton Roads business and industry scene. Sharp prognosticators that we are, we've been fortifying our economic base with a hot-bed of back-office operations and the "fulfillment" industry. Enter mega-companies like United Services Automobile Association (USAA) with a brand new corporate complex in Norfolk. Household International Inc. is putting down credit card processing roots in Chesapeake – where it will employ 1,400 – to neighbor its Household Finance Corp., 700 employees strong.

Adding even more computers and telephones is our "fulfillment" industry. Think Lillian Vernon Corp. and the QVC Network (the shopping channel). The retail front claims more than 133,000 workers, and general service sector employees number 191,000 at last count.

But for employment giants, look to the sea. To Newport News Shipbuilding which counts more than 25,000 workers on its payroll, Virginia's single largest private employer. To the Port of Hampton Roads, the East Coast's busiest, where 75 shipping lines ship an estimated $9 billion in annual exports that give another 115,000 residents a place to hang their hard hats. Then, of course, there's the military, with more than 100,000 active duty personnel. Add in local, state and federal government employees and that number swells to over 272,000.

We can't talk sea-biz without applause for the thriving cash crop of our watermen. Virginia's seafood business is a $442 million industry, and we can claim an annual haul of 103 million pounds of oysters, clams, crabs and fin-fish, making us the third most productive fishing region in the country.

The sea brings us industry from other lands as well. A global melting pot for international business, more than 60 foreign-based firms have set up Hampton Roads operations just in the last decade, bringing the list of foreign owned or operated firms to 125. From Japan: Canon Virginia, Mitsubishi Kaisei Virginia/Kaisei Memory Products, Inc. and Sumitomo Machinery Corp. of America. From Germany: Stihl Inc., whose U.S. headquarters is in Virginia Beach. In Chesapeake, find Volvo Penta Production, Inc. and look no further than your local Food Lion to find the Belgian connection.

Speaking of food, we can't neglect to recognize our agricultural community. While we city folk find their ways mysterious, they alone are responsible for maintaining the productivity of our fertile farmlands, first nurtured nearly 400 years ago. Peanuts, soybeans, corn and livestock thrive in our temperate climate, and support landowners with generations of farming in their blood.

Unfortunately, our suburban sprawl has encroached upon much of the rich soil formerly earmarked for cash crops, dwindling the usable acreage and putting many farmers out to pasture. Many other farmers who work in the shadow of the city are getting urban-smart, however, inviting us onto their land for pick-your-own strawberries and veggies. If you're a newcomer, or visiting during a harvest season, this is one down-country experience that is a treat for the whole family.

And lastly, there's tourism, a $1.5 billion Hampton Roads industry.

If you're a visitor to our region, we want you to know that you are supporting more than 40,000 full- and part-time workers who hustle to spit-polish our more than 40 historic sites and museums, three theme parks and as many state parks. We thank you, and the four million others, who choose our area as a vacation spot every year.

Want to take an advanced course in Hampton Roads business? Follow through this brief city-by-city tour of the industry that supports our pro-business environment backed by the state's right-to-work laws:

Norfolk

Traditionally the region's financial center, Norfolk is secure in this claim by being mid-Atlantic headquarters for NationsBank, the result of a merger of Sovran Financial Corp., Atlanta-based C&S and NCNB of Charlotte, North Carolina. It is home based in the 21-story office tower that forms the nucleus of the downtown area.

Rising two-stories higher than the NationsBank building is the gorgeous new Marriott Hotel and adjacent Waterside Convention Center, and under construction at this writing are two new downtown landmarks-to-be. Harbor Park, a state-of-the-art ballpark facility that will be home to the Norfolk Tides AAA baseball club, and National Maritime Center, a multi-million dollar world-class marine showcase of interactive exhibits and displays along with working labs and the Hampton Roads Naval Museum. Look for its grand opening in early 1994.

Mr. Peanut

In 1913 Italian immigrant Amedeo Obici decided to move his fledgling Planters Nut and Chocolate Co. from Pennsylvania to Virginia. He chose Suffolk as the best location and borrowed $25,000 to finance the relocation.

Obici's new Suffolk processing plant put him in the heart of where large Virginia peanuts flourish. Suffolk soon became known as "The Peanut Capital of the World."

By 1916 Planters needed a corporate symbol so it created a contest that offered a prize of $5 to the person submitting the best sketch. The winner was a 14-year-old Suffolk boy who drew a peanut with arms and crossed legs and labeled it "Mr. Peanut." Later a commercial artist added a monocle, top hat and cane to give the mascot his distinctive look.

Today Planters is owned by RJR Nabisco. The Suffolk plant, whose 500 workers roast and package nuts, is part of the company's Planters Division. Fourteen cast iron statues of the dapper Mr. Peanut line the fence outside the 1913 plant. By late 1994 Planters will replace the aging plant with a new one across the street. In the meantime Mr. Peanut aficionados can check out his memorabilia in a small museum in the old factory at 200 Johnson Ave. Hours are 8 AM-4:30 PM Monday through Friday. Other Mr. Peanut artifacts are on display in the basement of Riddick's Folly, a historic home in downtown Suffolk. It is open 10 AM-5 PM Tuesday through Friday and 1-5 PM on Sunday.

Portsmouth

The mainstays of the Portsmouth economy are the government-operated Norfolk Naval Shipyard, the Portsmouth Naval Hospital, and a Coast Guard installation.

If you think that's a weird economic mix, weigh the success of Olde Towne, the city's revitalized historic district with rebricked streets and quaint gas lamps, to Portsmouth's push to be host city to Virginia's first Thoroughbred horse-racing track.

Chesapeake

Once the rural agricultural hub of the region, Chesapeake has traded coveralls for pin-striped suits, tractors for computers, grain silos for glitzy shopping malls. The city's 10 bustling office parks play host to business concerns from 31 countries, with a large concentration of Japanese manufacturers. This influx of ready-to-spend workers has birthed numerous new retail shopping strips, restaurants and service related businesses, along with acres of new residential communities.

Suffolk

The most rural city in the region, "Surprising Suffolk" lays claim to more land than any city in Virginia, and just recently was selected as the site for the new Naval Sea Combat Engineering Station, a consolidation of three posts in other parts of Hampton Roads. It is renowned for its amazing peanut crop (don't miss the Suffolk Peanut Festival!) and is also a strong manufacturing base for plants that produce Hills Bros. coffee, Planter's peanut snacks and Lipton Tea.

Virginia Beach

With tourism and conventions an enviable mainstay of the Virginia Beach economy, this resort city has beached the total inner-tube mentality for the serious conquests of the manufacturing, distribution and service industries. With more office space than any city in Hampton Roads, plus wide open spaces primed for industry seeking inexpensive acreage and a reliable work force, Virginia Beach has landed such respected companies as Lillian Vernon, who continues to expand operations and employment opportunities.

Virginia Beach has show-biz in its blood, too. It is home to Pat Robertson's Christian Broadcasting Network, producers of the 700 Club, and to The Family Channel, one of the country's fastest-growing cable networks that just recently made its debut on the New York Stock Exchange. 1991 saw the grand opening of the $36 million Founders Inn and Conference Center, and the continuing expansion of the Regent University complex.

New business and industry does not find Hampton Roads by accident. There are several high-powered organizations whose sole mission is to aggressively pursue more and more business investment in our market. Anticipating reductions in Department of Defense spending in the Hampton Roads region, the impact of the current recession on employment, and growing competition in the global marketplace, our Chamber of Commerce is in the earliest efforts to develop what it calls "Plan 2007," a blueprint for the region's future economy.

Matching the vision of our extremely active Chamber of Commerce, there's Forward Hampton Roads, the Chamber's umbrella marketing and information resource organization that supports valiant municipal and state efforts to seduce large corporations to the region.

For small business, there's no lack of assistance either. The Small Business Development Center of Hampton Roads stands ready to provide business advice, counseling and assistance at no cost. The Entrepreneurial Center at Old Dominion University is a fertile incubator for emerging companies, offering administrative and office support in the formative years of development. Lastly, there's the state of Virginia supported Center for Innovative Technology, a superlative resource for business, utilizing a worldwide data base and academic network to help business solve technology-based problems.

For more information about the state of the Hampton Roads economy, we will direct you to the following sources:

Departments of Economic Development:
Norfolk   441-2941
Portsmouth   393-8804
Chesapeake   523-1100
Virginia Beach 430-4567
Suffolk   934-2303

Hampton Roads Chamber of Commerce:
Regional Headquarters 622-2312
Norfolk Office   622-2312
Portsmouth Office   397-3453
Chesapeake Office   547-2118
Virginia Beach Office   490-1221
Suffolk Office   539-2111

Other excellent information sources:
Forward Hampton Roads 627-2315

Small Business Development Center of Hampton Roads   622-6414

The Entrepreneurial Center/Old Dominion University   683-3000

Better Business Bureau 627-5651

Inside
Media

*H*ampton Roads residents are a very nosy bunch. We want to know what's happening and where, when and why. And, we want to be thoroughly entertained...twenty-four hours a day.

No problem. In fact, Hampton Roads is one of the most fiercely competitive media markets in Virginia. In just the radio category, we can boast more stations than markets twice our size. Flip on the tube, and you'll find not only the big three, but more than 50 cable channels all fighting for your attention. In print, there are daily newspapers as well as scores of weekly specialty publications that appeal to everything from parenting to partying, marine life to metaphysics, home searching to higher consciousness.

No matter what you want to know about the heartbeat of Hampton Roads, it's as close as a flick of a button or the black and white of a tabloid. Whether it's a helicopter traffic report at six in the morning or a radio talk show at midnight, plug into Hampton Roads' media and, in no time at all, you'll sound just like a native.

Radio

Every market has its own favorite radio personalities that they love, and love to hate. We're no different. Local celebs have earned their notoriety by a) being outspoken, b) being on-air for more years than they, or anyone else, can remember, and c) being one taco short of a combination platter. Talk radio's Pat Murphy riles us every morning, WCMS's Joe Hoppel is our answer to Mr. Country-Western, and what can we say about Henry "The Bull" Del Torro, a real piece of work whose antics on and off air match wits with the hutzpa of the Energizer Bunny.

Beach music and Bach, hard rock and sharp talk, fast jazz and easy listening...it's all here on your dial in Hampton Roads.

The programming listed here for each station is current as of this writing, but stations jockeying for higher ratings have been known to change formats overnight.

FM Stations

WAFX 106.9

Here comes "The Fox" with round the clock classic rock, local news and traffic. Boogy, boogy.

WCMS 100.5

Country music, old and new, and one of the most listened to stations in the market. When it comes to country, no one sings a sweeter song than WCMS. ABC, local news, traffic reports. Continuous.

WFOG 92.9

Always a rating leader, with easy listening that's quite a relief from hard rock. Add in a unique blend of vocal favorites, golden oldies and light jazz. AP, local news, continuous.

WFOS 88.7

The oldest high-school radio station in Virginia, WFOS, operated by the Chesapeake school system, mixes classical programming with a touch of big band and jazz. Mutual Broadcasting System and AP. 6 AM to midnight.

WGH 97.3

"Eagle 97" is taking the market by storm with all new country. Local news, continuous.

WHOV 88.3

Operated by Hampton University, this eclectic student-manned station broadcasts some of the best jazz around, with a little classical and hot salsa thrown in for good luck. Local news, 10 AM to 1 AM.

WHRO 90.3

The mainstay of this Public Broadcasting affiliate is classical music. Local news, continuous.

WHRV 89.5

WHRO's sister station, here you'll find all your NPR favorites, like All Things Considered, the National Press Club and the popular Morning Edition. Local news, traffic reports, continuous.

WKEZ 94.1

It's time for your favorite easy listening, big band sounds, 24 hours a day. AP, local news and traffic.

WLSV 96.1

Contemporary Christian.

WJQI 94.9

Joy 95 brings us soft adult contemporary sounds all day and night. Local news and traffic, too.

WQSF 96.5

Easy listening, plus AP, local news. Continuous.

WLTY 95.7

Oldies are us. "Oldies 97" features AP, UPI, local news and traffic. Continuous.

WMXN 105.3

"Mix 105" is adult contemporary, with all the hits.

WKOC 93.7

New rock defines "The Coast." NBC, local news, continuous.

WNOR 98.7

If there's a stick to the good old rock and roller in town, it's FM 99. Classic and current rock, plus bad boy Henry "The Bull" Del Torro and sidekicks Tommy Griffiths and Gigi Young get your mornings started. UPI, local news and traffic. Continuous.

WNSB 91.1

Jazz, big band and blues. UPI news; 7 AM to 1 AM.

WNVZ 104.5

Z-104 is for the Top 40 gang. Contemporary hits, local news and traffic around the clock.

WODC 88.5

Local and satellite ministries, along with Christian music and children's programs.

WOWI 102.9

More than 50,000 ears are tuned into #1-ranked 103-JAMZ every weekday morning for The Supreme Team of Chase "The Commander-in-Chief of the Base," Stan "The Man" Verrett and Cheryl Wilkerson. This station is hip all day long with urban contemporary music.

WWDE 101.3

If you want to be an Insider, catch Dick Lamb and his Breakfast Bunch every weekday morning on 2WD. Captain Crunch will get you going, with adult contemporary music filling the rest of the station's 24-hour broadcast day. CBS, local news and traffic.

WYFI 99.7

Christian Music, BBN, local news. Continuous.

WXRI 107.7

Continuous business news.

AM Stations

WBSK 1350

Black urban adult music. AP, NBN and local news, continuous.

WCMS 1050

Spins country hits just like her sister station on the FM dial. ABC, local news, continuous.

WESR 1330

Christian programming and music, along with AP news from 6 AM to midnight.

WGH 1310

All sports, all day. Continuous.

WJQI 1600

Adult soft contemporary music, just like sister station Joy 95, from sunrise to sunset.

WLPM 1450

Golden oldies between regional, state and national news. Continuous.

WKGM 940

Christian programming and music with Satellite Radio news. Sunrise to sunset.

WNIS 850

"The Big One" is talk radio in Hampton Roads. Local advocate Pat Murphy takes mornings; Rush Limbaugh grabs the afternoon hours. CBS and local news, continuous.

WNOR 1230

Catch the simulcast of "The

Bull" on 1230 each weekday morning, then settle in for '60s and '70s hits for the rest of the day. UPI and local news.

WPCE 1400

Political and religious leader Bishop L. E. Willis calls the shots at this station for gospel programming. Sheridan Broadcasting. Continuous.

WPEX 1490

Music from the '50s, '60s and '70s, plus Cable News Network and local news. Continuous.

WPMH 1010

Inspirational music and programs. USA radio news. 6 AM to 9 PM.

WTAR 790

The oldest radio station in town, 790 offers full service news and information, along with NBC news, weather and special sports broadcasting. Larry King carries the entire afternoon on weekdays. Continuous.

WTJZ 1270

Black contemporary inspirational. Read "gospel." Plus NBN, sports and local news. Continuous.

Television

Along with enough channels to make your VCR groan, Hampton Roads is home to three major electronic media companies. International Family Entertainment, based in Virginia Beach, owns The Family Channel, one of the top 10 cable channels in the country, which puts out popular original programming like "Big Brother Jake," taped right here in town. IFM is, in turn, owned by Christian Broadcast Network (CBN) patriarch Pat Robertson and son Tim, and although it shares the CBN complex, it is a for-profit company totally independent of the nonprofit CBN.

CBN is a world-wide network of Christian stations, most famous for it's popular "700 Club," produced at state-of-the-art facilities in Virginia Beach. If you'd like to watch a live taping of the show and take a tour of the studios, just call 424-7777 for ticket availability.

TeleCable Corp. is a Norfolk-based Landmark Communications spin-off that operates 21 cable TV systems in 15 states. TeleCable has gained national recognition as a pioneer in the field of multiplexing, the technology that allows premium cable channels to offer subscribers multiple screens.

TV Stations

(Listed in order of appearance on your dial)

WTKR CBS/Channel 3

The first television station to sign on the air in Hampton Roads, WTKR is where you'll find ratings-winner "60 Minutes," along with the rest of the CBS line-up. Long respected for their news reporting, the station is home to some longtimers like Ed Hughes, celebrating 25 years in the news biz. If you hate to wait for your evening news, there's "Live at 5" along with the succinct "Eleven at Eleven," which gives sleepy-heads eleven minutes of uninterrupted news, weather and sports at the eleven o'clock hour.

WAVY NBC/Channel 10

All your favorite NBC hits are here, from "The Today Show" to "Tonight with Jay Leno," along with a young, aggressive and well-respected local news team led by Terry Zahn and an attractive bunch of news, weather and sports professionals.

WVEC ABC/Channel 13

"The Spirit of Hampton Roads" gets much of its umph from long-time news anchor Jim Kincaid, a folksy kind of guy with some super solid broadcasting experience. His "notes" at the end of the ABC affiliate's 5:30 PM broadcast are popular favorites, mixing anecdotes about his family's farm in little Elam, Virginia, with insightful responses to the many letters he receives and comments on current events. This is one of local sports fan's best places to park on a chilly Monday night, when "Monday Night Football" crashes into your living room's red zone.

WHRO PBS/Channel 15

Our Public Broadcasting affiliate and champion of exceptional children's, educational and how-to programming. Catch Big Bird on "Sesame Street," the news team on "McNeil-Lehrer News Hour" and numerous specials on nature, the performing arts and more. WHRO has also produced many award-winning educational shows that have been seen around the country.

WGNT Independent/Channel 27

Catch your syndicated favorites on this independent station, along with "The 700 Club" with Pat Robertson and troop. In fact, this is the station, formerly known as WYAH, where Dr. Robertson launched his television ministry career.

WTVZ Independent/Channel 33

While Channel 33 is an independent station, here's where you'll find your favorite programming from the FOX Network.

Cable TV

Over 50 channels zip right into your home when you're cable

Insiders' Tips

Hot off the 1993 presses for all you military folk, a full-color beauty called *The Flagship* has just dropped anchor. The Navy Capital's only authorized newspaper, 45,000 copies will be published every Thursday and available free of charge at Navy and Marine Exchanges plus 500 other outlets throughout Hampton Roads.

connected, ranging from MTV to good old CNN and A&E. HBO, Showtime and Cinemax are popular premium add-on's, and pay-per-view is slowly establishing a following, especially for sports freaks who are denied access to ultimate showdowns in regular programming. Several cable companies operate in Hampton Roads. Contact the one that services your city for specific rates and installation fees.

Cox Cable, Norfolk, Virginia Beach, Portsmouth, 497-2011

Tele-Communications of Virginia, Inc., Chesapeake, 424-6660

Virginia Beach Cable Television, Virginia Beach Oceanfront, 425-0586

Falcon Cable TV, Suffolk, 539-2312

Newspapers & Magazines

What flavor do you want? Hipspeak on the hot band that's playing this weekend? Who's making the social scene in big style? How to potty-train without angst? These, and answers to many other pressing questions, will be answered to the fullest in one of Hampton Roads' newspapers and tabloid magazines. From the plethora of specialized publications that come (and sometimes go) from our market from week to week, you can be sure that if you're thirsty for knowledge, you'll not have any further to go than your local grocery store's pick-up rack to take a big drink. Here are the major pubs that appear with continuity, offering different spins on their respective themes, and keeping all of

us abreast of the newest, latest, hottest and most controversial subjects in the community.

Of special note to those who, because of disabilities, cannot see or hold printed material, Hampton Roads Voice is a free reading service heard on public radio station WHRV FM. The 24-hour service is supplemented by programming from Touch Network based in New York and provides daily readings of local, regional and national newspapers, special publications, monthly magazines and periodicals. Special equipment is needed to receive the closed circuit programming, and there is a waiting list. For more information call 489-9476 or 881-9476.

VIRGINIAN PILOT AND LEDGER STAR

The daily newspaper serving all of Southside Hampton Roads.

What you might miss in *The Virginian-Pilot* in the morning, you'll catch in its afternoon sister, the *Ledger-Star*. Owned by Norfolk based media giant Landmark Communications, it's basically the only "daily" game in town for both news lovers and advertisers. With the largest circulation of any daily newspaper in Virginia, *The Virginian-Pilot*, along with the *Ledger*, has a long tradition of excellence, with even a few Pulitzers to its credit. What it lacks for in competition is competently made up for in special interest supplements...community-oriented tabloids for each of the five Southside cities.

Also of note, is the recent addition of "Venture," a sports freak's utopia that lists every conceivable sporting event, class or tournament that's in the hopper for upcoming days. With a cover story aimed at a seasonally popular sport, it's in the sports section every Thursday.

For TV couch potatoes, there's the "Green Sheet," the ultimate TV listing guide each Saturday. And, for those who must party, party, party, check out "Preview" each Friday for all upcoming performances and complete movie and theater listings and reviews.

Pin-striped suit types get a full dose of business news each Monday in "Business Weekly." Anyone house hunting must have the latest copy of Saturday's "Real Estate Weekly" for the latest on-the-market reports as well as updated mortgage information from local lenders.

Community tabloids that focus on the haps in a smaller spectrum, and are published along with both morning and evening editions include:

Norfolk	*The Compass*
Virginia Beach	*The Beacon*
Portsmouth	*Currents*
Chesapeake	*Clipper*
Suffolk	*The Sun*

THE SUFFOLK NEWS-HERALD

Daily newspaper for Suffolk and surrounding areas

A general interest newspaper, *The News-Herald* features local happenings along with major international news of the day. It's at racks throughout the city or by subscription.

PORT FOLIO

Lifestyle Magazine, published by Landmark Communications

Don't let the fact that it's a free weekly fool you. This is the "bible" for those on the way up...and for those who are already there. Along with timely cover stories that highlight (or expose) a local personality or event, inside is a wealth of info about where to dine, to party and to meet the person of your dreams. Make sure you check out the first edition of every month. Inside is "Home," a voyeur's peek inside some of the most gracious and glamorous homes in the area. And, then there's the monthly "Health & Fitness" special, packed with all the information to make you feel guilty if you're not running laps before work. All in all, it's a slick piece of work that never fails to come up with topical, fascinating tales about who's making news in Hampton Roads.

MILITARY NEWSPAPERS OF VIRGINIA

Weekly publications for the major military bases

There are plenty of authorized weeklies that are distributed free on major military installations. They include: *The Casemate*, serving Fort Monroe; *The Flyer*, serving Langley Air Force Base; *The Wheel*, for Fort Story and Fort Eustis; and *Soundings*, for all Naval installations.

Also with military appeal:

The Gator, the official base newspaper of the Naval Amphibious Base, Norfolk

Jet Observer, official Base newspaper for Oceana Naval Air Station in Virginia Beach

Navy News, a privately-owned tabloid dealing with Navy-related issues

Service to the Fleet, a bi-weekly tabloid published by the Public Affairs Office of the Norfolk Naval Shipyard in Portsmouth

BYERLY PUBLICATIONS

Weekly community newspapers

Byerly has long been known for its commitment to the important little things in life, like what's going on next door. Cover to cover, these are decisively hometown papers, and a must for newcomers who want to get the full, and positive, picture of their new community. The Byerly publications include:

The Chesapeake Post, published each Wednesday

The Portsmouth Times, published each Thursday

The Virginia Beach Sun, published each Wednesday

VIRGINIA BUSINESS MAGAZINE

Here's a state-wide publication targeted at our slice of corporate America. Special editorial sections on travel, hospitality and the medical industry, to name a few, are especially helpful to a newcomer trying to get a firm handle on the workings of our business community.

Real Estate Magazines

Even if you've snagged the best Realtor in town, there are a number of real estate publications to help you focus before jumping in the car for the major open house assault. All are free, and multiplying at a rack at the grocery or drug store nearest you.

They include: *Home Search, Harmon Homes, Real Estate Digest, For Sale By Owner* and the Tidewater Builders Associations' *New Homes and Apartment Guides.*

Specialty Publications

There are numerous specialty publications in our market, each dealing with a specific hobby, avocation or interest. All are free and available at racks throughout the cities of Hampton Roads. Some of the most popular include:

FLASH

Hampton Roads' Music Magazine

This will tell you where to go and when to be there to make the music scene in town. With caustic rock notes, hot disc reviews, rock flash calendar and ads from the leading lyrical places in Hampton Roads.

GHENT MAGAZINE

For residents and want-to-be residents in Norfolk's most eclectic neighborhood. With in-depth business, resident and restaurant profiles, it's our area's *New Yorker* clone in tabloid size for avid readers.

VIRGINIA PATHWAYS

For those seeking guidance from a source other than the Insiders' Guide, this alternative monthly for holistic thought is for you. New agers will want to journey afar to snag the latest issue, filled with remarkably insightful dialog concerning higher consciousness of body, soul and spirit.

InSyte Magazine

Devoted to African-American culture and news, *InSyte* covers the gamut from movie and book review to fashion to political affairs.

Tidewater Parent

Anyone living with a human person under three feet tall should tuck a copy of this pub in the diaper bag. Published monthly, it is the definitive guide to child-rearing in Hampton Roads, with articles aimed at education, constructive play and mommy-relief.

The Compass Rose

The boating services guide for Hampton Roads and the lower Chesapeake, don't leave shore with out it. Marinas, dockside dining guide and boat-accessible calendar of events are all here.

Starboard Tack

Sailing the Chesapeake and beyond is the theme song for this free tabloid available at local marinas, yacht clubs and water-logged restaurants. It includes everything including the galley sink for the novice and experienced sailor.

Inside
Worship

*T*here are more than 500 churches and synagogues in Hampton Roads – enough to fill up nine pages of listings in the Yellow Pages directory. Worship options range from established main-line churches that are centuries old to nondenominational congregations started only a few years ago.

In recent years area churches and synagogues have seen a resurgence of young families coming back to the religion they abandoned during their teenage and college years. Many churches have been quick to respond to the needs of these younger members. Potluck family dinners, parenting classes, strong youth programs and free babysitting during committee meetings are just a few of the inducements that help keep the 30-something crowd hooked on religion.

Hampton Roads' religious heritage is more than 300 years old. A 1637 entry in the records of Lower Norfolk County, which yielded Virginia Beach and other area cities, ordered that a "penance of the church" be carried out by a local resident. At the time church services were held in private homes, but in 1639 Lynnhaven Parish church was built in what is now Virginia Beach.

Until the Revolutionary War began in 1776, the Anglican religion was the only one officially recognized in British-controlled Virginia. However, Rev. Frances Makemie introduced the Presbyterian religion to Norfolk while living here between 1684 and 1692. In Norfolk, First Presbyterian Church traces its roots to The Church on the Elizabeth River, which was founded before 1678.

Today there is still an Anglican church in Newport News. But there are also dozens of other religions represented here – from African Methodist Episcopal Zion to United Pentecostal. Besides the basic Baptist, Catholic, Episcopal, Jewish, Lutheran, Methodist, Presbyterian and Unitarian churches, there are numerous nondenominational churches. The region also has congregations affiliated with the Friends, Greek Orthodox, Mennonite and Muslim religions. Jewish synagogues include conservative, messianic, orthodox and reformed congregations. Temple Beth El on the outskirts of Suffolk dates from the early 1900s and is noted for having a congregation composed of African-American Jews.

Congregations range greatly

in size. Some have fewer than 50 members while others' rolls number in the thousands. Among the largest are First Baptist Church of Norfolk, Atlantic Shores Baptist Church and the Rock Church. All are in the Kempsville area of Virginia Beach and Norfolk. First Baptist has 6,000 members and relocated to the suburbs from downtown Norfolk in 1970. Atlantic Shores is an independent Baptist church with about 5,000 members. Rock Church is nondenominational with about 3,000 members. Anticipating more growth, it is building a new 5,000-seat sanctuary.

One major influence on the area's religion is having The Christian Broadcasting Network based in Virginia Beach. CBN's world headquarters includes studios that broadcast worldwide the "700 Club" TV talk show hosted by Rev. M.G. "Pat" Robertson, CBN's founder. Robertson's home is on the Georgian-style CBN campus as is Regent University, the Founders Inn and Conference Center and the Family Channel cable network. Although CBN isn't affiliated with any one religion, it has hundreds of employees and many followers in the region who lean toward fundamentalist churches. Therefore, there are quite a few of them in the populous Kempsville area near CBN.

If you're a newcomer, finding the right church involves checking out different ones to see what suits your needs. Get recommendations from friends and neighbors and scout out your neighborhood to see what churches are nearby. Then take your time attending services, classes and getting to know the members.

You can learn more about area churches by reading *The Virginian-Pilot/Ledger-Star's* Saturday religion page. Besides discussing topics of current interest, it includes listings of upcoming special programs and services at area churches. For recommendations on specific churches, contact the following offices of religious organizations:

Bahai Faith – 467-4008
Catholic Diocese of Richmond – 588-2941
Church of Jesus Christ of Latter Day Saints – 488-2239
Episcopal Diocese of Southern Virginia – 423-8287
Lutheran Council of Tidewater – 622-0125
Norfolk Baptist Association – 463-6525
Presbytery of Eastern Virginia – 423-2193
United Jewish Federation of Tidewater – 489-8040
United Methodist Church, Norfolk District – 473-1592

Some of the region's older churches have fascinating architecture and are a real treat to see. The downtown areas of Norfolk, Portsmouth and Suffolk have a concentration of massive church buildings dating from the 19th and early 20th centuries. The following are some of the more historic churches.

Norfolk

*Christ and St. Luke's Church, Olney Road and Stockley

Gardens (627-5665). Originally known as Christ Church, this Episcopal church is noted for its Gothic Revival architecture. It was built in Ghent around 1910 and features an ornate square bell tower.

*Freemason Street Baptist Church, Freemason and Bank streets (625-7579). This is Norfolk's oldest Baptist church. Its building was dedicated in 1850. When it was built the church was noted for its steeple, which had dozens of weathervanes and was the tallest structure in town. After it blew down in a storm in 1879 the steeple was replaced with only one weathervane on it.

*St. Mary's Catholic Church, 232 Chapel St. (622-4487). This is Norfolk's oldest and most elaborate Catholic church. Its majestic steeples are a downtown landmark. The current church was built in 1858 to replace one that burned. Inside are elaborate paintings, marble sculptures and stained-glass windows. One noted architect who

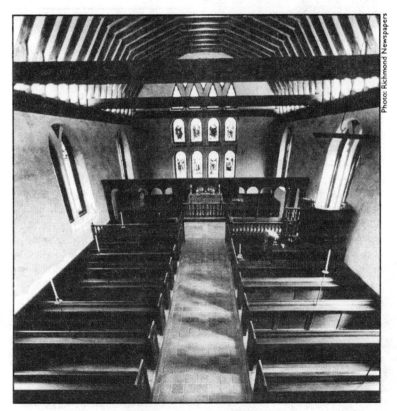

Photo: Richmond Newspapers

St. Luke's Church in Smithfield is the nation's only original Gothic church and the oldest existing church of English foundation.

visited the church in the early 1900s called St. Mary's "the best antebellum Gothic workmanship in the South."

*St. Paul's Episcopal Church, 201 St. Paul's Blvd. (627-4353). The church was built in 1739. After the burning of Norfolk in 1776, St. Paul's was the only building left standing in the city. The church still has a Revolutionary War cannon ball wedged in one wall and retains its original box pews. It also is noted for its Tiffany windows. Outside, a brick wall surrounds a peaceful, tree-shaded burial ground.

Virginia Beach

*Nimmo United Methodist Church, 2200 Princess Anne Rd. (427-1765). This is a traditional white-frame church that sits in the rural part of Virginia Beach on the way to Pungo. It was built in 1791 on land purchased for five shillings from Anne Nimmo. Although the building has had several additions, it retains its original charm.

*Old Donation Episcopal Church, 4449 N. Witchduck Rd.

(497-0563). This is the only surviving colonial church in what was Princess Anne County. Originally part of the Church of England, it affiliated with the new Protestant Episcopal Church of Virginia in 1785. Except for holding about one service a year, the church was abandoned for 40 years until 1882. The current building is the third one on the same site. It is a classic structure built in 1916. The church still owns several silver communion pieces it was given in the early 18th century.

Chesapeake

*Oak Grove United Methodist Church, 472 N. Battlefield Blvd. (547-2319). Founded in a home in 1770, this is one of the oldest churches in what was Norfolk County. It became a Methodist church in 1840, and two years later a small building was put on wheels and rolled a mile to the present location. The current church dates from 1852. The building is a traditional white frame structure that shares its design with Christ Church in Alexandria and Old St. John's

Church in New York.

Portsmouth

*Emmanuel AME Church, 637 North St. (393-2259). This is a historically black church whose congregation dates back to 1772 when it was a Methodist Episcopal Church. In 1871 the congregation affiliated with the African Methodist Episcopal Church. The red brick church dates to 1791. The interior features elaborate stained-glass windows and hand-carving, much of it done by slaves.

*Monumental United Methodist Church, 450 Dinwiddie St. (397-1297). This was the first Methodist congregation in Portsmouth, and its roots extend to 1772 when Portsmouth residents heard the first Methodist sermon preached south of the Potomac. The church was built in 1876 after another building was destroyed by fire.

*St. Paul's Catholic Church, 518 High St. (397-7066). Established in 1824, St. Paul's has had several buildings. This one is built of stone in an elaborate Gothic style with flying buttresses. The granite church was completed in 1897.

*Trinity Episcopal, 500 Court St. (393-0431). The church dates to 1762. It sits on land designated in 1752 for a church when the city of Portsmouth was first laid out. Outstanding features include Tiffany windows, an 18th-century burial ground and a brick wall around the churchyard that dates to the 1820s. The church has a stained-glass window dedicated in 1868 in memory of those who died "...in defense of their native state, Virginia, against invasion by the U.S. Forces." Protests by the U.S. Navy forced the church to remove the window and edit its message. The replacement window installed in 1870 is still there. However, the offending message is framed and resting on the windowsill.

Suffolk

*First Baptist Church, 237 N. Main St. (539-4152). The church was organized in 1827 with its first building constructed a year later. The current brick church was built in 1890 in a typical style of the day with an elaborate sanctuary.

*Glebe Episcopal Church, 4400 Nansemond Parkway, and St. John's Episcopal Church, 828 Kings Highway (255-4168). These two small churches are part of the same parish and are the only colonial-era churches remaining in Suffolk. The Glebe Church was built in 1738 and replaced an earlier structure. St. John's Church was the third built on this site. It was completed in 1756 and remodeled in 1888 to the appearance it has today.

*Main Street Methodist Church, 202 N. Main St. (539-8751). Modeled after a cathedral in England, this church was constructed in 1914. Its congregation dates to 1801, making it the oldest Methodist church in Suffolk. The red brick building has 14 stained-glass windows.

Photo: Richmond Newspapers

Loved ones await the arrival of the USS Shenandoah returning from the Persian Gulf War.

Inside
The Military

The minute you arrive in Hampton Roads you most likely will know this is a military community. But in case you're not sure, here are some clues:

*If you flew in, chances are good that you spotted at least a few Navy uniforms on the plane.

*If you're driving into downtown Norfolk or Portsmouth, you'll see gray-hulled Navy battleships docked at ship repair yards. A hodgepodge of shipyard cranes stand at attention ready to lower supplies to shipyard workers.

*Cross the Hampton Roads Bridge-Tunnel from Hampton to Norfolk and you can glimpse ships anchored at Norfolk Naval Base.

*Look skyward in Virginia Beach and you're likely to see a trail from an F-14 Tomcat or other fighter plane based at Oceana Naval Air Station.

*Arrive here by private boat, and you'll glide past miles of shipyards and Navy bases that hug the shoreline.

With this visual introduction, it won't take long to learn that Norfolk Naval Base is the largest Navy base in the world. Team it up with all the other branches of the Armed Forces located here – Army, Marine Corps, Air Force and Coast Guard –

– and you have one of the United States' largest concentration of military might.

Throughout the entire region there are more than 125,000 military personnel, 50,000 civilian Department of Defense workers and an estimated 44,000 military retirees. The region has seven of the country's 60 largest military installations. Its 20 shipyards, which rely heavily on military business, are the United States' biggest concentration of repair yards.

Norfolk is headquarters for the North Atlantic Treaty Organization command that oversees the Atlantic area. Attached to the NATO command are military officers from Canada and 10 European countries who come here to live and work.

In 1991 the Department of Defense spent $6.6 billion in the region, making it the backbone of the economy. That year Virginia ranked third in the country in Department of Defense spending with $17 billion coming into the state – the bulk of it in Hampton Roads and Northern Virginia. On a per capita basis, Virginia was first in defense expenditures.

The region's history is intertwined with that of the Revolutionary War, World War I, World War II and every other major war or conflict (see History section). During Operation Desert Storm in 1990 and 1991, more than 40,000 military personnel shipped out to the Persian Gulf and stifled the local economy. Before the battle groups left, ship repair yards, ship chandlers and other local companies worked around the clock to gear up for war. When the war heroes returned in 1991, they were greeted by thunderous celebrations not seen here since the end of World War II.

Since you'll encounter the military everywhere you go, you may be surprised to realize that it has loosened its grip on the economy in recent years. New industry coming into the area in the past decade has brought jobs that have nothing to do with the Department of Defense. A 1992 study by the Hampton Roads Planning District Commission shows that in 1969, 45 percent of all the region's employment was defense related. By 1990, less than 28 percent of jobs had direct ties to the military.

This economic diversity is a boon to the region as it waits anxiously to see how it will fare during military budget cuts. Local optimists prefer to believe the region will benefit as obscure bases in other parts of the country are consolidated into larger operations like the ones we have here. The Planning District Commission study gives some credence to that idea by showing that in 1971 less than 3.9 percent of the United States' armed forces were stationed in Hampton Roads. By 1990 that percentage had grown to more than 5 percent.

The region received good news in early 1993 when the Joint Chiefs of Staff Chairman Gen. Colin Powell recommended that Norfolk become the training center for all joint military operations. This would make Norfolk second in prominence only to the Pentagon.

The military gives Hampton Roads a unique flavor. Your neighbors will be people who have lived all over the world. However, they may move away within a few years to new duty stations. The comings and goings of large battle groups affect everything from rush hour traffic to business at area malls.

The following are the region's major military bases:

NORFOLK NAVAL BASE

This far-flung complex is in the Sewells Point area of Norfolk. It got its start in 1917 when the U.S. government purchased 474 acres of the old Jamestown Exposition Site for a Navy base. Another 300 acres were soon added by filling in adjacent waterways, and the base has expanded from there.

The base's naval station is homeport for 104 ships. During the year there are nearly 2,500 arrivals and departures from the station's 15 piers. Nearby is a submarine base that has 158 subs homeported there. A naval air station is home to about 25 aircraft squadrons. With an aircraft taking off or landing every three minutes, this is one of the world's busiest airports.

The Naval Public Works Center serves Navy operations in the Atlantic Ocean and Europe while the Naval Supply Center keeps ships

The Hampton Roads Naval Museum has exhibits focusing on significant naval events and the history of ship construction.

throughout the world stocked with 800,000 different items.

The biggest operation on the base is the Naval Aviation Depot (NADEP) whose 4,000 employees work in 90 buildings doing maintenance, engineering and other services in support of tactical naval aviation. NADEP is the largest employer in Norfolk.

Other major commands include the Atlantic Division of the Naval Facilities Engineering Command (LANTDIV), the Training Command of the U.S. Atlantic Fleet, the Fleet Training Center and the Atlantic Fleet Marine Force.

Located just down the road from the base are the headquarters for the Commander-in-Chief Atlantic Fleet (CINCLANT), which commands more than 220,000 personnel. The command supplies and services more than 300 ships and 2,000 aircraft.

Adjacent to the Atlantic Fleet headquarters is that of NATO's Supreme Allied Commander Atlantic (SACLANT). This command watches over ships and personnel in 12 million square miles of Atlantic Ocean – from the north Pole to the Tropic of Cancer and from North America to Europe and Africa.

LITTLE CREEK NAVAL AMPHIBIOUS BASE

This is the major base for the amphibious forces of the United States Atlantic Fleet. It is home to about 30 ships. The Norfolk base is on 11,000 acres next to the Chesapeake Bay. It is headquarters for the 4th Marine Expeditionary Battalion and is the East Coast base for the Landing Craft Air Cushioned craft (LCAC). More than 10,000 military personnel and civilians work at the base.

OCEANA NAVAL AIR STATION

This is home to the Navy's East Coast squadrons of F-14 Tomcats and A-6 Intruders. Twenty squadrons operate out of the 5,000-acre complex in Virginia Beach. This master jet base has a plane land or take off every two minutes. There are more than 10,000 civilians and military personnel at Oceana.

FLEET COMBAT TRAINING CENTER, DAM NECK

This 1,100-acre, oceanfront base has one of the best beaches in the area. Its real purpose, however, is to teach young recruits or boot camp survivors. It has a curriculum of more than 100 courses offered to about 15,000 sailors a year. Approximately 6,000 people are affiliated with the base.

NORFOLK NAVAL SHIPYARD, PORTSMOUTH

In 1992 the shipyard celebrated its 225th anniversary, making it the country's oldest naval shipyard. It occupies a four-mile stretch along the Elizabeth River in Portsmouth and has more than 800 buildings. The yard has the country's oldest dry dock, which opened in 1833. It employs about 11,000 workers who repair and improve everything from missile systems to berthing compartments on Navy ships.

NAVAL SECURITY GROUP ACTIVITY NORTHWEST

This activity operates on 4,500 acres in Chesapeake. It is a high-security intelligence base that monitors communications from around the world. It has about 500 Navy and Coast Guard personnel.

PORTSMOUTH NAVAL HOSPITAL

This is the oldest Navy hospital in the United States and is the second largest one in the country. Its first patients were admitted in 1830. The 500-bed hospital has a full range of services and operates several clinics. This hospital is in the midst of a $330 million renova-tion and construction project that will include a new 464-bed hospital to be completed in 2001.

ARMED FORCES STAFF COLLEGE

The college is part of the National Defense University, which started in 1946. Its Norfolk campus prepares mid-career officers for joint and combined staff duty during six overlapping sessions a year. Each has about 120 students who come for three months of intense study.

FORT STORY

This Virginia Beach Army base is located where the Chesa-

Help for Newcomers

The best source of help for new military families is Navy Family Services Center. It has a wealth of information and services for Navy and Marine Corps members and their dependents. The center has a Relocation Assistance Unit that has welcome packets and other information. If you get here ahead of your household goods you can rent cookware, cribs, cots and other necessities. Navy Family Services also has information on child care, jobs for spouses, counseling and many other services. The center is at 8910 Hampton Blvd. in Norfolk. Call 444-2102. To reach the center's 24-hour hotline call 444-NAVY.

If you arrive here by flying into Norfolk International Airport, look for the Airport Information Booth. There usually is a Navy representative stationed there to answer questions and help get you going in the right direction. There also is a Navy Welcome Center in Janaf Shopping Center in Norfolk.

To help get you oriented, read some of the free weekly or bi-weekly newspapers geared toward the military, available on base, in shopping centers and other public areas. They include *Soundings* and *Navy News* for the Norfolk Naval Base, the *Jet Observer* for the Oceana Naval Air Station and *The Wheel* for Fort Story.

Insiders' Tips

peake Bay meets the Atlantic Ocean at Cape Henry. It was created in 1917 and has 1,451 acres that include a great beach open to the public on weekends. The base is an installation of the U.S. Army Transportation Center Fort Eustis in Newport News. Fort Story has more than 2,000 military and civilian workers who maintain amphibious craft.

FIFTH COAST GUARD DISTRICT

The district is headquartered in Portsmouth and coordinates lifesaving efforts in the waters off Virginia, Maryland, North Carolina and the District of Columbia.

U.S. ARMY CORPS OF ENGINEERS

The Corps of Engineers' Norfolk District headquarters oversees several field offices around the state. The corps is involved in dredging and in issuing permits for construction in wetland and coastal areas. The office typically has had more than 300 employees, most of them civilians. But it is expected to expand to more than 700 as part of a nationwide consolidation of corps offices.

CAMP PENDLETON STATE MILITARY RESERVATION

Camp Pendleton is used mainly as an air defense artillery range. It is in Virginia Beach on the oceanfront and is the Virginia National Guard's summer training camp. Its 120 buildings can hold 1,700 troops.

PENINSULA BASES

Across the Hampton Roads Bridge-Tunnel are several other major bases that are included in the region's military complex. They are the Yorktown Naval Weapons Station in Yorktown, Langley Air Force Base in Hampton, Fort Eustis in Newport News and Fort Monroe in Hampton. Both Fort Eustis and Fort Monroe are Army bases. Newport News also has Newport News Shipbuilding, a private company that makes aircraft carriers and submarines. With more than 26,000 employees, the shipyard is the state's largest private employer.

Insiders' Tips

Guided tours of the Norfolk Naval Base are operated by Tidewater Regional Transit. You can board a TRT bus either at The Waterside festival marketplace or at the Naval Base Tour Office at 9079 Hampton Boulevard. Summer tours start every half hour. Tours are given less frequently during the rest of the year. But even in winter there is at least one tour a day. The cost is $4.50, $2.25 for children and retired people. For information call the tour office at 444-7955 or TRT at 623-3222.

Inside
Service Directory

Community Service Information

Police 911

Information Center of Hampton Roads 625-4543

Red Cross Language Bank (translators) 446-7760, 446-7756

Volunteer Action Center of South Hampton Roads 624-2400

United Way of South Hampton Roads 629-0500

United Way Help Line 627-1000

Battered Woman's Hotlines 625-5570, 393-9449

Response – Sexual Assault Support Group 622-4300

Tidewater AIDS Crisis Task Force 626-1027

Time of Day 622-9311

Medical

Emergency 911

Ask A Nurse 398-4454

Poison Control Center 1-800-552-6337

Physician Referral

Norfolk 622-1421
Virginia Beach 481-4516, 398-4454
Portsmouth 398-2131, 398-4454
Children 628-7500
Regional 1-800-SENTARA

Regional Resources

Better Business Bureau 627-5651

Forward Hampton Roads 627-2315

Hampton Roads Chamber of Commerce headquarters 622-2312

Chesapeake office 547-2118
Norfolk office 622-2312
Portsmouth office 397-3453
Suffolk office 539-2111
Virginia Beach office 490-1221

Hampton Roads Planning District Commission 420-8300

Retirement

American Association of Retired Persons (AARP) 481-7438

Southeastern Virginia Areawide Model Program (SEVAMP) 461-9481

Surfing Information

Surfing Regulations 428-9133

Surf Report 428-0404, 422-6015

Tourism

AAA of Tidewater Virginia Chesapeake office 547-9741
Norfolk office 622-5634
Portsmouth office 393-6471
Virginia Beach office 340-7271
Emergency 622-4321, 340-0533, 397-5941, 547-9742

Norfolk Convention & Tourism Bureau 441-5266, 1-800-368-3097

Norfolk Visitor Information Center 441-1852

Portsmouth Convention and Visitors Bureau 393-8481, 1-800-338-8822

Virginia Beach Department of Convention and Visitor Development 437-4700, 1-800-VABEACH

Virginia Beach Visitor Information Center 437-4888

Transportation

Amtrak 800-872-7245

Chesapeake Municipal Airport 421-9000

Hampton Roads Airport 488-1687

Hampton Roads Bridge-Tunnel
Traffic Report 640-0055
Office 627-6206

Norfolk Airport Shuttle 857-1231

Norfolk International
Airport 857-3200

Suffolk Municipal Airport 539-8295

Tidewater Regional Transit (TRT)
627-9291, 623-3222

Utilities

Cox Cable 497-2011

C&P Telephone 954-6222

Falcon Cable TV 539-2312

Hampton Roads
Sanitation District 460-2491

Southeastern Public Service Authority (recycling) 420-4700

TCI of Virginia 424-6660

Virginia Beach Cable Co. 425-0586

Virginia Natural Gas 466-5550

Virginia Power 858-4670

Waterworks
  Chesapeake 547-6352
  Norfolk 441-2334
  Portsmouth 393-8524
  Suffolk 925-6390
  Virginia Beach 427-4631

The Insiders' Guides Collection

The Insiders' Guide
to the Outer Banks

WRITTEN BY
DAVE POYER AND JAYNE DEPANFILIS

The Insiders' Guide to the Outer Banks is the only total guidebook to North Carolina's outer Islands. It is the standard reference for the traveling public. Whatever your budget, age or special interest, it will take you straight to the most exciting people and places the Outer Banks has to offer. Whether you come for business, pleasure or to find a new lifestyle, this book will save you time and money every day you use it. The 1993 edition marks the 14th anniversary of this guide! $12.95.

The Insiders' Guide
to Greater Orlando

WRITTEN BY
CYNTHIA GROSS &
CATHARINE COWARD

Orlando, Florida, is the vacation capital of the South as well as one of the fastest growing areas in the country. This indispensable 500-page guide will tell you everything you'll want to know about the sunny city and its surrounding neighbors. There's plenty of information on the major attractions, plus facts and insights into other enjoyable sites and activities the area has to offer.

Newcomers will feel as if they know the quickly-changing region better with the Insiders' Guide in hand. $12.95

The Insiders' Guide
To North Carolina's
Crystal Coast and New Bern

WRITTEN BY
TABBIE NANCE & SHERRY WHITE

For years, the Crystal Coast area – Morehead City, Atlantic Beach, Emerald Isle, Beaufort, Salter Path, Down East and other small communities – have drawn loyal visitors. Now there's a guide book to make those visits even better. You'll find it an indispensable guide to all the brightest and best this beautiful area has to offer. $12.95.

The Insiders' Guide
to Williamsburg

WRITTEN BY
MICHAEL BRUNO &
ANNETTE MCPETERS

Here's another great Insiders' book that helps visitors to this colonial capital city get the most out of their stay. Written by two insiders, it gives information on accommodations, restaurants, attractions, campgrounds, shopping and more on Williamsburg, Jamestown, and Yorktown. It has been totally rewritten for the 1992 edition.

The Insiders' Guide to Greater Richmond

WRITTEN BY
PAULA KRIPAITIS NEELY & DAVE CLINGER

The city of Richmond is considered by many to be one of the most beautiful and interesting of Southern cities. With close to 500 pages, this new Insiders' Guide will help visitors and locals alike experience Richmond to its fullest. History buffs, newcomers, business travelers and visitors will all find chapters to enrich and enhance their experiences in Virginia's capital city. $12.95.

The Insiders' Guide to Virginia's Blue Ridge

WRITTEN BY
LIN CHAFF & MARGARET CAMLIN

The Blue Ridge of Virginia, including the Shenandoah Valley region, is one of America's most visited areas. Let this Insiders' Guide take you to the beautiful country inns and bed and breakfasts, to the world-class resorts and top-rated restaurants, and introduce you to the many recreational activities offered here. The book will give you information on ski resorts, wineries, attractions, annual events and festivals, real estate and so much more. $12.95

The Insiders' Guide To Charleston

WRITTEN BY
ANNE JERVEY RHETT & J. MICHAEL McLAUGHLIN

South Carolina's Lowcountry draws thousands of visitors each year and none will want to go without this 500-plus page guide to the area. Included is information on history, architectural preservation, the arts, attractions, annual events, shopping, restaurants, bed and breakfast inns and other accommodations, recreation, real estate, retirement, day trips and more. It will show you around this beautiful Southern destination (and her surrounding cities) from a local's point of view. $12.95

Also Available

The Insiders' Guide to the Triangle of NC ($12.95) and The Insiders' Guide to Charlotte ($12.95).

Coming in 1993

The Insiders' Guide to Myrtle Beach, The Insiders' Guide to the Civil War and The Insiders' Guide to Washington, D.C.

Use our convenient order form on the following page to add to your collection of Insiders' Guides.

ORDER FORM

Use this convenient form to place your order for
any of the Insiders' Guides books.

Fast and Simple!

Mail to:
Insiders' Guides, Inc.
P.O. Box 2057
Manteo, NC 27954

or

for VISA or Mastercard orders call
1-800-765-BOOK

Name ————————————————————————————

Address ——————————————————————————

City/State/Zip ————————————————————————

Quantity	Title/Price	Shipping	Title/Price
	Insiders' Guide to the Outer Banks, $12.95	$2.50	
	Insiders' Guide to Richmond, $12.95	$2.50	
	Insiders' Guide to Virginia Beach / Norfolk, $12.95	$2.50	
	Insiders' Guide to Orlando, $12.95	$2.50	
	Insiders' Guide to Williamsburg, $12.95	$2.50	
	Insiders' Guide to the Crystal Coast of NC, $12.95	$2.50	
	Insiders' Guide to Charleston, $12.95	$2.50	
	Insiders' Guide to Virginia's Blue Ridge, $12.95	$2.50	
	Insiders' Guide to the Triangle, $12.95	$2.50	
	Insiders' Guide to Myrtle Beach, $12.95 (Summer '93)	$2.50	
	Insiders' Guide to Charlotte, $12.95	$2.50	

N.C. residents add 6% sales tax.

GRAND TOTAL ————————

*Payment in full (check, cash or money order) must accompany order
form. Please allow 2 weeks for delivery*

Index of Advertisers

Index

INDEX

The Atrium

21st & Arctic Ave • Virginia Beach, VA 23451

(804) 491-1400
1-800-96-SUITE

424 Atlantic Ave • Virginia Beach, VA 23451

(804) 425-2200
1-800-955-9300

10% OFF
WITH THIS COUPON
Based on availability. Not valid on holidays.

The Atrium

21st & Arctic Ave • Virginia Beach, VA 23451

(804) 491-1400
1-800-96-SUITE

424 Atlantic Ave • Virginia Beach, VA 23451

(804) 425-2200
1-800-955-9300

10% OFF
WITH THIS COUPON
Based on availability. Not valid on holidays.

DISCOVERY YACHT CRUISES

$1⁰⁰ OFF
Lunch & Sightseeing

$2⁰⁰ OFF
Dinner Cruises

• Adult fare only
• Valid thru 8/30/93
• Not valid with any other offers.

DEEP SEA FISHING

Va. Beach Fishing Center

$1⁰⁰ OFF
For Sightseeing or Fishing

To
Virginia Beach/Norfolk

Offer subject to modification by supplier without notice.
Unless otherwise stated expires: 9/1/94

To
Virginia Beach/Norfolk

Offer subject to modification by supplier without notice.
Unless otherwise stated expires: 9/1/94

To
Virginia Beach/Norfolk

Offer subject to modification by supplier without notice.
Unless otherwise stated expires: 9/1/94

THE
INSIDERS'®
GUIDE

To
Virginia Beach/Norfolk

Offer subject to modification by supplier without notice.
Unless otherwise stated expires: 9/1/94

THE
INSIDERS'®
GUIDE

To
Virginia Beach/Norfolk

Offer subject to modification by supplier without notice.
Unless otherwise stated expires: 9/1/94

THE
INSIDERS'®
GUIDE

To
Virginia Beach/Norfolk

Offer subject to modification by supplier without notice.
Unless otherwise stated expires: 9/1/94

Kiptopeke State Park
a natural part of your Eastern Shore visit

($2.50 value on weekdays • $4 value on weekends)
Park location: 3 miles north of Chesapeake Bay Bridge-Tunnel
on the Eastern Shore.
For information, call the park at 804/331-2267.

signature of user _____

date used _____